The Return of the Native

The Return of the Native

American Indian Political Resurgence

Stephen Cornell

New York   Oxford
OXFORD UNIVERSITY PRESS

Oxford University Press

Oxford New York Toronto
Delhi Bombay Calcutta Madras Karachi
Petaling Jaya Singapore Hong Kong Tokyo
Nairobi Dar es Salaam Cape Town
Melbourne Auckland

and associated companies in
Berlin Ibadan

Copyright © 1988 by Oxford University Press, Inc.

Published by Oxford University Press, Inc.,
200 Madison Avenue, New York, New York 10016

Oxford is a registered trademark of Oxford University Press

Library of Congress Cataloging-in-Publication Data
Cornell, Stephen E. (Stephen Ellicott), 1948–
  The return of the native: American Indian political resurgence/Stephen Cornell.
  p. cm. Bibliography: p. Includes index.
  ISBN 0-19-503772-3
  ISBN 0-19-506575-1 (PBK)
  1. Indians of North America—Government relations.
2. Indians of North America—Government relations—1934–
3. Indians of North America—Race identity. I. Title.   87-22896 CIP
E93.C79 1988 973'.0497—dc19

Some of the material in this book originally appeared, in somewhat different form, in the
following publications:

Stephen Cornell, "Crisis and Response in Indian-White Relations, 1960–1984," *Social Prob-
    lems* 32, no. 1 (October 1984): 44–59. Copyright 1984 by the Society for the Study of
    Social Problems, Inc. Used by permission.

Stephen Cornell, "The New Indian Politics," *The Wilson Quarterly* 10, no. 1 (New Year's
    1986): 113–31. Copyright 1986 by The Woodrow Wilson International Center for
    Scholars. Used by permission.

9 8 7 6 5 4

Printed in the United States of America
on acid-free paper

Preface

This is not a book about Indians; it is about Indian-White relations. I claim no particular expertise regarding American Indians themselves. Quite the contrary: In my associations with them and in my field work, I have become increasingly aware of how little I know and understand. The experts on Indians are Indians, and this book claims neither to speak for them nor to present them to the world.

What it tries to do instead is to examine and illuminate, from a sociological perspective, aspects of Indian-White relations. It is a study of relationships and of the ways in which relationships shape collective action.

I began work on this book in graduate school. I still remember the day I told one of my professors, Ira Katznelson, that my interest was in the militant political activism of Native Americans in the 1960s and early 1970s. Why and how, after decades of relative quiet, did Indians suddenly become so involved in political action? He thought about that for a moment and then suggested that a much more interesting and intellectually fruitful question would be why they *hadn't* turned to militant politics a lot sooner. They had always had grievances; why had they taken so long to act?

People resist their torments in myriad ways, of which rebellion is only one. In fact, Indians did a great deal long before the 1960s to change their situation. And this was partly Professor Katznelson's point. The issue was not why Indians finally became angry or desperate enough to become militant in the 1960s, but how one might account for the much longer-term pattern of responses—some militant, some not, some obviously political, some not—that Indians had made to the forces which had come to dominate them.

The effect of his remark was to reorient my thinking and to direct it to matters of structure and constraint. Structure, according to David Apter, can be thought of as "the relationships in a social situation" which limit choices of action "to a particular range of alternatives."* The issue, then, became understanding concrete historical relationships and the ways in which they had shaped political actors, their opportunities, and their capacities to act. The whole of Indian-White relations and the historical pattern of Indian action became my subject.

This change necessarily led to an active search for generalities amid the overwhelming quantity of historical specifics. A second factor had a similar effect. The Indian experience is, and always has been, remarkably various. To some degree this book helps to sustain a curse that has haunted Indian peoples for generations: the persistent Euro-American inclination to see the Indian population as monolithic instead of as a collection of exceedingly diverse nations and constituencies. But the scope of the subject, combined with the limits of time and space, left relatively few scholarly options. The result has been a tendency to pass over the exceptional in search of a larger pattern. In Indian-White relations, however, exceptions are often the norm, so that the overall pattern seems merely a historical mean, abstracted from a host of divergent cases.

The ultimate question, of course, is how much violence the written result has done to the facts. Generalization involves distance, a vantage point somewhat removed from the details of the materials. The trick is to avoid being so removed that the materials themselves—real people and their enterprises—disappear altogether in the haze, while the generalizations become so abstract as to lose their utility. This book may not entirely escape this problem, but critical commonalities remain within the Indian experience that increasingly link Native Americans with each other and to a common political trajectory. That they remain important and worthy of examination is a central thesis behind this study.

A word about terms. I have used "Indian" and "Native American" interchangeably throughout to refer to the indigenous peoples of the Americas and their descendants. Both terms are widely used by Indians, and it is by no means clear which is the preferred usage. In general, "Indian" is more common on reservations and in urban Indian communities, while "Native American" appears to be preferred in universities, among many intellectuals, and in some Indian organizations. Even in the last, however, usage is by no means consistent. I have chosen a middle ground.

This book has been a long time in the making, and my debts are many. Most of this work is based on library research. Less apparent is the effect of field research—largely interviews and extended conversations with Indians—carried out in a number of locations in 1978–79, 1981, and 1984. While such field work produced a good deal of specific information, its primary effect was to force me to rethink much of what I had read and thought about Indian-White relations and Indian politics. I am grateful to the National Science Foundation, Grant #SOC 77-15475, for support in

* David Apter and Harry Eckstein, eds., *Comparative Politics* (New York: Free Press, 1963), p. 732.

1978–79, and to the Harvard Graduate Society Fund and the Clark Fund of Harvard University for support in 1981 and 1984.

The actual seed of this book was planted by Bill Pensoneau during college days twenty years ago, in a series of conversations about Indian political action, in which he later became substantially involved. He has remained friend, informant, critic, and occasional host in the intervening years. I owe him a lot.

It was not until graduate school, however, that I followed up on those early conversations. When, as a student in the sociology department at the University of Chicago, I first proposed a dissertation on contemporary American Indian political activism, Professor William Julius Wilson responded with enthusiasm and encouragement—a critical moment in the life of this book. Its conception and shape owe much to Bill's generous commentary and to his insistence on the value—indeed, necessity—of holistic, historical analysis in the study of intergroup relations. Ira Katznelson, then Professor of Political Science at Chicago, also gave me crucial support, while his teaching, both in class and in dialogue, became a formative part of my whole graduate experience. I am indebted as well to Professors Arthur Stinchcombe, James Coleman, and Raymond Smith, and to Terry Straus for her advice and her enthusiastic bludgeoning of my more fanciful ideas.

Richard La Course, from the moment I met him in Rapid City in the fall of 1978, provided advice, friendship, relentless criticism, and an extraordinary quantity of information. During the early days of my research, he struggled to make me understand the gravity and meaning of the matters I was dealing with, not only as intellectual issues but as the measure of people's lives. There is much here with which he would no doubt disagree, but I learned a great deal from his encyclopedic knowledge of recent events in Indian affairs, his sense of history, and his compassionate sensitivity to the personal effects of highly impersonal processes.

It has become common in academia to show one's work to just about everybody one can think of before submitting it for publication. Surely this has slowed the pace of academic production, and I wonder sometimes about its impact on quality. In my own case, however, I have no doubts: I have learned from my friends. At Chicago, Kathleen Gille read early versions of much of this work, and her occasionally devastating criticism significantly improved it. At Harvard, as I struggled to turn an unwieldy dissertation into a more wieldy book, Duane Champagne, Tamara Hareven, David Harris, James Ito-Adler, David Karen, Rebecca Klatch, Ethel Klein, Katherine McClelland, Heather McCollum, Lisa Peattie, and Jeff Weintraub either read portions of the manuscript or discussed it with me, very much to my advantage. Students in my course on the sociology of Indian-White relations provided ample skepticism, while some offered important insights from their own experience of being Indian in America. Jerry Karabel gave me some much needed help.

I am indebted also to several others, both Indian and non-Indian, with whom, at various times, I discussed the events and developments that form the subject of this book. Some, either by choice or because I never knew their names, must remain anonymous. Others include Pat Ballanger, Herb Blatchford, Lisa Chavez, Rupert Costo, Vine Deloria, Jr., Andy de los Angeles, Thomasine Hill, Pat Locke, Charlie Lohah, Bettie Rushing, Vicky Santana, David Small, Sam Stanley, Gene Stone, Vern Stone, Robert Thomas, Stan Throssel, Chuck Trimble, and Gerald Wilkinson. Their observations and responses to my questions had a profound effect on my thinking, and I hope I have not abused their generosity. I alone remain responsible for what is said here.

Susan Rabiner, Valerie Aubry, and Marion Osmun at Oxford University Press have been patient, encouraging, and extremely helpful.

Finally, my deepest thanks go to Douglas and Judithe Cornell for their patient support; to Heather McCollum who, during a difficult time, believed in this book and helped me to believe in it also; and to Rand Edwards, Kathy Gille, David Harris, Bob Johnston, Rebecca Klatch, Ethel Klein, the late Bill Holt, and David Karen for the remarkable quality of their friendship.

Cambridge, Mass.   S. C
August 1987

Contents

For my father and in memory of my mother

Chapter 1

The New Indian Politics

On December 28, 1890, a few miles west of the Badlands in South Dakota, a band of exhausted Sioux Indians, including a hundred or so warriors and some 250 women and children, surrendered to troops of the U.S. Seventh Cavalry and agreed to travel with them to the Indian agency at Pine Ridge. The joint party camped that night at Wounded Knee Creek, twenty miles from their destination. Surrounding the Indian tipis and tents were nearly five hundred soldiers and four pieces of Hotchkiss light artillery.

On the morning of the twenty-ninth, the Indian men were gathered together and told to turn in their arms. Few did so, and the troops began to search the tents. Reports of subsequent events vary, but tensions were high. A scuffle ensued, and an Indian, intentionally or not, fired a gun. Instantly both soldiers and Indians fired at each other at close range; within moments the Hotchkiss guns were pouring explosive shells into the Indian camp.

Most of the warriors died in the opening volleys. Others, along with large numbers of women and children who survived the first moments of carnage, fled down adjacent ravines as the firing continued, the troops in quick pursuit, leaving a trail of Sioux bodies—men, women, children—that eventually stretched for miles. By the time the firing ended, some two hundred Indians—perhaps more; estimates vary—had been killed and many of the rest wounded; of the original band, precious few escaped.[1]

The survivors of this slaughter were among the last Indians to be brought under the direct administrative control of the United States. Confined on reservations, they joined thousands of other Native Americans, not only on the western plains but across the country, in a state of despondent dependency, wards of a government they had learned not to trust.

A little more than eighty-two years later, late on the night of February 27, 1973, a group of Oglala Sioux from the Pine Ridge Reservation in South Dakota and activists from the American Indian Movement seized

3

the reservation village of Wounded Knee, site of the 1890 massacre, in protest against corruption in the tribal government at Pine Ridge; against U.S.
violations of the 1868 Fort Laramie Treaty, which formally recognized
Sioux sovereignty over much of what is now the Dakotas, Montana, Wyoming, and Nebraska; and against continuing federal controls over Indians
themselves. Within twenty-four hours the village had been surrounded by a
force of 250 FBI agents, U.S. Marshals, and Bureau of Indian Affairs police; in subsequent days they were joined by more federal officers equipped
with everything from M-16 rifles to Armored Personnel Carriers.

The siege lasted ten weeks. It included night-long firefights and other exchanges of gunfire that left two Indians dead and caused injuries on both
sides. In May, after lengthy, on-and-off negotiations between the occupiers
and the federal government, an agreement was reached. The second battle
of Wounded Knee finally came to an end.[2]

The inherent drama of these events is obvious; each, in its day, was major news. Their ultimate significance, however, lies not in the events themselves but in the tale they tell between them.

The 1890 massacre brought an era to a close. For most Native Americans it was an era that had already ended. The Euro-American advance
across the continent had long since destroyed the prosperity and autonomy
of most Indian nations. For those few tribespeople still coursing the northern plains, the guns of the Seventh Cavalry merely emphasized a fact already well established elsewhere: Indians would no longer meaningfully
choose their future; it would be chosen for them. As Black Hawk, war
leader of the Sac and Fox, had said of himself a half century earlier, "He
is now a prisoner to the white men; they will do with him as they wish."[3]

The 1973 occupation likewise marked the passing of an era, and again it
was a passing already well advanced. Once more the Indians were surrounded at Wounded Knee, but this time it had a different meaning. The
activists of 1973 provided the most sensational evidence yet of the return
of Native Americans to the political arena, of their defiant claim to the
right once again to make their own choices.

THE NEW INDIAN POLITICS

One might ask just how much, by 1973, had really changed. Six years earlier Clyde Warrior, a Ponca Indian and president of the National Indian
Youth Council, had virtually repeated Black Hawk's words. "We are not
free," he had argued. "We do not make choices. Our choices are made for
us."[4] Yet both Warrior and his organization were testimony to the far-
reaching changes that in fact had occurred: pioneering practitioners of a
genuinely new and genuinely Indian politics.

Of course there has always been politics *about* Indians. For the most part
it has been non-Indian politics, carried on in Washington or the capitals of
Europe, among the governors of western states and territories, in corpora-

tion board rooms and chambers of commerce and among missionaries, reformers, and bureaucrats.

Its history is longer than that of the United States. During much of that history it was not only politics about Indians but politics that was, to some extent at least, Indian-made. Certain Indian nations—among them the tribes of the Powhatan Confederacy in what is now Virginia; the Pequots in southern New England; the Iroquois, Creeks, Cherokees; later the Sioux and other tribes—were central actors in the political drama. While they seldom were involved directly in decision making, they often set the terms on which decisions were made. Thus in the seventeenth and eighteenth centuries the French and English were forced to compete with each other for trade and alliance with the Iroquois, who controlled much of the Ohio River Valley and the eastern Great Lakes, while King George's Royal Proclamation of 1763, which briefly closed lands west of the Appalachians to white settlement, was a response to Indian outrage at white penetrations and to Pontiac's war against the forts of the northwestern frontier. A century later Sioux resistance forced the United States to abandon the Bozeman Road through the Dakota and Montana territories, and led to changes in Indian policy.

In time, however, U.S. power and numbers prevailed, and the Indian influence in Indian affairs rapidly declined. Struggles between sovereign powers were replaced by rigid patterns of dominance and subordination. "The Indians are children," Horace Greeley wrote in 1859.[5] Certainly policymakers were determined to treat them that way. From the end of organized Indian resistance in the nineteenth century until the last few decades, Native Americans have been barred systematically from meaningful participation of almost any kind in those decision-making processes most affecting their communities and lives.

The situation today is dramatically different. At the root of that change lie altered politics as well as altered policies: the distinctive actions of Native Americans themselves. Since the 1940s—and particularly in the last two to three decades—Indians not only have demanded a voice in decision making, but they have *appropriated* such a voice for themselves, forcing the surrounding society to respond once again to their actions and agendas.

Reversing the usual order of things, Sioux author Vine Deloria, Jr., chose *"We Talk, You Listen"* as the 1970 title of one of his books.[6] But Indians had more than words to toss into the political arena; by then their actions had become at least as loud. "Fish-ins" in the Pacific Northwest in the early 1960s when Indians asserted their treaty rights by fishing in traditional sites in defiance of state regulations; the takeover of Alcatraz in 1969 and of other lands and buildings in subsequent years; the seizure of the Bureau of Indian Affairs headquarters in Washington, D.C., in 1972; the Wounded Knee confrontation a few months later: these and other events signaled the arrival of a style of Indian political action that, if native to those generally turbulent times, had long been absent from Indian affairs.

Nor was this new assertiveness restricted to sensational events. It was equally apparent in the rapid increase in Indian-initiated litigation on behalf of treaty rights and other claims; in the appearance of a new, fiercely nationalistic Indian news media; in the rapid proliferation of Indian organizations, many with regional or national political agendas; and in growing Indian participation in conventional politics. "This vanishing remnant of a race," as Joseph Dixon called them in 1913,[7] not only had failed to vanish, but had returned to the political arena with unexpected, often defiant force, and in the process had reversed the four-hundred-year trend of declining Indian influence and power. Coming on the heels of decades of apparent quiescence, this activist surge thrust Indians into the headlines and the consciousness of the public and shook the White establishment, which for years had been running the Indian business.

At the same time, the new Indian politics of the last three decades lacked the coherence of an organized political movement. It was rather a composite of organizations, groups, interests, and events—a population of less than two million persons caught up in a vast array of often disconnected political activities. Yet despite this remarkable diversity it remained a singular phenomenon: a far-reaching attempt by Native Americans to regain some measure of control over their lives, their future, and their place in American society.

It is this political resurgence that forms the subject of this book.

INDIAN PROBLEM AND INDIAN RESPONSE

This resurgence may only recently have become apparent, but it is a subject that leads well beyond the last few decades. The suddenness of the new Indian politics is partly illusion, a result, in the 1960s and 1970s, of a more confrontational style that captured media attention. In retrospect it can be seen gathering strength as early as the 1940s, and its beginnings go back further still.

But there is more to it even than this. The new Indian politics is part of an old Indian struggle. It is the resurgent phase of a diffuse, fragmented movement of Indian resistance, a movement that has continued in one form or another for generations. And, like the other phases of that resistance, it has been shaped by specific and steadily evolving relationships between Native Americans and European newcomers to the North American continent.

For four centuries non-Indians in North America have had an "Indian problem." In its most basic form this problem has had three aspects. First, it has been an economic problem: how best to secure access to Indian resources, land in particular. Second, it has been a problem in cultural transformation: how best to accomplish the cultural transformation of Indians into non-Indians. Third, and consequently, it has been a political problem: how to maintain an effective system of controls over Indian groups so that problems one and two could be satisfactorily resolved.

These concerns have been more prominent during some historical periods than others—pressures on Indian lands, for example, diminished substantially in the 1920s and 1930s—and from time to time other issues have been more salient, particularly in the twentieth century. Today, policy-makers tend to be preoccupied with problems of reservation poverty and ill-health, urban Indian adjustment, education, economic development, and related topics. But these problems are themselves part of the legacy of the centuries-old effort to solve the more fundamental "Indian problem," a problem that has by no means disappeared, as contemporary efforts to gain access to Indian natural resources testify.

Indians, on the other hand, have had what might be called a "Euro-American problem." In its essence this problem seems to have been tribal survival: the maintenance of particular sets of social relations, more or less distinct cultural orders, and some measure of political autonomy in the face of invasion, conquest, and loss of power. Again, many Native Americans, particularly in recent years, have had other concerns than these. In the face of often astonishing poverty they, too, have focused much of their energy on jobs, improved standards of living, and the rewards offered by the larger society. Few, however, have been willing to sacrifice the goal of tribal survival—itself a social and political as much as an economic objective—for purely economic gains.

The working out of these two inverse and conflictual agendas has given context and shape to Indian-White relations. The history of those relations can be viewed as a record of the attempts of each group—Indians and Whites—to solve the particular problem they have had to face. Those attempts have not proceeded independently. On the contrary, they have conditioned each other. In the long drama of Indian-White interaction, each actor has been forced to respond to the actions of the other or to the consequences of those actions, manifest in concrete social conditions and relationships.

While mutual, this conditioning process has been uneven. Although in the early years Native Americans on occasion exerted considerable influence over the actions of the invaders and the shape of events, over time they found themselves increasingly constrained, caught in an ever more elaborate mesh of circumstances and relationships beyond their control.

In the pattern of their subjugation lies the shape of their resistance. Human beings, as Karl Marx pointed out in a famous passage, make their own history, but under circumstances not of their choosing and with materials handed down from the past.[8] New histories are built on the foundations of the old; only with time do they transcend—or remake—their origins. The ways Indian groups have been linked to larger political and economic structures have continually refashioned those groups, their political opportunities, and their capacities to act on those opportunities. Indian action, in other words, bears the indelible imprint of the changing situations in which Indians have found themselves. Actors, opportunities, capacities, and the changes in all three—these are the key themes in the argument of this book.

Yet the pattern of influence moves in more than one direction. Groups act not only *within* limits set by forces beyond their control, including their own distinctive histories. They also act *upon* those limits. In the process they may remake both themselves and the world in which they live, and thereby the conditions under which they act.

Such, indeed, is the significance of contemporary Indian political resurgence. In the 1960s, 1970s, and 1980s, the Indian world has been changing. This much is hardly new; it has been changing all along, and often quickly. What is new is that for the first time in a long while it is Indians who have been making those changes happen. They by no means dictate the outcomes, but they have turned the world of Indian-White relations upside down. The road from one Wounded Knee to the next has been a road from powerlessness to a modest form of power. Importantly, however, and inevitably, that road has been built on the residues of the past.

Thus the agenda of this book. The object here is to understand the evolution of contemporary Indian political resurgence. The method is to trace the history of political and economic relationships—here referred to as patterns of incorporation—linking Native American groups to emergent Euro-American society, and to examine the effects those relationships have had on Indian groups and on their opportunities and ability to act.

The intended result can be read in different ways. At one level it is simply a sociology of collective action: an attempt to account for changing pattern and form in Indian resistance. Yet its method links it to a broader agenda. It may be viewed also as an exercise in historical sociology, an effort to better understand the intricate interplay between systems of social relationships on the one hand and patterns of social action on the other, what Philip Abrams calls the "shaping of action by structure and transforming of structure by action."[9] To trace the evolution of incorporation and response in the Indian case is to attempt to capture—in a single extended illustration—the historical development of that exchange.

Part I

INTO THE DARK

Chapter 2

Exceptional Beginnings:
The Fur Trade and Indian Labor

In the sixteenth, seventeenth, and eighteenth centuries, Europe spun a web about the world, and in the process the world was remade. During those and subsequent years, various peoples, nations, and ideas would struggle within the grasp of that web. Some would flourish, some would disappear; but few would entirely escape the ever-expanding network of connections that made this world so very new.

The architects of the web were themselves diverse—Portugal, Spain, France, England, the Netherlands—and they acted far more in conflict with each other than in concert. Nonetheless, their product was a single system of relationships, frayed a little here, sagging a little there, but ultimately binding together continents and peoples whose lives would never be the same again.

It became eventually a web of many parts: ideas, cultures, institutions. But most importantly it was a web of politics and markets, a network built to funnel fuel to the thirsty engines of mercantile and industrializing Europe. Over time it captured the human and material resources of much of the world, incorporated them in its emergent system, and bent them to its many tasks.

The resultant patterns of incorporation—the particular ways peoples or groups were fit into that web and linked to its architects and their successors—varied widely across the world, so that a single global history is composed of a thousand different parts. This is true even within the reduced geographical scope of North America, whose indigenous peoples were gradually drawn into the European web, but in myriad ways. Within those multiple patterns, however, there is apparent a larger design, one that brings the various experiences of Native American groups into a common

11

historical frame and that in turn becomes the context in which Indian political responses have been made.

This incorporative process linking Indians to the Euro-American political economy can be divided into six major periods. These can be distinguished by the prevalence in each of more or less distinct sets of economic and political relationships linking Indian nations to Euro-American polities and economies.

The first of these periods, which might be called the market period, lasted from shortly after Indian-White contact into the last half of the eighteenth century. Its centerpiece was the fur trade of the eastern woodlands, which incorporated Indians, as producers of peltry, into a European market and, as potential allies, into the system of competitive trans-Atlantic European politics.

The second, or conflict, period, taking shape during the latter years of the eighteenth and early years of the nineteenth centuries, was based on the direct incorporation of Indian resources into the developing economy of the United States. Its centerpiece was the forced expropriation of Indian lands, accompanied for the most part by the exclusion of Indians themselves from that emergent American economy.

The third period might be called the reservation period. It dates from different times in different places, but generally from the mid- to late nineteenth century into the 1930s, and begins with the confinement of Native Americans on reservations. It is characterized by gradually diminishing demands for Indian resources, already largely lost, and by the imposition of severe, tutelary, administrative controls over Indian peoples.

The fourth period lasts only from passage of the Indian Reorganization Act (IRA) in 1934 to the late 1940s. Its major features include both the organization of formally constituted and federally supported tribal governments and an effort to resuscitate reservation economies. It is followed by a fifth, equally brief termination period, from the 1940s to about 1960, which saw a retreat from the supportive political and economic policies of the IRA, a major federal effort to dismantle the reservation system, and a renewed push for the individual assimilation of Indians into the larger society.

The sixth, contemporary period begins sometime in the 1960s, but has been slow to form. It is marked by policies of Indian self-determination, resurgent demands for remaining Indian economic resources, growing political conflict between Native Americans and non-Indian organizations and interests, and consequently a substantial reorganization of contemporary Indian-White relations. How long this latest period will last remains to be seen.

In each of these periods, Indian responses to incorporation likewise have been distinctive. The market period was one of willful Indian participation in the fur trade and extensive Indian diplomatic efforts to exploit unusual political opportunities and maintain their own autonomy. In the conflict period, faced with radically altered political conditions, Indian diplomacy and negotiation were accompanied more and more by armed resistance. The resultant struggle shattered Indian political capacities. With few choices left, in the last years of conflict and in the reservation period Indians turned away from overt resistance, looking increasingly to the supernatural and to their own, rapidly changing cultures for help. A host of religious movements emerged designed either to transform a world gone wrong or to help people live with a new reality. The result was a hiatus in secular political activity that lasted, with some exceptions, including some legal cases, into the 1930s.

With the Indian Reorganization Act of 1934, the door opened once again to large-scale secular politics. In that period and the following, an Indian political resurgence of striking proportions began to emerge. The 1960s found this resurgence at flood tide. New political opportunities and the regenerate political capacities of Indian groups combined to produce the activist politics of the contemporary period.

These patterns of incorporation and response are summarized schematically in Table 1. Of course fitting four centuries of interaction among such diverse peoples into any six-part scheme inevitably involves simplification. Native Americans came into contact with Europeans at different times and in different ways. Not all groups, for example, experienced all six stages. Some had little involvement in the fur trade; others today lack the kinds of resources that might bring them fully into the latest stage of incorporation.

The pattern of Indian response likewise challenges the precision of such a scheme. Despite the popular image of Indian horsemen battling blue-clad troopers throughout the West, not every Indian nation entered into conflict with the invaders. And while the subsequent years on reservations were quiet ones, they included the founding of the Society of American Indians and the Indian Defense League of America as well as the Pueblo struggle against congressional legislation threatening Pueblo lands.

Nor can the lines between these periods always be so neatly drawn. The fur trade, for example, remained important in some areas long after it had passed in others, while the process of land dispossession began soon after contact.

Such variations are important; an overview must not overlook the polymorphous character of this extended encounter between New World and Old. The object here, however, is not to exhaust the variety of Indian-White interactions, but to point to the dominant features of the changing incorporative process and indigenous responses to it.

The scheme also serves a larger purpose. The study of Indian-White relations generally has concentrated on watershed policies and legislation. Indian removal, the General Allotment Act of 1887, the Indian New Deal, the termination policy, and other events have provided reference points for the examination of Indian affairs. The approach taken here uses such points but attempts to place them in a larger framework of dominant-group goals and intergroup relationships. It is a necessary kind of sim-

Table 1.   Patterns of Incorporation and Response in Indian-White Relations

Period	Economic Incorporation	Political Incorporation	Response
Market (c. mid-16th to late 18th centuries)	Voluntary integration into fur markets based on Indian labor and consumption	Competitive European politics; substantial Indian autonomy; alliance	Diplomacy; some armed resistance
Conflict (c. late 18th to late 19th centuries)	Forced expropriation of Indian lands; exclusion of Indians from larger economy; little demand for Indian labor	American hegemony; increasingly restrictive treaty relations	Armed resistance; negotiation under stress
Reservation (c. late 19th century to 1930s)	Continued land loss through allotment; welfare dependency; eventually declining demand for Indian resources	Comprehensive U.S. administrative control of reservations; forced assimilation; citizenship	Secular intergroup politics sporadic at best; growth of religious movements
IRA (1930s to late 1940s)	Efforts to stabilize land base and develop reservation economies; support for reservation communities	Establishment of federally sponsored tribal governments; political support	Increased political participation through tribal governments; some supratribal activity
Termination (late 1940s to early 1960s)	Some demand for Indian lands; federal promotion of urban migration; withdrawal of support for reservations	New assault on tribal sovereignty; some states gain jurisdiction over Indian lands; imposed assimilation	Growth of supratribal politics; new constituencies appearing; opposition to termination
Contemporary (1960s to present)	Resurgent demands for Indian economic resources; major efforts to develop reservation economies; increased labor integration	"Self-determination" for Indian tribes; support for tribal governments; repression of radicals	Rapid growth in political activity of all kinds; eventual decline of radical activism

plification: the location of background continuities and transformations that may lend coherence to actual events.

The first of these six periods was exceptional in two ways. First, the pattern of incorporation gave genuine power to certain Indian nations. It did so by placing them in a pivotal position in an emergent trans-Atlantic political economy. As producers of furs and customers for European goods, they became the linchpin in the fur trade, itself both foundation and rationale of early colonization in North America. At the same time, as potential enemies and allies, they achieved a central position in the competitive interstate politics that emerged as the European powers battled for North American resources and their benefits. While this dual role lasted, some Indian groups retained substantial influence over their own destinies.

Second, and related to the first, it was only in these early years that Indian labor was a critical element in Indian-White relations. In subsequent periods land and its resources became the centerpiece of Indian affairs, a fact that takes on substantial significance in the analysis of Indian political resurgence.

The remainder of this chapter examines that first period, the factors that led from labor to land and from the first stage of incorporation to the second, and the significance of the labor/land distinction for Indian-White relations and Indian politics.

THE FUR TRADE AND THE EUROPEAN POWERS

"The invasion of America," as Francis Jennings has aptly described it,[1] was before all else a commercial and political enterprise. It was the search for a shorter route to the riches of the East that led Columbus westward in 1492. Over the next century the riches of the Americas were found to be prodigious in their own right, and Spain's quest for gold and silver as well as souls carried her captains and conquistadors deep into both continents within a few decades of Columbus's landfall. England likewise turned to the West in search of prosperity and power. The institutional model for English colonization, writes James Lang, was the great trading company, as trading and colonization "were seen as part of the same basic process—the extension of English commercial strength."[2] Jamestown was England's first success after several failed efforts to found a colony in North America. It was financed by a group of London merchants. As for Plymouth, "the prospect of quick returns from the fish and fur trade," writes Francis Moloney, "led English merchants to finance the venture of the Pilgrims." These merchants even promised to ship food from England so the colonists might devote more of their time to trading and less to agriculture. Regarding the Dutch in America, Jennings remarks that the trade of Dutch manufactures to the Indians for furs was New Netherland's "whole reason for existence." Seventeenth-century French explorations of the St. Lawrence River and surrounding country were primarily trading ventures, searches for furs and a passage to the Pacific that could carry French ships to the Indies. Early French settlements were trading posts, predicated on the region's potential for sustained Indian-French commerce.[3]

At the root of this commercial impulse was the competition among European powers for economic and political dominance in the rapidly expanding world economy of the sixteenth, seventeenth, and eighteenth centuries. North America, with its apparently abundant resources, became a central arena of European competition, and the new colonies the loci of extensive commercial enterprise directed at the control of those resources and their export to Europe. At stake were money metals as well as whatever other minerals that might be found, timber, fish, agricultural produce, and animal hides or furs. These last are of particular interest here. For a substantial part of the colonial period, competition among the European powers in North America, and particularly between England and France, was centered on the fur trade.[4] At the center of that trade were the Indian nations.

The demand for furs began to increase substantially in Europe in the late sixteenth and early seventeenth centuries in response to expanding prosperity and changing fashions. Beaver hats, fur linings and trim, and outer clothes made of fur or hides became increasingly popular, producing a rising demand for pelts. With the opening of New World fur resources, European hatters and furriers saw their business boom.[5]

The result was a classic mercantilist activity. European traders in contact with North American native groups purchased beaver, coney, marten, otter, rabbit, fox, and other furs from the Indians with European manufactured goods. This trade brought to the European states from their own colonies products they largely lacked and had formerly obtained from northern European or Asian sources. It provided both raw materials for the manufacture of profitable and exportable luxury goods and—in the other direction—a profitable outlet for a variety of European manufactures.

The Indian market for such manufactures was substantial. Preferred trade items included some luxury goods, mainly alcohol and tobacco, and decoratives ones such as glass beads, but the bulk of demand commonly was for items of practical use in the Indian environment: firearms, powder and lead, knives, axes, kettles, blankets, and so forth. Once these goods had been introduced, Indian demands grew rapidly. Remarks Harold Innis: "The task of continuously supplying goods to the Indian tribes of North America, of maintaining the depreciation of those goods, and replacing the goods destroyed was overwhelming." Jennings finds evidence that the "demands of Indians as consumers shaped imperial policies and influenced the development of England's greatest industry, the wool trade." "Indian customers," he goes on to say, "were the more appreciated because English woolen exports to the continent were encountering difficulties in the seventeenth century."[6]

The importance of the fur trade, however, was not only economic. It was very much a political activity as well. Although control of the economic benefits derived from the trade was a central object of intra-European conflict in the New World, there was more at stake than simply furs and related markets. The potential wealth of North America had been a subject of discussion in Europe since the earliest explorations; besides furs there were surely mineral and agricultural opportunities, fortunes to be made in shipping, endless expanses of land. The European powers were eager to tap these various resources, and the fur trade was a central pivot on which competition among them turned. Its very nature, combined with the political realities of the time, gave it a decisive role in the shaping of European destinies in the New World.

Interaction among the European powers in North America did not occur in a political vacuum. Particularly in the seventeenth and eighteenth centuries and in some cases until after the American Revolution, certain Indian nations, individually or in concert, were significant powers in their own right, effectively controlling both the hinterlands and the resources therein. Eager for European goods, they were also politically and economically shrewd, searching for the best prices for their furs and for support in their own affairs with other Indian nations. Both geographically and politically their opportunities were limited, and at times they were forced into alliances they might not otherwise have chosen. Nonetheless, their support was often critical in intra-European conflicts. They came to the Europeans, but the Europeans, equally, came to them. Thus the trade produced more than furs. Politics and pelts were intertwined; at one time or another, success or failure for the various European powers, whatever the object, depended substantially on Indian alliance.

As a consequence intra-European struggles were waged at least in part through the Indians. Jennings has shown how the Mohawk attack on the Susquehannocks in 1650–51, made with the benefit of Dutch-supplied arms, was part of a Dutch effort to dislodge the Swedes from Delaware Bay. The English and French competed for favor with the Iroquois Confederacy throughout much of the seventeenth and eighteenth centuries. While both European powers had claims to western New York and the eastern Great Lakes and Ohio country, each realized that without the friendship of the Iroquois, who controlled large parts of the region, their claims had little practical substance or effect. For the English, according to Allen Trelease, eventually "the economic importance of the Iroquois was subordinated to their political and military value as buffers and allies—even mercenaries—against the French." Significantly, England's success among the Iroquois during much of the period resulted in part from the price advantage of English manufactured goods at Albany over French goods at Quebec and Montreal, emphasizing the substantial freedom of the Iroquois to direct their trade where they pleased. Of course this European competition was of no small advantage to the Iroquois. Not only did it exert upward pressure on prices for their furs, but long after their own strength had been surpassed by both English and French, they maintained some degree of independence through the shrewd diplomatic exploitation of their strategic position astride major trade routes and between European powers.[7]

Indians entered similarly into intra-European politics on the western slope of the Appalachians. There also, conflicting French, Spanish, and English claims and designs were substantially dependent on trade relations with the Choctaws, Chickasaws, and other tribes.[8]

Thus Indian relations—more precisely, trade relations with Indians—

became both object and means of expanding European influence and opportunity in North America. At issue immediately were the economic rewards of the trade itself, but it served also as a political tool in the more comprehensive struggle for the New World, a struggle related to the larger conflict for position and power in the evolving world order of the time. England, of course, emerged the victor through the conquest of New France, the Ohio Valley, and the upper Mississippi. Among the fruits of that victory was the achievement, through the Treaty of Paris in 1763, of a virtual monopoly over the North American fur trade east of the Mississippi and from Florida to Hudson Bay.

THE FUR TRADE AND THE COLONIES

The fur trade, however, was by no means solely a metropolitan affair. Indeed, its economic importance was substantially greater in the colonies, especially in Canada and New York but occasionally elsewhere as well. This was true particularly in the early years, before the development of other trans-Atlantic commerce, and seldom so true as at the founding. "English, French, and Dutch colonizers counted heavily upon the profits of this trade to underwrite their North American settlements," remarks Wesley Frank Craven. And Edward Channing argues that the trade was essential to the survival of the Plymouth colony. It was through the trade that the new colony managed eventually to pay its debts. William Penn counted heavily on trade with the Indians of Pennsylvania to meet the expenses of establishing a colony there. The Dutch did likewise. Trelease identifies the fur trade as New Netherland's chief source of revenue. In 1687, more than twenty years after the English drove the Dutch from the area, New York's governor warned that encroachments by Pennsylvania on the New York Indian trade threatened the financial basis of the colony. In Maryland, according to L. C. Gray, "in 1638 the principal settlers were more interested in the trade than in planting, and roanoke and beaver were employed as currency."[9]

Furs were less important in the southern colonies, but played their part nonetheless. With the decline in tobacco prices brought about by the Navigation Acts of 1660 and after, Virginia encouraged the development of alternative industries, and a substantial leather business grew up based largely on Indian trade in deerskins. According to Craven, the Virginia trade presently came to rival New York's both in its profits and in its geographical reach.[10]

Furs were linked to other aspects of early colonial economic development. In particular they provided much of the capital necessary for economic expansion and diversification. The development of agriculture in the southern colonies, argues Gray, was dependent on trade profits. According to Philip Brown, South Carolinians of the late seventeenth and early eighteenth centuries "amassed great wealth in the Indian trade, providing that colony's initial capital accumulation which would later be invested in rice and indigo plantations and in the black slave trade." Similarly in Plymouth, according to Moloney, the development of cattle raising was based on income from the fur trade.[11]

As an extractive export industry the trade was critical also in the colonial balance of payments. Trade deficits are chronic in colonial situations owing to an early dependence on metropoles for manufactured and other goods, including, in some cases, foodstuffs. Much of the purchasing power of the early North American colonies was derived from furs, which were relatively easy to obtain and greatly in demand in Europe.[12]

Of course the economic importance of the trade declined in most of the colonies as larger proportions of both population and commerce—themselves rapidly growing—became involved in other economic activities. Only in Canada, New York, and the Russian settlements in Alaska did the trade retain much economic significance in the eighteenth century. It provided more than a quarter of the value of New York's exports to England in the first half of the century. By the 1750s, however, with the New York economy diversifying and trade with the West Indies steeply on the rise, its importance had greatly diminished.[13] Fur markets were less to blame for this general decline—beaver hats, for example, remained in fashion in Europe until nearly the mid-1800s—than were the growth and development of colonial economies.

Meanwhile the trade continued to serve prominently in another capacity. No longer central to colonial economic life, it remained the leading edge of European expansion over the continent. By the end of the eighteenth century the heart of the fur trade had moved west of the Mississippi, and traders were moving up the Missouri in search of beaver, buffalo, and other pelts. When Lewis and Clark led their exploration of newly acquired western lands, they carried with them instructions from President Jefferson to seek "a commercial intercourse with [the Indians]; confer with them on the points most convenient as mutual emporiums, and the articles of most desirable interchange for them and us."[14] It was the vision of trade profits, not settlement, that first drew Europeans across the plains to the western mountains and beyond.

But if the fur trade was of major importance to the Europeans, it was no less important to the Indians. While the trade flourished, both Indian and European—with some important exceptions—flourished as well. But when it declined, only the European survived. For the Indians the trade was decidedly ambiguous. It gave some groups unprecedented power and even, for a while, the means of survival in the face of European invasion. But it also transformed their environments, their cultures, and their lives, and linked them irrevocably to an evolving economic order that ultimately had no use for them.

THE FUR TRADE AND THE INDIANS

Through the fur trade the Indians of the eastern interior of North America were incorporated into a mercantile economy dominated by a few European states. That incorporation involved two separate but intimately related economic identities: the Indian as producer for a world market, and the Indian as customer for European commodity goods.

As a producer the Indian invested considerable technical skills, capital in the form of tools, and prodigious amounts of time and labor in the procurement, processing, and transport of furs. Francis Jennings, in a fascinating account of the Indian side of the trade, describes the operation as a complex manufacturing process.

> Labor was varied in a number of operations and was performed by both men and women. Men in work gangs traveled for months away from home and lived at their site of operations. They located the special kind of raw material incorporating their desired commodity—the beaver and other fur-bearing animals—and extracted the raw material from its site. This extraction involved a number of processes hidden under the rubric "hunting," and it required skilled labor as well as the expenditure of operating capital. Having acquired his raw material, the Indian hunter turned skinner, spending more labor on extracting the commercially valuable part of the material from its associated waste product. He then became porter and freight manager to get his peltry back to his village, and on the way he might be obliged to turn soldier to protect it from hijackers. At the village further work was done, comparable to a tanner's, to dress the skins. Then the Indian transported his product once again—sometimes for distances of hundreds of miles—to the marketplace maintained by a European merchant, and there the Indian turned trader.[15]

Operating capital was essential in the form of proper tools. Some were procured from Europeans, often on credit: knives, hatchets, awls, and so forth; others, such as canoes, were manufactured by the Indians, requiring additional specialized skills. Processing itself was a lengthy business. The most prized fur in the hat industry of Europe, for example, was known to the French as *castor gras d'hiver*: prime winter beaver, dressed, scraped, treated at length with animal brains, bone marrow, or other substance, trimmed, sewn in batches of several skins into a robe, and then worn next to the skin for a few months to loosen the longer hairs and soften the shorter fur—all done by Indians prior to the consummation of trade. Deerskins likewise required complex treatment. Preparation for the top classification, known as "Indian drest," involved soaking, scraping, heating, scouring, twisting, and drying the skins in specified ways. Peltry, writes Jennings, "was raw material for further processing only in the sense that a bolt of cloth is raw material for tailoring."[16]

This process took place under Indian control. The commodity Indians sold was not their labor but its product; they worked as independent producers within the embrace of their own societies and territory, meeting

Europeans not at the point of production but in the marketplace. Incorporated as traders into a transsocietal economy, as producers they remained autonomous.

Indians were involved in the trade in other ways as well. Some Canadian tribes in particular became dealers in food, provisioning the trading posts. In 1808 agents for the Northwest Company remarked of the Indians, "They alone supply all the food on which the company's servants subsist."[17]

More common was the Indian as middleman. Nations that had exhausted local fur supplies often turned to neighboring or more distant groups for furs; others found they could more easily gain European goods in the middleman role than by trapping for themselves. In the process they conveyed European goods far beyond the limits reached by Europeans themselves. The Hurons, located on the southeastern shore of Georgian Bay, traded both European goods and homegrown corn for furs they then carried east. They guarded their middleman role closely, going to considerable efforts to keep the French from bypassing them and establishing independent trade relations with Indians elsewhere; the Potawatomi in Michigan did the same. By 1750 the Assiniboine and Cree southwest of Hudson Bay were trading European goods for furs with groups as far west and south as the Canadian Rockies and Montana, and had long since established themselves in the middleman role astride major trade routes leading to the bay posts. The Iroquois, strategically located and militarily powerful, eventually controlled most of the trade coming to Albany and at times to Montreal as well. According to Trelease, in 1644 three out of four Huron trading parties headed for Montreal were captured by the Iroquois; for years other tribes as well had no choice but to deal with them.[18]

Indian trade participation—as either producer or middleman—becomes fully comprehensible, however, only in light of the second role Indians filled, that of customer for European commodities. The fur trade was founded on Indian needs and desires for goods available only from European sources. Aboriginal Indian material culture was based largely on stone, clay, wood, fiber, hides, and bone. Such materials were adequate to Indian needs; they provided the means for highly efficient technological adaptation to the environment. But the introduction of European goods, particularly metal implements, firearms, and woolens, rendered certain aspects of Indian material culture obsolete. Indians were quick to recognize superior convenience or utility, and as contact with Europeans and their commodities spread, demand for these goods rapidly rose. Furthermore, Indians quickly developed new wants. James Clifton's summary of the Potawatomi "shopping list" from the mid-1700s includes everything from steel axes to mirrors, ribbons to borax, flavored tobaccos to calico.[19]

This consumer demand was the motor force of the trade. Without it there would have been little or no North American fur industry until Europeans learned the skills necessary to produce peltry themselves and gained practical control of areas bearing sufficient quantities of furs. Given the financial role of the fur trade in the early life of the colonies, it seems fair to say that the entire colonial enterprise was substantially made possible by the continuing Indian market for European goods.[20]

Thus Native Americans were incorporated into a mercantile trans-Atlantic and European economy on the basis of European demands for Indian-produced peltry and Indian demands for European-produced goods. As trading networks spread outward from the colonies, Indian nations with no direct contact with non-Indians were brought into that expanding economic system. For nearly all of them, the consequences of incorporation were revolutionary.

Native American societies and cultures were by no means static. European invasion, however, at first through the medium of trade relations, greatly accelerated the pace of change. It also redirected change in a number of ways.

European commodities themselves initiated a substantial transformation. As Indian material goods were replaced by European ones, some traditional crafts and technologies fell into disuse. Eventually some were forgotten. Trade items once considered luxuries or conveniences became necessities. At the same time new wants emerged that could be satisfied only by European products. The result for many tribes was growing dependence on trade. By the mid-1700s, for example, the Cherokees acknowledged that trade with Europeans was key to their survival; seventeenth-century Potawatomis found their freedom constrained by the need for good relations with French traders, their only source of firearms, iron knives, and other goods. A century later, their fur supplies exhausted, the Potawatomi began leasing and selling land in order to maintain trade and political relations that had become indispensable to Potawatomi life. By the 1820s, according to Charles Bishop, Canada's Osnaburgh Ojibwa had become "totally reliant on the trading post for survival," while the Blackfeet, writes John Ewers, likewise found themselves dependent on traders for goods they could not make themselves and now considered necessities.[21]

Consequently, the production or procurement of furs came to dominate more and more of Indian life. New commodities and trade activities tended to reorganize the bases of prestige and authority. New, trade-oriented leadership roles emerged; gender relations changed; new sources of wealth appeared. The trade had a social as well as an economic impact.[22]

It also subordinated indigenous trade patterns to the emergent European ones, often reorienting the entire system of intertribal commerce. As Indian societies were transformed, these new trade relations took on monumental importance; losing them could be devastating. In 1763–64, Pontiac's War threw New York and the Ohio River Valley into turmoil and substantially affected a number of tribes that, according to Norton, after two years of disrupted trade "desperately needed European goods."[23] This crisis was the product of an increasingly specialized and dependent economy tied to limited markets.

Of course the degree of dependence varied greatly among Indian nations. In some cases survival was at stake, while in others the use of European goods remained a matter of choice. "Adaptation," as James Axtell reminds us, "is less often a sign of capitulation than of capitalization."[24] Those who turned to the trade were seizing an opportunity, exploiting newly available means of meeting concrete needs. Indians had always been dependent, if only on each other; the shift was from dependence on one set of technologies and relationships to dependence on another. But now Indians were tied into a vastly different economic and political system, and were vulnerable to new and unusually potent social forces from which, eventually, there would be no escape.

Hunting grew in importance, to the detriment of agriculture. Crucially, it was hunting on an increasingly commercial, instead of subsistence, basis. The purpose of the hunt was no longer simply to secure food, hides, and other products for home consumption, but to sustain trade relationships with Europeans.[25] As Indian demands for trade goods rose, the hunting of fur-bearing animals intensified. The efficiency of Indian hunters also increased with the coming of firearms, a major item in the fur trade.

The ecological effects were severe. Intensified hunting destroyed game populations. Phillips reports that commercially exploitable populations of fur-bearing animals were gone from the lower St. Lawrence area by the 1630s, from New England by 1690, and from virtually the whole of the British colonies east of the Appalachians by 1744. By the 1770s fur trade regulation in the southern colonies was no longer a problem; there were too few deer left.[26] With the depletion of game some tribes became dependent on the Europeans not only for trade goods but for food as well; others could scarcely find enough furs for their own clothing, much less for trade.[27]

Intertribal warfare increased as groups competed for shrinking fur supplies and for control of trade routes and access to European merchants. Struggles over northern fur supplies and French trade relationships, for example, led to the virtual annihilation of the Huron by the Iroquois in 1648–49.[28]

Through such contests, and thanks to the political nature of the trade itself, Native Americans were incorporated not only into the trans-Atlantic economy but also into the system of European and colonial politics. In a sense it was a reciprocal relationship: just as the Europeans used the Indians as political instruments in their designs, groups such as the Iroquois made effective use of the Europeans. But it was a reciprocity weighted eventually against the Indians. Struggling to maintain their independence, they found their choices of action steadily reduced. The Five, later Six, Nations of the Iroquois League, threatened by both English and French encroachments on their lands and liberty, became adept at balancing one power against the other, but their own freedom eventually came to be limited by the necessities of the diplomatic act. The fall of New France upset the balance and presaged the fall of the Iroquois. In the mid-seventeenth century the Mohawks built their power on Dutch support, but when the English conquered New Netherland, the structure of Mohawk politics collapsed.[29] The blessings of the trade were bountiful but insecure.

The fur trade also paved the way for European settlement and Indian dispossession. Traders established posts; posts became settlements; settlements became towns. Some Indians actively encouraged penetration of traders deeper into the continent; it shortened the distances furs had to be transported, bypassed middleman groups, and assured the proximity of European goods. New emphases on hunting and the corollary decline in sedentary agriculture fueled the arguments of colonial settlers that the Indian was merely a nomadic savage who did not cultivate the soil and must step aside in favor of the agrarian Whites. With the depletion of game in eastern regions there was no longer an economic argument, from the European point of view, for leaving Indian lands to the Indians; only where furs remained could the Indian continue to produce and the trader continue to profit.

The trade had other effects—often substantial—on Indian social organization, culture, and geographical distribution. But it is the changes in Indian-White relations that are of more immediate interest here. For the better part of two centuries, from the latter part of the sixteenth century until well into the eighteenth, the fur trade defined the structures of Indian-White relations for probably a sizeable majority of those Indians in contact with Europeans. Through the trade they were incorporated as producers into the trans-Atlantic political economy.

For the most part they did not resist that incorporation; on the contrary they pursued it.[30] They saw its benefits, which were immediate and concrete, more readily than its costs, which were less tangible at first and took longer to appear. But the benefits were only temporary; the costs were essentially permanent.

Politically, the trade was a relationship between powers that began more or less as equals. Yet Indian strength—vis-à-vis the Europeans or tribally among themselves—came to depend on the trade more and more, while the Europeans, their own economic activities diversifying, came to depend on it less and less. Thus the power of the European grew while the power of the native, like the trade itself, slowly slipped away.

Economically, the results were no less uneven. Europeans depended on the Indians for luxury goods and money income; they invested capital and labor in the trade and commonly drew a handsome return. Indians came to depend on the Europeans, in some cases, for the material means to survival; they invested in the trade not only capital and labor but much of their culture besides. Once in, they found that the costs of getting out were high. Their ultimate returns were dependency and dispossession.

FROM LABOR TO LAND

Major transformations of social structure commonly do not occur over-night, even in revolutions, and the patterns of Indian incorporation are no exception. The change from the first phase to the second occupied most of the eighteenth century, and even then it is difficult to say just when it was complete. By the time of U.S. independence the primacy of trade in most Indian-White relations was over. Within a few decades the incorporation of major Indian groups into a world market on the basis of their own production, and the political integration that accompanied it, would be something largely of the past. The new pattern of incorporation would be built around the direct acquisition of Native American resources—primarily land—in their raw state, rapidly declining Indian power, and the exclusion of Indians themselves from the newly emergent economy of the United States.

The transition to this second phase of incorporation involved a number of factors, some internal to the fur trade, others embedded in political and economic developments external to the trade and the everyday world of Indian-White interaction. Of the internal factors these have been noted already: increased Native American dependence on European goods and a consequent decline in Indian autonomy, and the virtual extermination of fur-bearing animals in large areas of eastern North America. The latter development not only destroyed the trading economy just as Indians had become dependent upon it, but also forced many groups—and the trade it-self—westward in search of new resources.

Also important was the end of the Indian monopoly on fur production. From the beginning of the trade, Indians had monopolized the hunting and processing of furs; Europeans had depended on Indian skills and Indian knowledge of the animals and the land. Even the French *coureurs de bois,* who made the deepest early penetrations of the hinterlands, were primarily traders, searching not for live beaver but for Indians from whom already processed furs could be obtained.

Just when this dependence on Indian skills changed is unclear. Jennings suggests that Kentucky hunters such as Daniel Boone "revolutionized the trade, late in the eighteenth century, by substituting themselves in the Indians' roles." Nonetheless, the original pattern seems to have prevailed into the early nineteenth century as the trade moved into the upper Missouri River basin, where it remained dependent for a time on Indian labor. Although as early as 1807 basin traders like Manuel Lisa were trading *and* trapping for furs, it was not until the Ashley expeditions to the Rocky Mountains in the early 1820s that trapping became the dominant method of obtaining pelts. The Rocky Mountain trade, except that with the Blackfeet and a few others, was not really a trade at all but essentially a trapping enterprise. This distinguished it from the trade for buffalo robes on the northern plains, where production remained for a time largely an Indian activity. But in the mountains, remarks David Wishart, "the Native American played only a supplementary part, occasionally trading furs to the trappers or furnishing food and shelter for the trappers during the winter season."[31]

It was not that Europeans lacked the requisite skills. Ray and Freeman report, for example, that Hudson's Bay Company men trapped marten in large numbers around Fort Albany in the winter of 1715–16.[32] It seems more likely that what was lacking during the heyday of the trade was the labor force and organization, ready access to fur regions, and the knowledge of the hinterland environment necessary to reproduce Indian hunting efficiencies. But regardless of the timing of the transition from Indian labor to White—which probably occurred in different areas at different times—what is important is that by early in the nineteenth century, except on the northern plains, Indian skills and, therefore, Indian participation were of declining importance to the trade. The critical factor for the fur industry was quickly becoming direct access to raw materials—not to Indians, that is, but to Indian lands.

Still more important in this transitional period were external developments that altered the Indians' role in colonial and European economies and left them increasingly vulnerable to political pressure. Politically these developments had to do with the changing European power structure in North America; economically they had to do with land.

Pressure on Indian lands was hardly new. Particularly in the English colonies it had been part of Indian-White relations since contact. By the eighteenth century some tribes located near the seacoast, in New England, and in parts of the Atlantic interior already had sold their lands, opened them to European settlement, or had simply been displaced by superior force or the effects of disease. Growing colonial populations and expanding agriculture produced mounting White demand for land throughout the colonial period. Most of the major tribes of the eastern interior managed to resist substantial encroachment on their lands during much of this period through a fortuitous combination of elements: military strength, European alliance, and practical economics. The Iroquois and certain of the southern nations—Creeks, Choctaws, Chickasaws, and Cherokees—were potent military powers, and were recognized and respected as such by the Europeans, who could not afford, during much of this period, to confront them directly. But the deterrent effect of that power lay not so much in its ability to intimidate outsiders as in its ability to upset the European political balance. It was the threat of Iroquois-French alliance, for example, that forced the English to honor Iroquois claims; the threat of an Iroquois-English alliance had a like effect upon the French. Strength lay not only in arms but also in the anxieties of one's friends. Finally, the economic health of the fur trade depended significantly on good relations with those nations that either controlled the trading routes in middleman roles or brought their own furs to the trading posts.

The developments of the latter half of the eighteenth century left this fragile equation in a shambles. Politically, the precipitator was the final collapse of the French presence in North America, ending the competitive politics that had been the basis of Indian political power. In the Treaty of Paris in 1763, closing the Seven Years' War, France ceded to England her territory east of the Mississippi River, including Canada, and gave her western territory to Spain. Suddenly the Indian nations could no longer play the European powers against each other in pursuit of their own aims. This did not mean that a triumphant England could simply ignore Indian concerns, but it did mean that the Indian nations no longer controlled the balance of power in North America, and it left them politically vulnerable to English and colonial designs. The eastward retreat of the French opened the door to the west.[33]

In the meantime the colonial demand for land was growing and the fur trade was in decline. While both settlers and traders envisioned prosperity in western lands, their interests were essentially in conflict. The fur trade was dependent on precisely those ecological conditions that were the antithesis of White settlement. Opening western lands to settlers would drive away both the animals, who were the objects of the trade, and the Indians, who still provided the bulk of its labor. But the role of trade in colonial and British economies was already much diminished. The growth of the colonies had made them far more valuable as markets for English goods than as suppliers of raw materials. In the southern colonies deerskins were hard to find and profits were meager; labor and capital had long since turned to agriculture. The trade was increasingly an affair of the northern colonies, and even there, except only in Canada, its support could not compete with cries for land. Economically, as politically, the dramatic Indian role had become a minor part.[34]

The Revolutionary War brought a respite of sorts. Once again, for example, the Iroquois were able to play one party off against the other, although ultimately the pressures of the diplomatic game, combined with other developments, undid the League, some nations siding with England, others with the colonies.[35] From the Indian point of view the British defeat was a disaster. In the articles of peace ending the conflict, Britain transferred its claim to all Indian lands east of the Mississippi River to the United States. The Iroquois and other groups, recognizing no sovereignty over their lands save their own, were outraged at such presumption. But in the next few years there was more to come. The Continental Congress, laden with debts after years of war, saw in this newly acquired expanse of territory a source of revenue, a form of currency, a means of paying troops. Speculators saw new vistas opening to them; farmers and homeseekers saw new homes. Peace was followed by a scramble for land.[36]

The affected groups resisted encroachment as best they could, but found themselves bereft of allies and diminished in power. In a series of conflicts and treaties in the decades following the Revolution, their lands and freedom rapidly declined.

As for the fur trade, the independence of the colonies left the most productive Canadian lands and the bulk of the trade in the hands of the British. The American trade continued for a time. With the Louisiana Purchase its attention moved west of the Mississippi, and by the 1820s American traders and trappers were harvesting the resources of the Rocky Mountains. Here, in new form and environs, the trade continued to attract adventurers and entrepreneurs; but though it brought fame and fortune to some, its economic impact on the emergent nation was slight.

Politically, on the other hand, the trade retained some significance. It was American trappers who first tested U.S. boundaries with Spain in the Southwest and Britain to the north, and it was trappers also who shaped the earliest contacts between the United States and a host of western Indian nations. Even so, the pivotal place of the trade in Indian-White relations was gone, disappearing with the era of colonialism and intra-European competition on the North American continent. Gone as well, more and more, was the participation of the Indians themselves, on whose labor the industry had once depended. Trappers and traders continued to obtain furs from Indians, especially on the northern plains; certainly many native groups were eager to sell. But in the nineteenth century it was increasingly White labor, not Indian, on which the western trade was built.

ON INDIAN LABOR

This first phase of Indian-White relations, dominated by the fur trade, was the only time in which the widespread incorporation of Native Americans into larger economic and political structures was based primarily on the need for Indian labor. This distinguishes the Indian experience in the United States and Canada from that of many indigenous peoples south of the Rio Grande. In Mexico, the Caribbean, and most of Central and South America, labor was a primary, determinative basis of relations between indigenes and Europeans and their descendants. But in North America, by late in the eighteenth century, Indians were rapidly becoming superfluous—indeed, a hindrance—to the economic system on which they had come to depend. Land was increasingly the object of incorporation, and no Indian assistance was needed to exploit it or its many resources.

This is not to say that aside from the fur trade Indian labor played no part in Indian-White relations.[37] In the seventeenth century New England colonists enslaved Indians as a form of criminal punishment, and Indians taken captive in war were occasionally exported to the West Indies as slaves. Indian enslavement was most common in South Carolina. In 1707 there were 1,400 Indian slaves in the colony, out of a total enumerated population (free Whites, White servants, Black slaves, Indian slaves) of 9,580. At times the colonial administration encouraged Indian enslavement, especially for export to the West Indies in exchange for Blacks. Of course slavery was not unknown among the Indians themselves. Some southeastern tribes sold their own captives to the Europeans, who encour-

aged them to war on each other for this purpose. In 1619 the Chicka-
hominy chief Opechancanough invited the British to join in a raid against
his western enemies; part of the anticipated booty would be captives who
could be enslaved.[38]

Indian labor was a salient feature of Indian-White relations in the Southwest. Spicer reports that the Spanish government and the Catholic church
competed with each other for access to Indian labor in the region in the
seventeenth century. In California the Spanish put thousands of Indians
to work in communal and peonage labor systems, and the enslavement of
Indians remained common after the Americans took over. As late as the
1850s and 1860s, Californians were raiding Indian rancherias for women
and children to be sold in the cities as domestic help.[39]

Yet in the long history of Indian-White relations, Indian enslavement
emerges as a largely incidental business. Winthrop Jordan raises the question of why it was not more widespread, especially in comparison to the
enslavement of Blacks, against which it was numerically insignificant. He
points to the differing European conceptions of the two, formed in quite
different contexts. Englishmen certainly viewed Indians as fundamentally
different from themselves, but they saw them as different from Africans
as well. From very early on, Indian groups, unlike Blacks, were dealt with
as sovereign nations. Especially in the early years it was important to
retain the friendship of those nations, many of whom were capable of
costly reprisals. Gary Nash draws a similar distinction, pointing out that
for nearly three centuries, in trade, in negotiations, in war, "the Anglo-
American confronted the native as an adversary rather than a chattel."
The uncertain nature of power distributions between Indian and White
groups made relations between the two very different from those between
Black and White.[40]

The nature of much Indian slavery in the Atlantic colonies supports
these views. In general it involved either retribution for crimes, captives
taken in "just wars," or Indians already enslaved and sold by other tribes.

Other factors were involved as well. Several authors have pointed out
that Indian cultures and social structures probably made most Indian
groups less enslavable than Africans. Indians, says Jordan, "were less used
to settled agriculture, and their own variety of slavery was probably even
less similar to the chattel slavery which Englishmen practiced in America
than was the domestic and political slavery of the West African cultures."
Eugene Genovese refers to the Latin American experience, "where a sustained effort to enslave Indians was successful only where they had previously developed an agricultural society."[41] Such arguments may carry some
weight in the North American case, although many eastern Indians were
no strangers to farming. Marvin Harris points also to Indian susceptibility
to European diseases. Lacking the immunities acquired by Blacks over
centuries of indirect European/African interactions, "Indian slaves died
by the thousands while engaged in labor on behalf of their conquerors."[42]

Disease exacerbated another drawback: the lack of numbers. Even if

Europeans had managed to turn Indian populations into a disciplined agricultural labor force, in North America those populations were too small to satisfy the needs of the emergent colonial and American economies.

Perhaps most important, however, was the problem of control. Enslaved in or near familiar territories, and often near their own free communities, Indians would be more prone to attempt escape and more likely to be successful. Peter Wood notes that "when Indians were sold to an unfamiliar region where they were less likely to run away, their value as slaves went up."[43]

Of course many Indians, throughout the history of Indian-White relations, have sold their labor for wages. On farms and in urban areas, from the colonial period to the present, Indians have sought and found employment. As their old ways of life were swept away, some turned to the culprit itself, the wave of White settlement, for economic survival. Albert Hurtado claims that in the late 1840s the California labor force included perhaps ten thousand Indians, a substantial proportion. Indians, along with much larger numbers of Chinese, Irish, and others, were employed in construction of the transcontinental railroad. By the 1860s Paiute Indians already had become an important source of cheap labor for Nevada farmers and ranchers. Much the same happened in the Southwest by late in the century, where Mexican and Anglo employers began to use Indian labor in transportation, mining, and agriculture.[44]

Policy was also a factor in Indian employment. Especially in the nineteenth and early twentieth centuries it was widely believed that Indians would be civilized only as they were taught the work habits and motivations of White Americans. The allotment policy, which distributed reservation lands to individual tribesmen, was predicated in part on just such sentiments, while government administrators tried to involve Indians on many reservations in wage labor. In 1874 Congress went so far as to require Indians to work in return for annuities often guaranteed by treaty.[45]

In the twentieth century Indian wage labor became commonplace. In the early 1930s the Bureau of Indian Affairs organized a Guidance and Placement Division that placed Indians in off-reservation jobs. During the same period the Civilian Conservation Corps had an Indian Division; over nine years it provided training and/or employment to some eighty-five thousand Indians.[46] World War II provided perhaps the greatest single push into wage labor: thousands of Indians either joined the armed forces or took jobs in wartime industry. Also, throughout the period, faced with poverty, Indians sought out employment both near reservations and in the cities of the land.

Despite such labor experience, the central point remains. With the exception of the early Southwest, only in the fur trade was Indian labor either critical to colonial, U.S., or trans-Atlantic economies or a foundation of Indian-White relations. This has some significance for the larger topic of this study. The ways Indians have acted politically reflect—directly or indirectly—the particular ways they have been incorporated into larger economic and political structures. Much the same could be said of any group in American life. For example, one of the critical factors in the historical emergence of a Black racial consciousness in America was slavery, not simply because of the common experience of oppression, but because the enforced mobility and mixing of slaves shattered group boundaries and identities carried from Africa and facilitated the emergence of a more comprehensive consciousness.

No Indian experience had comparable effects until the middle of the twentieth century, when off-reservation employment and the massive urban migrations of the 1950s and 1960s played a central role in the emergence of a politically aware supratribalism. Even then, the preservation of tribal homelands, among other things, meant that an emergent "Indian" consciousness became an adjunct to, not a replacement for, tribal identities. Had Indian labor remained fundamental to the incorporative process in the period following the collapse of the fur trade, it seems likely that Indians would have been much more widely integrated as individuals into local or regional economies. Such individual incorporation would have increased Indian geographical mobility, more thoroughly undermined indigenous communities, and perhaps hastened the appearance of a supratribal identity while greatly reducing, if not eliminating altogether, the influence of the tribe on Indian self-concepts and action. That the fur trade did not have this effect reflects the fact that, until very late in the game, fur production remained a group activity that was more or less freely entered into, took place under Indian control, and was linked to European actors at the marketplace, not in production.

The relative lack of any large-scale demand for Indian labor in later years, combined with the high demand for Indian land, had another consequence as well. Ironically, it left Indians a land base. Eventually removed from lands coveted by Whites, Indians retained the unwanted ones. Had labor been the object of incorporation, it is unlikely that Indian populations would have been concentrated on reservations or that the later assimilation effort (see Chapters 3 and 4) would have focused on retaining an Indian land base, if only to distribute it among independent Indian farmers. It seems more likely that assimilation would have been accomplished through the integration of an Indian labor force into non-Indian economic activities, and Indians would have been removed as individuals to the mines and rich agricultural lands where their labor was most needed, and not as groups to lands viewed as worthless or distant from White settlement.

In this regard, then, the fur trade is exceptional in Indian-White relations. For two centuries or more it dominated those relations, and at the heart of it lay Indian labor: the procurement and processing of furs. Through the trade the Indians of North America were incorporated into the economic and political system of rapidly evolving Euro-American society. The transformative effects of that incorporation on Indian societies and cultures were often drastic, comprehensive, and essentially permanent. The particular form of incorporation, however, was temporary. By the middle of the eighteenth century, the heyday of the fur trade was decades past; other riches—the land itself—had long since taken the place of furs. It would be nearly two centuries before Indian labor would be sought on such a scale again, and then it would be not because of a need for Indian skills, but because Indians had gained enough political power, tenuous though it may be, to insist that their resources not be exploited without their participation.

In another way, however, the fur trade was part and parcel of a long-term trend in Indian-White relations. It marked the beginning of a long decline in Indian political autonomy and economic self-sufficiency. While the basis of incorporation changed, the nature of its effects had been firmly established. Even among the more remote groups, whose contact with the trade was slight, the pattern was becoming clear. Increasingly, Indian action would take place within constraints set by the actions, growing political power, and emergent economic interests of Whites. In this sense the fur trade was not exceptional at all, but a harbinger of what was yet to come.

Chapter 3

Solving "the Indian Problem"

I know what the misfortune of the tribes is. Their misfortune is not . . . that they are a dwindling race; not that they are a weak race. Their misfortune is that they hold great bodies of rich lands.

—Senator Eugene Casserly, 1871[1]

The consequences of the fur trade were devastating, in their own way, for the Indian nations, but they emerged in a context of willful Indian participation. In contrast, Native Americans fiercely resisted the second phase of incorporation, whose consequences were far more costly. Again a commodity lay at the heart of the matter. This time it was land.

Land occupies center stage in the historical theater of Indian-White relations. Around it the drama moves. Its leading role was supported by a multiplicity of values. To the Europeans land meant subsistence, wealth, freedom, power. It defined the promise of the New World, whose very name, now commonplace and merely geographical, suggested then regeneration and abundance, a singular opportunity to refashion social and political life. For Indians, land—perceived through a radically different cultural prism—bore meanings no less significant, but rooted in continuity instead of change.

The practical significance of land for Euro-Americans—paramount in an agricultural society—was magnified by its composite character. In both the colonies and the young United States, land at various times was a form of currency, a means of paying debts, the major source of American government revenues, and a common determinant of suffrage. Land, power, and fortune were natural partners; commercial agriculture and land speculation were major sources of early American wealth. As James Truslow Adams remarked, "In all the colonies, land and ever more land was the goal of

33

those who wished to advance in the most rapid way possible both their financial and social position."[2]

It should hardly be surprising, then, that land became the centerpiece of Indian-White relations. American land was Indian land, and in the eighteenth and nineteenth centuries the need for this elemental commodity drove White America westward into conflict with the Indian nations.

INDIAN LAND, WHITE DESIGN

In 1783 the Treaty of Paris brought the American Revolution to a close and established the territorial boundaries of the United States. According to that treaty, the Mississippi River formed the western boundary of the new nation, yet the frontier—the line of White settlement—still lay substantially to the east. As late as 1800, after nearly two hundred years of European colonization, White penetrations beyond the Appalachian Mountains were few. Practically speaking, the vast bulk—more than 80 percent—of what is now the contiguous forty-eight states was still Indian land.

One hundred years later fewer than eighty million acres remained, less than 5 percent of the 1800 holdings. While the twentieth century saw substantial further reductions, by the end of the nineteenth the aboriginal land base was almost entirely in non-Indian hands.

During the same period the United States emerged as the world's leading economic power. That these two processes, American economic development and Indian land dispossession, should occupy the same approximate period is of course no mere coincidence. The two are closely related. At one level that relationship is obvious and elementary: any economic activity on the North American continent was ultimately dependent, directly or indirectly, on access to land. As land was removed from Indian control it became available for non-Indian settlement and economic enterprise.[3] Dispossession, in other words, not only fueled economic development; it was essential to it.

The character and quantity of American land affected economic development in less obvious ways as well. In colonial America, for example, land availability was fundamental in maintaining the standard of living. The colonies, write Susan Lee and Peter Passell, sustained an increase in population of more than 600 percent "without a decrease in living standards," an extraordinary achievement. The availability of land was a critical factor: "high-quality farmland was always available to accommodate a growing labor force. Labor productivity did not decline; the frontier was simply pushed westward."[4]

Land and its associated resources were the great American blessing. From early on the American economy was characterized by a relative abundance of land and a relative scarcity of human and capital resources. Land provided an essential resource base for growth, and its availability led to increases in more scarce productive resources. Capital and labor poured into America in response to the economic opportunity offered by the natural riches of the continent, and in turn fueled agricultural expansion, mineral development, and infrastructural construction.[5]

Yet this abundance of land, largely assumed in texts on American economic history,[6] was itself dependent on dispossession of the original inhabitants. Land may have been ample, but it was largely inaccessible until the social formations of Native American societies, which bound land to communities and practices very different from those of the emergent United States, could be altered, removed, or destroyed.

This process of gaining access to Indian lands weaves its way through much of American history, and its geographical contours, especially in the first half of the nineteenth century, frame the topography of economic development in the United States. The cotton economy of the South, for example, which itself provided much of the motor force of early American economic growth, expanded only as fast as the acquisition process would allow. From 1815 into the 1830s the growth of cotton cultivation and production followed the changing map of Native American land cessions.[7] Markets for southern cotton fueled demands for land on which to expand production; demands for land promoted dispossession. It was the promise of increased cotton profits, for example, that led the acting governor of the Arkansas Territory to demand extinction of the Quapaw claim to Arkansas lands in 1823. Mississippians rejoiced at Andrew Jackson's election in part because Jackson's program to remove Indians from the southern states would mean expanded cotton production.[8]

Elsewhere the relationship is less immediately obvious but no less fundamental: Indian resources were essential building blocks in the rise of the United States to economic power. Indian-White conflict, then, was substantially a struggle over those resources, made inevitable by their relative scarcity measured against the conflicting demands of Indian and non-Indian populations. But there was more to it. Indian-White conflict arose also and fundamentally out of an epic confrontation between two kinds of society. In each, land was of great importance but served a distinctive role. The struggle between Indian and White, therefore, was not only over who would have access to resources, but over the nature of the resources themselves and their place in social relations and cultural order.

Europe's grand venture into the New World involved more than people. It involved as well an emergent economic system: the gathering forces of mercantile and industrial capitalism. In such a system economic growth and capital accumulation are dependent on the market availability of the various factors of production, on the commercialization of land, labor, and capital. They depend, in other words, on the transformation of land, labor, and capital into commodities that can be freely bought and sold on the market.

This requirement poses a distinct challenge to precapitalist societies. In so-called primitive and feudal societies labor and land are bound up in a network of social relations—kinship, custom, obligation between peasant and lord, and so forth—which substantially determine their uses. Commercialization means that labor and land are no longer controlled by social bonds or cultural practice but are subject instead to market forces, available for the best price: labor for wages, land for purchase or rent. It means also that the various social and cultural uses of the land become increasingly subordinate to its economic exchange value, to the value inherent in the exchangeability of the land or its products, be they agricultural, mineral, or social. Where once the value of the land could be measured in terms of its multifaceted contribution to the maintenance of the social organism, under capitalism its value is measured in terms of the monetary, or equivalent, return that can be realized from it.[9] The market becomes the arbiter of value for the land as for labor and other things.

Thus the Euro-American quest for resources involved more than simply a change in the occupancy and control of lands. Its intention and its effect were to transform those resources into commercial quantities, to wrest them from the grasp of indigenous cultural practice and thrust them onto the market.[10]

At the same time the economic uses of the land, which more than anything else brought Indian and European into conflict with each other, were only one part of the calculus of dispossession. Also involved were an array of cultural concepts and an evolving body of political thought, rooted in Europe but bearing the imprint of the uniquely American landscape and experience. The relationship was an interactive one: the ideas Europeans brought to America and the economic forces embodied in those ideas shaped their perceptions of American land, but the land itself, and in particular its apparently pristine immensity, also shaped their ideas of themselves and their purposes. Sensing the opportunity for social construction on a grand scale, the Europeans' concepts were self-consciously creative. "Men, it seemed," writes Michael Rogin, "could regain Eden from a position of control instead of dependence."[11]

This American vision—what Robert Berkhofer calls "the ideology of Americanism"[12]—involved economic prosperity and powerfully intertwined as well ideas of progress, nationalism, religious mission, and individual liberty. Land played a major part in it. One of its central themes in the latter portion of the eighteenth century and early decades of the nineteenth was agrarian social theory.[13] Its most distant roots were classical and biblical, but it had been nourished in European social thought, in particular the Scottish Enlightenment and among the French physiocrats. In the New World it gained an aura of imminent reality: here the liberal ideals of the age might at last be realized.

As political economy, it placed agriculture at the heart of national development, viewing it as the most productive sector of the economy and the primary source of national wealth. As creed, it found the highest expression of civilization in the individual farmer: sturdy, industrious, subduing nature with hoe and plow. This exalted status of the cultivator was combined with particular notions of property. Following the Lockeian view, private property was conceived not only as a natural right, but also as the basis of civilized society; the freehold farmer was the icon of civilization.

Agrarianism was a prominent theme in the social and political thought of the early United States, and it found perhaps its most elaborate political expression in the thinking of Thomas Jefferson. Jefferson placed his emphasis not, in the manner of John Locke, on individual rights to property, but on its social functions. He viewed political independence as best preserved through economic security and social equality. The broad distribution of wealth assured an economically interested and therefore politically responsible public; and land was the key. Widely distributed throughout the population, it would offer to Americans something no longer possible in Europe: the social foundations of republicanism. A nation of farmers would be a nation of independent, self-sufficient individuals, protected thereby from the impositions of the State.

There was also a moral aspect to Jefferson's agrarianism. "Those who labor in the earth," he wrote, "are the chosen people of God. . . . Corruption in morals in the mass of cultivators is a phenomenon of which no age nor nation has furnished an example. . . . While we have land to labor, then, let us never wish to see our citizens occupied at a workbench, or twirling a distaff."[14] For Jefferson, notes A. W. Griswold, agriculture "had a sociological rather than economic value."[15]

Nor was Jefferson alone. Similar sentiments were common among many early American thinkers and statesmen—James Madison, John Adams, George Mason, Noah Webster, and others. "The only possible way," wrote Adams, ". . . of preserving the balance of power on the side of equal liberty and public virtue, is to make the acquisition of land easy to every member of society; to make a division of the land into small quantities, so that the multitude may be possessed of landed estates."[16]

Agrarianism, then, saw in a nation of farmers a nation of economically independent, politically autonomous, morally virtuous citizens. Land became the basis of prosperity as well as morality, social equality, and democratic government. Access to land, and its more or less equal distribution, was therefore crucial to the preservation of the body politic. The implication is clear. For political, social, as well as economic reasons, growing populations made expansion imperative. Only increasing quantities of readily available land could assure the maintenance of democratic institutions and the equality of economic opportunity.

Land thus became the object of mixed but complementary purposes. Expanding populations and economic interests looked to western lands for future fortune, bending the natural resources of the continent to the purposes of capital accumulation. At the same time political philosophy also promoted the commercialization and appropriation of land, but on behalf of social equality and political freedom. Eventually the economic interest and the social ideal came in conflict; the fortunes of the former flourished in westward expansion while those of the latter gradually declined.[17] But the conflict between them is of less moment here than their convergence: both made the incorporation of Indian land a fundamental intermediary goal of the emergent American system.

There were other ideas that at one time or another fueled westward expansion: manifest destiny, dreams of empire and visions of Progress, the image of America as Garden of the World. "The untransacted destiny of the American people," wrote William Gilpin in 1846, expressing the convictions of many, "is to subdue the continent—to rush over this vast field to the Pacific Ocean . . . to establish a new order in human affairs."[18] While the precise nature of the historical project varied through the nineteenth century, the exalted sense of mission remained, as did the vast geographical scope of the enterprise. But enough said. Economically, politically, conceptually, by late in the eighteenth century land had become a critical part of the American adventure, shaping the encounter between Indian and White.

LAND AND COMMUNITY IN NATIVE AMERICA

On the other side of that encounter stood the Indian nations. While in social organization and culture those nations were profoundly diverse, they—like most "primitive" or "tribal" societies—shared certain commonalities that set them apart from the European invaders, among them a relationship to land quite different from that emerging in modern Europe.

This distinctive land relationship reflects a particular social organization. "The economy" in tribal societies is difficult to locate; there is no set of activities that can be viewed as solely or even primarily economic. Consequently it is also difficult to treat the factors of production in isolation from the rest of the social order. Land, labor, and the productive process are inextricably bound up in webs of kinship, ritual, and custom, which themselves render the different aspects of social reality mutually intelligible and interdependent. Discussing tribal economy, Marshall Sahlins argues that "structurally, 'the economy' does not exist. Rather than a distinct and specialized organization, 'economy' is something that generalized social groups and relations, notably kinship groups and relations, do. Economy is rather a function of the society than a structure." Elsewhere he writes, "What are in the conventional wisdom of economic science 'exogenous' or 'noneconomic' factors, such as kinship and politics, are in the tribal reality the very organization of the economic process. . . . They *are* the economy."[19]

The form and function of economy in such societies tend to coincide. All social relations are engaged in economy as a matter of course, for economy involves "the process of provisioning society (or the 'socio-cultural system')." Economy is "the material life process of society rather than a need-satisfying process of individual behavior."[20]

Land and labor under such conditions are organized not so much for the production of wealth as for the maintenance of community. Economic activity is oriented typically to the production of use value as opposed to exchange value, where "use" refers to subsistence utility as well as to the contribution of an object, of the productive process, or of human interaction through production and exchange, to the maintenance of social relations.[21] It is not to the market that land and labor are bound, but to the preservation of the social organism itself and of a particular, meaningful mode of existence. They are inseparable from the intricate web of relations and meanings that constitute the society as a whole.

This means that land and labor lack the "freedom" that, as commodities, they enjoy in market-based societies. The freedom of the market is freedom from constraints on the production and transfer of goods, including the factors of production, other than those constraints imposed by market forces of supply and demand and subsequently by contract and ownership. In these terms land and labor in tribal societies are not free at all. Land is not something one controls as a consequence of individual action, but something with which one shares a particular relationship by virtue of membership in a particular community.[22]

Native American attitudes toward specific lands may well have changed in the course of their interactions with non-Indians. As some lands were threatened by invasion, attachments to them may have gained salience, while reduced resources were more fiercely defended than more plentiful ones.[23] But whatever the variations among groups and over time, at a conceptual level land and community were often intimately linked. Just as land held diverse meanings for Whites, for Indians likewise its significance was multivalent. For them, too, land not only offered subsistence and freedom, but shaped and was shaped by identity and self-concept.

"Most groups," writes French sociologist Maurice Halbwachs, "engrave their form in some way upon the soil and retrieve their collective remembrances within the spatial framework thus defined."[24] Of course the physical impact Native Americans had on the land, while hardly negligible, was often slight compared with the transformations wrought by Europeans. Nonetheless, Indians worked their own conceptual transformations, mixing their ideas of places and their ideas of themselves. Thus, for example, Chief Joseph of the Nez Perces: "The earth and myself are of one mind. The measure of the land and the measure of our bodies are the same." History was written in place names and stories that gave space definition in relation to the group, and vice versa. "Every part of this soil," said Seathl, Suquamish chief, in 1854, "is sacred in the estimation of my people. Every hillside, every valley, every plain and grove, has been hallowed by some sad or happy event in days long vanished."[25] To be a member of the group was, among other things, to share in this history, to make particular use of the land not only economically but culturally, as part of a structure of ideas. Space and identity were thereby intertwined; place and group, in Halbwachs's words, "each received the imprint of the other."[26]

In their own way, of course, Europeans did much the same, but for them the American land signified a new beginning and enabled a break from the past. For Indians, it assured the continuity of their own distinctive way of being, and quite literally embodied a past that told them who they were. As Curly, the Crow who served with Custer, said, "The soil you see is not ordinary soil—it is the dust of the blood, the flesh, and bones of our ancestors. . . . You will have to dig down through the surface before you can find nature's earth, as the upper portion is Crow."[27]

To summarize: at both practical and conceptual levels, the land relationship in Native American societies, while varied, was an attribute of membership in a particular community and of participation in a particular cultural order. Furthermore, that relationship was at odds with the market; capital accumulation could not proceed until land was set free of the encompassing restraints of social relations and cultural conception. The incorporation of Indian resources required either a fundamental transformation of Native American societies or their removal from the scene.

THE PROCESS OF DISPOSSESSION

Thus "the Indian problem": how to gain access to Indian resources. Of course, there was more to Indian affairs than this. For federal and state authorities, for policymakers and philanthropists, Indian-White relations were more complex than so simple a statement implies. For them "the Indian problem" was variously one of protecting the frontiers from the Indians; protecting the Indians from the unscrupulous; keeping peace among Indians themselves; promoting Euro-American civilization; negotiating treaties and land cessions; distributing education, Christianity, food, annuities, and other odds and ends among the tribes; and coping with the many persons and interests making claims to some part of the Indian business. But all of these aspects of Indian-White relations were in one way or another derivative of their essence: U.S. expansion over Indian lands and consequent Indian resistance.

At a rather abstract level methods of acquiring Indian land fell into two broad categories: assimilation and removal. The premise of assimilation as a mode of land acquisition was that Native Americans, in contact with or under pressure from non-Indians, could be persuaded to abandon nomadic or seminomadic hunting economies and "communal" patterns of landholding in favor of settled agriculture, private property, and other aspects of Euro-American society. Vast hunting lands thereby would be made superfluous to Indian livelihood and available to Whites. Acquisition by assimilation was dependent, in other words, on the transformation of tribal life and culture or on the willingness of large numbers of individual Indians to abandon that life in favor of Euro-American cultural designs.

Removal was less complicated.[28] It involved not culture change but culture relocation: Native Americans would give up a piece of land and go somewhere else. This might be accomplished through negotiated land purchase (the usual case), conquest, legislative fiat, or some combination of these, particularly of the first two, with conquest or the threat of it providing a favorable climate for tribal land sales. While removal itself was not dependent on alterations in tribal society, it often had traumatic consequences for the tribes, undermining tribal economies, intertribal relations, and cultural practice.

Both methods were common and often complementary aspects of U.S. Indian policy. Indeed, the effectiveness of assimilation as a means of obtaining Indian land lay not so much in the successful assimilation of Indians into non-Indian society as in the support that the more expedient removal policy gained from the widely endorsed goal of bringing civilization to the tribes. The assimilation of Indians into non-Indian society, as policymakers quickly discovered, took time and money. A cost-conscious government and a relentless White advance meant neither was easy to come by. Removal, by insulating Indians from frontier confrontation, could buy time for the assimilative process.

Thus the goal of assimilation helped rationalize removal. It was not until late in the nineteenth century that a program of assimilation—the allotment policy—was itself systematically used to obtain Indian lands. But whether as rationale or independent instrument, assimilation was very much part of the dispossession process, and the two methods supported each other in pursuit of the larger goal, the incorporation of Indian resources.

At the same time, efforts to bring civilization to the tribes were not always intended to facilitate land acquisition. Robert Berkhofer has pointed out that the foremost concerns of American policymakers consistently have been *both* the extinction of native land title *and* the replacement of Native American cultures with White.[29] That success in the latter advanced the former was opportune. Nevertheless, the primacy of the first consideration—access—has been evident throughout most of the history of the Indian-federal relationship.

Policy responded to interest and circumstance. Relocation was the method favored by settlers and other interests whose primary concern was simply land acquisition. Assimilation was the choice, first, of those liberal and religious reformers more concerned with saving "savages" and spreading the American way of life than with the land itself and, second, of governmental and other actors whenever Indian resistance derailed efforts at relocation.

In the years immediately following the American Revolution, for example, policy toward the Indian nations was based on the terms of the Peace of Paris, by which Great Britain transferred to the United States its claims to Indian lands east of the Mississippi River. Assuming the right of conquest, Americans moved to take from Indians in western New York and the Ohio River Valley, in consideration of their defeat as British allies, those lands believed needed by the people of the United States. But the Indians, feeling neither defeated in war nor bound by the peace, forcibly resisted both the efforts of the government and the encroachments of White settlers. Faced with a frontier war and lacking the means to wage it, the government was forced to reconsider. The result was a return, in 1789 and subsequently, to the British and colonial practice of purchasing from the Indians the right to the soil.

An additional result was the appearance, as an integral part of Indian policy, of the belief that in return for their lands Indians should be offered the benefits of American civilization. These were to include private property holding and the agricultural arts, traits that, if adopted, would much reduce Indian needs for land and would make what was left more accessible to the market.[30]

This program of civilization—or, in effect, assimilation—offered a solution to several problems. If properly executed it would spare the nation a costly and difficult conflict with militarily powerful adversaries, one that might find new and dangerous alliances developing between Indian nations and the English in Canada or the Spanish in Louisiana. At the same time it would both facilitate land acquisition and provide considerable benefits to the Indians. Finally, it would avoid the disturbing specter of the United States, founded on principles of freedom and equality, setting out to destroy Indian nations for the sake of real estate. Henry Knox, secretary of war in the first administration, was explicit on the point. A policy of purchase and civilization, he remarked, would reflect favorably on the United States in the eyes of the world. Robert Berkhofer dubs the program "expansion with honor."[31]

Removal, on the other hand, first appeared as an element in American policy in 1803, following the Louisiana Purchase, when Thomas Jefferson suggested that newly acquired western lands be given to eastern tribes in exchange for lands east of the Mississippi River.[32] As White demand mounted and Indian power declined, such exchanges, along with simple land cessions and group consolidation within reduced territories, became increasingly the object of treaty negotiations. By the 1860s removal had produced an early version of the reservation system: the concentration of Native American groups in the Indian Territory (now Oklahoma) or on remnant lands elsewhere, where assimilative programs ideally could proceed under supervisory federal controls. The following decades saw the pattern spread throughout the West, and the reservation system in approximately its present form came into being.[33]

But it was not until the 1880s that assimilation and removal joined hands in a single policy. Their convergence was momentous. In 1887 Congress passed the General Allotment Act, also known as the Dawes Act. Applicable to most Indian reservations, the act authorized the allotment of reservation lands, in severalty, among members of occupant tribes, at such time as the president believed it to be in the best interests of those tribes. In most cases heads of households would receive 160-acre parcels, with smaller tracts going to single individuals. Lands thus allotted were to be held in trust for the allottee for twenty-five years, during which time it could be neither sold, leased, nor willed. Lands surplus to the allotment requirement would be put up for sale to White settlers, with proceeds held by the government for the benefit of the tribe. In effect the Dawes Act provided for the dissolution of the reservation system and the end of tribal landholding.[34]

The idea was not new. Some early treaties had provided that individual parcels of land be given to chiefs or headmen and occasionally to others. But allotment did not appear as a central element in Indian policy until fairly late in the nineteenth century. Support for it was widespread. Much of it came from a diverse but growing body of what Robert Mardock calls "social-gospel humanists," many of them veterans of the abolitionist struggle, "deeply concerned with the welfare of their fellowmen."[35] Beginning in the late 1860s the attention of these humanitarian reformers focused increasingly on Native Americans. Their struggle was for Indian rights, by which they meant natural rights to equality of political and economic freedom and responsibility in a liberal democracy. In their own minds the issue was Indian survival; theirs was a desperate effort to save the Indian from extinction at the hands of land-hungry settlers, corrupt government officials, an inept and faithless Congress, and the more decadent elements of frontier society. They viewed Indians as inferior, not by nature but by culture, and their program, therefore, was one of advancement through acculturation. The attributes of Euro-American civilization would be taught to Native Americans; by those attributes, they would be saved.

Their primary target was tribal organization. In the view of the reformers, the tribe was an inferior social formation dominated by tradition, senseless and immoral rituals, communal ownership of property, and hereditary forms of government, all of which inhibited individual freedom. In such societies individual self-interest could not function freely; therefore, the members of the group could not advance. Released from the bonds of the tribe, schooled in non-Indian behaviors, Indians could make their own way successfully in the non-Indian world as free and enlightened individuals. What they advocated, in effect, was a program of forced cultural replacement, in which a Christian education, informed by classically Protestant and individualist values, held the key.

In the years immediately following the Civil War, these reformers, some of them involved in the federal Indian affairs bureaucracy, had defended the reservation system because it isolated Indians from the more harmful influences of the non-Indian population, especially along the frontier, and facilitated a concentrated educational effort. In time, however, the reservation itself came to be viewed as a central part of the problem. It hindered the influence not only of harmful elements in the larger society, but of beneficial ones as well. Isolated from Whites, Indians could hardly be expected to emulate them. Furthermore, the reservation fostered dependency on the federal government, which not only administered the system, but often had to sustain those nations whose economies had been destroyed. Worst of all, it supported tribalism, maintaining communal forms of property holding and use and obstructing individual enterprise.

In the long-term scenario of both reformer and government agent, Indians were to become farmers, something believed impossible under conditions of tribal land tenure and communal social structure. "It is doubtful," wrote Commissioner of Indian Affairs John Smith in 1876, "whether any high degree of civilization is possible without individual ownership of land." An effective program of land allotment would break down the tribal edifice, destroy the system of dependence, and bring Indians into close contact with civilized life. In the process it would foster in them a higher set of values. The allotment system, according to another commissioner of Indian affairs, Hiram Price, would create "individuality, responsibility, and a desire to accumulate property."

This last seemed to figure most prominently in the reformers' thinking. The desire for wealth and property was held to be the source of progress. As Merrill Gates, prominent educator and member of the Board of Indian Commissioners, remarked in 1885, "True ideas of property with all the civilizing influences that such ideas excite are formed only as the tribal relation is outgrown."[36]

Support for allotment came from other quarters as well. White settlers, commercial interests, and the governments of western states and territories all saw Indians as obstacles to their designs. Late in the nineteenth century in Minnesota, Wyoming, Nebraska, Nevada, the Indian Territory—indeed, throughout the West—demands for the dissolution of reservations and the removal of Indians from their lands were on the rise.

In light of such pressures, allotment was perceived as an alternative means of securing to the Indians, via individual titles, at least some of their remaining lands. It was a compromise between eastern concerns for justice and Indian welfare and western desires for land. Allotment in severalty would preserve a reduced land base and promote the civilizing process, while the opening of "surplus" lands would satisfy western economic interests.[37]

The policy had opponents. Indian opposition was widespread and ignored. Non-Indian opposition included cattlemen, many of whom leased grazing lands from tribes and saw allotment as a threat to the large tracts of open land essential to their industry. A few reformers—in particular the National Indian Defense Association—also opposed it, along with some congressmen, senators, and others who viewed the policy as overly ambitious, hasty, or ill-conceived; but their voices were faint against the chorus of support.[38]

Thus assimilation and removal eventually found a common ground, while the goal of civilizing Indians, originally a response to the practical problems of American expansion, eventually took on a life of its own and by the end of the nineteenth century became the dominant idea in Indian policy. But it was as a vehicle of land dispossession that allotment proved most effective. Between passage of the General Allotment Act in 1887, and 1934, when the policy was officially abandoned, eighty-six million acres—more than 60 percent of the remaining Indian land base—passed into non-Indian hands. Much of it went under the surplus lands provision, much of the rest through debt, fraud, and deception or as a result of legislative alterations that facilitated individual sales. The common ground of policy became the Indians' Dismal Swamp.

DESCENT INTO POWERLESSNESS

The coming of allotment also provides a marker of sorts. If treaty-based land cessions are the characteristic form of dispossession in the conflict years, allotment is the characteristic form of the reservation period. Land loss itself continued, but the process was very different, reflecting a new set of political relationships between Indian and White. Indeed, these two stages of incorporation are distinguished, one from the other, more by political than economic criteria. For Native Americans the transition from conflict period to reservation was a transition from relative power to powerlessness. While some groups went through the transition quickly, as an aspect of Indian-White relations it occupied most of the nineteenth century. Allotment was merely part of the evidence, late in the game, that the transition was complete.

The incorporation of Indian resources into the developing economy of the United States necessarily involved a complementary process of political incorporation: the reorganization of political relations between Indian nations and the larger society. Both access to Indian resources and the assimilation of Indians were dependent on such a reorganization, on the assumption by the United States of authority over Indian communities and lives. In other words, the problem of economic incorporation and the problem of cultural transformation were at the same time problems of control.

Non-Indian control faced three related obstacles: Indian military capacities, or the capacity for armed resistance, whether highly organized or not; Indian structures of self-government, that is, structures capable of coordinating group action and sentiment;[39] and national sovereignty. Clearly these are not of a piece. Military power is physically tangible, while structures of self-government are institutionally realized, whether those institutions are formally constituted and readily apparent or not. Of course the two—military power and governmental structures—may not be wholly distinct. Sovereignty, on the other hand, is a relationship, essentially intangible, between human groups and their environment, a measure of a people's claimed and recognized right to think, organize, and act freely to meet their own needs as they see them.[40]

The sovereignty of the Indian nations was recognized, in theory at least, from very early in the history of Indian-White contact. In the sixteenth, seventeenth, and eighteenth centuries European writers on international law generally agreed that the Indian nations were sovereign powers with legal title to the lands they occupied. This position was the basis of treaties of land cession concluded between the colonial powers and Indian

nations and, despite some attempts to ignore it, the basis of early U.S.–
Indian relations as well. As Felix Cohen, long the preeminent authority on
Indian law, wrote, "From the earliest years of the Republic the Indian
tribes have been recognized as 'distinct, independent, political communities,' and as such, qualified to exercise powers of self-government, not by
virtue of any delegation of powers from the Federal government, but
rather by reason of their original tribal sovereignty." This means, says
Cohen, that "those powers which are lawfully vested in an Indian tribe are
not, in general, delegated powers granted by express acts of Congress, but
rather inherent powers of a limited sovereignty which has never been extinguished."[41] This recognized sovereignty of Native American groups was
an obstacle in the sense that Congress or the courts had to extinguish
that sovereignty or otherwise reduce it in order legally to assert control
over Indian nations.

These three components of Indian political autonomy—military power,
structures of self-government, and sovereignty—became the primary targets
in a continuing effort to solve the control problem, an effort intended not
only to undermine Indian capacities for self-government and resistance,
but also to replace indigenous governing structures with structures controlled by non-Indians. Of course the control problem may not have been
perceived in just such terms by those who wrestled with it, nor was this
agenda necessarily explicit. The imposition and elaboration of U.S. political controls over Native Americans was hardly the work of a moment
or a few minds. It was a cumulative process spread out over many decades
and a vast geographical space, and its peculiar shape was determined more
by the exigencies of particular situations than by grand and conscious designs. The only grand design—and it was the product of social forces, not
of conscious thought—was that of Euro-American civilization itself, which
over four centuries has needed Indian resources in order to grow. The
problem of control and the approaches taken to it were products of that
larger imperative.

The resolution of the control problem can be traced in the gradual assumption by the United States of ever greater degrees of authority over
Indian life. In the conflict years that assumption was realized primarily
through treaties signed between the United States and the Indian nations,
supplemented increasingly by congressional legislation and judicial decisions.

Treaties, of course, are political phenomena. They specify relationships
between negotiating parties. They do so in two ways: first, through their
very existence, which constitutes recognition by each party of an essential
equivalence between itself and the other; and, second, in their provisions,
which govern certain actions of each party relative to the other.

Indian treaties were political in just this way. Aside from the maintenance of peace, the primary objective of most treaties was to accomplish
and legitimate major transfers of land from the Indian nations to the
United States. In the process of achieving that objective, however, and

along with related legislation and court decisions, they also specified political relationships. They both constituted formal recognition of Indian nations as sovereign powers with whom the United States could negotiate and specified an increasingly dependent relationship between those powers and the United States. Over time they became more and more intrusive, chipping away at the autonomy of indigenous peoples.

The first target was external affairs. In early treaties Native American groups typically agreed, among other things, to maintain diplomatic relations exclusively with the United States and form alliances with no other power, accepted U.S. regulation of trade relations, relinquished certain jurisdictional rights, and accepted some limits, through land cessions, on tribal mobility and land use. In a 1785 treaty, for example, the Wyandots and other tribes acknowledged "themselves and all their tribes to be under the protection of the United States and of no other sovereign whatsoever." The treaty promised also that any Indian committing robbery or murder against a U.S. citizen would be delivered by the tribe to the United States for punishment according to U.S. law. Four years later the Wyandots and others promised to sell their lands to no power other than the United States. A Cherokee treaty, also signed in 1785, gave the United States "the sole and exclusive right of regulating the trade with the Indians and managing all their affairs as they think proper," while the Kaskaskias agreed in an 1803 treaty to refrain from making war on any other tribe or foreign nation without first obtaining "the approbation and consent of the United States." In return Indian nations might receive guarantees of peaceful relations with the United States, assurance against trespass, trade commitments, offers of education or protection, and so forth.[42]

In these and similar treaties the Indian nations granted certain of their sovereign powers to the United States and accepted some limits on their activities, but maintained a substantial degree of freedom in their movements, in their relations with other tribes, and in their internal affairs. But the distinction between internal affairs and external relations did not last long. An early sign that the boundary was hazy came with the Indian Trade and Intercourse Act of 1790, which asserted federal jurisdiction over non-Indians in Indian territory and placed limits on Indian land transactions. Subsequent Trade and Intercourse Acts further undermined that boundary, while it virtually disappeared in the effort to remove Indians from eastern lands to lands west of the Mississippi River, an effort that was the central concern of treaty making for the better part of thirty years following the War of 1812. In the late 1820s and early 1830s the Five Civilized Tribes—Cherokees, Choctaws, Chickasaws, Creeks, and Seminoles—resisted pressures to sign treaties providing for the cession of their lands in the southeastern United States and their subsequent emigration west. In response, three states—Georgia, Mississippi, and Alabama—adopted measures extending their laws over the Cherokees, Choctaws, Chickasaws, and Creeks within their borders, in effect—and in violation of established Indian treaty rights—declaring their tribal governments null and void. When the tribes appealed to Washington for support of their treaty-guaranteed rights, the federal government simply added its own pressure to that of the states. In 1830 President Jackson warned the Chickasaws to emigrate or be forced to abandon their tribal customs and be made subject to the laws of Mississippi. When the Supreme Court ruled in 1832 that the actions taken by the State of Georgia against the Cherokees were unconstitutional and violated Cherokee treaty rights, Georgia, with at least tacit support from Jackson, defied the Court and allowed harassment of the tribe to continue.[43]

Direct interference in internal affairs, then, was used as a threat in order to force Indian compliance with non-Indian interests. In this particular case the tribes managed to maintain some degree of political autonomy through emigration—something less than a victory—but encroachment on their sovereignty continued. In the treaty of 1835, by which, under extraordinary pressure and with only a fraction of the nation represented, the Cherokees finally relinquished their lands and agreed to move west, it was stipulated that they might establish whatever laws they wished in their new country, but those laws must be consistent with the Constitution of the United States and could not be extended to U.S. citizens and soldiers traveling or residing by permission in that country.[44]

In the early 1830s the Supreme Court, in two major decisions—*Cherokee Nation* v. *Georgia* (1831) and *Worcester* v. *Georgia* (1832)—affirmed the inherent sovereignty of the Indian nations. Yet both congressional legislation and treaties continued to undermine Indian autonomy. In 1837 Congress passed legislation ending direct payment to the Indian nations for lands they ceded or sold to the United States.[45] From then on such proceeds were to be kept in the Treasury and used for the benefit of the Indians. There was a persuasive logic to such legislation: many tribes had little, if any, experience with a cash economy and little conception of the sums they received. Congress would be better able, perhaps, to husband and usefully dispense such moneys. But the result was to remove Indians from the decisions regarding the use of their own resources. Having relinquished much of their material resources—the land—they now were denied control over much of what they received in return. The result was a net loss in autonomy. Furthermore, the uses Congress saw as beneficial to the Indians seldom supported Indians in their chosen modes of existence, but were far more likely to operate against such modes and support congressional programs of enforced cultural change. Such programs, especially in education or agriculture, may have had Indian support, but such support was seldom a consideration in congressional action.

In the 1840s and 1850s the expanding role of the United States in the internal affairs of these nations became increasingly apparent. In a series of actions Congress began an extended effort to individualize tribal property, as, for example, through the distribution of treaty-guaranteed annuities directly to heads of families instead of through tribal leaders, bypassing indigenous governments.[46] Treaties also contributed to the process. In 1849, for example, treaties signed with the Navajo and Ute Indians, typical of the time, allowed the United States to "pass and execute in [the Indians'] territory such laws as may be deemed conducive to the prosperity and happiness of the Indians."[47] Of course the provisions of any treaty applied only to signatory tribes, but the provisions of one often became models and objectives of negotiation for others. More comprehensive was legislation passed by Congress in 1858 authorizing the commissioner of Indian affairs to "remove from any tribal reservation any person found therein without authority of law, or whose presence within the limits of the reservation may, *in his judgment,* be detrimental to the peace and welfare of the Indians."[48]

Unusual for its time, but indicative of what was coming, was a provision in the 1857 treaty with the Tonawanda Band of the Senecas requiring that attorneys appointed by the Tonawanda Council be approved by the secretary of the interior.[49] The Tonawandas, living in New York, were further advanced down the path to powerlessness than were more isolated, western nations like the Navajo, but their experience would soon be repeated farther west.

The power of the United States to reshape Indian society was carried still further when a series of treaties, beginning with the Oto and Missouri Treaty of 1854 and foreshadowing the allotment policy thirty years later, authorized the president to distribute tribal lands to individual Indians. This not only continued the effort to individualize tribal property but, in moving land distribution and use out of tribal control, undermined a critical tribal function and a central element of community cohesion. The importance attached by Congress to allotment and the reformation of Indian property relations can be seen in 1862 legislation that provided for punishment for trespass on Indian allotments by Indians who had not taken up individual allotments themselves. Of particular interest: if the trespasser was a headman or chief, the law provided for his removal from office for three months, revealing the extent of the congressional assumption of power over tribal processes.[50]

Later treaties continued the trend. Some of those signed in the 1860s gave agents of the Bureau of Indian Affairs power to settle intrareservation disputes and authorized the United States to pass and extend to Indian communities laws pertaining to property alienation, descent, and other matters of reservation government. The treaty of 1866 with the Cherokees simply gave to the president veto power over laws passed by the Cherokee Nation and control over actions of the general council of tribes in the Indian Territory.[51]

In 1871 treaty making came to an end. In March of that year, in an appropriation bill, Congress declared "That hereafter no Indian nation or tribe within the territory of the United States shall be acknowledged or recognized as an independent nation, tribe, or power with whom the United States may contract by treaty." The provision resulted not so much from a desire to further reduce the already severely limited sovereignty of the Indian nations, although the congressional debate took up the issue, as from House dissatisfaction with Senate prominence—thanks to its singular role in treaty ratification—in the formation of Indian policy.[52] Indeed, the federal government continued to make formal agreements with the tribes. But the measure was indicative of the growing role of legislation in Indian affairs, at the expense of negotiation. In this it both underlined and tacitly acknowledged the increasingly unilateral character of Indian-White relations.

It reflected also the radically changed distribution of power. Behind the imposition of U.S. control lay the reality of military force: it was the collapse of armed resistance that ultimately left the tribes vulnerable to acts of Congress and the pressures of treaty negotiators. The central elements in that collapse were the overwhelming strength of Euro-American numbers and, eventually, technology; the destruction of native economies through land loss and wildlife decline, which left Indians dependent on the invaders; and the inability in most cases of the various Indian nations to come together in sustained, united action.

The erosion of Indian autonomy continued—in executive actions, legislation, and the courts—in subsequent years, but by the 1870s the Indians were rapidly disappearing as major actors on the intergroup stage. Those in the eastern United States had long since ceased presenting a threat to non-Indian interests. Only a few groups—some of the plains tribes, Apaches in the Southwest, the Nez Perces in the northern mountains, and a few others—could still mount significant resistance to the Euro-American advance. Their final struggles were often sensationally heroic, but their days were growing short. In another decade the last of them were being brought to heel, and the conflict years, already past for nations farther east, came to a close for them as well. In 1878 the Shoshone chief Washakie, echoing the words of Black Hawk forty years earlier, captured the essence of the change. "Our fathers," he said, "were steadily driven out, or killed, and we, their sons, but sorry remnants of tribes once mighty, are cornered in little spots of the earth all ours by right—cornered like guilty prisoners and watched by men with guns."[53]

Thus "the Indian problem"—or at least the economic problem at its core—was solved. Certainly the process of dispossession went on, but by the 1920s there were few resources left; the demand for Indian land was fading, and the allotment effort with it. Nearly half a century would pass before it would be realized just what riches actually remained in Indian hands, and "the Indian problem" would reappear in its original form. But by then Native Americans would be climbing back from powerlessness, just in time to make solving "the Indian problem" once again a very complicated business.

Chapter 4

"They Carry Their Lives on Their Finger Nails"[1]

In 1889, a year before the first battle of Wounded Knee, Sitting Bull, the great Hunkpapa Sioux medicine man, was furious at his tribespeople for agreeing to a treaty and land cession he had long opposed. "Indians!" he announced with disgust. "There are no Indians left now but me."[2]

He was very nearly right. Although his anger was not with numbers but with capitulation and betrayal, his words were an unwitting paraphrase of a complementary tale. "The discovery of America," William Denevan remarks, "was followed by possibly the greatest demographic disaster in the history of the world."[3]

It was followed also, eventually, by the exclusion of Native Americans from the emergent economy of the invaders, by a systematic assault on indigenous patterns of social organization, and by a desperate Indian search for adequate ways of responding to a world in crisis.

"WHEN YOU COME, WE DIE"[4]

The demographic facts are uncertain. How many Indians were there? How many are there now? Even today U.S. Census enumerations chronically undercount the Indian population[5] and only approximate its precise geographical distribution. The farther back one looks, the less certain the facts become.

For a long time the generally accepted estimate of the pre-Columbian population of America north of the Rio Grande was that of ethnologist James Mooney in the 1920s, compiled on a tribe-by-tribe basis and later modified by A. L. Kroeber. Both men reached a total of just over one million. Subsequent scholarship has revised this figure dramatically upwards, with estimates sometimes reaching ten million or more, although in recent years they have tended to range between two and five million aboriginal inhabitants.[6]

While the starting point may be in doubt, the trajectory is clear: contact and conflict with Europeans had a catastrophic impact on the Indian nations. Contact was by far the greater villain, although conflict has received the publicity. Disease was the sword with which the New World was devastated. European afflictions such as smallpox, tuberculosis, plague, and influenza, unknown to the Americas, found in the aboriginal population highly susceptible victims and proved stunningly efficient killers. Sherburne Cook estimates that in the years 1630 to 1730 diseases introduced by Europeans reduced the native population of New England by approximately 80 percent. In only five years—from 1615 to 1620—between 75 and 90 percent of the Massachusetts tribe died of plague; a decade later more of them succumbed to smallpox. The Western Abenaki of New Hampshire and Vermont virtually disappeared: 98 percent of the estimated ten thousand in the aboriginal population are believed to have died; less than three hundred apparently survived the biological assault. In the first half of the seventeenth century, writes Francis Jennings, "specific figures for the Huron Indians, confirmed in a variety of ways, show a decline from a minimum of 32,000 persons to about 10,000 in ten years, largely from the effects of epidemic."[7]

Of all the diseases introduced by Europeans, smallpox was the most grimly effective. A persuasive argument can be made that smallpox was the single most important factor in the decline of Native American population and power and, therefore, in the success of the European invasion. Successive epidemics swept over the Americas, occasionally yielding fatality rates in single tribes of 90 percent or more. In the late eighteenth and early nineteenth centuries major epidemics, often carried to the Indians by fur traders, crisscrossed the Great Plains, devastating numerous groups. Both the Assiniboines and the Arikaras are believed to have lost half their numbers to smallpox. The Mandans fared even worse. There were approximately nine thousand of them in 1750. In subsequent decades three waves of the disease struck and virtually annihilated them. By 1837, writes Edward Bruner, "there were only twenty-three male survivors."[8] In some cases disease so reduced native populations that areas that once supported substantial communities were left totally uninhabited and were discovered so by Europeans, whose diseases had silently preceded them. Observes Francis Jennings: "Europeans did not find a wilderness here; rather, however involuntarily, they made one."[9]

Disease was not the only culprit. The economic impact of invasion sometimes led to malnutrition and even famine. These in turn increased Indian susceptibility to infection. The Micmacs of Canada's Maritime Provinces lost 90 percent of their numbers in the first century after contact with Europeans. A turn from agriculture to the fur trade, along with other economic disruptions and dietary changes, produced a deterioration in Micmac provisioning and health that greatly reinforced the impact of imported diseases. In the 1860s and 1870s Mormon settlers monopolized the fertile lands of the Arizona Strip, driving the Kaibab Indian population into starvation. A flood of White settlers had a similar effect in California, where the loss of major food resources, along with disease and more or less organized White efforts at extermination, led to a disastrous decline in Indian numbers between 1848 and 1860. Cook estimates that by 1865 an aboriginal California population of three hundred thousand had been reduced to only twenty-five to thirty thousand persons.[10]

Warfare also took its toll, especially on young males. There are reports, for example, of substantial drops in the ratios of males to females among the Mescalero Apaches late in the nineteenth century, apparently as a consequence of conflict with U.S. troops.[11] Nonetheless, while conflict certainly contributed to Indian demographic change, it was clearly secondary to disease.[12]

This massive drop in numbers, begun in the earliest contact years, went on until nearly the beginning of the twentieth century.[13] Again, the date and size of the nadir population are matters of debate, although 1890 to 1900 seems reasonable, with a population of two hundred fifty thousand or less.[14] Of course the nadir came at different times for different groups, some beginning to recover much sooner than others. But whatever the details, the dimensions of the collapse are extraordinary: from several million—possibly more—in 1492 to less than three hundred thousand by the end of the nineteenth century, a reduction of more than 90 percent in four hundred years. It came perilously close to extinction.

Indeed, under the circumstances some nations simply disappeared. Others, their numbers vastly reduced, found their social organization by necessity simplified: villages ceased to exist, while individual clans were extinguished or had so few survivors that they were forced to join others less affected by the decline. The same thing happened to entire communities. Driven by disease and warfare to the brink of extinction, they were absorbed by neighboring or related peoples. Not only were Indian numbers thus reduced, but disappearance and remnant consolidation led to a decline in the number of distinct Indian groups.

Those who remained faced a struggle of another kind. Around their remnant communities and lands a new world was coming into being. As time went on they became more and more dependent on that world. Increasingly, however, it had no place for them.

THE PROCESS OF EXCLUSION

In the nineteenth century Indian land fueled American economic growth. But dispossession had an opposite effect on the Indian nations. While it led to American economic development, it led to Indian underdevelopment: the reduced capacity of Native American societies to sustain themselves. In little more than a century it destroyed the aboriginal economic base as White settlers appropriated the most fertile lands, restricted Indian hunting territories, increased the pressure on game, diverted waters to irrigation, and in numerous ways altered the existing environment.

Caught in a vastly enlarged and increasingly violent competition for choice natural resources, Native Americans struggled to adapt. But indigenous economies were coming to pieces and the alternatives were few: the process of dispossession was also a process of exclusion. Indian lands were essential to U.S. economic development; Indians were not. While the Indian land base was incorporated into the American economic structure, most Indians, whether by circumstance or design, were excluded from it. The result, emerging in the conflict years and dominating the reservation period, was economic marginalization and dependency.

The obstacles facing Native Americans were enormous. In many cases the bases of their own economies had been destroyed. Loss of the buffalo to non-Indian hunters and destruction of grazing lands, for example, locked the plains nations into marginal reservation-based economies and left them dependent on non-Indian sources of canvas for tipis, cloth for garments, and even food. But even groups that tried to adjust to changed conditions found major hurdles in their path. After ceding much of their land to the United States, the Cherokees of Georgia, whose traditional economy was based partly on horticulture, took to full-time farming with alacrity and notable success, only to discover that Georgia had no intention of allowing them to stay in the state, farmers or not. In the 1830s they and others of the Five Civilized Tribes were forced out of Georgia and the Southeast and driven westward to the Indian Territory, their aboriginal lands occupied by Whites. Decades later, when these same nations realized that the railroads could not be turned away forever from their new territorial lands, they set out to charter their own railway companies and other enterprises so as to retain control over development and reap its benefits. Their attempts were well within their demonstrated abilities, yet they were blocked by Congress and a group of railroad and other interests determined to gain the rewards of territorial development for themselves.[15]

Under the allotment policy, Indians could select their individual lands from those set apart by the federal government for allotment. But lands suspected of substantial mineral potential were often closed to Indian selection, ostensibly because such lands would provide wealth without the civilizing discipline of hard work. Corporations, hoping to exploit the mineral potential themselves, campaigned to keep such resources out of Indian hands. In the Indian Territory rich Choctaw coal lands—440,000 acres of them—were withdrawn from allotment entry, denying the Choctaws perhaps their most valuable economic resource.[16]

In the Southwest during the latter part of the nineteenth century, growing markets for agricultural goods briefly integrated some Indian farmers into the expanding regional economy, but not for long. Groups such as the Gila Pimas, which had been important suppliers of food to Anglo settlers in Arizona, rapidly lost irrigation water and land to those same settlers. "The interests of Anglos and Mexicans," writes Edward Spicer,

> became focused on acquiring Indian land and water, which they justified on the ground that Indian farming was too inefficient to warrant the Indians holding even as much land as remained to them. . . . The result was that Indians wherever they engaged in farming ceased to produce for the expanding market, and in fact, as they were limited to smaller and more marginal tracts, produced less and less even to the point of not being able to supply their own needs. By the early 1900s few were any longer even reasonably secure subsistence farmers.

The Apache farmers on the San Carlos Reservation, dependent on the Gila River for irrigation, were forced to abandon farming and search for wage labor when Mormon settlers upstream so reduced the flow of the river that adequate irrigation became impossible.[17]

Indian economic enterprise was discouraged also by the quality of land left to them. The salient motive of Indian policy for most of the nineteenth century was the acquisition of economically valuable land; it is hardly surprising, then, that what remained was marginal. Programs designed to turn Indians into farmers often failed to take this into account. Efforts to make farmers of the Sioux, for example, came to grief in the harsh environment of the Dakota plains, where cultivation was often impossible with the agricultural technology of the time. Non-Indians did no better. After successfully demanding that Sioux lands be taken from the Indians and opened to them, homesteaders flocked into the Dakotas; within two decades many had abandoned their own, hopeless struggle to wrest a living from the soil and were moving on.

Things weren't much better on the southern plains. In the 1870s, at the insistence of the federal government, Comanches in the Indian Territory reluctantly attempted farming. But the rains proved undependable and the attempt failed. The crop yields on the quarter sections allotted to Southern Cheyennes and Arapahoes "were too low to support even efficient white farmers," much less tribespeople with neither experience nor interest in farming. Even those groups that were relatively successful, such as the Arapahoes at Wind River in Wyoming, had difficulty retaining their lands in the face of continuing local and congressional pressures for cessions and sale.[18]

But the greatest setback to Indian attempts to respond to economic disaster was that dream of nineteenth-century reformers and civilizers: allotment. The claim of allotment, the centerpiece of Indian policy after 1887, was that it would turn Indians into farmers, bring them into the mainstream of American economic life and culture, and end their dependence on the government for support. In practice it had the opposite effect. Indian farming in fact declined with allotment as the most fertile lands were taken by Whites and numerous allotments were leased or sold.[19] Not all Indian lands were allotted, nor did every reservation experience the process. Particularly in the Southwest, some were wholly spared. But while reservations, some tribal lands, and tribalism itself survived the allotment experience, the impact on Indian resources—in terms both of the magnitude of the loss and the quality of the lands remaining—was devastating. The results were crippled economies, increasing poverty, and deepening dependence.

There was another dimension to dispossession. As Indian resources were incorporated into the developing economy of the United States, not only their economic but their cultural uses were denied to Native American societies.[20] The more obvious examples of such losses include buffalo and other game and the flora that played a role in healing practices, ceremonies, or social relations. Less obvious were losses of particular lands or places that had significance in group histories or ceremonial practice. Far from underutilizing the land base, as Europeans believed, Native Americans "used" these lands in many different ways in the complex process of sustaining themselves and their societies. As a result, dispossession was itself transformative, stripping away the physical foundation of entire ways of life. Just as the conflict over resources was cultural as well as economic, so the outcome bore on culture as well as economy.

TRIBALISM UNDER ATTACK

The assault on indigenous society and culture was not only circumstantial. It was an organized effort that eventually became the focal point of policy.

By late in the nineteenth century, the shape of "the Indian problem" was changing. The bulk of Indian lands had been transferred to non-Indian ownership or occupation. With few exceptions Indians themselves no longer presented significant obstacles to the flow of White settlement and commerce. The emphasis in Indian policy, long determined by the acquisition agenda, was changing as well. Certainly acquisition remained a goal: powerful settler and commercial interests continued to put pressure on Indian lands. But for policymakers the object was increasingly cultural transformation. "The Indians," said Thomas Morgan, Indian commissioner, in 1889, "must conform to 'the white man's ways,' peaceably if they will, forcibly if they must."

The key to this transformation, as far as policymakers were concerned, was the systematic destruction of tribal organization. Claimed Morgan, expressing a common sentiment: "The tribal relations should be broken up . . . and the family and the autonomy of the individual substituted."[21]

This detribalizing effort took the form of an elaborate set of tutelary, administrative controls over Indian lives, coupled with the attempted abrogation of indigenous systems of governance. The main protagonist in this new drama was the Bureau of Indian Affairs (BIA), also known at various times as the Indian Office or the Indian Service. Established originally in the War Department in 1824 and transferred to the Department of the Interior in 1849, by the end of the nineteenth century the BIA had become a surrogate government for the Indian nations, its presence apparent in every aspect of Indian life.

Treaty provisions and legislative acts alone fail to convey the full extent or impact of BIA interference. Charged with the civilizing process, the BIA adopted a course designed to force its recusant and often unruly wards into the sociocultural molds preferred by the larger society. While Congress and the courts stripped the substance from Indian decision-making power, the BIA went after those social structures and cultural practices that, even under conditions of powerlessness, sustained the tribal community.

Traditional chiefs and councils, unless they favored the adoption of new ways of living, were primary targets. Agents of the BIA used their control of food rations and the threat of army troops to enforce their decisions against the will of tribal leaders. Beginning in the 1860s tribal police forces were recruited from among reservation tribesmen. Responsible to the agents, they were used to maintain order, enforce BIA regulations, and bypass traditional leaders. They became enforcers as well of civilization programs, charged with, among other things, ending gambling and dancing, enforcing school attendance, and ending the influence of shamans and traditionalists. By the mid-1880s such police units had been established at forty-eight of sixty agencies.[22]

The BIA established Indian courts as well. In 1883 the commissioner of Indian affairs issued a set of rules defining "Indian offenses," among them feasts and dances, polygamy, and assorted religious practices, all cultural activities that seemed to distinguish Native Americans from Whites. Courts of Indian Offenses, composed of Indians appointed by the agents, were set up to enforce these rules and assume other judicial functions, replacing, in conjunction with the agents, traditional forms of dispute resolution. Like the police forces, these courts were vehicles for enforced acculturation. Regulations issued in 1892, for example, provided "that if an Indian refuses or neglects to adopt habits of industry, or to engage in civilized pursuits or employments, but habitually spends his time in idleness and loafing, he shall be deemed a vagrant" and punished accordingly.[23]

The agents' positions gave them other powers. They controlled the distribution of jobs on and often near the reservations, usually the only available wage work near where Indians lived. The distribution of food rations was also in the agents' hands; many used their power to promote acculturation and maximize their own influence. Roy Meyer reports, for example, that at both Sisseton and Devils Lake reservations in the Dakotas "the agents discriminated in the issuance of rations between the industrious and the 'disobedient or indolent,' as one called them." At Devils Lake, "the latter group received the basic issue of pork, flour, and tobacco, but only the workers were entitled to soap, sugar, coffee, tea, candles, and kerosene."[24] Such discrimination had the formal sanction of the BIA. Commissioner of Indian Affairs William Jones directed in 1901 that rations be given "only in return for labor performed," arguing that the Indian "must be made to realize that in the sweat of his face he shall eat his bread."[25]

Many agents systematically discouraged tribal decision making. In its place they tried to foster individualized planning and action or took over decision making themselves. They urged tribal members to move onto individual parcels of land, breaking up the older band or village residential patterns and reducing the influence of traditional leadership.[26] Indigenous social organization capable of coordinating action or mobilizing opinion was often ignored or replaced. On the Gila Pima Reservation in Arizona, for example, the superintendent took over agricultural planning, an activity long carried out by indigenous Pima organizations. The old village structure was replaced by a new organization controlled by the superintendent and the missionaries. On the San Carlos Apache Reservation, as on many, land assignments were made by the reservation superintendent, who also took over the planning of economic resource development. Traditional parental relations at San Carlos were undermined as children were placed under strict discipline in a reservation boarding school. Band settlements were broken up and the population dispersed. "By the 1930s," writes Edward Spicer, regarding San Carlos, "the result was an extreme breakdown in traditional forms of authority with the substitution of no authority except that of the superintendent and his staff."[27]

Yet the agents could not wholly ignore their charges. They needed at least some cooperation from the Indian populace if order was to be maintained and the reservations smoothly run. When they could not get such cooperation from existing tribal leaders, they passed them by. On the Pine Ridge Sioux Reservation a council of traditional chiefs had survived into the early 1900s. But during the winter of 1917–18 the council and the agent quarreled; the agent ordered the council dissolved.[28] Some agents singled out more progressive leaders and solicited their support and assistance; others found men who had no traditional leadership positions or standing in the tribe but who generally supported the agents' programs, and promoted them into positions of authority.[29] At times agents went so far as to form committees to act as liaison between themselves and the populace or to function as "representatives" of the tribal interest.

Such was the genealogy of the Business Council on the Navajo Reservation, where oil was discovered in the early 1920s. The treaty of 1868 with the Navajos required tribal consent for the granting of leases, yet there was no body that could speak for the whole tribe when the question of oil leases arose. In 1922 the secretary of the interior appointed a "Business Council" of three Navajos to act on behalf of the tribe. The council was neither representative of nor controlled by the Navajos. Its function: to approve oil leases.[30]

Other processes also were affecting Indian self-government. Land loss and competition for reduced resources made many traditional economic activities obsolete. Such activities had often been central to the larger cultural fabric; as they became pointless or were replaced, the social mechanisms that had sustained them atrophied. Decision-making processes deteriorated not only through suppression, but also from lack of use: many important tribal decisions—when to move camp, when to plant, where to hunt this year, and so forth—had become irrelevant or had been removed from Indian hands. Warrior societies, religious organizations, and even some kinship structures lost influence and vitality once their collective activities had been prohibited or preempted by the Indian Bureau. Such organizations and activities, while perhaps not obviously "political," were in fact the foundation of self-government. It was through them that the social organism was maintained and the activities of the group coordinated and controlled. As they were suppressed or abandoned, indigenous self-government became tenuous or disappeared.

But the defining feature of the reservation years was not so much the arrogation of rights and powers—that had begun long before—as it was the organized attack on tribal organization and allegiance and the consequences of this attack for the incorporative linkages between Indians and the larger society. The critical element was allotment.

The General Allotment Act of 1887 marks the acme of U.S. political control over Native Americans. Allotment and subsequent legislation specified a new set of incorporative relationships, relationships anticipated by prior legislation and some treaties but now made the formal object of policy. Indians were to be able to retain significant control over land and related resources, but only via allotment—that is, only as individual land-holders—and then only under regulation set out by the Congress and the secretary of the interior. Furthermore, the law provided that every Indian taking up allotment (which was to include, ideally, all Indians) become a citizen of the United States and of the state or territory in which he or she resided, subject to its criminal and civil laws. In other words, the act envisioned both the individualization of tribal property and the dissolution of tribal polity. Indians were to be incorporated *as individuals* into both the economic and political structures of the larger society.[31] It was the ultimate form of control: the end of the tribe itself as a political and social entity.

The link between allotment and citizenship was later relaxed, and in 1924 Congress passed the Indian Citizenship Act, declaring all noncitizen Indians citizens of the United States, regardless of their allotment status. But the overall design remained: Native Americans might gain access to the dominant social order—indeed, they were to be forced into it—but on terms imposed from without, over Indian opposition.

INCORPORATION AND RESPONSE

Structures of incorporation are structures of opportunity. In the relationships between groups lie patterns of political possibility, options human beings face as they attempt to deal with the situations in which they find themselves. In other words, incorporative structures are gateways, opening the way to certain kinds of actions, closing it to others.

During the fur trade years Native Americans faced both European invasion as well as uncommon opportunities. European competition within North America, the European market for furs, and the Indian monopoly on technical skills and access to fur resources allowed many Indians to play, for a time at least, a rare game of political and commercial alliance, and to play it for their own distinctive ends.

But the rules of the game eventually changed. The collapse of fur markets, the rising demand for land, and the emergent hegemony of the United States altered the incorporative pattern and with it the structure of political opportunity. Narrower options required different strategies. The conflict years tested Indian ingenuity to the utmost as the tribes searched for ways of dealing with the White advance. Armed struggle and negotiated land cession, the one usually following the other, were each, in their own ways, forms of resistance, attempts to halt the erosion of space, economy, and freedom. But as lands and resources were lost, as the power of the United States grew, as the wave of non-Indian settlement moved relentlessly westward, Indian autonomy became more and more circumscribed. Some groups capitulated; some fought back; all eventually were forced to submit.

Reservation dependence and confinement drastically reduced Indian choices of action. Armed resistance had become suicidal. White hunters had devastated the vast buffalo herds, leaving the plains and some of the mountain nations dependent on the reservations and the government for food. The reservations themselves inhibited intertribal alliance, while Indian Bureau agents and the army kept close watch on the more dangerous tribes.

Indians faced other obstacles as well: legal constraints encircled them; non-Indian authority bound them at every turn. But more than restricted opportunities were to blame. Indian political capacities had collapsed. The suppression or cooptation of indigenous systems of self-governance had left most groups incapable of mounting large-scale political activity of almost any kind: the requisite organizational structures were crippled or gone, while few groups had sufficient skills or experience to deal effectively with federal bureaucrats and congressional committees.

The result for most tribes, in the secular realm at least, was a period of political quiescence characteristic of the reservation years. It begins at different points in the eighteenth and nineteenth centuries, earlier for eastern and West Coast tribes, later in the Southwest and on the plains, and continues into the twentieth century.

There are numerous exceptions to the pattern. In the first two decades of the twentieth century a few tribes waged important court battles on behalf of land claims and other objectives. But most of the exceptions, then and earlier, were local affairs: efforts by often shrewd, determined, but politically handicapped tribal leaders to maintain their own authority in the face of official usurpation or to follow their own sense of their peoples' needs and interests against the obstructionism and disapproval of reservation agents, superintendents, and the BIA. They include struggles over everything from the size of allotments and annuities to the suppression of ceremonial activities, from compulsory schooling to demands for further land cessions.[32]

In effect these were holding actions, attempts to preserve some measure of control in the internal affairs of the Indian nations. They required stamina and political finesse, and included a share of Indian successes, but they took place largely outside the national arena of policy making and deliberation, an arena that paid little attention to Indian views not backed by the threat of force or the mobilization of non-Indian constituencies. Indeed, almost the only major secular political activity among Native Americans in the last years of the nineteenth century occurred in the Indian Territory, where for decades the Five Civilized Tribes had carefully preserved an unusual degree of autonomy and in the process had become expert in the politics of Indian-federal relations. From the 1870s until after the turn of the century the governments of these nations, often in concert with other tribes in the Indian Territory, tried to construct a set of political institutions that would preserve some of that autonomy within the political framework of the United States. In a series of conventions and charters they attempted to create either a federated Indian territorial gov ernment or an Indian state.[33] Ultimately they failed, their efforts blocked by Congress and a variety of national and local interests, including Indian ones. In the last years of the nineteenth century Congress moved to dissolve the national governments of the Five Civilized Tribes, and in 1907 the territory—that would-be Indian state of Sequoyah—became Oklahoma instead.

Regardless of its outcome, the effort these nations made was politically significant and exceptional for its time: a multitribal attempt to find a non-military political response adequate to the continuing threat to tribal lands and sovereignty. It was also the last gasp of political collapse, a desperate and unsuccessful bid to stave off the disasters that had already come to Native Americans elsewhere. It was not until the 1920s that substantial organized secular political action again took place on Indian land, and much longer before such action became common.

Yet many Indians continued to resist. A common consequence of failure is innovation. The European invasion of America presented Native

American societies with an extraordinary challenge: the scale and profundity of the changes taking place were, for the most part, unprecedented in their experience. In response, they did what societies the world over have done: they tried well-tested methods of solving societal problems, and when those failed or came to grief on the rocks of circumstance, they invented new ones or looked for solutions in the repertoires of other peoples.

The attempt by the Five Civilized Tribes to form an Indian state is an example of such innovation, in this case in the realm of secular politics, reflecting the particular characteristics and opportunities of those groups.[34] But innovation occurred outside that arena as well. As economic and social order began to collapse through the dual disasters of military defeat and forced cultural change, Native Americans looked to their own cultural roots—and in particular to the supernatural—for solutions to crisis.

STRATEGIES OF TRANSFORMATION AND SURVIVAL

Early in 1889, in the course of a solar eclipse, a Paiute Indian named Wovoka on the Walker River Reservation in western Nevada had an extraordinary experience. As he later reported to ethnographer James Mooney, during the eclipse Wovoka was taken up into the spirit world. There he saw God and the dead of his nation, happily alive in a beautiful land abundant with game. He returned with messages for his people, telling them, among other things, to work hard and to live in peace with the Whites and that eventually they would be reunited with the dead in a world without death or sickness or old age. He brought back also a dance that if conscientiously performed, would occasion this transformation in the fortunes of his people. This dance, and the movement that Wovoka inspired, came to be known as the Ghost Dance.[35]

News of Wovoka's prophecy quickly spread, not only among the Paiutes, but to other nations to the north in Idaho and Wyoming, into Utah, and east across the Rockies to the plains. In the process the Ghost Dance was altered; the tribes that took it up interpreted it in their own ways, fitting the fundamental prophecies into their own cultural designs and practice and orienting it to their own situations. The Sioux and Pawnee, for example, gave to the prophecies a hostile content: in their versions the Whites were to be annihilated by a massive whirlwind, and the Sioux in particular made much of the expected return of the buffalo—of little concern to the Paiutes—and great herds of horses.[36] It was Sioux participation that eventually gave the Ghost Dance its notoriety. Their enthusiasm spread panic among reservation agents and White settlers, who believed it a prelude to war. Army troops were sent to suppress the new religion, a mission that led ultimately to the 1890 massacre at Wounded Knee.

Both doctrine and ritual varied from tribe to tribe. The unity of the movement lay not in its attitude toward Whites nor, certainly, in organizational linkages, but in genealogy and eschatology, in the inspiration of the prophet and his teaching: resurrection and transformation, the coming of a new world.

Such expectations also provide taxonomic links between the Ghost Dance and predecessor movements throughout the country. In 1881, for example, an Apache shaman named Nakaidoklini promised to raise from the dead past leaders of his nation. When his efforts faltered, he claimed that the Whites undermined his powers and prophesied their imminent departure from the land. Certain dances were prescribed as part of the process. Fearful of a general uprising, the army sent troops to arrest Nakaidoklini at his camp near Cibecue, Arizona. The confrontation became a full-scale battle in which the shaman was killed, and the movement subsequently died.[37]

In the early 1870s a young Comanche medicine man named Eschiti, or Isatai, likewise claimed extraordinary powers, including the ability to make himself and others bulletproof and raise the dead. He saw himself as a savior sent to deliver the Comanches from the oppression of the Whites and from the fate of other nations that had chosen the white man's path. His influence rapidly spread for a time, but his medicine failed at the battle of Adobe Walls when a force of Comanches, Cheyennes, Kiowas, and Arapahoes had to abandon their siege of a group of buffalo hunters in the Texas Panhandle in 1874.[38]

Of much longer duration than either of these was the Smohalla religion, or Dreamer Movement, which became prominent among the Sahaptin peoples of the Pacific Northwest in the 1850s, 1860s, and 1870s. It, too, promised resurrection of the dead, world rebirth, and the eventual annihilation of the Whites. Named for the Wanapum prophet—and passionate opponent of land cessions—who first revealed the prophecies and their attendant rituals, the religion combined older Sahaptin traditions with elements of Christianity, although in its teachings, revealed to its followers in dreams, it called upon them to abandon the ways of the Whites and return to those of their ancestors. It survived in one form or another well into the twentieth century.[39]

Not all were restricted to ritual practice. In some cases prophecy emboldened resistance and became a foundation of militant action and intertribal alliance. The Delaware Prophet, Neolin, taught in 1762 that the Indians had been corrupted by the sins of the Whites; purified behavior would restore their power and enable them to drive the invaders from their country. His prophecies were crucial in Pontiac's effort to unite the Ottawas, Potawatomis, Hurons, Chippewas, and other nations in the massive Indian uprising against European settlements in the Great Lakes and Ohio River Valley in 1763. Tecumseh and his brother the Shawnee Prophet similarly organized supratribal resistance half a century later, while Smohalla's teachings, though not militant, may have facilitated the alliance of northwestern Indian nations that joined in the Yakima War of 1855–56.[40]

The link between religion and action in these movements and others was by no means new; that link had always been there. Action gained power from the spirit world and appeals to the sacred were a common component of daily life. In many nations ritual practices were means of tapping the power held by the universe and directing it to mundane ends. Nor, in most cases, did these movements make radical departures from traditional practice or belief. Their mobilizational success depended on their resonance with traditional conceptions of how the world worked.[41]

Where they seemed to depart from the past was in their attempt to cope specifically with the White invasion and its effects, their millennialism, and their timing. They were typical of the transition from overt conflict toward the reservation years and arose under conditions of society-threatening stress. Eschiti's influence among the Comanches came at a time of major trauma: the tribe was under growing pressure from White settlers and the army; treaty rations had been scarce the previous winter and their buffalo-based economy was taking a beating at the hands of White hunters. Eschiti claimed to have been given extraordinary powers that could be used to resolve a growing and intractable crisis. The Sioux similarly took up the Ghost Dance at a time of desperation, when a whole way of life hung in the balance and their choices of action were few.

But the movements failed. The bullets did their deadly work, the promised resurrections never came, and the White invaders swallowed the country whole. And in place of these a very different set of responses began to emerge, new movements and religions—many still vital in Native American societies today—that promised less and delivered more. Some were outgrowths of millennialist cults. The Pawnee Ghost Dance, for example, eventually abandoned its vision of cosmic metamorphosis, but continued, transmuted into quite different ceremonial forms, as a vehicle of national assertion, stimulating in the last years of the nineteenth century a Pawnee cultural renaissance. Likewise the Drum Cult of the Potawatomis and Ojibwas, which in the 1870s and 80s had promised that "a great drum will tap in heaven" and their lost lands would be repossessed by them, in time revised its expectations and ultimately offered something else instead, of different but equal value: the ritually based exercise and affirmation of a national culture and identity.[42]

Others, such as peyotism, the Handsome Lake Religion of the Iroquois, or certain versions of the Sun Dance, combined older and sometimes revised traditions with borrowings from the Europeans or from other native groups to articulate in various ways new codes of behavior and provide new ritual practices, which in turn might equip individuals and communities to survive the rigors of a world that had changed beyond the capacity of indigenous practice and belief to cope with alone. The Code of Handsome Lake, for example, based on a series of visions and pronouncements by a Seneca named Handsome Lake in the years 1799–1815, sought to reverse the declining fortunes of the Iroquois. It forbade the drinking of whiskey, urged the preservation of social unity and peace and the retention of the remaining land base, modified certain ritual practices while urging the preservation of others, and encouraged acculturation, particularly in education and agriculture, while seeking simultaneously to preserve national Iroquois identities, tribal landholding, and village communalism.[43]

The most prominent of such movements was peyotism, or the Peyote Religion, which used the bud of the peyote cactus as a source of individual vision and power and spread from the southern plains late in the nineteenth century through much of Indian America. Rooted in aboriginal religious practices among Mexican peoples, the Mescalero Apaches, and southern plains tribes, peyotism eventually served a number of functions as it was adopted by successive groups in the United States and adapted to their own needs and religious traditions. In its later manifestations, at least, it served as a vehicle of relief for individuals and societies caught in the maelstrom of social and cultural upheaval, a means of dealing with persistent individual and social problems through new behavioral codes, ceremonial action, and sacred power. In doing so it combined new ideas and practices with materials from the aboriginal past to fashion yet another strategy of adjustment.[44]

Such movements were transformative in their own way, but of individuals and communities, not of the world-at-large. Where the earlier movements often had been hostile to the surrounding society, these were largely pacific in their doctrines, introverted in their orientation, and accommodating in the nature of their resistance.

The pattern is familiar. Pacifism on the part of the oppressed, often interpreted as inherent passivity or contentment, more often reflects severely restricted opportunities for action, and a decision to spend energy in the more productive and likely enterprise of community maintenance and revitalization. Beneath the veneer of passivity, in other words, often lies an extraordinary effort to reorganize and reconceptualize personal and social life and experience, so that apparently unalterable conditions can be made tolerable. "If a people," writes Eugene Genovese, "finds the odds against insurrection not merely long but virtually certain, then it will choose not to try. To some extent this reaction represents decreasing self-confidence and increasing fear, but it also represents a conscious effort to develop an alternative strategy for survival."[45]

Genovese's concern in these words is not with Indians but with slaves, and in particular with the distinctive Christianity of American slaves, a Christianity that formed one such strategy: a set of beliefs, interpretations, and modes of action that provided enslaved Blacks with means of retaining dignity, some degree of freedom, and a distinctly positive sense of themselves in a world that sought to deny them precisely those things and that they felt they could not, at present, substantially change.[46]

The latter responses of Native Americans can be seen in similar terms. Faced with continuing crisis, declining capacities for secular action, and a political arena effectively closed to them, a number of Indian groups chose other strategies directed, first, to the transformation of the world and then, when such efforts failed, to the tasks of survival, to the maintenance of culture and community as means of lived resistance to the effects, if not directly to the system, of oppression.[47]

Viewed in such terms, virtually all these movements, while appealing to the supernatural, are fundamentally political. A consequence of the failure of politics and of traditional modes—political or otherwise—of coping with stress in individual and social life, they nonetheless had as their central object the reestablishment of Indian control over Indian lives. In other words, they were about power, although it was power largely perceived and pursued—as traditionally in Native American societies—not as a relationship among persons or institutions, but as the spiritually given capacity of objects, persons, or other natural phenomena to order and reorder relationships, events, or the world itself.[48]

These movements sought power via the few cultural resources Indians still controlled: definition, interpretation, belief. What is most significant about them is not their departures from aboriginal roots, but their continuities. They were innovative and conservative at once: invention for the sake of preservation. Against the assault on tribalism, the dismissal of indigenous culture, and the usurpation of Indian freedom, they asserted in their various ways the value and beauty of traditional belief and native forms of cultural practice, the power of the spirit world, the sanctity of land and community, and the essential sovereignty of native peoples. As traditional life designs proved unable to deal adequately with altered conditions, Native Americans—in these and other adaptations—retooled those designs, searching for order in the midst of radical disorder, for coherence in a world made incoherent by the onrush of cataclysmic events, for a means to articulate and affirm their own distinctive identities. They were attempting to construct, in Anthony Wallace's terms, more effective or satisfying cultural designs,[49] but designs that were fundamentally generational: descended from the past, from aboriginal practice and perception, responding to the present.

It was a powerfully assimilative colonialism Native Americans faced. Here was a society determined to reproduce itself in them, with their participation, and thereby, perhaps, to reassure itself of its own superiority. "This civilization may not be the best possible," claimed Indian Commissioner Thomas Morgan, "but it is the best the Indians can get."[50] With determination and brute force, it stripped away the physical and much of the social foundation of their "otherness," but the ideological foundation, as evidenced by these responses, proved both resilient and creative. With equal determination, and together with the cultures of which they were so much a part, these movements defied the official, dominant-group accounts of past, present, and future events and resurrected or constructed in their place alternative conceptions or interpretations that could guide action in distinctive and affirmative ways and provide ideological bases for the preservation of peoplehood.

In so doing they provided what Roberta Ash calls "a cognitive framework for opposition."[51] Resistance had moved from the political arena—as that is generally understood—to the ideological: long after the warrior had retired from the field, the battle continued on the terrain of ideas, identity, and interpretation. Decades down the road that battle would still be going on, but no longer in isolation from the political arena it had once, perforce, ignored.

Part II

THE FOUNDATIONS OF POLITICAL RESURGENCE

Chapter 5

The Transformations of the Tribe

"Our power is gone and we are dying, for the power is not in us anymore." Thus said Black Elk, the Oglala medicine man, to John Neihardt in 1931.[1] And perhaps it was so. Black Elk had seen the dead and dying at Wounded Knee and had fought briefly there. He had witnessed in his own life the passage of the Sioux nations from freedom to dependency. In his youth the spirits of the Lakota had given him a magnificent vision, calling him to give aid and leadership to his people, and he felt he had failed in his appointed task. Yet his words of despair came at what, in retrospect, appears to have been a critical time, the start of a decade that would see some crucial developments in an extended Native American renaissance.

It is a recurrent irony of history that renaissance and ruin are so closely intertwined. The new Indian politics owes its particular character to diverse influences, but not least to the patterned ruins of the Indian past. The forces that led to nineteenth-century political collapse laid much of the foundation of twentieth-century political resurgence. They did so in a variety of ways, but most prominently in their impact on the organization and identity of Native American peoples.

Incorporative processes are inherently transformative of the peoples they embrace. They not only reorganize relations among groups and between groups and larger societal systems, and thereby reorganize political opportunities; they also transform the groups themselves. This is as true for Indians as for others. The spread of Euro-American civilization over the North American continent placed intense pressures on the indigenous inhabitants to reorganize and reconceptualize themselves. Some of those pressures were intentional, directed ultimately toward the assimilation of Native Americans into the larger population. Others were by-products of economic and political forces indifferent to the peoples they swept before them. But whatever their genesis, their effects were momentous: the reshaping of social life as well as of the bases on which social life was organized and experienced. Some groups were changed more than others, but few escaped unscathed.

This is not merely a historical curiosity. It is crucial to an understanding of Indian political resurgence. The subjects of history are likewise its objects. The agents of collective action are not given to the world; they are made by it. Through the unfolding of incorporative processes such as those involving Native Americans, groups of people come to occupy common positions within a particular social order and to share distinctive interests or historical experience. As an outcome of that process, and of the clash of ideas attendant upon it, they also come to see themselves and their world in particular ways and, consequently, to act on specific bases: as the poor, the working class, Blacks, women, farmers, even as individuals without attachment to larger, solidary wholes. Group formation, in other words, lies at the heart of collective action, squarely between the impersonal forces of historical change and the concrete, collective responses of human beings.

Two such formative processes have powerfully shaped the pattern of Indian political resurgence. These might be termed, inelegantly, Indianization and tribalization. The first refers to the growth of a supratribal consciousness and constituency, to the eventual emergence of "American Indians" as a politically self-conscious population. The second refers to the process by which tribes came to be what they are today as political organisms and as focal points of Indian identities.[2]

Both processes began, to a large degree, in the European mind and only later came to be realized in the self-concepts and actions of Native Americans. It is this realization, however, that is important here. Indianization is largely a phenomenon of the twentieth century and will receive its share of attention later. Tribalization, on the other hand, has been a more lengthy and complicated affair. The consolidation and politicization of the tribe as the dominant category of Indian group organization and self-concept is a process with roots reaching back to the early stages of incorporation. While it has continued to the present day, by the reservation years its fundamental shape was already apparent.

ORGANIZATION AND SELF-CONCEPT

Understanding processes of group formation and transformation among Native Americans requires a distinction between two dimensions or aspects of groupness: the organizational and the conceptual. These processes involve, first, the restructuring of patterns of group organization and, second, the reformulation of group identities. The first of these refers not specifically to patterns of kinship organization—though these often are involved—but to political structures, the ways groups are organized as collective actors. The second refers to the ways they conceptualize themselves.

With relatively few exceptions Native American societies, like most "tribal" societies, generally lacked what are called polities: formally distinct institutional structures in which secular authority in civil affairs is vested. This is not to say that they lacked political authority, but only that both the sources and functioning of such authority cut across fixed institutional distinctions, distinctions difficult to apply to tribal social organization in any case. Clyde Kluckhohn and Dorothea Leighton illustrate the point in their discussion of the Navajos. The Navajos, they write,

> have a set of categories altogether different from that of white Western culture. The category "government," something fixed and powerful to white people, is foreign to Navaho thinking. Authority, to their minds, extends only indefinitely and transitorily beyond the established rules of behavior between sex groups, age groups, and, especially, classes of relatives. There are headmen, but the sphere of their influence widens and narrows with the passage of time, the emergence of a new leader, the rise of a new faction. The prestige of some headmen often spreads beyond their own local region. Through channels excessively informal they can sometimes "swing" most of the population of a number of local groups to a given course of action. By and large, however, control of individual action rests in The People as a group and not in any authoritative individual or body.[3]

While the details of this statement are particular to the Navajos, the view of authority it describes is, or was, more generally applicable among Indian groups. Describing Potawatomi leadership, for example, James Clifton writes:

> What we are dealing with here is a variety of interlocked leadership roles with none having much ascribed, legitimate power. Leadership was largely expressive of kinship ties: some key okamek [broadly, leaders] drew their support from and were responsive to the needs of their clans. Governance consisted of all varieties of leaders coming together in open council and there deliberating on their opinions and wishes until some consensus position was achieved. They were not isolated from their followers. Indeed, there were no followers. Leaders did not have the power to command, although they might suggest, encourage, or point out possible directions or solutions.[4]

In these groups and others, individual and collective activity was guided not so much by hierarchical authority structures as by custom, historically evolved practice, and agreed-upon modes of action. Authority, as socially legitimated control exercised by one or several individuals over the actions of others, tended to be temporary, limited to certain activities, or both. There was, of course, variation from this norm, with some groups—the Pueblos, the Natchez, some of the eastern tribes—having more elaborate hierarchical governance, but these were more exception than rule.

Nonetheless, political organization of some sort existed nearly everywhere: groups acted as groups. The shape of such political organization is of less interest here than its extent. The enterprise is not the extraction of particular structures of political organization from encompassing social wholes, but to find the locus of political organization in each case or, more precisely, to find at what level of the social order the effective and more or less continuous coordination of group action took place.

This level, or locus, of political organization varied a great deal. Some groups, regionally concentrated and sharing both language and culture, lacked political integration of any kind beyond the extended family or the temporary village settlement, often of fewer than fifty persons. Such minimal political organization (minimal in its inclusiveness) was found particularly in the Arctic, northern California, and among Great Basin groups such as the Paiutes and western Shoshones. At the other end of the spectrum were such multitribal confederacies as the League of the Iroquois, in which a limited degree of comprehensive political organization united distinct tribal groups.[5]

Most fell somewhere between these extremes, with everything from village- and band-based political organization to what might loosely be called tribal organization, in which language and other cultural features, kinship boundaries, self-concept, and territorial and political organization more or less coincided. This last type, however, seems to have been rare prior to contact with Europeans. Perhaps the outstanding example of comprehensive tribal political organization—in which decision making often took place at the tribal level—was the Cheyennes, where a council of forty-four peace chiefs united ten major bands and functioned as "the keystone of the Cheyenne social structure," primary locus of authority in Cheyenne civil affairs.[6]

Much more common were groups in which political power, such as it was, was concentrated in the village or band. These villages or bands, often quite large, might join together in occasional or seasonal enterprises such as hunts or ceremonies, but in general, while they shared language, culture, and to some extent territory, they were autonomous, lacking political integration at the tribal level, as that level is commonly perceived. Viewed historically by non-Indians in monolithic terms and functioning today in most cases as political units, these groups had no such *political* identity until contact or later. Prominent examples include the Comanches, Navajos, the Apache groups, and many others.[7]

Yet political organization was only one aspect of groupness. However restricted in scope political organization might be, many such groups were carriers of identities reaching well beyond the limits of political integration. Far from being merely fragmented associations of disparate villages and bands, they formed what Edward Spicer has called "peoples": "determinable set[s] of human individuals who believe in a given set of identity symbols."[8]

The Indian population was divided into just such sets: groups of individuals bound together by, among other things, their collective participation in common symbolic beliefs, cultural practice, and social networks and interactions that established and sustained their common identity and subjectively distinguished them from the rest of the world. The particular sets of symbols, relationships, and interactions involved in such collective identity systems might vary widely from group to group. At the heart of most lay real or assumed lineal ties and systems of religious or cosmological belief, as well as language and other cultural phenomena and historical and often territorial continuities. But whatever the particular structure of the identity system, the point is the product of collective participation in its various elements: a self-conscious peoplehood.

A. L. Kroeber, using slightly different criteria, called such groups nations, "possessing essentially uniform speech and customs and therefore an accompanying sense of likeness and likemindedness."[9] The nation was a larger, more comprehensive grouping than the village or band.

Peoplehood or nationhood bound together politically discrete social units. Wallace and Hoebel give an excellent example in their discussion of the Comanches, who comprised a varying number of autonomous bands and family groups.

> "Tribe" when applied to the Comanche is a word of sociological but not political significance. The Comanches had a strong consciousness of kind. A Comanche, whatever his band, was a Comanche. . . . By dress, by speech, by thoughts and actions the Comanches held a common bond of identity and affinity that set them off from all other Indians—from all the rest of the world. In this sense the tribe had meaning. The tribe consisted of a people who had a common way of life. But that way of life did not include political institutions or social mechanisms by which they could act as a tribal unit.[10]

As much could be said of many other Indian nations. Robert Lowie remarks, for example, on the "sense of solidarity" among politically autonomous Crow bands, while Morris Opler writes that the Chiricahua Apaches, though divided into three autonomous bands, shared "a very real unity" and considered themselves "one people." The more northerly Jicarilla Apaches, according to Opler, were divided into two bands and numerous local groups, yet "there was a consciousness of tribal territory and solidarity." Basehart reports the same for the Mescaleros. The Hopis, while divided into fully autonomous villages, apparently had a sense of common identity, while the essentially autonomous rancherias of the Colorado River groups, according to Spicer, typically had "a strong sense of tribal identity" and some capability of united action.[11]

Lowell John Bean, in his study of the Cahuilla Indians of California, notes that Cahuillas were aware of membership in a culturally, linguistically, and historically distinct group, although prior to White contact the group had apparently never functioned as a single unit. Below this "maximal level of social identification" were other, more precisely defined levels: clans, moieties, lineages. As among most southern California Indians, however, the basic political unit was the lineage.

Potawatomi political organization was embedded in more or less autonomous, clan-based villages, but these shared a more comprehensive national identity, were linked through a variety of kinship and other organizational bonds, and often acted in concert. Likewise the Shawnees, divided into autonomous bands, had a more inclusive concept of themselves as a people, although the extent of actual cooperation and organization among these bands is unclear. In the Southeast, the numerous Cherokee towns were for the most part politically independent, but they were symbolically integrated. While Cherokee group organization, like that of all Indian groups, adapted when necessary to the demands of the social and physical environment, a comprehensive sense of nationhood is evident, along with a "capital" or symbolic center in one village.[12]

Of course there were many groups in which such relatively large-scale self-concepts were either poorly developed or absent. The Navajos, for example, had a common name for those who spoke the Navajo language, but the sense of what today would be called "tribal" identity seems to have been minimal and of little importance. Both identity and political organization were concentrated in much smaller band structures and groupings of families.[13] Likewise, in both the Northwest and along the northern Atlantic coast such comprehensive identities apparently were rare.

But whatever the specifics in each case, the point is twofold. First, the organizational and conceptual bases of group life were often not coincidental. "Peoples" may have been but were not necessarily politically integrated groups. Second, the conceptual dimension was often the more comprehensive of the two, embracing much less inclusive political units.

TRIBALIZATION IN THE CONFLICT YEARS

The European invasion inevitably had an impact on these patterns of group organization and identity. One aspect of that impact was political consolidation: the eventual establishment or solidification of comprehensive "tribal" political organization, accompanied in most cases by the decline of less comprehensive, autonomous political units. In other words, the organizational and conceptual dimensions of grouphood converged as political integration expanded toward the maximal level of self-concept. In some cases also, political integration led to the emergence of a new collective identity where none previously had existed.

Consolidation was neither immediate nor ubiquitous; indeed, often the early effect of societal interactions was just the opposite: the deterioration of comprehensive political organization. Groups reorganized—and occasionally broke up—in order to take advantage of new economic opportunities, to deal with threats to lands or livelihood, or as a consequence of military defeat. But the overall pattern was eventually consolidational: autonomous bands, villages, clans, and family groups either disappeared or became, for the most part, "tribes."

In cases of European–non-European contact around the world, group consolidation generally is a consequence of four factors: first, the ignorance and prejudice of newcomers. Early European travelers and settlers, often insensitive even to relatively gross differences among other cultures and prone to a view of humankind as divided most significantly between the civilized (us) and the barbarians (them), tended to make distinctions among native peoples based on their most general and accessible characteristics: somatic features, language, territorial distribution. Furthermore, in their dealings with those peoples they searched for political structures similar to their own: individuals or councils with authority to act on behalf of the nations or peoples they encountered. Where such comprehensive political structures were absent, they encouraged their development, trying to reproduce the processes of interstate politics by which their own external relations were governed.

Second, contact between Europeans and indigenous peoples often involved cultural interactions and economic developments that led to organizational transformations, including the emergence of more comprehensive sociopolitical units. Trade opportunities, for example, might encourage changes in settlement patterns leading to group consolidation at local trade centers. Third, indigenous peoples often found it in their interests, for purposes of defense or negotiation, to join together against the European invasion. And, fourth, as the Europeans extended their hegemony over the world's continents, the exigencies of political and economic control had a leveling effect on native organization: larger political units emerged—were either reinforced or in effect created by Europeans—as convenient territorial and administrative units that, regardless of their often tenuous relationship to indigenous political or conceptual realities, had a persuasive logic in the European system of domination.

These factors are amply evident in the tribalization of Indian peoples. Changes in material culture had some effects. The introduction of horses, for example, in some cases brought villages into closer contact; local problems became regional as intercourse increased.[14]

Other influences were transmitted more directly. Trade with Europeans often had centralizing impacts. The early stages of the fur trade, for example, led to changes in Chippewa sociopolitical structures in the Great Lakes region. Large villages replaced local clans as primary units of social authority and coordination, although subsequently this centralizing process was reversed. The complexities of expanding relations with European governments and traders apparently contributed also to a process of political centralization among the Cherokees in the eighteenth century, reducing the traditional autonomy of the Cherokee villages.[15]

Another centralizing influence came from missionaries, primarily through the active promotion of European political culture with its emphasis on separately institutionalized governments and formal codes of law. Missionaries often encouraged Indians to elect or appoint ruling councils, to centralize authority, and to adopt laws defining and protecting private property, and introduced organizational patterns and procedures that facilitated more comprehensive political structure.[16]

At the heart of tribalization, however, were activities that became ever more prominent in Indian-White relations: diplomacy, negotiation, conflict. Over time, the centralizing tendency increasingly reflected either Indian responses to changing political circumstances or the specific demands made by Whites.

Of course conflict as a source of unity certainly preceded European contact. Indian groups lacking political integration above the rancheria, village, or band level on occasion did cooperate nationally—that is, at the tribal level—for warfare or in response to attack. Indeed, such situations were often the only occasions when national identity took practical form in substantive political organization. Such conflict also on occasion promoted the consolidation of distinct tribal groups. At the end of the eighteenth century, for example, Sioux raiding was a major factor in the reorganization of Mandan and Hidatsa villages on the Missouri River. This and other developments led to a process of gradual amalgamation of the two groups that continued well into the nineteenth century.[17]

Conflict with Whites elicited similar patterns of action. While often a source of division and factionalism as Native Americans struggled to find effective ways of coping with the consequences of invasion, conflict produced alliance as well. This occurred not only among tribes but within them, as bands and villages joined together in defense of territory or, especially in later years, searched for political structures capable of responding to a situation of sustained crisis.

The centrality of land in these conflicts also contributed to tribalization. The extent of tribal land claims varied. Some groups had a powerful sense of exclusive tribal territory. Others, writes Imre Sutton, "came to articulate a territorial claim only when pressured by white demands for land cessions."[18] Tribal land, which often had no counterpart in tribal political organization, suddenly became a political object or, more precisely, the object of politics. As such, it "often triggered the need for articulation of tribal-wide government."[19]

U.S. government representatives asked in effect for two things: that tribes indicate which lands they claimed and that there be some political structure that could ensure the effectiveness of negotiated settlements. The latter requirement in particular was crucial; all too often treaties concluded with one band or village were repudiated or ignored by related but autonomous groups whose claims to the same territory, either unknown to or dismissed by U.S. negotiators, had not been released. Both government tactics and Indian avarice exacerbated such difficulties. If one "chief" could be persuaded to sign away land rights on behalf of his band or village, this might be considered a sufficient basis for the forced expulsion of all related but unrepresented groups from the same lands. Bribery was common. If one group or leader refused to part with particular lands, another who could be bought would serve as well.[20]

All the same, the frequent lack of a tribal polity was a source of constant frustration to European and American negotiators, who searched for and often assumed comprehensive structures of authority or hierarchical political organization where, often enough, they did not exist. As Indians were confronted with such assumptions and were pressed to respond within the framework of the White illusion, more comprehensive political organization was circumstantially encouraged.[21] Writing about the evolution of Potawatomi governing structures, Clifton remarks that the role of chief "was undoubtedly built upon older Potawatomi ideas and practice concerning the selection and responsibilities of clan leaders. But just as certainly it took on a new form in consequence of French expectations, ideas, and preferences."[22]

Comprehensive political organization at times was even made a prerequisite for negotiations. At the Fort Laramie treaty council of 1851, for example, the U.S. commissioners demanded that the Sioux and Arapahoes each select a "head chief." The Arapahoes complied; the Sioux at first refused. Similar efforts, successful or not, were frequent, while Whites themselves sometimes made the selections for the reluctant Indians. Army officers negotiating with the Mescalero Apaches chose a "principal chief" with whom they communicated, although the Mescaleros refused to recognize him as such. John Wesley Powell finally succeeded in establishing the position of tribal chief among the Kaibab Paiutes, while the first attempts to establish a Navajo tribal government appear to have been made in the 1860s by the army and the Indian agent as a control mechanism when the Navajos were confined at Fort Sumner.[23]

Some nations fought the official fictions, but once established they proved tenacious. When William Henry Harrison, governor of the Indiana Territory, negotiated with the allied Sac and Mesquakie (Fox) nations, he assumed he was dealing with the "united Sac and Fox tribe" and wrote the 1804 treaty accordingly. A generation later, when the Mesquakies realized what had happened, they found officialdom oblivious to the facts and reluctant to recognize their independence.[24]

Of course tribalization could have advantages for Indians. They, too, had political agendas; they also were in pursuit of peace, secure borders, access to resources available only from their adversaries. Centralized political structures, often including new leadership positions, had advantages in dealings with European and American governments and their representatives. As such dealings came to play a larger role in Indian life, specialized political organization became increasingly advantageous. It also offered opportunities to ambitious individuals or factions seeking to expand their influence or power.[25]

Thus conflict and negotiation fostered—even if they did not always produce—tribal political organization. They put the group in a position where it needed to act, and was expected by non-Indians to act, as a single political unit, encouraging the emergence of tribe as primary functional and conceptual unit in Indian-White relations. But the end of conflict and negotiation brought no end to tribalization. The extension of U.S. hegemony over Native American peoples brought new forces to bear upon them, but with comparable effects. The circumstances changed, but in the crucible of the reservations, the process went on.

INADVERTENT TRIBALIZATION:
THE RESERVATION YEARS

Of course the goal of federal Indian policy was precisely the opposite—the destruction of the tribal edifice—and at no time more so than during the reservation years. The federal objective was to dismantle kinship and other communal structures and to substitute in their place individualistic political and economic philosophy and organization. The allotment policy inaugurated with the Dawes Act in 1887 was both cornerstone and exemplar of the federal design. By distributing tribal lands to individual tribal members, granting U.S. citizenship to allottees, and making the United States the trustee not, in many cases, of tribal lands but of individually held allotments, the Dawes Act set out to destroy the tribe as a territorial, economic, and political entity.

The campaign was only partially successful, although the costs to Indians were enormous and by no means limited to land. Allotment, the prohibition of certain ceremonies, the forced dismantling of indigenous authority structures, and other policies of the period in many cases precipitated political collapse. Collective decision-making processes atrophied as meaningful decisions were taken out of Indian hands, while much of the substance of decision making under conditions of freedom—hunt organization, camp moves, interband and intertribal relations—was no longer relevant. The institutional substance of tribal life was dissolving under the impact of imposed sociocultural change.

Even so, much survived. The community organization of a few groups was relatively less affected by U.S. control, particularly in the Southwest. The village organization of the Pueblos remained largely intact, while the Navajos and Papagos, comparatively isolated on vast expanses of land, for the most part were spared rigorous controls on their internal affairs until the 1920s. Neither of the latter two, however, had anything like tribal political organization until well into the period of U.S. domination; what survived were more or less traditional systems of local autonomy. Not all southwestern groups were so lucky. The political organization of both the Pimas and the Apaches, for example, were either dominated or transformed by missionary and BIA controls.[26]

Other factors mitigated the impact of these decades. In some cases, as with the Pueblos, traditional structures of religious and political authority—the two were virtually indistinguishable—survived in some fashion by going underground, hidden away from government officials and religious reformers. Allotment itself was only incompletely instituted, and some tribal lands were not affected at all. Finally, as the whole history of Indian-White relations demonstrates, Indian group identities, while scarcely impervious to the assaults of policy, were not solely dependent on economic, political, or territorial continuities, nor on the retention of material ways of living in the world. More important to their survival were other social and cultural continuities: patterns of kinship relations, modes of thought and action, systems of meaning and interpretation. Thus rooted, Indian identities have proven to be complex, resilient, and adaptable; despite substantial changes in the outward manifestations of culture, much survived, including distinctive self-concepts and world views. Surviving with them, though often greatly changed in numbers, lifestyles, and activities, were Indian peoples.[27]

At the same time, tribal survivals were not products solely of Indian isolation or secrecy, the intrinsic durabilities of Indian identities, or even equivocation in government administration. However inadvertently, federal policy circumstantially sustained the tribalizing process. The reservation system both reinforced already existing tribal identities and created new ones, at the same time making the tribe increasingly the focus of political relations between Indians and Whites. The reservation became both setting and instrument of a new phase of tribalization in a context of non-Indian control.

Whether or not individual tribes had their own reservations was of little inherent interest to the federal government, which preferred to concentrate Indians as much as possible in a single area, such as the Indian Territory. But few tribes had readily agreed to leave their homelands, and many had negotiated from a position of strength. By the time the power of these tribes had been reduced, the logistical and political problems of moving them had become substantial. What's more, there was evidence that such transfers could be catastrophic for tribes from very different physical environments.

The result was that many groups ended up on their own reservations. Barring massive and permanent out- or in-migration, survival of these reservations assured survival of the tribal unit. It also meant that the reservation and, by virtue of coextension, the tribe became the principal units of Indian administration, continuing a pattern established by the treaty process.

More important, the reservation system, coupled with government desire for close supervision of Indian life, continued the geographical process of consolidation initiated earlier by conflict. On reservations wholly or largely occupied by a single tribe, bands that had once been territorially discrete often were forced to settle side by side or together on the same spot. Villages were moved and consolidated; widely dispersed rancherias, their lands ceded to or taken by Whites, found themselves concentrated within sharply circumscribed areas. On the San Carlos Reservation in Arizona, traditional Apache band organization was ignored as new patterns of settlement and a unitary administrative system were imposed on the groups gathered there, gradually undermining traditional sociopolitical boundaries. In Minnesota, following the Sioux uprising of 1862, the Santees were removed to the Crow Creek Reservation in South Dakota and eventually to Nebraska. Under the stress of removal, concentration in new territory, and the hands of White administrators, the traditional band organization collapsed and was replaced by more comprehensive political arrangements.[28]

A similar process followed Comanche confinement on a reservation in the Indian Territory. Within a few years, reports William Hagan, "the original band lines were blurring and Indian spokesmen were emerging more and more as Comanches rather than as Quahadas or Yamparikas [band identities]." In the Northwest during the contact period, the Nez Perce Indians comprised four informal and loosely organized groups, each in turn made up of more or less autonomous bands. In the 1860s and 1870s, through treaty negotiations and subsequent conflict, Nez Perce lands were drastically reduced. In the process two of these regional groupings, along with their constituent villages and bands, lost their lands and essentially disappeared as identifiable groups. Over time and largely as a result of outside forces, more and more inclusive political structures steadily displaced indigenous Nez Perce sociopolitical organization.[29]

Similar changes occurred among more sedentary agricultural groups. The Papago Indians of Arizona were originally a loose collection of distinct village groups or tribes. The formation of the Papago Reservation in 1917 encouraged the Papagos to think of themselves as a distinct people. "Their growth to tribal self-consciousness," writes Henry Dobyns, "was the direct result of the enforced geographic segregation of the reservation policy."[30]

In these and other cases, not only did subtribal political organization deteriorate, but subtribal identities did as well. Those tied to particular bands, villages, clans, and the like did not necessarily disappear, but, as Hagan suggests for the Comanches, they gradually gave way to more inclusive, tribal ones.[31]

Not all reservations, of course, were occupied exclusively by one people. In order to maximize land availability, minimize administrative structures, and ease the White Man's Burden, distinct—sometimes even hostile—groups often had to share a restricted land base. In the 1850s, for example, treaty commissioners on the Northwest Coast "were directed to combine little tribes into big tribes and locate as many as possible on single reservations."[32] While groups combined in this manner often retained distinct identities, for administrative purposes the reservation population came to be treated as a single unit, in many cases taking on a tribal designation that might be at odds with the subjective Indian reality but encouraged the emergence of a concomitant identity.

This development was characteristic of the Northwest, where some treaties created tribal "confederations." The Yakima Indians—today the Confederated Tribes and Bands of the Yakima Nation—are in fact descendants of fourteen separate tribes and bands, including the Yakimas, sharing neither political nor conceptual unity, who were placed on a single reservation created in south-central Washington by the Yakima Treaty of 1855. In the same year the Warm Springs Reservation in north-central Oregon was established by treaty with several bands from two distinct peoples, the Wy-um-pum and the Wasco Indians. Following military campaigns in 1866–68, a small band of Paiutes from southeastern Oregon was moved to the reservation as well. These three groups eventually came to be known collectively as the Warm Springs Indians.[33]

The Flathead Reservation in western Montana, also established by an 1855 treaty, became the home of Flathead, Salish, Kootenai, Pend d'Oreille, Spokane, and other Indians, taking its name from the most famous of these groups. Among them they spoke several different languages, but administratively they were treated as a single tribe. When allotment came to the reservation, for example, the population was listed on a single tribal roll. The Indians also found that in defense of their reservation lands they needed to act together; in 1916 an informally constituted tribal council was formed. In the course of a controversy over dam construction on the reservation, the Indians were referred to both by themselves and others as the Flathead Indians, although the Flatheads proper were outnumbered by other groups. "The reservation," writes Ronald Trosper, "had become a source of identity."[34]

There were other outcomes as well. Consolidation was not everywhere the case, and for some groups the processes of conflict and confinement led to disintegration. The Mississippi Choctaws and the Eastern Cherokees in North Carolina are remnant bands of the Choctaws and Cherokees who were forced to move to the Indian Territory in the 1830s. When the Great Sioux Reservation was broken up into five parts in 1889, the various Teton groups were mixed and scattered to varying degrees among the new reserves. By the mid-nineteenth century the Potawatomis, driven from most of their western Great Lakes homelands, were dispersed in locations from Ontario to Oklahoma, while the Senecas of the League of the Iroquois were divided ultimately into five parts, three in New York— two of them functioning today under a single government—a Canadian group, and a segment removed to the Indian Territory.

Despite this diversity, however, the trend overall was toward increasingly inclusive political organization and tribal identities. The reservation gave physical reality to tribal boundaries once primarily culturally defined or helped create such boundaries where they had not previously existed. These boundaries now separated not so much Indian from Indian as Indian from White, but did so on the basis of the tribal unit. Federal administration paid little attention to subtribal divisions except where they could be exploited for purposes of control. What rights Indians retained were attached to them now through treaties usually made on a tribal basis; their legal standing was derived from tribal identifications or more generally from Indianness. Relations with the rest of the world, once largely the concern of bands, villages, or lineages, were now tribally defined. Those relations went on largely outside Native American control; nonetheless, to the extent that they left any room at all for expressions of group sentiment or group action, they encouraged tribalism. Administratively treated as tribes, Indians found it made sense to respond the same way.

Thus tribal identification received circumstantial support from the external framework of relations within which the tribe was situated, even as the internal supports of tribal community and consciousness came under attack. Of course the atomistic thrust of Indian policy in the late nineteenth and early twentieth centuries threatened even such remnant communalism as the reservations managed to preserve, particularly as the Indian land base was eaten away through allotment, sale, and fraud, and as a destitute dependency replaced native maintenance activities. The tribe was surviving as an administrative unit, but, however slowly, the community or communities it embraced were being broken down.

Moreover, while tribalization was sustained by administrative practice, this very fact testified to its impotence. Tribal identifications were reinforced, but the tribe remained powerless, both victim and by-product of the structure of subordination.

FRAGMENTATION

Coming together, the tribe also began to come apart. The structures and processes that give it political unity left it conceptually divided.

Much has been made of factionalism among Indians. "Why can't those Indians get together?" is a recurrent and revealing query, betraying a persistent belief in common interests and in the power of such interests to bridge uncommon lives.

Indian factionalism is an old story that predates European contact. Internal rivalries and disagreements were hardly unknown and often led to conflict; they sometimes led as well to fission, the emergence of new villages or bands as dissenters went their own ways. But whatever the incidence of factionalism prior to the European invasion, that event gave it a considerable boost. From the native point of view, Indian-White relations presented at least as much of a problem as they did to Whites. With the European advance and the decline in native power, it became increasingly difficult for Indian nations to find and agree upon appropriate courses of action. Traditional modes of response to crisis appeared more and more inadequate. Land pressures often led to fierce disagreements within Indian groups over the desirability of negotiation and the terms of cession. Non-Indians demanded unified action in circumstances that often made it almost impossible to achieve.[35]

Political tribalization heightened factional difficulties. Tendencies toward centralization inevitably reduced the influence of some groups and individuals and increased the power of others. As political power within Indian societies became more concentrated, competition for it increased. The reservation system in particular was a natural setting for factionalism. Indigenous power was minimal, precious, and often dependent on White administrators. Competition for influence with the agent could be intense. The ability to deal successfully with non-Indians became an ever more desirable qualification for leadership, a development that favored more acculturated tribespeople. Already apparent divisions between "conservative" and "progressive" factions within many tribes were deepened as agents bypassed traditional leaders in favor of younger men or those more disposed to cooperate with BIA policies and programs. On many reservations factional conflict became chronic along "conservative," less acculturated, or "full-blood" versus "progressive," more acculturated, or "mixed-blood" lines. In some cases mixed-blood groups organized councils or other bodies in an attempt to influence the agent, improve reservation services, or simply gather power. Such councils had the effect of replacing, often with administrative encouragement, the older, kinship-based or other traditional leadership, promoting new models of leadership selection and authority derived from non-Indians.

Not all factionalism followed full-blood/mixed-blood lines.[36] Some disputes reached back centuries, involving particular families or clans while interfamily conflict often underlay other factional disputes. Missionaries introduced new sources of discord. Much of the conflict they stimulated was of a Christian-versus-pagan sort, but competition between Christian sects occurred as well. White land interests also encouraged factionalism and were quick to exploit it whenever it appeared, rewarding groups viewed as favorable to their goals.[37]

The loss of traditional means of dealing with conflict made the effects of factionalism still more severe. Prior to U.S. hegemony and reservation confinement, serious internal conflicts often led to separation. The disaffected might leave to form a new band or village. Without a centralized structure of power to be fought over and with generally available sustenance resources, factional conflicts could be more easily resolved without generating exclusive sets of winners and losers.

Reservation confinement raised the stakes and narrowed the means of dispute resolution. Now there were central positions of limited power to be won or lost and diminishing resources to be controlled, while separation was no longer an option. The result was not necessarily an increase in factionalism, but almost certainly an increase in its intensity and often a bitter legacy. By early in the twentieth century many reservations were deeply divided, if not by long-standing cleavages given fresh salience in a radically transformed world, then by entirely new ones generated by subordination and decline.[38]

Thus the historical pattern of incorporation set in motion two very different processes: a gradual consolidation of group boundaries on the one hand and the introduction of new intragroup divisions on the other. But there was a third process involved as well. The two dimensions of groupness—organization and self-concept—remained asymmetrical, as they had been at contact, but their asymmetry was being turned inside out. Where once a single conceptual design had embraced political complexity, now a simplified—and in some ways inadvertent—administrative design struggled to contain a ramifying conceptual mosaic.

But the reservation years did not see the end of the process. Tribalization would continue, eventually giving shape to the Indian-White politics of the mid-twentieth century. But unlike the process in the conflict and reservation years, it would become explicitly intentional, the product of yet another transformation, this time in policy. In a startling reversal of long-standing objectives, in the 1930s Indian policy not only offered to formalize emergent tribal structures, but invited these reconstructed entities into the political area, made newly accessible to their participation.

Chapter 6

New Music, New Partners, A New Dance

Ira Katznelson has suggested that the study of intergroup relations can profit by attention to what he calls "critical historical periods." These are times when structured linkages between groups—links that shape the distribution of power, the opportunities for action, the pattern of domination and subordination—are set in place or transformed.[1]

Such periods may be of varying duration. Some, like the elaboration of Jim Crow segregation in the American South late in the nineteenth century, occupy a decade or more. Others are compressed into moments, realized abruptly in the passage of a single law, a turnabout in policy, a sudden revolt.

There have been a number of such periods in Indian-White relations, pivotal times when the patterns of incorporation changed. The early ones tended to be lengthy. The conflict phase emerged gradually out of the collapse of fur markets and interstate competition; the reservation period likewise took shape incrementally as the various Indian nations were subordinated to Euro-American designs.

The critical periods of the twentieth century look very different: moments, relatively speaking, when the reorganization of intergroup relations is captured in a few events, when large-scale transformations and their effects are compressed into a brief time. This shift from the elongate periods of one century to the compressions of the next is a consequence of latter-day unilateralism: uncontested ground gives way more quickly. The critical periods of the nineteenth century took form in an adversarial context, but those of the twentieth, up until the 1960s, took place on a policy-making terrain from which Indians were largely absent. What conflict there was occurred primarily among those making the decisions, that is, among Whites.

Yet some of those decisions, unilateral though they may have been, had crucial consequences for Indian political resurgence, and none more so than the Indian Reorganization Act of 1934, commonly known as the IRA. Passage of the IRA and its implementation in succeeding years form a critical historical period in Indian-White relations because of their lasting impact on the pattern of political incorporation linking Native Americans to the larger society and on the political structures of the Indian nations.

In the conventional academic view of political development, groups are incorporated politically into a society insofar as they participate in the institutionalized political arrangements by which the society is governed. Put somewhat differently, political incorporation can be measured "by the degree of responsiveness of the political system to the grievances of the group."[2]

The emphasis here is different. Political incorporation refers not to the degree of group participation in larger political structures or the responsiveness of those structures to group concerns, but more generally to the political relationships that link the group to the larger system, whether those relationships are responsive to group concerns or not. There are not so much degrees of political incorporation as types; groups are not more or less incorporated, but are differentially incorporated on terms that provide different degrees of political opportunity and thereby facilitate or inhibit collective political action of various kinds.[3]

At the start of the twentieth century, the political links between the Indian nations and the larger society were restrictive in the extreme. Indigenous structures of self-government, accountable to their own populations, had been undermined, destroyed, or ignored, replaced by administrative structures imposed from without, controlled by and accountable to non-Indians. These new structures, unlike the indigenous ones they replaced, were devoted not to the maintenance of the tribal community and the conservation of tribal resources, but to the transformation of that community and the incorporation of its resources into the dominant economy, with or without Indian participation. Furthermore, they formed the only link between Indian groups and the national political system. This link, therefore, was unilateral in nature, effectively excluding Indians as groups from participation in the political processes that ultimately governed their affairs. The result was that Native Americans lacked almost any independent means of pursuing group interests. Although a few tribes were able to pursue their political agendas through the courts, most could do little more than try to influence local BIA representatives who were largely unaccountable to their charges. Doing much more required organizational resources most groups now lacked as well as independent access to alternative sources of power.

As individuals, on the other hand, Indians could escape, at least theoretically, much of the formal system of control and enter the national polity. In fact, however, given their lack of organizational resources and experience as well as the formal and informal controls ubiquitous on the reservations, individual entry into the larger system produced little increase in collective political capacities. Nor was it intended to. Individualization was proposed as an antidote to tribalism, not to powerlessness. Citizenship and allotment were viewed, and indeed functioned, as educational tools, as vehicles of cultural transformation, not as gateways to collective political power. Even in the Indian Territory, where the Five Civilized Tribes in particular had managed to retain substantial political capabilities—in part by adapting dominant-group institutions to their own needs and political ends—the tribal structure came under attack. The group was held in bondage while the individual, theoretically, was set free.

In the 1930s these terms of political incorporation changed. While the full effect of that change took some time to appear, its primary accomplishment was rapidly apparent: it opened the door to large-scale collective Indian participation in the political arena of Indian–White relations. While the federal government still called the tune, the political dance was never again the same.

THE IRA

Nineteen thirty-four was a pivotal year—the twentieth century's watershed—in Indian affairs. It appears abruptly, this radical shift in Indian policy, but long before the legislative realization there were indications, in the underlying forces that traditionally had shaped Indian-White relations, of impending change. Demand for Indian land was waning. Allotment, which peaked between 1906 and 1910, declined irregularly thereafter, although there was a flurry of activity in the late 1910s and early 1920s. But remaining Indian lands were of little apparent value and land prices were falling. Partly as a result of declining agricultural profits, prices for U.S. farmland fell through most of the 1920s, and in 1933 hit their lowest point between 1906 and the present. Homestead entries likewise were low.[4] The motor of Indian policy—land acquisition—was running out of gas.

Changing circumstances brought other societal forces to the fore. A movement for reform in Indian policy had been gathering momentum in the 1910s and 1920s. It grew from various roots. Those years had much to offer the reformer in the way of ideology: social-justice progressivism, a new awareness of cultural diversity and a new interest in cultural pluralism as an American model, a growing concern with the shape and persistence of community in social life. Indians were attractive objects for these ideas, being both less numerous and more American than the southern European and Asian immigrants who tested the limits of enlightened ideology in those years.

Events also had an impact. In 1922 the Harding administration sponsored legislation in Congress in an effort to settle conflicting White and Indian claims to Pueblo lands in New Mexico. The provisions of this legislation, known as the Bursum Bill, clearly favored non-Indian claimants and threatened both Pueblo lands and water resources. A number of liberal non-Indian organizations, including the General Federation of Women's Clubs and the newly established American Indian Defense Association, angered by the government-sponsored threat to the Pueblos, came out in opposition to the bill and were joined by members of the artistic and intellectual community of northern New Mexico. D. H. Lawrence, for example, writing in the *New York Times,* claimed the bill played "the Wild West scalping trick a little too brazenly." The legislation ignited Indian action as well, triggering the revitalization of the All Pueblo Council, a coalition of the Pueblo villages that had lain dormant since the revolt against the Spanish more than two centuries before. Leaders of the council argued that the bill "will complete our destruction" and headed for Washington to protest in person. After a protracted conflict Congress adopted a substitute measure, the Pueblo Lands Act, which shifted much of the burden of proof of ownership to non-Indian claimants.[5]

Reformers were setting their sights also on the Bureau of Indian Affairs. Popular and intellectual periodicals carried a number of articles in the 1920s charging the government with mismanagement of the reservations and interference with religious rights and community life. When the BIA tried to prohibit some of the surviving tribal dances and ceremonies in the 1920s, claiming they were immoral, physically dangerous, or simply wasteful of time better spent in economic enterprise, it found itself in conflict with reform organizations as well as Indians.

Eventually the criticism proved too much. In 1926 the secretary of the interior asked the Institute for Government Research to carry out a survey of the social and economic conditions of American Indians. The result, two years later, was the Meriam Report, named for Lewis Meriam, who directed it: "a masterpiece of reform propaganda in the best sense of the word."[6] The report documented, in scientific survey style, the staggering degree of poverty, ill health, poor education, and community disorganization that generally prevailed on the reservations. "An overwhelming majority of Indians," said the report,

> are poor, even extremely poor. . . . The income of the typical Indian family is low and the earned income extremely low. . . . The number of Indians who are supporting themselves through their own efforts, according to what a white man would regard as the minimum standard of health and decency, is extremely small. . . . Many of them are living on lands from which a trained and experienced white man could scarcely wrest a reasonable living."[7]

Among other things, the report criticized allotment, labeling it a failure and deploring its effects; advocated support for Indian community life and stronger protection of Indian property rights; and proposed major new efforts in the areas of Indian education and health. It showed unusual ambivalence on the question of assimilation, concluding that "the object of work with or for Indians is to fit them *either* to merge into the social and economic life of the prevailing civilization as developed by the whites *or* to live in the presence of that civilization at least in accordance with a minimum standard of health and decency."[8]

In 1929 a new commissioner of Indian affairs, responding to the Meriam Report and independent congressional investigations, attempted to implement a number of changes, especially in the areas of health and education. But it was not until Franklin Roosevelt's election and the appointment in 1933 of John Collier as Indian commissioner that a genuinely new Indian policy began to take form.

The Indian Reorganization Act was the product of a relatively rare historical phenomenon: the conjunction of propitious conditions and visionary persons. The conditions in this case were the felt need and public support for a significant change in Indian policy, combined with the diminution of both the economic imperative and the cultural presumption that for so long had shaped Indian affairs. The visionary was John Collier.

Collier was a veteran of social welfare and community work in the first two decades of the century and of the protests over Indian rights in the 1920s. He had been executive secretary of the American Indian Defense Association and an architect of the fight against the Bursum Bill and cultural interference. His experiences with Indians in the Southwest, then and earlier, had reinforced his almost mystical belief in the organic community and in the need to revitalize community life and spirit, not only among Indians, where he believed they yet prevailed over the fragmenting individualism of competitive American society, but for the sake of the United States itself. Collier viewed traditional Indian societies as characterized by cooperative enterprise on the basis of shared values and a vital community aesthetic, ideals he believed had disappeared from the society at large. And it was precisely these qualities, he believed, that needed to be protected and preserved in Indian life. Native American communities should be supported, not undermined, and Indian societies, he argued, "must be given status, responsibility, and power." He viewed provision for Indian self-government and the stabilization and even expansion of the Indian land base as crucial steps toward these essential ends.[9]

In the early years of the New Deal, Collier and others in the new administration who advocated policies of community revitalization found support for their ideas and an opportunity to put them into practice. In Collier's case the result was a massive effort to reorient the whole of Indian policy. The cornerstone of that effort was the IRA.

In its original version this legislation, drafted by Collier and his associates, made a radical break with the past. It provided, for example, for Indian school courses in native history and cultures and special training for Indians to run their own affairs; it vested extensive powers of home rule in tribal corporations and mandated the consolidation under tribal ownership of allotted and heirship lands. In terms of implementation, however, it embraced past practice: most of the reforms it envisioned were to be imposed upon Indian communities. Congress, recognizing a need for change but wary of Collier's ideas and the antiassimilationism they implied, tempered the extremes. In particular it modified Collier's proposals for self-government and land consolidation and diluted his emphasis on native cultures. It also subjected implementation to tribal approval: the IRA would not apply to any tribe in which, via a special election called by the secretary of the interior, a majority of the adults rejected it. In this provision alone—to say nothing of the rest of the act—it departed dramatically from the past. For the first time in more than half a century, Native Americans were back in the decision-making process.

While Collier did not get anywhere near what he wanted in the act as passed, the final version included a number of critical changes.[10] It ended the policy of allotment, authorized the return to tribal ownership of lands withdrawn for entry by homesteaders but never entered, and authorized the secretary of the interior to acquire additional lands for the tribes with funds provided for that purpose. It encouraged the conservation of Indian resources and established a revolving credit fund from which tribes could borrow for economic development purposes.

Most important from a political viewpoint, the IRA provided that "any Indian tribe, or tribes, residing on the same reservation, shall have the right to organize for its common welfare" and to adopt a constitution for that purpose. In addition to already existing tribal powers, tribes so organized were to have the power to employ legal counsel, subject to the approval of choice and fees by the secretary of the interior; to prevent the sale, lease, or encumbrance of tribal lands and other assets without tribal consent; and to negotiate with federal, state, and local governments. Furthermore, tribes could organize as business corporations for the management of their resources.[11] Native Americans were not only reentering the decision-making process; they were also being offered specific tools with which to participate in the political arena. The door to a genuine Indian politics, slammed shut the century before, had begun to open.

Yet Indian reaction to the IRA was decidedly mixed. In conferences with Collier in the months preceding passage many tribes responded coolly. Their objections were diverse. Where group traditions and communities had been most deeply undermined by the years of allotment, administrative controls, and schooling in non-Indian society, some tribespeople objected to what they saw as a step backward. To those oriented economically and culturally to the world outside the reservations, the IRA was an anachronism, an attempt to preserve something they no longer believed in. They protested that Collier's proposals would lead to increased federal supervision and hinder the assimilation process, which was their best hope of economic success. At the opposite end of the spectrum were Indians, including some less acculturated "full-bloods," who were afraid they would be forced to relinquish their allotments, the only land they had managed to retain after a century of dispossession. Some tribes feared Collier's plans would adversely affect land claims, while others, mindful of past experience, held virtually all Indian-related legislation suspect, seeing in it a disguised attempt to strip them of yet more land. There were other concerns as well: the Pueblos worried that the act might change their still-surviving system of government, while others, joining with some non-Indian opponents, accused Collier of promoting socialism.[12]

Modifications in the original proposals overcame some of these objections before the legislation was passed and put to tribal referenda. Yet the results reveal marked ambivalence among the Indian nations. While some two-thirds of them approved the IRA, substantially fewer actually organized under its provisions. The largest tribe in the country, the Navajos, rejected it.[13]

On the other hand, the IRA had a dramatic impact on policy. In ending allotment, it reversed the commitment, dominant in Indian policy for the better part of a century, to the individualization of tribal property as the centerpiece of assimilation. The new policy set out not only to maintain the tribal land base, but to expand it. In effect the IRA recognized that tribal communities still existed and endorsed their right to exist.

Collier's lengthy tenure as Indian commissioner (1933–45) was perhaps as important as the act itself. Despite the failure in Congress of some of his most ambitious ideas, he used his administrative powers to implement many of them and to extend certain benefits of the IRA to nations that had rejected it. Among the important changes: much of the monopolistic control of Indian lives and affairs by the BIA was curbed, at least for a while, and the powers of the agents were checked; cultural preservation was encouraged and the suppression of indigenous religion reduced. It is no wonder that the IRA and Collier's other programs became known as "the Indian New Deal."[14]

THE AMBIGUITIES OF POLICY

The irony, however, is that despite these advances, the basic assumption of Indian policy was little changed. Neither IRA nor Indian New Deal challenged the fundamental belief that Indians would, and probably should, be assimilated ultimately by the society around them. They looked rather for a means of easing the process of change and giving Native Americans some measure of control over it. "The basic idea of the IRA policy," writes Edward Spicer,

> was that the cultural assimilation of Indians, individual by individual, as conceived in the former policy of land allotment and boarding-school education, disorganized both Indian personality and communities, and that influences from Anglo culture could be best assimilated through the medium of the tribe as an organized entity set up to deal as a unit with the outside influences. It was in a sense a concept of transitional community.[15]

Native culture was no longer to be discouraged—indeed, it was to be given support, and interference in internal tribal affairs was at least somewhat reduced—but the thrust of the policy was acculturational. In the implementation of the IRA, tribes were asked to choose between an alien constitutional form of government and the uncertainties of the pre-IRA period. The institutions provided for through the IRA were Euro-American in origin, applied more or less uniformly to a hugely varied mosaic of cultures and in widely divergent local situations. The form of political organization the tribes were encouraged to adopt, with its representative government, electoral districts, tribal officers, and so forth, was derived from political and legal traditions very different from theirs. As Spicer observes, it was a pattern "in the image of the conquerors' nation," designed to prepare Native Americans "for participation in the national political life."[16]

Collier himself expressed his faith that in the American democratic ideal Indians would find a new freedom: "The experience of responsible democracy," he said, "is, of all experiences, the most therapeutic, the most disciplinary, the most dynamogenic and the most productive of efficiency." In 1954, twenty years after passage of the IRA, when the policies he initiated were under attack from the right, Collier responded to the ominous political atmosphere with a reaffirmation of his belief: "the Indian Reorganization Act in its historical reference is the American way, and in its future reach it is a seeking by Indians and for Indians of full entry to, full participation in, that American way."[17]

Of course a return to wholly traditional forms of self-government was probably impossible. Both ecologically and culturally the Indian world was vastly different in 1934 from even half a century earlier. While some groups—the various Pueblos, the Arapahoes, a number of others—had managed to maintain effective tribal governments of one kind or another, in many places a structure of economic and political dependency was long and well established and the breakdown of indigenous forms of social organization far advanced. Then, too, a portion of the Indian population viewed assimilation as the only appropriate and desirable course. Many of those who opposed the IRA did so out of fear that it would hinder their progress in adapting to White society.

But the point lies elsewhere. The IRA and the Indian New Deal set out to grant to Indians a limited but enlarged degree of control over their affairs and destinies, but did so in the service of ends preselected by the dominant society and through methods given by that society, after its own models.

The important change, rather, was in the focus of policy, which had moved from the individual to the community, from the liquidation of native cultures to a policy of cultural pluralism within a framework of political and economic integration. Where once the community had been viewed as the primary obstacle to assimilation, through the IRA it became the vehicle through which assimilation could proceed. Instead of trying to break up the tribal mass and insert individual Indians into the institutional structures of the larger society, those structures would be built into Indian communities themselves. Furthermore, they would be built into those communities through the medium of self-government. As Indian tribes voluntarily formed constitutional governments, undertook the development of their own resources, and joined with the federal government in the assault on poverty and ignorance, assimilation would necessarily follow. American economic and political institutions would be reproduced within Indian societies, as a result of Indian efforts. The tribe, as a political construct, might well survive and, conceivably, at least some of what remained of Native American cultures along with it, but survival would take place within the institutional structures of American society, newly realized in the tribal context. And those structures, in turn, would inevitably promote acculturation.[18]

Thus the Indian New Deal altered the means but not, fundamentally, the ends of Indian policy. On the other hand, it did increase Indian political power. It did so not so much via expansion of the actual powers of self-government. Those inherent sovereign powers not yet surrendered by the Indian nations remained with them before the IRA was passed, and the act did not add measurably to these. Although it gave to those tribes that ratified it a power of veto over some federal and other actions, as in the provision for tribal consent to land sales, as well as the right to negotiate with other governments within the federal structure, it did not fundamentally increase federal accountability to Indians and it gave the secretary of the interior power of review over the constitutions adopted by the tribes as well as amendments thereto, a power that has been used to justify broad secretarial review powers over tribal actions. But until the IRA those powers Indian tribes did possess were largely ignored.

Furthermore, owing to the collapse of indigenous political organization and to the controls prevailing in the reservation years, many nations lacked the means of asserting what powers they had. The IRA gave legislative recognition to the already existing powers of self-government and provided a mechanism by which such self-government could be organized. It empowered tribal councils to negotiate on behalf of their peoples and thereby reestablished, albeit in a limited form, what Collier called "the fundamentally bilateral nature of the Government-Indian relationship."[19] In other words, the IRA facilitated and legitimated Indian political mobilization. It legitimated the entry of Indians *as groups* into the political arena and enlarged their capacities for action, and it is here that its political significance lies.

Those capacities, however, remained limited. The new political structures were not only organizational frameworks, but structures of control as well. The IRA facilitated and legitimated mobilization, but channeled it specifically into tribal governments and business committees modeled on dominant-group political forms. Even where the IRA had been rejected, the BIA pressured tribes to alter whatever political structures they had to better fit the BIA's conception.[20] Furthermore, in their genesis and activity the new councils were the progeny of Congress and subject to Interior Department approval. Despite the doctrine of inherent sovereignty recognized by U.S. courts and the tribal referenda that were necessary for adoption of both the

IRA and tribal constitutions, in practical terms these governments drew their political power from the consent of the Congress and the Interior Department, not from their own peoples. While tribal members could decide, via free elections, whether or not their governments actually represented their interests, the ability of those governments to promote those interests and, indeed, to govern remained subject to the approval and cooperation of non-Indian organizations and actors.

What's more, tribal governments still lacked linkage to other political structures except through the BIA. They could express their opinions, but their actions took place within the administrative hierarchy of Indian affairs. The IRA incorporated Indian nations into that structure but still excluded them, ultimately, from the seats of power. To be sure, some important things had changed, yet the form of self-government was more impressive than the substance.[21]

THE IRA AND TRIBALIZATION

Quite aside from its impact on Indian political opportunities and capacities, the IRA accomplished yet another significant reversal. It endorsed the tribalizing process previously supported by circumstance alone.

Formally constituted governments already existed for some tribes. Others had informal councils with limited authority in tribal affairs that served as liaison between reservation populations and BIA superintendents. But with the passage of the IRA and the shift in policy emphasis from individual assimilation to community institution building, the establishment and support of tribal political organization gained explicit federal favor. Tribalization was no longer the inadvertent by-product of a policy with opposite intentions; it had become a central component in the new federal design.

That design, however, remained flawed. The IRA had defined a "tribe" as "any Indian tribe, organized band, pueblo, or the Indians residing on one reservation."[22] Graham Taylor has pointed out, however, that "this definition was not very helpful to administrators," who had little knowledge of existing Indian political structures. "In practice, therefore, the reservation became the focus for organization."[23]

This not only undermined the effort to resuscitate and protect indigenous communities—a core element in Collier's vision—but it also ignored Indian sociohistorical realities. While tribalization was well advanced, there were cases such as the Shoshones and Arapahoes at Wind River, or the Fort Berthold Reservation in North Dakota, shared by Mandans, Gros Ventres, and Arikaras, where the reservation was merely a geographical space embracing distinct, often unrelated peoples. Even on reservations occupied by a single tribe, the new organizational structures often came into conflict with surviving traditions of subtribal autonomy. The effect of organization influenced by the IRA was to formalize a political unity superimposed on cultural and political diversity within single reservations. While it attempted to give Indians some control over their own affairs, it did so within a framework already established by administrative practice: with few exceptions, reservations, not actual Indian communities, were the organizational units in the new federal-Indian relationship.[24]

The IRA had a similar direct or indirect effect across reservations. It sought political and economic uniformity across widely varied reservation situations. To be sure, some effort was made—more in some cases than in others—to accommodate the peculiarities of individual Indian contexts, but the models of economic and political development promoted by the IRA were dominant-group models, put forward within an essentially assimilationist framework.[25] Far from protecting diversity, they undermined it. Under the IRA, tribalization came to mean homogenization, a homogeneity not of cultures but of structures.

At the same time the Indian New Deal had another profoundly significant effect: despite its neglect of community as organizational basis, it reversed for a time the anticommunity bias of federal policy in favor of tribalism, at least as an intermediary stage on the path to assimilation, and gave implicit recognition to the value of traditional custom and, to some extent, indigenous institutions. A critical change had been made: the purposive erosion of the tribal edifice had been stopped. Through the IRA and related legislative and bureaucratic actions, tribal autonomy began to expand and Indian cultures began to reemerge—albeit in much modified form—from the repression of the preceding decades. Tribal boundaries might change, but within them a revivified tribalism could surface. Robert White's comments on the Sioux are indicative of the results for many tribes: "Sioux tribalism had never really ceased to exist during the reservation period, but it began to take on new institutional expression with the policies [of the New Deal]: the establishing of the tribal councils, the restoration of rituals such as the Sun Dance, and, in general, a much more favorable attitude toward Indian nativism."[26]

As a political process, tribalization culminated in the IRA and its immediate aftermath. The process of organizational consolidation begun, in some cases, two centuries earlier was now complete, formalized in tribal governments organized for the most part under IRA provisions or independently under the influence of the new federal policy. For many Indian groups these governments were the first *tribal* political organizations in their history.[27]

THE IRA AND FRAGMENTATION

These governments also bore the burden of that history. It was a history, as already shown, in which two opposing tendencies kept uneasy company. On the one hand was organizational unification. Distinct groups had been joined together, first circumstantially or as an indigenous response to circumstance, later through the imposition of the administrative structure of the reservations. More often the unifying process occurred within single nations, as less inclusive sociopolitical boundaries gave way to more inclusive ones.

On the other hand, the resultant unity was often more apparent than real, an illusion produced by the construction of relatively rigid administrative frameworks that assumed an already existing unitary tribal structure. By the time of the Indian Reorganization Act, many reservations in fact were deeply divided, either by the aggravation of long-standing cleavages or by the emergence of new ones. The IRA, which gave formal sanction to the first of these tendencies, was poorly equipped to deal with the second.

The legislation itself did not always help. The IRA was in substantial part a response to the dismal economic prospects of most Indian nations in the 1920s; it was intended, among other things, to provide the organizational structures necessary for economic revitalization. The result, however, was "a basic problem of the Indian New Deal: how to generate real community participation in the framework of a program which for economic reasons must be oriented toward larger units of organization."[28] Its success depended to a large extent on a degree of group identification and commitment that in some cases had never really existed.

Furthermore, by formalizing and advancing the consolidational process, the IRA antagonized subtribal communities and constituencies whose autonomy or power were at stake. Its introduction of Anglo-American political institutions, for example, often antagonized traditionalist groups. The new forms of government usually institutionalized a separation of religious and political authority that was radically new. This secularization alienated both religious leaders and conservatives, not least, presumably, because it threatened to strip them of much of their power. In resultant conflicts the BIA tended to side with secular authority, reinforcing the idea that the new governments, lacking traditional roots, were merely agents of BIA domination.[29] Such notions were common especially in the first decade or so under the new tribal constitutions. They often had merit, as the early councils in many cases remained virtual administrative adjuncts of the BIA, reflecting both BIA power and Indian uncertainty under the new system. In areas where strong traditions of village or other local autonomy persisted, as among the Hopi, tribal government also met with powerful resistance.[30]

The IRA was not everywhere divisive. At Santa Clara Pueblo, for example, the organization of an IRA government apparently reduced simmering conflicts by formally separating religious and political affairs.[31] But whatever its often substantial benefits, the IRA inevitably encountered difficulties as it tried to create comprehensive political structures among peoples often lacking comparable political traditions.

In the years since passage of the IRA, factional conflict, whatever its nature, has tended to concentrate on control of the tribal councils, which have become the primary centers of significant political power available to Indians on reservations, including what little power they can exercise over processes of development and social change. In many cases these new councils were quickly dominated by mixed-blood factions. While attitudes toward the IRA did not necessarily correlate with the full-blood/mixed-blood distinction, the form of the new governments, once established, inherently favored more educated and acculturated Indians who better understood its workings and often were more willing participants in non-Indian institutions. Traditionalists who refused to take part were ignored. In effect, the IRA institutionalized progressive/conservative divisions, which often came to represent not only cultural distinctions but a differential distribution of power.

On the Sac and Fox Reservation in Iowa, for example, according to a report made soon after the adoption of the IRA, "most of the old men have held tenaciously to the traditional system while the young, trained in school and in closer contact with the whites, have gradually adopted the new ways. Re-organization has tended to emphasize this cleavage and set up irreconcilable groups." In 1945 the BIA reported that on Montana's Blackfeet Reservation, where mixed-bloods had taken control of the tribal council, antagonizing many conservatives, "the Indian Reorganization Act has placed a legal tool in the hands of the ruling clique . . . that more or less formalizes the struggle for control on a plane that makes full-blood resistance almost an act of treason." At Pine Ridge the new tribal government became the focal point of factional struggle between the full-blood "Old Dealers" and the mixed-blood "New Dealers." Old Dealers viewed New Dealers as favoring assimilation into White society and as insensitive to traditional values; New Dealers viewed Old Dealers as retrograde. These lines of conflict eventually came to dominate Pine Ridge politics.[32]

The problem, however, goes beyond power struggles. Writing about the Oglalas of Pine Ridge, Raymond DeMallie speaks to the larger issue on many reservations:

> The tribal organization has been made to accept administrative responsibility for the whole reservation, but it seems certain that the local people, the Oglala living in the various district communities, do not as a whole believe in a representative form of government. They do not identify with the tribe as a political group and would prefer to run their own affairs at the local level, under the direction of local leaders whose support comes from community faith in their abilities.[33]

Duane Champagne suggests that even where such comprehensive political identities exist, the structural problems remain substantial. The political institutions of the larger society assume a high degree of institutional differentiation; there are clear boundaries between the political system and other social institutions: kinship ties, religion, economy, and so forth. Decisions are made by a subset of community members who, once selected, operate independently of the rest of the society. But traditionally in Indian societies the level of institutional differentiation is low; the links among polity, kinship, religion, and other institutions are complex and independent governance is rare. Contention within and around tribal governments often reflects this fundamental disjuncture: the incompatibility of two distinct institutional traditions.[34]

Some groups have responded to these problems by withdrawing. At Pine Ridge in 1969, less than 30 percent of eligible voters took part in tribal elections. One study in the late 1970s blamed small voter turnouts among Papagos in Arizona on the fact that "the entire elective system of government, as exemplified by the tribal constitution, is foreign to traditional Papago political systems." In eastern Oklahoma, according to two longtime students of the Cherokees, "full-blood" or "tribal" Cherokees simply ignore the official tribal government, which is not of their making and is dominated by an essentially non-Indian population with ancestral links that make them legally defined members of the Cherokee tribe. "Tribal Cherokees," these observers say, "are neither interested nor participant in the affairs of the tribal government. On the whole, they neither support it nor oppose it, and their psychological distance from it is enormous." A somewhat similar situation is apparent among traditional Mohawks in New York.[35]

Elsewhere the result has been a sometimes uneasy coexistence of dual power structures, one embedded in traditional social organization and customs, the other an elected government formally recognized by the BIA. These structures may operate in more or less distinct spheres of influence, as in the Navajo case in the 1950s (and to some extent today), where traditional forms of authority persisted in the daily affairs of local residence communities, while the tribal council operated largely in the expanding sphere of tribal-wide concerns and relations with the larger society. Alternatively, the two structures may compete directly for power and influence, a situation found in varying form among the Hopi, the Western Shoshone-Goshute, and other tribes.[36]

To some degree these divisions reflect continuing conflicts—some of them interfamilial—over the distribution of political and economic resources within the tribe, conflicts aggravated by the passing of traditional ways of determining those distributions. But many are symptomatic of a more fundamental phenomenon: the breakdown of consensus within many Native American groups over the nature of the tribal community and the content of the identities its members ostensibly share.[37] Societies that once were relatively homogeneous culturally have become increasingly heterogeneous, while the established means of coping with diversity, of mediating disagreements, of combining individual freedom with collective continuity, in many cases have been undermined. Attempts to find new ways of accomplishing these goals have not always been successful.

Given the extraordinary pressures produced by conquest, tutelary external controls, and rapid cultural and economic change, such a breakdown was perhaps inevitable. It has been exacerbated by the process of political tribalization, replacing relatively fluid indigenous systems of social coordination and authority with relatively rigid ones rooted in non-Indian traditions.

The labels attached to the resultant factional viewpoints—traditionalist, conservative, progressive, and so forth—are doubly unfortunate. First, as Warren d'Azevedo has observed, they are value laden, expressing the perspective of the dominant society.[38] Second, in many cases they obscure both the more substantial diversity of Indian self-concepts and views and the nature of the divisions themselves. Frequently those divisions have less to do with favoring or opposing change than with the various ways—political, economic, cultural—of defining the community and with the freedom of these variously conceived communities to make their own ways in the world. The tribe has been institutionalized as the primary political unit in Indian-White relations, but the nature of that unit and its appropriate role in Indian life remain unclear.

THE TRANSFORMATIONS OF THE TRIBE

What, then, of tribalization? The cast of actors had changed somehow; new partners were engaged in a new dance. But who were they now and how had they changed from what they had been before?

Historically, though the experiences of particular nations have been hugely diverse, the tribalizing process has generally involved a kind of triple transformation, a transformation in both the organizational and conceptual dimensions of groupness and in the relationship between the two.

In the years of Indian-White conflict, tribalization occurred largely as a native response to invasion and its consequences and to the assumptions and practices of non-Indians. The tribe gradually emerged as the basis of official dealings between the United States and the Indian nations. But however new it may have been as a political structure, the roots of the tribe as a circle of identity often lay in aboriginal patterns of community and thought. For many groups the tribe was already a conceptual reality; for some it was a political reality as well. But contact and conflict made the tribe increasingly the focus of both identity and organization.

With the end of military conflict and the establishment of reservations, the indigenous substance of tribalism—that is, the substance of community life—came under direct attack. The tribe was reduced to an administrative category in a program of enforced cultural change. Tribalization now occurred not as a native response to invasion, but as the by-product of a particular formal structure of dominant/subordinate group relations.

Finally, with passage of the IRA and related events, the tribe was given formal status and support as the basic unit of Indian political and community organization. Having been stripped during the reservation years of much of its indigenous institutional substance, it was reinstitutionalized politically, but now after dominant-group models and on dominant-group terms. Structures of authority and decision making, once embedded in the fabric of aboriginal societies, were now attached, as it were, from the outside, institutionally separate from the structures of kinship and custom and modes of thought that had "governed" Indian peoples and still in varying degrees survived.

The tribe changed definitionally as well. Once largely a conceptual and cultural construct, defined for Indians in terms of a sense of peoplehood and shared cultural practice, by the mid-twentieth century it had become a political and legal construct, a definitional element of the jural status of Native American groups and of their relationship to the institutions of American society. Tribal membership, once synonymous with tribal identity, had become a distinct legal, as opposed to cultural or conceptual, category.[39] As it came to mean less in cultural terms, it came to mean more as a foundation for the assertion of individual and group rights to land, services, or exemptions guaranteed by treaty or legislation.

Thus there are fundamental discontinuities between tribal polity and membership today and their precontact counterparts. As already shown, with some exceptions, tribal political organization—that is, political organization commensurate with the sense of peoplehood—was either absent or occasional among most Indian groups prior to contact. The European invasion initiated a process of political tribalization that continues to the present day. Politically, the contemporary tribe is a product of that process. In most cases it represents the adoption of increasingly inclusive forms of political organization. The process has been consolidational: the creation of formal political unities in place of multiple autonomous units.

Along the other, conceptual dimension, however, the process of tribalization has been both different and more complex. Parts of it, certainly, look the same. Especially in the reservation years there tended to be a decline of older, subtribal identities in favor of more comprehensive self-concepts. There are cases, particularly in the Northwest, of tribes created by fiat, composites of distinct nations given unity by external powers, a unity that eventually became the focus of identity for all the constituent parts. The Yakimas and the Makahs, to different degrees, are examples. But for the most part the comprehensive identities that were circumstantially encouraged through the years of conflict and confinement had aboriginal roots. Peoplehood was neither a novelty nor a recent development from previous, less inclusive attachments. Its origins lay in a more distant past.

In these cases, as a conceptual entity, the tribe is not a creation of Indian-White interaction but a survivor of it. Through interaction with Euro-Americans and their institutions, Native American identities were focused increasingly at the maximal, tribal level. That it was the *tribal* level of identity, and not some other, that received reinforcement is due in large part to the nature and shape of that interaction; but in most cases the identity itself was already a significant element in Indian lives.

At the same time, within the broad boundaries of tribal identity, there has been in many Indian groups a process of fragmentation. The cultural and conceptual content of tribal identity was once largely the same for all members of the tribe, but is no longer so. Change in the focus of identity has been convergent; the point of convergence has been the tribe. But change in the content of identity has been divergent. Many persons may identify themselves as Navajo, or Oglala, or Cherokee, but what that means to each one may be very different.

Some of those meanings are essentially continuous with the past, changed by time and circumstance and the influences of both Euro-Americans and other Indians, but rooted still in aboriginal modes of thought and action and structures of social relations. Others are anchored in the specific historical experience of the group and are subjective products of incorporation. Still others may involve little more than the legal definition of tribal membership. For some tribal members, the preservation of distinct ways of seeing and being is of paramount importance; for others, it is the preservation and development of the tribal estate; for still others, what matters may simply be access to the economic and political rights and rewards that tribal membership provides.[40] The political unity of the tribe often embraces a disunited people.

Finally, change has occurred not only along these two dimensions of groupness, but in the relationship between them. Originally, in most cases, the conceptual was the more comprehensive of the two. Autonomous political units were bound together in the conceptual framework of a single people. Now the roles are reversed: diverse concepts of peoplehood are bound together in a single political framework. The conceptual community, once salient in Indian relationships with the rest of the world, has been subordinated to the political community—its form derived not from the Indian past but from the White—which now dominates Indian relationships with the larger society. Aboriginally the two were not the same, nor are they now, but both the differences and the relationship between them have changed (see Figure 1).

These transformations have implications for Native American political action. Certainly the institutionalization of the tribe has facilitated political action of various kinds. The tribe has become not only the focal point of

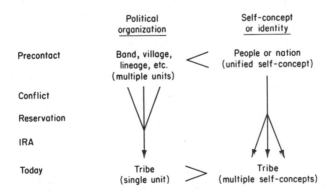

Figure 1. Tribalization

Indian rights and jural status, but also a political structure capable of defending those rights and pursuing Indian interests within the framework of U.S. political and legal institutions. Tribalization also has facilitated cooperative relationships among diverse and distant peoples. Contemporary organizations such as the National Congress of American Indians (NCAI), the Council of Energy Resource Tribes (CERT), the National Tribal Chairmen's Association (NTCA), and various regional organizations are products in part of a convergence of political interests and of structures capable of articulating those interests in a larger arena.

On the other hand, especially in the larger tribes, the centralization of power within a rigid tribal political structure has meant a loss of autonomy for subtribal communities. Political questions no longer have to do so much with what particular Indian communities want as with what "the tribe" wants. The needs and interests of culturally defined communities have been subordinated to the needs and interests of legally defined, political entities. The determination of what and whose interests will be defended, and how, has become a problem, made all the more significant by the tribe's emergent prominence.

Under these conditions intratribal conflicts tend to ramify. Some subtribal or nonreservation communities find it difficult to pursue their interests within the formal structure of Indian-White relations, a structure in which the tribe is the only political entity of consequence. As a result they may go outside the tribal framework in pursuit of their goals, reducing their legitimacy in the eyes of the larger society, or at least in the eyes of federal authorities. This problem is probably most acute for traditionalist groups and urban Indians.

But there is more involved here than loss of autonomy. Originally the ability of Indian political structures, tribal or otherwise, to resolve internal disputes was substantially dependent on the fact that the form and existence of those structures were themselves seldom at issue. That has changed. Today the form and existence of tribal governments are sometimes very much at issue. To the extent that this is so in any particular situation, tribal government loses much of its ability to resolve internal conflict.

All this indicates a twofold effect of tribalization in the political arena. On the one hand it has created a formal, more or less homogeneous set of political actors—tribes and their governments—recognized as legitimate representatives of Indian interests. The institutionalized, "legitimate" field of Indian-White relations involves ongoing interactions between these actors (and certain supratribal organizations, such as NTCA and CERT, whose relevant members or referents are tribes) and non-Indian bodies: federal and state governments, corporations, the courts, and so on.

On the other hand, and quite inadvertently, it has created a host of new constituencies who feel inadequately represented by these formally recognized actors or who fit poorly into the established structure of Indian affairs. These new constituencies are in many cases products of the breakdown of consensus and the process that led to that breakdown: yeasty residues come to life in the nutrient bath of tribalization. They are hardly of a piece; often what they most notably share is a lack of power. But as they have become both more numerous and more active in the decades since the passage of the IRA, they have vastly complicated the political arena of Indian-White relations.

These constituencies demand attention. In the continuing dance of Indian-White relations, they are the ones who have most often tried to change the tune. But first there is another process of collective redefinition that needs elaboration here. In the twentieth century another, parallel development was taking place, different from tribalization but with equally profound political consequences: the gradual emergence and growth of a supratribal American Indian consciousness.

Chapter 7

Toward A Supratribal Consciousness

When Christopher Columbus, sailing westward in 1492, concluded that he had struck the Indies and accordingly designated the peoples he encountered "los Indios," he gave birth to a misnomer—"Indians" in English—that soon came to embrace all the native inhabitants of the Western Hemisphere. It was a label at odds not only with the geographical facts, but also, in its implied uniformity, with the subjective perceptions and sociological realities of the inhabitants themselves. As Hazel Hertzberg has pointed out, culturally the peoples of the Americas were more diverse than the Europeans.[1] This fact was not entirely lost on the White newcomers, but it was the differences between Indians generally and themselves that struck them more forcefully. Their perception was value laden: Europe was culture, intellect, Christianity, and power; the New World was nature: pagan, savage, nearly dumb.[2] The breadth of such antipodal categories rendered native diversity insignificant.

Yet there was no equivalent native term for "Indian." European notions of similarities among the native peoples of the Americas had no counterpart in Indian self-concepts or worldviews. Quite the contrary: Indian groups were well aware of the innumerable differences that separated them. Their very names are indicative of the fact; at what John Lowell Bean has called the "maximal level of social identification," Indians demonstrated a powerful ethnocentrism. Many groups identified themselves with names that meant simply "persons," "people," or "human beings." By implication other groups were something else. Some names granted equal generic status to others while at the same time establishing a first-among-equals uniqueness. *Kiowa,* for example, meant "principal people," and the Delaware *Lenni Lenape* meant "true men." The Cherokee referred to themselves as *ani yun wiya,* "real human beings." Anthropologist Robert Thomas, himself a Cherokee, suggests that while the name implies the existence in the world of other humans, "the Cherokees were the 'realest.' "[3] Such names delineated group boundaries. Beyond those boundaries there might be other human beings, or there might be something else, but whatever it was, it wasn't "us."

Thus Indians were as capable of ethnocentric bias and generalization as were Europeans, but they lacked the basis for making the kinds of classifications Europeans made. There was no sense of the continental geography, the more or less uniform technological development, the "civilized"/"uncivilized" dichotomy, or the concept of race that, among other things, encouraged Europeans to gather native peoples under a single term. While the White newcomers, despite their own diversity, could see themselves as Europeans, Native Americans lacked, subjectively, the common identity so blithely bestowed upon them. "American Indians," as anything other than a European taxonomic construct, did not exist.

Today "American Indians" do exist, not simply in the minds of government administrators or the American public, but as a self-conscious population. That population is not necessarily coextensive with either the Census or Bureau of Indian Affairs categories or with the popular conception of just who is an Indian. It is composed of those descendants of American aborigines who act self-consciously on the basis of Indianness. They need not do so always; in fact, few of them do. For most, tribal identifications remain at least as strong and usually stronger. But increasingly for large numbers of Indians, Indian identity—as distinct from tribal identity—has become a conscious and important basis of action and thought in its own right. A host of "American Indian" and "Native American" organizations testify to its salience, as do the numerous cooperative political efforts by Indian groups and organizations on behalf of both tribal and supratribal interests.

Indeed, it is supratribalism that has made such politics possible. An Indian consciousness provides a distinctive basis for political action, and in the twentieth century it has transformed the politics of Indian-White relations.

The development of a supratribal consciousness and constituency is the subject of this and the following chapter. Far more than tribalism, whose shape was at least partly apparent in aboriginal times, that development is a product of the incorporative process. Much the same forces that led to Indian underdevelopment and dependency eventually gave substance to the European myth and made American Indians a reality.

It was a lengthy business. Although in many ways "the American Indian" is a contemporary phenomenon, supratribal identity and action did not appear unheralded in the twentieth century. Their development took place gradually and intermittently through the early years of contact and conflict with non-Indians, expanded more rapidly and in new directions in the reservation years, and finally flourished on a large scale in the mid-twentieth century. What distinguishes this century and in particular the last few decades from earlier years is not the appearance of a supratribal identity, but its rapid diffusion among large numbers of Indians and its attendant politicization: the swift transformation of condition into consciousness, consciousness into constituency. Whereas in previous years supratribal activity had been limited largely to regional tribal alliance or to religious and cultural activity, in the present century Indian identity joined tribal identity as a basis for political action on a large scale.[4]

CONTACT AND CONFLICT

The antecedents of Indian identity are centuries old. Long before contact with Europeans, elaborate Indian trade networks stretched over hundreds of miles. In some areas, as along the Columbia River, groups would gather to trade in multitribal camps. The interaction was not only economic; cultural practices also were transmitted from one group to another. Such relationships helped lay a basis for later supratribal sentiment and action in the face of the European challenge. A perception of similitude and common interest beyond the bounds of nationhood is evident also in federations such as the League of the Iroquois and other alliances, as well as in intertribal visiting and ceremonial participation.

Despite these activities, however, for many Indians the world beyond the boundaries of peoplehood seems to have been an alien one, a world of unintelligible languages and unfamiliar cultural practice, of beings often dramatically different from themselves. In such a world the first Europeans may have been less remarkable than a retrospective view of the encounter suggests. In the earliest years of contact most Indian groups, while uncertain of just who the Europeans were or where they came from, probably classified them similarly: another variety of stranger.[5] But the actions of these new strangers, their vast numbers, and the relentless quality of their advance soon drew increased attention and encouraged a growing sense among native peoples that they faced a common and unusual enemy.

The result was both unity and division. In the 1600s some eastern tribes banded together to resist the invasion. Attempts to create multitribal federations by the Wampanoag "King Philip" and the Pamunkey Opechancanough ultimately failed, but they were early examples of a growing recognition among Indian nations that their interests and ways of life were collectively at risk. "Brothers," said a Narragansett to old enemies from another tribe in 1642, "we must be as one as the English are, or we shall all be destroyed." In the Southwest the Pueblo villages, after nearly a century of Spanish encroachment on their lands, economies, and religious freedom, finally responded with unprecedented collective action in the Pueblo Revolt of 1680, a coordinated military uprising that drove the Spanish from the region. Both unity and triumph, however, were short-lived; by 1696, exploiting divisions and disputes among the villages, the Spanish were back, reestablishing control of the Pueblos along the Rio Grande. More ambitious yet in terms of intertribal outreach were the self-consciously supratribal alliances established by Pontiac shortly before and Tecumseh some years after the American Revolution. But in both cases unity proved difficult to maintain and their success was brief. Such efforts gained strength to the extent that they could arouse among diverse peoples a consciousness of kind, could articulate persuasively a common cause, and could do so well enough to overcome divergent interests and long traditions of independent action. Their failures were products of many factors, including colonial efforts to arouse or reinforce intertribal enmity, but they are indicative also of the magnitude of the differences that in fact separated Native American groups.[6]

Alliance was made problematic also by the divisive effects of European settlement and expansion. During much of the colonial period, competition among the European powers for Indian allies occasionally divided friendly nations. Such competition was a major factor in the collapse of the League of the Iroquois late in the eighteenth century. Economic opportunities had similar effects: competition for the fruits of the fur trade, for example, sometimes pitted nation against nation. Faced with unprecedented political, cultural, and economic challenges, the tribes often found themselves deeply divided over the best responses to make. Gradually beaten back or forcibly removed from aboriginal lands, they also found themselves competing for a shrinking land base and diminishing resources, a competition that hindered their growing awareness of the equivalence of their situations. But that awareness eventually came. Perhaps its most striking manifestation was the late-nineteenth-century attempt by the Five Civilized Tribes and others to turn the Indian Territory into a self-governing Indian commonwealth or state.

Also important were the prejudices of non-Indians. Just as Euro-American ideas about group structures and intergroup politics promoted tribal self-concepts, so the racial emphasis in non-Indian thinking about Indians encouraged Native Americans to think in similar terms. Especially as the United States expanded westward and encountered Indian resistance, the treatment of Indians as a largely undifferentiated racial category, and one clearly inferior to Europeans, became both more salient and increasingly important as justification for the White advance.[7] Intentionally or not, U.S. agents and treaty negotiators, with their talk of the Great White Father and his Red Children, were nourishing the roots of a new identity, laying the early foundations of what one day would become a new political opposition.

Through such interactions the seeds of supratribal consciousness and action were planted and began to grow. Their early harvest was a sparse and often bitter one; it formed only one aspect of indigenous response to invasion, and a largely unsuccessful one at that. But while supratribal action—such as it was—ultimately failed, part of its legacy was the nascent Indian identity that inspired and infused it and was in turn encouraged by it. Yet, as Hazel Hertzberg observes, it remained fragile, "lacking the rich and deeply rooted associations of tribal identity. The tribe represented the way of life of the people; *Indian* was a way of differentiating aborigine from European."[8]

It had a substantive content nonetheless. Differentiation between European and Indian was not a matter simply of political opposition. In the recorded comments of nineteenth-century tribespeople and leaders a more profound understanding is evident. Charlot, a Flathead chief, talked in 1876 of how the Indian perception of Whites had changed:

> We were happy when he first came. We first thought he came from the light; but he comes like the dusk of the evening now, not like the dawn of the morning. He comes like a day that has passed, and night enters our future with him. . . . To take and to lie should be burned on his forehead, as he burns the sides of my stolen horses with his own name. . . . No, no; his course is destruction; he spoils what the spirit who gave us this country made beautiful and clean.

Or, more simply: Daykauray, a Winnebago, said in 1829, "The Great Spirit made the white man and the Indian. He did not make them alike."[9]

As the Indians' knowledge of these new Americans increased, their own ways of life were set in sharp relief. The European invasion was reproducing among Indians the original European conception: they also were learning now to think of two very different kinds of peoples, facing each other across a cultural crevasse.

THE RESERVATION YEARS

U.S. hegemony and the reservation system brought intertribal political activities and alliance to an abrupt end. Overt conflict, to date the major stimulus to supratribalism, disappeared as the Indian nations were stripped of political power in their external affairs, not least by the physical boundaries imposed upon them. An Indian identity continued to develop, but it did so now in a very different context and with a rather different content. With national and intertribal political arenas essentially closed to Indian participation, supratribalism became less an aspect of politics than of social interaction and cultural practice. Despite government and church opposition, social activities became focal points in emergent intertribal networks. While not in themselves generally political, such networks continued to promote an Indian identity that one day would be mobilized into politics.

Among these activities were the religious movements that had begun to appear late in the conflict years. While varying from tribe to tribe, many fostered intertribal linkages and brought diverse groups into common frameworks of action and belief. Some spoke explicitly to a supratribal consciousness. The Ghost Dance, for example, prophesied a specifically *Indian* renaissance: "The great underlying principle of the Ghost dance doctrine is that the time will come when the whole Indian race, living and dead, will be reunited upon a regenerated earth, to live a life of aboriginal happiness, forever free from death, disease, and misery."[10]

Peyotism in particular became a source of supratribal sentiment. Commenting on Washo peyotism, for example, James Downs writes, "Because peyote meetings were intertribal they were conducted in English and gave the Washo a sense of identity with other Indians."[11] It also led to supratribal action. To be sure, as noted in Chapter 4, peyotism was not so much oppositional as, in David Aberle's term, redemptive. Largely accepting the dramatic changes in Indian situations, it sought to help individuals and societies adjust to new conditions and cope with profound personal and societal trauma.[12] But as it spread through the Indian world in the late nineteenth and early twentieth centuries, it not only established a shared religious practice among diverse peoples, but also became the focal point of political mobilization.

Opposition to peyotism was widespread among government and church officials, and often among Indians as well. As the religion continued to spread and Indian enthusiasm for it grew, so did the non-Indian alarm. Viewing peyote as a harmful drug that undermined Indian health and morals, the BIA, churches, and organizations working in Indian affairs and education set out to eradicate the practice. The Hayden Bill, introduced in the House of Representatives in 1918, would have outlawed the use of peyote by any Indian under BIA jurisdiction. The bill was never enacted, but its introduction had an important effect: the legislative threat prompted formal institutionalization of peyotism in the Native American Church, incorporated in Oklahoma in October 1918. This was essentially a political attempt by Oklahoma peyotists, urged on by ethnologist James Mooney, to gain a better legal footing for their defense of the religion. Its charter spoke in terms of "Indian" religious beliefs and of "union" among the Oklahoma tribes. As opposition to peyote continued, peyotists in other states also incorporated, some in tribally specific churches, others in supratribal organizations. Over time a network of links developed among a number of these bodies. Peyote thus not only became a vehicle for the expansion of a specifically Indian identity, but contributed, by force of circumstance, to the supratribal *political* consciousness that was beginning to grow among diverse Indian populations.[13]

There were other supratribal currents in the reservation years, though few carried the political significance eventually attached to peyotism. Growing numbers of Indians, especially in the plains, took part in intertribal social gatherings and festivals known as powwows. Sponsored by a particular tribe, they typically drew Indians from other reservations, some quite distant, for several days of ceremony, socializing, and dancing. Lurie argues that these played an important role in establishing bonds and shared perceptions among Native Americans generally, while Kurath, reporting on Great Lakes intertribal festivals, argues that "the Indian participant is for the duration a member not only of the tribe but of the great Pan-Indian community."[14]

The other—and essentially non-Indian—factor at work in these years, as in previous ones, was non-Indian perceptions, especially as those perceptions informed government policy, public debate, and Indian education. As noted already, one effect of contact and conflict was to reproduce within the Indian population the kinds of group classifications favored by non-Indians. The influence of such classifications on Native American self-concepts did not end with conflict; if anything, it became more intense.

The binary and value-laden Indian-White distinction that dominated thinking in the United States was a persistent one. It was accompanied by a related and equally tenacious practice. Writes Robert Berkhofer, "Not only does the general term Indian continue from Columbus to the present day, but so also does the tendency to speak of one tribe as exemplary of all Indians and conversely to comprehend a specific tribe according to the characteristics ascribed to all Indians."[15]

Even anthropology, although one might expect otherwise, contributed to the myth. Nineteenth-century social thought, heavily influenced by evolutionary theory in the natural sciences, came to view societal development also in evolutionary terms. Social theorists such as Herbert Spencer and early anthropologists such as E. B. Tylor and Lewis Henry Morgan postulated a temporal sequence of stages in the development of human societies. Primitive savagery, barbarism, civilization, and their variations became categories into which societies and peoples could be placed, way stations along the cumulatively upward path of social progress. Indian societies supposedly occupied more or less common ground—in Morgan's scheme, for example, the lower and middle stages of barbarism. While such classifications required comparative analysis, it was a comparison ultimately of "them" and "us," informed by the assumptions of evolutionary social change and the conviction that European civilization represented the foremost advance thus far achieved in societal development.[16]

This evolutionary perspective dominated anthropological thinking through the early twentieth century, until the Boasian school of cultural anthropology rose to challenge both its premises and its implications. Its effect was to give at least tacit scientific support to the collectivist tendency, to discount diversity among Indian groups in favor of generalization, and to support the cultural racism that dominated both non-Indian attitudes and U.S. policy toward Native Americans.

These same tendencies were apparent in debates over Indian policy. In writings by the late-nineteenth-century reformers, for example—the self-designated "Friends of the Indian"—one is struck by the extent to which it is "the Indian problem," not the problems of particular Indians, that preoccupied the reform movement.[17] Given that reformers were concerned not so much with what the Indian was as with what he or she was not—that is, socially, economically, culturally White—the differences among Indians were of little importance. Indeed, the unitary conception was a predictable by-product of the place Indians occupied in the non-Indian calculus of Indian-White relations. At the heart of those relations lay both economic and cultural designs: the dispossession of Indians of their lands and their cultural transformation into Whites. In both contexts Indians were perceived categorically: either as non-Whites or as encumbrances on lands coveted by non-Indians. Neither category encouraged or required distinctions among Indian peoples other than those derived from their relative degree of cultural non-Whiteness or physical obtrusiveness in the path of progress.

Finally, there was the influence of changes in policy and administration. Until the end of the Civil War the Indian tribes had been considered—and treated with—as sovereign nations. Within the broad framework of a national Indian policy and administrative structure, relations were organized largely on a tribal basis. Contact and subsequent relations with each tribe presented distinct, if characteristic, problems. With the end of the Civil War, the resumption of the westward movement, the decline of the powerful western nations, and the consolidation of the reservation system, Indian relations became increasingly administrative in character. Diplomats, negotiators, and soldiers gave way to bureaucrats; extraordinary events were replaced by routine. By 1880 there were few cases left in which a single tribe or band retained enough power or freedom to dominate either the headlines or the concerns of policymakers. Certainly legislation still had to deal with specific reservation populations, but for the most part tribes had been reduced from relatively independent actors to a common, dependent status. Out of a vast historical and cultural mosaic, Euro-Americans had first imagined and then created a single category—Indians, wards of the federal government—and acted accordingly. Their dealings with Indians were increasingly just that, dealings not with distinct Indian nations but with Indians. They fostered in practice the prejudices that informed them.

Thus both the practical exigencies and underlying motivations of policy, as well as the implicit cultural values and intellectual premises of Euro-American thought, contributed to a unitary conception of the Indian population. Words, policies, and action all assumed homologies among Indian peoples that, beyond some circumstantial validity, often existed only in the minds of Whites.

Considered on their own terms, of course, these factors, while important for understanding Indian-White relations, have little apparent significance for the issue at hand, which is not the non-Indian image of Indians but the emergence among Indians of a supratribal consciousness. Toward the end of the nineteenth century, however, and much sooner in some areas, especially the East, Indians were coming increasingly in contact not only with the institutional agencies of White domination, but also with the conceptual and rhetorical paraphernalia of Indian policy and debate. Such contact promoted, or at the very least made available for Indian consumption, the prejudices Euro-Americans carried in their extended encounter with Indian peoples. The point is not that Indians were encouraged to disregard the differences among themselves, but that they were encouraged to look byond them, to see themselves in other than tribal terms.

Although for a time exposure to the attitudes that dominated nineteenth-century discussions of Indian affairs was limited to relatively few Indians, there was another factor that both greatly expanded such exposure and made a crucial contribution in its own right to the emergence of a supratribal consciousness. This was the rapid expansion of Indian education, and in particular the establishment of off-reservation boarding schools.

Education had long been considered the Indians' pathway to civilization. Until the 1870s, to the extent that it was in non-Indian hands, Indian education was largely under the control of missionary or church-related organizations. In the latter part of the nineteenth century, under new, federal controls, it began to receive vastly increased resources.

Boarding schools became the centerpiece of the federal effort. The first federal Indian boarding school was established on the Yakima Reservation in Washington in 1860, but it was not until the 1880s that such schools took over the larger part of Indian education. Boarding schools were the preferred institutional setting because they removed the Indian child from the daily reinforcement of tribal custom and language and offered the opportunity for sustained teaching of the habits of "civilized life."[18] By 1886 there were more than seven thousand Indians in federally operated or subsidized boarding schools, three times the number attending day schools.[19]

Of all the boarding schools the most important in the development of supratribalism were the off-reservation or industrial training schools. The majority of boarding schools were located on reservations, but as early as 1865 a congressional committee had recommended that boarding schools be established remote from centers of Indian population. In 1879 the first such school, the Carlisle Indian School, was founded at Carlisle, Pennsylvania. Over the next few decades Carlisle and schools like it constituted the elite sector of the Indian educational system. Their status had several sources: the relatively high quality of the teaching; the opportunity they offered for intensive training in industrial and agricultural arts; the "outing" system, in which Indian students at some schools were sent to live with selected Christian families in the local community; and in general their isolating and "liberalizing" influence, which, according to Indian Commissioner Thomas Morgan, writing in 1889, "breaks the shackles of tribal provincialism."[20] In 1885 five off-reservation boarding schools were in operation with federal support; by the turn of the century, there were twenty-five.[21]

These schools had several critical effects. First, like all schools for Indians but more intensely than most, they fostered the spread of English, providing individuals from different tribes with a common language, often for the first time.[22] Second, unlike the day schools and most of the reservation boarding schools, they brought together in one place a multitribal student population. This was a new experience for many Indians, and while the total number of students involved was relatively small, the results were significant. It was at these schools, for example, that an Indian, as opposed to tribal or community, journalism got its start.[23] Lasting friendships and even marriages were made across distant tribal boundaries. Such relationships helped to break down traditional barriers to a common Indian consciousness.

Third, while they inevitably facilitated intertribal bonds and communication, most of these schools—and others, though less effectively—worked hard to discourage tribal ties and indigenous cultural activities. Not only was this frequently their intention, it was considered perhaps their most important function.[24] Fourth, more thoroughly than most schools, they brought many Indians into close contact with the moral and intellectual premises that informed non-Indian thinking about Indian-White relations and more generally about the nature of progress. This was the result not so much of the curriculum as of contact with the surrounding non-Indian environment and with the philosophical doctrines that infused and justified the schools' very existence.

And finally, they produced a group of Indians from a wide assortment of tribes who, to use Hertzberg's words, "had sense of a common experience in the Indian and white worlds."[25] At these schools young Indian men and women, separated from family and tribe, often for the first time confronted the problem of defining themselves jointly as Indians and discovering what that meant.

Three of these boarding schools attained special prominence: Carlisle, founded in 1879; the Hampton Institute at Hampton, Virginia—actually its Indian Department—which first accepted Indian students in 1878; and the Haskell Indian School at Lawrence, Kansas, established in 1882. Their prominence extends as well to the issues under discussion here. For one thing, graduates of these schools were active in peyotism and in the incorporation of the peyote churches. More important, it was largely from these schools, and from Carlisle and Hampton in particular, that the first major, concrete evidence of a new *Indian* political consciousness emerged: a group of educated young Indians who together formed the nucleus of the first supratribal political organization of the postconflict period—the Society of American Indians.

THE SOCIETY OF AMERICAN INDIANS (SAI)

"The honor of the race and the good of the country will always be paramount." So stated the provisional constitution of the Society of American Indians, founded in 1911.[26] The statement captures the fundamental thrust of the organization. The SAI is important here for two reasons: first, as the earliest major political manifestation of an emergent supratribal consciousness and, second, as indicative of the limits supratribalism faced in the early decades of the twentieth century.

The society was the first successful attempt by Indians to form a national political organization. Its goals were to promote the welfare of Indian people and their contribution to American life. Founded and led by Indians, the SAI had three operating divisions—education, legislation, and membership—which, according to Hertzberg, "reflected the major concerns of the new Society and emphasized what the members believed they had in common: a commitment to education, to a broad legislative program affecting all Indians, and to building an organizational vehicle for the expression of common interests."[27]

The leaders of the SAI—they were a small group—were largely educated and professional men, and exceptional among the Indians of their time: doctors, lawyers, ministers, anthropologists, bureaucrats. While they often maintained close tribal connections, for the most part they lived their lives in a non-Indian world, a world in which many of them were notable for their individual accomplishments, regardless of their backgrounds. Many were graduates of or connected with Carlisle and Hampton. They had been schooled—formally or not—in the ideas of the Progressive Era:

> In principles and program the Society showed its deep commitment to the reform ideals of the time: to a vision which would transcend petty selfish interests, to a belief in progress, to the necessity for self-reliance and self-help, to expanding education as a vehicle for expanding opportunity, to government intervention on behalf of the weak, to uplifting the less fortunate, and to defining American nationality as a continually renewed and reinvigorated product of the best characteristics of the diverse American population.[28]

While acutely aware of the injustices of the past and fiercely proud of their heritage as Indians, these men saw the paths they had taken individually as exemplary of the desirable course for Indians in general: integration into the larger society accompanied by the preservation of a more or less abstract native identity and pride. Yet it was specifically an Indian identity they wished to preserve. For the most part marginal to the tribal world, they tended to be critical of tribalism, viewing it as an obstacle to individual progress and integration and ultimately as a source of division among Indians, where they sought unity.

They were believers in social evolution and the developmental potential of the "Indian race." This they intended to encourage, and their reform politics were directed to that end. They sought changes in Indian policy and education that would better equip Indians to contribute to their own and the national welfare. In the reservation system and the BIA they saw a virtual prison that, while giving refuge to older Indians who had grown up in another time, perpetuated dependency and helplessness. While they disagreed as to methods and timing, they tended to believe that both BIA and reservations should be abolished. In principle they favored the currently popular melting-pot model of American society, and in effect promoted the assimilation of Indians into the body social. At their founding conference, in a paper that aroused debate but found favor with many delegates, Seneca anthropologist Arthur C. Parker, long a central figure in the SAI, put it this way:

To survive at all [the Indian] must become as other men, a contributing self-sustaining member of society. . . . No nation can afford to permit any person or body of people within it to exist in a condition at variance with the ideals of that nation. Every element perforce must become assimilated. I do not mean by this that the Indian should surrender things and passively allow himself, like clay, to be pressed into a white man's mold. I do not mean, by assimilation, that his love of the great esthetic ideals should be supplanted entirely by commercial greed or that his mind should become sordid with the conventional ideas of white civilization. . . . I do mean, however, that the Indian should accustom himself to the culture that engulfs him and to the force that directs it, that he should become a factor of it, and that once a factor of it he should use his revitalized influence and more advantageous position in asserting and developing the great ideals of his race for the good of the greater race, which means all mankind.

In 1916, in the society's journal, which he edited, Parker wrote: "The future of the Indians is with the white race, and in a civilization derived from the old world."[29]

The SAI was thus a product of its times, and in its early years vigorously pursued its general program. In its origins, however, lay much of its limitations. Derivative of and dependent upon the reform movement, the society faltered in the late 1910s and early 1920s, as did reformism generally. The melting-pot model also was giving way in those years to a new academic interest in the distinctiveness and value of individual cultures, an interest that fit poorly with the supratribal intentions and doctrines of the SAI. Within the society itself a growing factionalism was evident as early as 1915, with the membership divided over a variety of issues, including the role of the BIA (some were BIA employees), peyotism, and the importance of the tribe. Gradually the organization lost its sense of purpose and its members fell to bickering. By the mid-1920s, well past its brief heyday, it had disappeared.

Beyond these problems lay a more fundamental difficulty. Vine Deloria, Jr., discussing the demise of the SAI and the rejection of its ideas by many Indians, places the blame in part on "a basic inability [among Indians] to proceed beyond the confines of tribal existence to a conception of nationalism."[30] That inability reflected the times. The leaders of the SAI were themselves products as much of the White as of the Indian world. The society, Hertzberg observes, was "the expression of an educated and acculturated elite."[31] As late as 1926, while more than 80 percent of school-age Indian children were in school, only 13 percent of these were in off-reservation boarding schools, the particular milieu out of which much of the SAI's leadership had come.[32]

In contrast, for most Indians the world remained a tribal one. The vast majority were still on reservations, living in historical and cultural contexts that, despite convergences and rapid change, remained diverse. The reservation system itself, while it inadvertently promoted tribal unity, hampered supratribal action. The few formal links between reservations and the national arena were controlled by non-Indians. With a few exceptions, those who were most self-consciously "Indian," such as the SAI's members, were quite removed—by education, occupation, residence, and often by choice—from reservation life. Their own sense of Indianness grew from a history and environment few tribespeople shared.[33]

The SAI forms a remarkable beginning, but the political base of supra-tribalism was too narrow to sustain it. The few instances of significant Indian political action in the 1920s, whatever their implications, were more localized affairs: the fight over the Bursum Bill in the Southwest, for exam-ple, and Iroquois battles for treaty rights in New York. Such activities surely contributed to the enlargement of that base, making Indians else-where aware of the potential of political protest in favor of Indian rights. But these were relatively isolated events. The failure of the SAI to attract support on the reservations and, ultimately, to establish an effective na-tional organization based on an explicitly Indian identity indicates just how far away a nationwide supratribal political consciousness, much less con-stituency, actually was.

"A SENSE OF POWER"

That situation soon began to change. The factors involved were various, but two in particular stand out. The first was the convoluted path of policy, which led eventually to large-scale Indian political involvement. The sec-ond was demographics.

The IRA initiated a major shift in Indian policy, but its momentum was short-lived. Opposition plagued it from the start. Part of that opposition was Indian, and it found its most sophisticated expression in the American Indian Federation (AIF), a supratribal organization founded in 1934 with the explicit intention of reversing New Deal Indian policy and abolish-ing the BIA, arguing that both perpetuated non-Indian controls over Indian communities and inhibited the individual integration of Indians into the larger society. The organization's Indian support was diverse but limited, thanks in part to its rather narrow and controversial goals, but it repre-sented one of the first major Indian efforts to redirect policy. Much of its rhetoric, however, parroted the right wing in the 1930s, and it attracted a number of extremists. With European fascism and World War II looming in the background, it quickly lost its appeal; by the early 1940s it was in rapid decline.[34] Nonetheless, it had an impact, encouraging the policy turn away from the Indian New Deal, a turn apparent as early as 1937, when six bills to limit or repeal the act were introduced in Congress.

More distant events also played a part in policy change, in particular World War II and its Cold War aftermath. During the war Indian affairs budgets were slashed—the BIA itself was moved out of Washington to make room for more pressing needs—and the programs Collier had set in place began to suffer from neglect. At the same time the tribes that had embraced the Indian New Deal needed information and assistance in order to take full advantage of it. As IRA programs faltered, a number of Indian leaders became increasingly aware of their common concerns and of the advantages of cooperation in pursuing shared interests. Out of that sentiment, in the mid-1940s, came yet another supratribal political organization with rather different goals and a much broader base of support: the National Congress of American Indians (NCAI).

Seventy-five delegates from some fifty reservations and tribes gathered at the NCAI's first convention in Denver in November 1944. Many of these men and women were similar to the leaders of the SAI: professionals, well educated, with a wide variety of experiences in the non-Indian world. Some were graduates of Haskell or Carlisle; a number were veterans. But the differences between the two organizations were more striking. The NCAI explicitly embraced both individuals and groups, including any "Indian tribe, band, or community" that wished to join. In effect it was an organization of tribes, and it emphasized the preservation of tribal rights and existence. Its constitution outlined its objectives: "to enlighten the public toward a better understanding of the Indian race; to preserve Indian cultural values; to seek an equitable adjustment of tribal affairs; to secure and to preserve rights under Indian treaties with the United States; and otherwise to promote the common welfare of the American Indians."[35]

Organizationally and conceptually the NCAI embraced both an emergent commonality of interests and the distinct tribal identities the Indian world comprised. Its emphasis on treaty rights and tribal cultures had little counterpart in the SAI or the AIF, and it was less concerned with Indian contributions to the larger society than with Indian rights and interests within it. In practical terms, it offered tribes assistance and information, advised them regarding the provisions of the IRA, and lobbied for Indian interests before Congress and the BIA. While it was powerless to do much more than this, it represented an important Indian effort to compensate for a critical shortcoming of the IRA: the lack of integration between tribal political structures and national ones. It was the first national Indian organization to attempt to link the tribes to national policy-making bodies, bypassing the intermediary BIA and Interior Department. With the NCAI Indians found something close to a national political voice.

This is not to say that Indian opinion was united in the new organization. Especially in its early years, it paid little attention to the concerns of traditionalist groups on the reservations, and its favorable attitude toward the IRA was by no means universally shared. It was, and remains, an organization dominated largely by Indians with considerable experience in tribal government and the day-to-day politics of Indian affairs. Its leaders have been most interested in the practical aspects of politics, using weapons offered by the dominant society to promote the interests of Indian peoples. This is reflected in its early concerns, such as legal aid for tribes, the establishment of the Indian Claims Commission, and the defense of Indian voting rights in the Southwest. But it campaigned at every level: national, regional, tribal. In its implicit support of both Indian and tribal identities and its concern with cultural matters and treaty rights, it made itself accessible to a broad Indian constituency and rapidly emerged as an important intertribal forum.

Organizations such as the NCAI, the regional organizations that followed—and in some cases preceded—it, and the new tribal governments themselves began to lay the organizational foundation of a more active Indian politics. Much of this development would not pay off for another decade or so, but by the 1940s and 1950s significant signs of resurgent politics—*Indian* politics—had begun to appear. In 1946, responding in part to NCAI lobbying, Congress established the Indian Claims Commission to hear and rule on claims made by Indian nations against the United States. A host of tribes entered such claims, largely land related, inaugurating a wave of Indian-initiated litigation that continues to the present day. Late in the 1940s the NCAI and other groups joined the battle for Indian voting rights, still withheld in New Mexico and Arizona, while in the 1950s the NCAI supported the Three Affiliated Tribes of the Fort Berthold Reservation in North Dakota in a lengthy, though ultimately unsuccessful, effort to stop construction of the Garrison Dam, which eventually flooded much of the reservation.

The war years contributed to this development in another, different, but crucial way. In what the Interior Department described at the time as "the greatest exodus of Indians from reservations that has ever taken place," at least 25,000 Native Americans joined the armed forces during the war, while 40,000 more, escaping the economic desert of the reservations, worked in a variety of wartime industries.[36] Even if the 1940 Census count of 334,000 Indians is low, as it surely is, something like a sixth of the Indian population entered into off-reservation, war-related work. For many this was their first extended personal experience with non-Indian society, and it had politicizing effects. While some Indians remained in the cities when the war ended, thousands returned home, bringing with them not only new experiences but a concrete sense of the Indian/White distinction, which took precedence over tribal identities in the non-Indian world.

Many returned also with a new political awareness, eager to use political and legal processes to secure rights and treatment to which they felt they were entitled. It was veterans who went to court for voting rights in the Southwest, and they were prominent in the NCAI. In 1952 the *New York Times* reported that "a new, veteran-led sense of power is everywhere in the Indian country."[37]

That sense of power was premature. It soon became apparent that the new Indian politics that had begun to surface in the 1930s and 1940s lay on a bed of sand.

"THE INDIAN FREEDOM PROGRAM"

In the decade following its passage, the IRA and associated events had led to a flurry of political organization among the Indian nations. The NCAI was part of this activity, and it marks the transition from tribal to supratribal terms. Yet none of these organizations had much in the way of concrete political power. This was largely a consequence of the political structure of Indian-White relations. The early tribal councils were little more than extensions of the administrative apparatus, giving Indians a role and a faint voice in Indian administration but little substantive power and no significant way of putting pressure on the existing sources of power in Indian affairs.

The impotence of these organizations in the face of external forces soon became apparent. By the mid-1940s the pendulum of Indian policy was retracing its arc, swinging back again toward the more directly assimilationist approach of an earlier time.

Part of the problem was the failure of the IRA to live up to its promise. Indian enthusiasm for it had never been great, and a number of more acculturated Indians had repeatedly asked Congress to repeal the act. Factional conflicts over tribal government didn't help, while the inadequacies of funding and the constraints on tribal government action severely handicapped IRA programs and fueled skepticism about the policy. A confused Congress had difficulty believing Collier's reforms had accomplished very much.

But there was also more profound opposition to the Indian New Deal, rooted in a belief that the IRA perpetuated an undesirably distinct status for Native Americans and was somehow corrosive of human dignity and American values. Against the backdrop of an emerging Cold War, a growing conservative viewpoint in Congress found in the tribalism supported by the IRA a shackle on individual initiative and in tribal communities the dread shadow of socialism. Nevada's Senator George Malone complained that while the country was "spending billions of dollars fighting Communism," it was simultaneously "perpetuating the systems of Indian reservations and tribal governments, which are natural Socialist environments."[38] The exceptional status of Native Americans—tribal citizens and wards of the federal government—seemed to violate American ideals of individual achievement and free enterprise. The solution, so the argument ran, was to dismantle the tribal edifice, remove the protective arm of government, and cast the Indian into the melting pot and the marketplace. Everyone would benefit.

More liberal viewpoints agreed, if for different reasons. In the liberal worldview the distinct status of Indians smacked of discrimination. Reservations were "rural ghettos" where individual rights were secondary to racial identity. The spectrum of Indian views included similar sentiments. Some Indians saw the BIA, tribal property, and tribal government as common elements in Indian bondage, restricting individuals in their drive to join the larger society on equal terms.[39]

The Hoover Commission on government reorganization shared the thrust of these notions and in 1949 proposed steps "to integrate the Indians into the rest of the population as the best solution of 'the Indian Problem.'" Among other things, the commission proposed the transfer of responsibility for Indian services to state governments and urged that Indians be encouraged to leave the reservations and, implicitly, the tribal framework and enter the economic and cultural mainstream. The commission's Committee on Indian Affairs was even more explicit. "Assimilation," it said, clearly intending an individual process, "must be the dominant goal of public policy. On this point there can be no doubt." Even if Indians themselves were opposed, "it would still have to be accepted as a controlling policy."[40]

By the 1950s it was. The new emphasis is first apparent, in embryonic form, in the Navajo-Hopi Rehabilitation Act, passed by Congress in 1950 in response to a deteriorating economic situation on the Navajo and Hopi reservations. The act authorized money for programs designed to lure industry to the reservations and to relocate Indian families to urban areas. It drew together two distinct approaches to Indian problems. While it returned to an individualist orientation—sending Indians to the cities, where they could join the existing economic and social structures of American life—in its provisions for reservation development it echoed the IRA emphasis on community survival. But the echoes were muted: the emphasis was not on tribal enterprise but on bringing industry to the reservations, that is, simply creating jobs. Even in reservation development, the individual was again the focus.

More drastic measures followed. In the so-called termination policy—an ominous moniker if ever there was one—Congress set out to end the federal role in Indian affairs by dismantling the reservation system, the programs and services that supported it, and the federal bureaucracy that administered it. Tribal communities were to be disbanded and their assets distributed among tribal members. Senator Arthur V. Watkins, an architect of the new program and a champion of urban relocation, called it "the Indian freedom program," a necessary antidote to the IRA, which, in its support for Native American communities, he saw as an obstacle to Indian progress. Indians would advance, he argued, only through "the full realization of their national citizenship with all other Americans," that is, through assimilation.[41]

In the summer of 1953 Congress made its move. In House Concurrent Resolution 108 it identified specific Indian groups that were to be removed from federal supervision "at the earliest possible time" and states where federal services to Indians were to be terminated. In Public Law 280, passed that summer, it transferred to five states civil and criminal jurisdiction on Indian reservations and provided that any other state could assume such jurisdiction if it wished, without Indian consent. In support of termination, federal services such as health and education, previously the responsibility of the BIA, were turned over wholly or in part to states or to other federal agencies.

Congress then proceeded on a tribe-by-tribe basis. Between 1954 and 1962 a series of legislative acts specified the termination of particular tribal-federal relationships. Typically they provided for a transition period, usually one to seven years, during which land would be transferred from trust status (held in trust by the federal government on behalf of individual tribes) to private ownership and tribal assets would be distributed among tribal members. Among the larger groups terminated were the Menominees in Wisconsin and the Klamaths in Oregon.[42]

Taken together, these actions were directed toward a complete restructuring of U.S.-Indian relations. Ideally, reservations would be eliminated along with special federal services to Indians; Indian lands would be removed from trust status and made fully taxable and alienable; and the sovereignty of the tribes, now lacking both a land base and any special relationship to the federal government, would become abstract and practically meaningless.[43]

The new policy represented a return to the past in another way as well. It abruptly abandoned the bilateralism—such as it was—of the IRA. Dissenting Indian viewpoints were to be ignored. Commissioner of Indian Affairs Dillon S. Myer's instructions to BIA employees were explicit. "I realize that it will not be possible always to obtain Indian cooperation," he wrote in 1952. Nonetheless, "we must proceed."[44] In an effort to relieve itself once and for all of the financial and moral burden of Indian affairs, the federal government reasserted full control of Indian lives and fortunes and fit them to its plan.

OPPOSITION AND RETREAT

It was a lousy plan. When Congress passed the Menominee Termination Act in 1954, the Menominee Tribe was riding high. Poverty on the reservation was substantial, but the tribe had reserves of cash and a thriving forest products industry providing many with jobs and income.

With termination, the reservation became a county. Tribal assets came under the control of a corporation in which individual Menominees held shares, while previously untaxed lands became subject to state and local taxes. The tribal hospital, once financed by Washington, was shut down and other services were cut. The corporation tried to step into the breach, but much of the tribe's cash had been spent planning for termination. In an attempt to remain solvent, the corporation began laying off mill workers, throwing more Menominees on welfare. Faced with rising taxes and unemployment, many began to sell their shares. Before long the corporation itself was leasing lands to non-Indians in an attempt to raise money. Soon it was selling the land in order to survive. By the mid-1960s the result was a shambles: accelerated Indian land loss, deepening poverty and economic chaos, and increased—not diminished—public expenditure as state and federal governments were forced to pick up the pieces. As more than one Menominee asked in frustration, "Why didn't they leave us alone?"[45]

By then much of Indian country had been aroused. As early as 1954 the NCAI had convened an emergency conference in Washington to protest the congressional moves, seen by many Indian nations as the greatest threat to their survival since the end of military action against them. Both substance and method were at issue. Not only did many Indians oppose the overtly assimilationist nature of termination, with its attendant losses of land and federal protection, but they were incensed at the lack of Indian input into either policy making or implementation, a mockery of the spirit of the Indian New Deal. The IRA may not have been satisfactory, but termination was no improvement. On the contrary, in its disregard for Indian viewpoints, treaty rights, and the survival of tribal communities, it seemed a colossal step backward.

The result was a major shot in the supratribal arm. Nancy Lurie has argued that it was not until the 1950s and termination that many Indians became fully aware of "the diametrical opposition between Indian and white objectives," of the essentially ideological confrontation between assimilationism on the one hand and the commitment many Indians still felt to preservation of nation and community on the other. "A common Indian opposition was spontaneously evoked" as the implications of the new policy became clear. Termination had touched a nerve, drawing Indian groups and leadership together in a concerted effort—much of it waged through the NCAI—to defeat or modify the termination program.[46] In the summer of 1961, when nearly five hundred Indians from seventy tribes gathered in Chicago for the American Indian Chicago Conference, they had in common, wrote D'Arcy McNickle, an anthropologist who was one of them, "a sense of being under attack, and it was this shared experience which drew them together." In its concluding statement the conference rejected termination and asserted the right of Indian communities to choose their own ways of life.[47] It was the largest multitribal gathering in decades, the most striking evidence to date of a supratribal consciousness making its way into politics.

And it had an effect. It was a long struggle, but the opposition to termination gradually grew. State governments, at first in favor, had second thoughts once they realized what was involved in assuming responsibilities once borne by the feds, while other critics attacked the lack of Indian input and the haste with which the policy was adopted. In 1958, signaling the beginnings of retreat, the secretary of the interior called termination without tribal consent—once official practice—"unthinkable," although termination remained government policy for another decade. But by the early 1960s Indian and non-Indian protest, coupled with the policy's failure to deal effectively with Indian problems, had killed its momentum. In 1970, in a message to Congress, President Richard Nixon repudiated it, and in 1973, in response to the protests of the Menominees themselves, Congress restored the tribe to its earlier status.[48] Indeed, the major accomplishment of the program was counter to its intention: it provided Indians with a critical issue around which to mobilize and it persuaded many of the value—indeed, the necessity—of united action and of organizational structures through which to act.

One other tributary to this supratribal current should be noted here. Its headwaters were the universities.

In 1932 the Indian Bureau could find only 385 Indian college students; only five colleges and universities offered Indian scholarships. The IRA provided loan funds for higher education, but it was not until the postwar years that the numbers really began to grow. Some of that growth was a product of the G.I. Bill, but tribes themselves, prompted in part by veterans, began to get involved, setting up scholarship funds of their own. Federal support also rose. In 1952 fifty-six Indians received BIA grants for higher education; by 1957 the number was over seven hundred. In the same year some two thousand Indians were attending college, more than five times the number in 1932.[49]

These students eventually had an impact on politics. In the early 1950s students at the University of New Mexico in Albuquerque founded an Indian club—the Kiva Club. It began as a social organization intended to bring together Indian students, many of whom had come to college direct from the reservations. It soon became more than that. In 1954 a group of these students and others gathered in Santa Fe to discuss Indian education and Indian affairs in concert with older tribal leaders. The gathering led to the establishment of similar clubs at other schools, of regional Indian youth councils, and eventually to a series of youth conferences that took up a variety of Indian issues. The largest, in 1960, drew 350 Indians from fifty-seven tribes. In 1961, shortly after the Indian Chicago Conference, 10 of these young Indians founded the National Indian Youth Council (NIYC), which quickly became a major actor on the Indian political scene.

Parallel to these developments was a series of annual summer Workshops in American Indian Affairs, begun in Colorado Springs in 1956. A group of young Indians gathered with Indian and non-Indian instructors for an intensive six-week examination of Indian issues. The workshops continued for more than a decade. The founders of NIYC were veterans of this workshop experience.[50]

The result of all this activity was the emergence of a group of young Indians with an explicitly supratribal perspective on Indian affairs. While many had roots in tribal communities and their commitment to tribalism remained substantial, they saw themselves, says Robert Thomas, who had run some of the workshops, "as acting on behalf of Indians."[51] Eventually they would act in new ways: it was this group, a few years later, who helped bring a new, confrontational style to Indian politics.

THE LIMITS OF SUPRATRIBALISM

In the 1950s, then, there was a convergence between political crisis and a growing disposition to act on a supratribal basis. Every nation was threatened as the IRA's promise faded and termination gathered force, yet each had little power. In unity lay, if not strength, then at least a louder voice, and one less easily controlled by the non-Indian administrative apparatus.

Tribal and supratribal identities were thus linked together. The survival of the tribe required an *Indian* consciousness, the ability to act as Indians and thus confront federal policy on its own terms. Indian policy, through its own organization and implications, had turned tribal politics into Indian politics, and in so doing had greatly increased the tribes' political capacities.

Despite its progress, however, Indianization—as a political process—had yet to reach very deeply within the Indian population. As late as the 1940s it is difficult to speak of American Indians as forming a self-consciously solidary group in the sense, for example, that Blacks did. Supratribal political activity, severely limited by the reservation system and administrative controls, had only recently reemerged on a significant scale. It remained largely limited to the as yet barely discernible intersection of federal policy making and Indian political life and involved, for the most part, tribal governments and a few Indian organizations such as the NCAI. It was not divorced from the tribal world, but it functioned at a level distant from daily reservation life, while the fragmented character of Indian-White relations—both as a structure of politics and as a structure of groups—continued to inhibit its diffusion.

At the same time, via peyotism and other movements, powwows, and networks of intertribal visiting, marriage, and exchange, a "pan-Indian culture" had appeared: a set of symbols and activities, often derived from plains cultures, that had come to be considered by many Indians and non-Indians as expressive of Indianness: ceremonies, styles of dress and dance, social events.[52] In the 1940s and 1950s these activities and symbols were persuasive indicators of an emergent Indian identity. But it remained an identity largely divorced from politics. It seldom involved sustained interaction with Whites, nor, generally, were its activities political in intent. Certainly they had political consequences and were in part a response to powerlessness and political frustration. But the identity embedded in "pan-Indian" cultural and social life, on the surface at least, was apolitical. Furthermore, most such activities occurred in a context of Indian-Indian, as opposed to Indian-White, interaction. In that context, participation often had the effect, even as it fostered a sense of Indianness, of reinforcing tribalism: the interaction itself sensitized groups to each other's distinctions. Its contribution was to enlarge the potential base of supratribal political organization through the elaboration of networks of acquaintanceship and a consciousness of kind, but it contributed little directly to supratribal action.

To summarize: two related but distinct developments had occurred. The first—multitribal social and cultural activity—while involving large numbers of people, was most characteristic of Indian-Indian relations, carried with it an underlying emphasis on tribalism, and was seldom self-consciously political. The second—a supratribal political consciousness—was characteristic of Indian-White relations and encouraged action on the basis of an Indian identity, but it remained limited in scope and directly involved relatively few Indians. The one embraced diversity and attempted to enrich Indian lives in a context of subordination and powerlessness. The other emphasized commonality and solidarity and sought to transform the context itself, but remained only poorly developed. "American Indians," in the sense of a distinct population or substantial portion thereof that both subjectively identified as Indians and consistently acted in the political realm on the basis of that identity, had yet to emerge.

In the 1950s and 1960s, in the cities of the United States, that population appeared.

Chapter 8

The Politics of Indianness

"Great cities," wrote Robert Park in 1925, "have always been the melting-pots of races and of cultures."[1] In the crucible of city life, peoples are transformed. But the term "melting pot" is misleading. It suggests something more than even Park seems to have intended. Cities have not so much destroyed groups as refashioned them. Feed groups—ethnic, racial, class—into an urban area, wait a while, and examine the result. Groups there will be, but they are likely to have changed. The bases of differentiation will be different; some will have disappeared; new ones will have emerged. The result will be no homogeneous mass, but a new collection of communities and peoples jockeying for advantage, position, status, and opportunity.

It is not the city that accomplishes this so much as the extraordinary shift in social environments. Something generically similar could be achieved by war or disaster, by massive economic change or demographic transition. The world we know disappears and in changed circumstances we are forced to construct new relationships, new responses, new strategies for survival and success, even new conceptions of who we are.

Native Americans, of necessity, have become expert in the construction of such relationships and strategies. Nowhere has that been more evident than in the cities of the United States.

Although the bulk of research on urban Indian populations has focused on the last few decades, there is tantalizing evidence of Indian communities in American cities and towns a century and more ago. Papago and Pima Indians, for example, have lived in or around Tucson, Arizona, since the founding of the city late in the eighteenth century; the city's first White settlements were adjacent to an Indian rancheria. In the 1850s Indians were reported to be a major source of labor in the fields around the village. In 1881 an area on the south side of town, called Barrio Libre, was identified in the *Tucson City Directory* as a slum district where Mexicans and Papago Indians lived.[2] Tucson may not have been much of a city at the time, but it became one, and its Indians urbanized with it.

Such developments were predictable in towns like Tucson or Santa Fe, close to substantial Indian populations, but there were Indians in other cities as well. Richard La Course has found Indian publications dating from the mid-1800s in Chicago and New York. Other cities—Buffalo, Detroit, St. Louis, Pacific Northwest towns—almost certainly had multitribal Indian communities at some point in the nineteenth century. Their early roles as trade and administrative centers would make such communities inevitable, and some would have survived the passing of the frontier. Of course the number of "city" Indians, relative to the Indian population, was tiny. Concentrated at the lower end of the socioeconomic scale and often transient, they were doubtless difficult to locate. The minimal efforts of the U.S. Census of 1900 found only a thousand, surely an undercount, but nonetheless suggestive: they were there, if just barely. The 1928 Meriam Report made no effort to count the urban Indian population, but commented at length on "migrated" Indians and guessed that the numbers were growing.[3]

What was then a trickle soon became a flood.

THE URBAN MIGRATION

The legacy of nineteenth-century land dispossession was underdevelopment: the shattered capacities of Indian economies to support their own populations. After the turn of the century, as Indian populations began to recover numerically, they put increased pressure on limited reservation resources. Many Indians owned lands that were useless for agriculture. Many more held claims to lands kept idle by minutely fragmented ownership. On most reservations unemployment was extreme.

For years many Indians responded to these conditions by seeking wage work just off the reservations, usually on nearby farms or ranches, on railroad gangs, or in the border towns. During World War I substantial numbers sought out industrial work in American cities; during World War II much larger numbers left the reservations to take advantage of urban job opportunities. Whether or not these migrants stayed in the cities at war's end or returned home, they helped establish new patterns of response to the economic pressures of reservation conditions. Relatives and friends followed after; others went to take their chances, too.

Large-scale urban migration begins in the World War II years. It was reinforced by another factor, this one indiscriminate in its treatment of Indian and White. In the 1940s many small farmers and ranchers began to find themselves unable to compete in agricultural markets increasingly dominated by large corporate producers. Most Indian families simply lacked the necessary resources for large-scale production, while fragmented ownership kept the size of typical agricultural operations small and, therefore, disadvantaged. Meanwhile, farm and ranch mechanization reduced employment opportunities.[4] More and more Indians, like non-Indians from farm economies, had to look elsewhere for work.

Economics and policy, here as elsewhere, were intertwined. In the 1930s studies conducted by the BIA and other organizations had revealed in detail for the first time the inadequacy of reservation resources—as known and developed—to support growing Indian populations.[5] Following World War II, with veterans and others returning to the reservations, the BIA searched for ways to expand economic opportunities. In 1948, responding to economic crisis on the Navajo Reservation, it initiated a job placement program, finding employment for single Navajo males in Denver, Los Angeles, and Salt Lake City.[6]

There had been earlier efforts to find off-reservation employment for Indians. In 1906, for example, the commissioner of Indian affairs reported at length on efforts to induce "young and able-bodied Indians who have no profitable work at home to leave their reservations and go out into the world to make a living as white men do." In South Dakota the Pine Ridge Reservation agent announced in printed advertisements that "800 Able-Bodied Oglala Sioux Indians Desire Employment." The agent later admitted the claim was extravagant, at least as far as "desire" was concerned, and there was some problem persuading Indians to accept employment once it was offered.[7] But the effort was being made. Of course in 1906 it was not so much economics as the civilizing mission that inspired such promotions. Then, too, the employment sought was usually close at hand. Major movement to the cities had not yet become an objective.

In the 1930s the BIA initiated a placement program intended to find off-reservation employment for Indians, especially the graduates of BIA schools. In 1931–32 it made 995 permanent placements, many apparently in urban areas, but the program was discontinued after a few years.[8]

In contrast, the Navajo program begun on a limited scale in 1948 quickly gathered momentum. In 1950 the BIA decided to extend placement services to other Indians. By late 1951 Field Relocation Offices had been set up in Denver, Salt Lake City, Los Angeles, and Chicago; offices subsequently were added in Oakland, San Jose, Dallas, and Cleveland. In 1952 the first Indian migrants began moving under the expanded program, with transportation, placement, and subsistence help provided by the BIA.

Urban-directed migration received further support from the Indian Vocational Training Act, passed in 1956, which initiated a number of vocational training courses at schools in urban areas and near the reservations. The majority of Indians taking part in this program, finding few opportunities on the reservations, eventually went job hunting in the cities.[9]

By the mid-1970s some one hundred sixty thousand Indians had taken part in the relocation program.[10] But relocation was not only a program; it was a policy. At the heart of it lay not only economic forces but a particular government orientation to Indian affairs. Relocation was intended to do more than just solve the economic problems of the reservations. It was a product of the termination years, part of a return to policies of individual assimilation and the discounting of the tribe and the community as critical elements in Indian lives.

Two strategies were available for dealing with the economic problems of the reservations: remove Indians to places with economic opportunities or improve such opportunities where Indians lived. Given the orientation of Indian policy in the 1940s and 1950s, it was perhaps inevitable that relocation would become the primary component of the policy response. Elaine Neils has compared BIA expenditures for reservation agricultural and industrial assistance (A and I) and relocation for the years 1952–65, showing dramatic increases in relocation funds through the period, much more gradual increases in A and I. In 1952 the BIA spent just over half a million dollars on relocation. In 1965 it spent eleven and a half million. In the same period A and I expenditures rose from just over one and a half million dollars to just under six and a half million, dropping from more than three times the relocation amount to a little over half as much.[11]

Whether or not the BIA viewed relocation as an aspect of termination remains an open question, but some policymakers did. The Hoover Commission's Committee on Indian Affairs saw relocation as a key element in its recommended program of assimilation and governmental reduction, while Senator Arthur V. Watkins of Utah, chairman of the Senate Committee on Indian Affairs during the Eisenhower years and a leading advocate of termination, claimed, "The sooner we can get the Indians into cities the sooner the government can get out of the Indian business."[12] Certainly relocation and termination shared a common logic: one way to deal with problematic tribal communities was to get rid of them.

Much Indian sentiment, on the other hand, was powerfully inclined toward community development. The NCAI, for example, attacked relocation as just another form of termination and offered its support for the program only if participation was voluntary and efforts were made first to develop reservation communities.[13] To some extent participation *was* voluntary; officially it was intended to be so, and many Indians eagerly took the road to the cities. In practice, sometimes it was not. On occasion students who had completed schooling and vocational training were asked to which city they wished to relocate. Returning to the reservation was not presented as an option.[14] Of course the alternatives were genuinely limited: as long as reservation economies languished, relocation had the force of necessity.

The cumulative effect of World War II, heightened economic pressure, and government policy was dramatic. In a period in which the populations of both the United States and the world have been becoming more and more urban, Indians have been doing likewise with a vengeance. From 1950 to 1960, when the urban population of the country rose 29.3 percent, the urban Indian population increased 160 percent. In the following decade it rose 144 percent, and from 1970 to 1980 it doubled again. Accord-

Table 2.   Indian Population Increases, Total and Urban, 1940–80

Year	Total Indian Population	% Increase	Urban Indian Population	% In- crease	Urban Ind. as % of Total Ind.	% In- crease in U.S. Ur- ban Pop.
1940	334,000	—	27,000	—	8.1	—
1950	343,000	2.7	56,000	107.4	16.3	20.6[a]
1960	524,000	52.8	146,000	160.7	27.9	29.3
1970	792,000	51.1	356,000	143.8	44.9	19.2
1980	1,364,000	72.2	719,000	102.0	52.7	11.9

[a] For purposes of comparability, figures using the old definition of *urban* were used in cal- culating the % increase in U.S. urban population, 1940–50. See Bureau of the Census, *Census of the Population: 1950*, vol. 2: *Characteristics of the Population*, Part 1: U.S. Summary, pp. 1–5, 9–12.

Source: Bureau of the Census, *Census of the Population: 1940, 1950, 1960, 1970, 1980*, vol. 2: *Characteristics of the Population*, Part 1: U.S. Summary.

ing to the 1980 Census, more than half the Indian population of the United States was resident in urban places (see Table 2). In thirty years Indians accomplished a demographic transition of remarkable proportions.

Indian labor has been less at issue in this development than the state of Indian economic resources. It has not been societal demands for Indian workers that has brought Indians to the cities in such numbers. Much of that movement, in fact, has occurred during a period of declining opportu- nities for unskilled or manual labor in American cities and rising unem- ployment among urban minority populations. Instead, it has reflected the dismal economic state of most reservations, combined with federal policies intended to solve the reservation economic problem and at the same time reduce the federal role in Indian affairs.

As an economic strategy it has had payoffs, although the winnings have been slight. Urban Indians fare better than their reservation counterparts: employment levels and per capita incomes are higher and housing, among other things, is generally better. Yet they remain poor, with per capita in- comes slightly ahead of urban Blacks and well behind urban Whites and unemployment figures twice those of the urban White population.[15]

In contrast, the political effects have been substantial.

URBANIZATION AND SUPRATRIBALISM

Early observers tended to view "pan-Indianism" as a sign of assimilation: a transitional stage between collapsing tribal cultures and the mainstream of American society. Some recent writers, concentrating on its urban vari- ants, have seen it differently, describing it, as one representative article does, as "one of the most important adaptive social mechanisms for easing the transition of migrating American Indians from rural reservation communities to urban centers."[16] It is this and more. Urban supratribalism has emerged as a political response to particular characteristics of the contemporary Indian situation.

The phenomenon itself is of an older vintage. "Pan-Indian" organizations and clubs certainly were extant in some cities—Los Angeles and New York among them—as early as the 1920s and may have existed there or elsewhere earlier still. Their major functions appear to have been social: the creation through regular social activities of an environment in which Indians could interact comfortably with each other and through which they could retain an Indian identity despite urban isolation.[17] Along with the off-reservation boarding schools, these organizations were probably the first incubators of contemporary supratribalism.

But the political contribution of urban supratribalism comes later, with the explosive growth of the urban Indian population since the 1940s. One factor was the emergence of a more varied Indian population. Certain major cities—San Francisco, Chicago, Denver, others—drew particularly widely from the reservations, especially as the relocation program took off. The result was multitribal populations of considerable diversity. A perhaps extreme but indicative illustration: a 1966 survey of three thousand Indians in Los Angeles found representatives of more than seventy tribes.[18]

Yet association alone would be insufficient to produce a durable and politically active supratribal consciousness, especially in the face of closely held tribal identities. The crucial additional component has been the urban context itself, the growing perception among urban Indians of the interests they shared and the problems and political conditions they faced.

Especially in the early years of substantial migration, the move from reservation to city, whether made autonomously or with federal assistance, involved for most Indians an unprecedented and dramatic transition. It entailed a shift not only from a rural to an urban physical setting, but also from a familiar social and cultural environment, dominated in most cases by kinship relations and the embrace of the tribe, to a largely alien, often industrial environment dominated by an individualistic worldview and a very different set of values. While most Indians had come in contact with at least some representative parts of that alien world on the reservations and in the border towns, few migrants had experienced before an entire social system made up of elements so different from those out of which their own, more accustomed world was constituted. Few knew how to operate effectively in this new environment, and there were few places to turn for help. Sources of assistance available to the rest of urban society were unfamiliar to most Indian migrants and, in any case, were ignorant of the particular problems Indians faced in city living.

Nevertheless, urban Indians by necessity are in frequent contact with urban bureaucracies: welfare agencies, BIA Employment Assistance offices, the police and courts, public health organizations, and so on. These bureaucracies not only are often insensitive to the peculiarities of the urban Indian situation, but for the most part view urban Indian migrants indiscriminately as "Indians." In itself this is unexceptional; Indian policy generally adopts such terms. On the reservations, however, these unitary categorizations are mediated by tribal organization and the encompassing tribal environment. In the city no such mediating factors operate. Once inside an urban bureaucracy Indians, for all practical purposes, are Indians. Moreover, their relationships to such organizations are individual relationships based on membership in no group other than the Indian population as a whole or the still larger body of the urban poor. Tribal membership means little.

Coupled with this is the effect of discrimination, which tends to ignore tribal boundaries. Although in general Indians appear to experience discrimination—in jobs, housing, and relations with public authorities—less frequently than Blacks, it is something many urban Indians face, particularly in cities near reservations. The results of the bureaucratic experience and discrimination are similar: an awareness of Indianness as an important, defining property of the urban experience, as more relevant than the tribe to many aspects of urban living.

In response to the problems of adjustment to urban circumstances, discrimination, and the lack of social services oriented to the Indian population, a set of institutions gradually emerged designed to meet urban Indian needs. Certain ones—Indian bars and some churches—were long established among the much smaller populations of the early to mid-twentieth century. By the 1950s and 1960s, with the dramatic growth in urban Indian populations, these were being joined by social service centers and other charitable organizations. While many of the early ones were started by non-Indian groups such as the Quakers, by the mid-1960s urban institution building was increasingly an Indian enterprise and eventually included schools, cultural workshops, health clinics, and professional groups.[19]

The organizational activity has been intense. In the mid-1970s the American Indian Policy Review Commission surveyed urban Indian service organizations. With only modest effort it found 167 organizations and centers in twenty-nine states and the District of Columbia. A more exhaustive survey would have turned up many more.[20] Some organizations are tribally specific, but the majority are intertribal, drawing from the urban Indian population at large. Many both supply social services to migrants and provide a social environment controlled by Indians and oriented to Indian needs. In the 1960s and 1970s they became the primary service organizations for much of the urban Indian population.[21]

Such organizations, acting as magnets and network nodes, evidence the emergence in many cities not only of multitribal Indian populations, but of multitribal communities as well. These communities are defined not by geographical boundaries or census enumerations but by informal social networks and institutional arrangements, by patterns of participation that loosely link a constantly changing population. The institutional structures are often tenuous, but the communities are not. They depend less on the persistence of institutions than on the social networks in which the institutions are embedded: that is, on the participants themselves. Furthermore, they work. They do not overcome all the problems faced by Indians in the cities, nor do they embrace the whole of the urban Indian population. For some persons tribal associations are more important, even in the urban setting; others associate only occasionally, if at all, with other Indians. But for large numbers these communities provide ways of coping with some of the more acute difficulties of urban living and offer a surrogate of sorts for the supportive tribal structures that either have been left behind or whose effectiveness has been reduced by lack of numbers.[22]

They also foster a supratribal identity. The various elements of the urban experience make two things dramatically clear for many Indians: the affinities among them and the differences between them and non-Indians. While the system itself, with its stereotypical categorizations, takes such affinities for granted, many Indians do not. But in the urban milieu it rapidly becomes apparent that the social and cultural distances dividing Indian and White are far greater than those that separate tribes. The result for many is a new sense of Indianness as a formative influence in everyday life, something experienced in the cities often for the first time. Even among those who do not actively take part in organized intertribal activities, there appears to be a widespread identification with the generalized Indianness these activities express.[23]

These conclusions may not be applicable to all urban Indians, nor to every city with an Indian population. But for the vast majority and for most cities with significant multitribal populations, emergent urban Indian communities appear to serve these functions and have these effects. Given the number of Indians who at one time or another in recent decades have spent more than a few months in such situations, the cumulative impact of this development is enormous. What has occurred in effect is the establishment for the first time of a sizeable self-consciously Indian population, bound together by a shared social environment and by a growing recognition of affinities in historical experience, social position, contemporary interests, and often worldviews, acting daily on the basis of a shared Indianness. Ultimately that development can be traced to the historical processes of incorporation that led eventually to large-scale urban migration.

But another factor may be still more important in the development of urban supratribalism. This is the simple fact that Indian affairs are formally structured in terms of tribal-federal relationships. This structure neither addresses the problems urban Indians face nor provides them with any effective framework for political participation.

The large Indian migration of the 1950s and, especially, the 1960s coincided with the growing disparity between white-collar and blue-collar employment opportunities in American cities. As jobs in the manufacturing sector and demands for unskilled labor declined, Indians often found themselves hard-pressed to find adequate work in urban areas. When they did find work, other problems of adjustment to the norms of industrial society often complicated the situation. For many, urban poverty replaced reservation poverty. At the same time, in leaving the reservation the Indian migrant lost those community services, such as health and education, provided by the BIA or other federal agencies. Obtaining similar services from city or state agencies often proved difficult. While the federal government denied responsibility for nonreservation Indians, many cities and states refused also to grant services on the grounds that *all* Indians are a federal responsibility. Indian institution building has been partly a response to this problem. Yet in the problem itself there is no compelling reason why the Indian response should be supratribal.

One possible explanation for the resultant supratribalism has to do with organizational ecology: the competitive advantage of larger scale. Competing with other urban groups for influence with large bureaucracies and power holders, Indians benefit from the greater ability of large-scale organization to mobilize resources and command attention. Supratribalism, in other words, is a logical organizational strategy, likely to be more efficacious than organization based on narrower tribal affiliations.[24]

This explanation, while surely valid, is incomplete in the Indian case. It says much about the organizational logic but less about the politics of the situation or the perceptions of individual participants. It is here that the formal structure of Indian-White relations becomes important and contributes further to an understanding of both the organizational dynamics and the patterns of individual participation. In leaving the reservation, the Indian leaves the only institutionalized political framework in which tribal identity has any practical meaning. In the cities the tribe is no longer relevant as a political category; the sociopolitical environment is organized in different terms. The vocabulary of urban politics and ethnic competition is set largely by non-Indians and has little room for the language of tribalism. In the urban Indian's struggle with city, state, and federal bureaucracies, the Indian population as a whole becomes the relevant political category, relevant not in terms of institutionalized structures that speak directly to Indian needs—such structures, other than those Indians create, are virtually nonexistent—but as the only logical basis for political organization and action.

Urban Indian organizations intuitively recognized this fact and organized accordingly. Their emphasis on a generalized Indianness represents not so much psychological marginality or cultural detribalization as an effort to adapt to social and political reality, an effort rooted in a logic that is at once organizational, political, and phenomenological. What has changed is not Indians or their objectives so much as the situations in which they have found themselves. Indians in cities were being integrated (not assimilated) as individuals (not tribes) into a new set of political and economic relationships. Urbanization did not bring politics into Indian lives; it brought Indians into new politics. Only with the recent urban migration did large numbers of Indians find themselves in political and social situations that not only encouraged but in a real sense also demanded that they begin to act on a supratribal basis as both individuals and groups. For the first time a supratribal identity not only made its way among substantial numbers of Indians, but did so in the context of political needs. Indianness became relevant to the daily lives of Indians. The result was a massive supratribal constituency.[25]

The effects of this development have reached far beyond the urban boundary. From the cities an enlarged and politicized supratribal consciousness has been carried back to the reservations, much of it via migrant returnees.

Census figures for urban Indians both tend to be low and by definition are time specific. They do not include substantial numbers of Indians who have left the reservations, lived in the cities, and returned, nor do they include many of those who move back and forth between the two in the fashion of long-distance commuters. Useful as an indicator of the urban Indian population at a single moment, census data are much less useful as an indicator of the extent of the Indian urban experience.

Both of these groups—sometime urban residents and regular "commuters"—appear to be large. The BIA reported that between 1953 and 1957 some 30 percent of those Indians moving to cities under the relocation program returned to their reservations before the end of the fiscal year in which they were relocated. In 1965 Joan Ablon estimated relocation returnees at 50 percent of those who went on relocation, while the Navajo Agency in 1961 found that 37 percent of Navajo relocatees between 1952 and 1961 eventually returned to the reservation.[26] Of course relocation is by no means the only source of urban migrants, but it has involved more than 160,000 Indians. However long they spent in the cities, the number of returnees from that source alone is large.

The other, perhaps overlapping group—those who alternate between urban and reservation settings—more difficult to quantify, is no doubt also substantial: that kind of commuting has been common among Native Americans for decades and is widely reported in studies of urban Indians. Today more than ever it appears that large numbers periodically come to the cities, stay a while, and return home, participating in what Herbert Blatchford calls "a usable cycle": procuring resources in one place, spending them in another. Others, who may spend the larger part of their time in the cities, make periodic returns to the reservation for a day or two, a few weeks, a month or more. The number of such commuters may well exceed the permanent, or "rooted," urban Indian population. In 1975 Hodge estimated that "at least 60 percent of American Indians are full or part-time residents of cities." Given the 1980 census finding of an Indian population more than 50 percent urban, a finding that surely picks up only a portion of the most mobile, the extent of urban residence seems likely to be larger still.[27] The implication is clear: while the magnitude of Indian urbanization, considered as the extent of urban experience in the Indian population, is unknown, it substantially exceeds that indicated by the urban Indian population at any given moment.

Obviously not every Indian who returns from city to reservation is a carrier, so to speak, of supratribal consciousness. But the experiences and points of view of returnees come with them and, in varying magnitudes, become inputs into the collective perceptions of the reservation community. Although many Indians, whether they live on the reservations or in the cities, may view the urban world as an alien one, by nature inimical to much that they value in their lives and cultures, these experiences and viewpoints cannot easily be rejected. By force of circumstance and number, they enter the community consciousness. With them comes an awareness of "Indian" concerns. Returnees themselves may become interpreters of those concerns and of events and problems in the areas they have left behind. Often accustomed to acting politically on the basis of Indianness, they bring that larger dimension to the consideration of reservation issues as well. Blatchford observes that a large number of contemporary tribal leaders and elected officials have been urban residents at some point.[28] Many learned their politics as much in the cities as on the reservations. As more and more reservation residents spend time in the city, the urban experience and its by-products increasingly contribute to the political perceptions and self-concepts of group members.[29]

Thus the conceptual and political effects of urbanization travel far beyond the cities. In the process they reveal the Janus-like character of urbanization itself. For many Indians the urban experience has been a painful one. Often it has involved loneliness, discrimination, and poverty as well as the disruption of ties to culture and kin. For substantial numbers, the move to the cities was not a choice in any meaningful sense, but the only possible outcome of economic processes beyond Indian control. At the same time, viewed in a group perspective, the urban experience has been a creative one. It has been central to the emergence of a supratribal consciousness, a new dimension of group identity and adaptation. These two apparently antipodal characteristics of Indian urbanization are connected. Supratribalism has been a response to particular modes of incorporation and their consequences, an effort, conscious or not, to enlarge the capacities of Indian groups to act effectively in the situations in which they find themselves. In that effort urbanization, despite its costs, has played a crucial role.

MEDIA AND SUPRATRIBALISM

Migrants are not the only vehicle of a supratribal consciousness. Also important has been the Indian press.

In 1828 a newspaper called the *Cherokee Phoenix,* printed in Cherokee and English, appeared in Georgia. It was the first of many. By the turn of the century, according to one count, "over 100 [Indian] newspapers had appeared from Alaska to Florida." In 1974 the American Indian Press Association listed more than two hundred active Indian news publications in thirty-three states and the District of Columbia, including tribal papers, urban papers, Indian center newsletters, and regional and national publications. By 1980 some Indian groups, including several tribes, had established radio and television stations or were otherwise involved in broadcast journalism.[30]

Until the last few decades most of these publications were concerned primarily with local issues. In contrast, the 1960s and 1970s saw the rapid growth of a national Indian news media specifically directed toward the largest possible Indian audience, covering both tribal and urban developments as well as issues of more general Indian concern. *Indian Voices,* published in Chicago from 1962 to 1968, the more recent *Akwesasne Notes,* published by the Mohawk Nation in New York State since 1968, and the reborn *Wassaja,* published intermittently since 1973 in San Francisco, brought to the reservations news of the entire Indian population. The latter two in particular have given close attention to political matters, and *Akwesasne Notes,* which claims a readership of one hundred thousand, continues to serve as a "prime voice" of Indian political activism.[31] In 1970 the American Indian Press Association (AIPA) was founded; for five years it operated a news service out of Washington, covering events throughout the country and functioning as a critical source of news for Indian and other publications nationwide. At one time it was sending news packets to more than 150 Indian newspapers.[32]

Indians with wide experience in both urban and reservation environments—some began their journalistic careers with major city dailies—played a role in this development. Many of their own concerns were supratribal; part of their agenda was to bring to the reservations news of national developments likely to affect all Indians. Much of their journalism was politically committed, not so much to specific issue positions as to the empowerment of Indian communities through the distribution of critical information once monopolized by the Indian affairs bureaucracy.[33]

These media efforts helped enlarge the scope of Indian political awareness and dialogue beyond the boundaries of tribe or region. The results are evident not least in the space devoted by many tribal papers to national Indian issues and news from other parts of the country, but also in the network of Indian journalists in close communication with each other and with tribal leaders and national Indian organizations.

URBANIZATION AND TRIBALISM

It is in the 1950s, 1960s, and 1970s, then, that a supratribal consciousness and constituency were finally made, that Indianization fully flowered. It was a protracted process and one of many parts, reflecting both a changing sociopolitical context made by outsiders and a political agenda—far more constant—made by Indians. Indeed, it has been a continuing product of the encounter between the two.

But what is the relationship between this emergent identity and the tribal identities that preceded it? On the one hand there is the progressively greater concentration of political organization and self-concept at the tribal level; on the other, the growth of a politicized supratribalism. Are these developments not somehow contradictory? Is Indianness replacing the tribe as a focus of identity among Native Americans? If not, how are the two related?

One way to approach these issues is to look first at urbanization. If urbanization has been a critical factor in the growth of supratribalism, what has been its effect on tribal identities? Some studies of Indian urbanization have suggested, in a kind of updated "vanishing Indian" thesis, that it heralds the end of the tribe and even the eventual disappearance of a culturally distinct Indian population. Thus Officer suggests that with long-term urban residence, ties to the tribe attenuate, while Yinger and Simpson, in a discussion of the integration of Indians into American society, list urbanization as a factor promoting cultural assimilation and a shared (Indian and White) identity. White and Chadwick, in a study of the Spokane tribe, found three factors highly correlated with White self-identification on the part of Indians, among them urban residence.[34]

These viewpoints and the conclusions derived from them are consistent with a traditional academic view of urbanization and its effects. In this view urbanization is an assimilative process in which ethnic and kinship ties and customary modes of behavior give way to interest-based group affiliations and new forms of behavior based on generalized, achievement-oriented, "modern" values.

Yet there is significant evidence from the Indian experience that challenges these viewpoints. An early study by Joan Ablon concluded that relatively few Indians in San Francisco were "assimilated." Chadwick and Stauss, in a study of Indians in Seattle, found a "fairly low" level of assimilation and found as well that length of stay in the city had little effect on degree of assimilation. Using several indicators of identity, they concluded, "Indians who had lived their entire life in the city were as traditional as those who had only recently left the reservation." Anderson and Harvey found evidence among Navajo migrants that urbanization led to an increased emphasis on traditional values. Krutz reported that Navajos in San Francisco brought important aspects of Navajo culture and social organization with them to the city, including an approximation of the local residential unit or "outfit" that continued to function in the urban setting as locus of social interaction and economic cooperation. Navajos sought out employment that, whatever its economic return, would require "minimal social contact with employers and maximal contact with other Navajos." He reported further that Kiowa migrants, coming from a very different, non-reservation, rural environment, worked hard to maintain Kiowa identity, used rural Kiowa society as an "anchor culture," and struggled to revitalize traditional Kiowa values in the urban setting. In neither the Navajo nor the Kiowa case, says Krutz, "was there severance of rural ties, a weakening of the bonds of kinship and the undermining of the traditional basis of social solidarity." He reports similarly for Sioux residents he studied in the Bay area.

Indians interviewed by Patrick in Dallas, most of whom had been there for at least five years, consistently used tribal self-identification and placed tribal loyalties above all others. Most looked on their stay in Dallas as temporary, viewed the reservation as home, and expected to return there. Makofsky reports that Lumbee Indians in Baltimore similarly have continued to emphasize the primacy of Lumbee identity in their lives and, even after years of urban residence, carefully preserve links to their homeland community in North Carolina. Stanbury's study of urban Indians in British Columbia found significant continuities in cultural identity as shown by a high incidence of attendance at traditional ceremonies, frequent visits to reserves, and other measures.[35]

But whatever the effect of long-term urban residence, for many Indians city living is either temporary, followed by return to the reservation, or recurrent, interspersed with periods of reservation living. Overall, the number of Indians for whom tribal ties are *not* powerful elements in their lives appears to be small.

Many of these studies are dated now, but little has emerged to refute them. Of course these data and observations may be no more valid as broad generalizations than those that find urbanization to be assimilative. Both draw on cases that may not be comparable, and no systematic, comparative study of Indian urbanization, embracing the variety of peoples and situations involved, has yet been undertaken. Nor would it necessarily resolve these apparent differences. Taken together, the materials on urban Indians most convincingly argue diversity, both in the effects of urbanization and in the patterns of Indian adaptation. Also unavailable yet are adequate longitudinal data, which will be critical. In the last few decades, as Sam Stanley and Robert Thomas point out, "a whole generation of Indians has been born and socialized in large metropolitan areas." This is the first substantial group of Indians to grow up in extensive contact with urban American institutions. Exactly *how* they have been socialized and how they now perceive the tribe is not fully known, but certainly their experiences are very different from those of their reservation-reared urban counterparts. Have they entered into the generalized urban culture and its attendant American identity, or a generalized Indian one, or some urban version of tribal culture and identity? These same authors note that "the vast majority of young Indians raised in the city do not know a tribal language."[36] Numerous reservation youth likewise speak only English; on the other hand, many live in a setting in which a tribal language survives. Their own ability to speak it may be less important than its presence as part of the tribal environment, a marker of the distinctiveness of their people. What effect does the absence of such markers have on urban tribalism?

These remain open questions, but it appears certain that for some urban Indians tribal bonds are rapidly disappearing. At the same time it is also clear that for many Indians in the cities tribal identity remains not only paramount, but a means of survival. Where urban tribal concentrations are substantial, tribal networks become important support mechanisms, facilitating the flow of information, jobs, transportation, housing, and social life. Tribal identity is sustained in part by its practical functions.

It is sustained also by the fact that few Indians remain separated from the tribe for long. Either they bring it with them to the city or, eventually, they make their way back to it. Many do both.

It is here again that the urban experience is a creative one. The starting point for most studies of Indian urbanization—and of urbanization generally—has been the assumption that when the migrant moves to the city, something in him or her changes. This is a valid assumption, given the magnitude of the transition. The program of most such studies has been the specification and measurement of that change. But there is another, equally valid starting point that, in concert with the first, might enlarge our understanding of Indian urbanization. This is the idea that when the Indian moves to the city, it is something in the "typical" patterns of urban life and social organization that is transformed. The patterns of living familiar to most urban residents are altered to fit Indian needs and perceptions. The focus of investigation becomes not the American Indian in urban society, but urbanism in American Indian societies: the ways in which Indians have incorporated the urban experience into their world.

This in effect is what Jeanne Guillemin does in her study of the Micmac Indians of Canada's Maritime Provinces, and the result is instructive. Large numbers of Micmacs travel regularly to industrial centers, particularly Boston, in search of employment to supplement meager reservation resources, and subsequently return. Yet they seldom leave the social organization of the tribe. Constant interactions with other Micmacs, kinship ties and obligations, a shared history and culture—these and other factors allow urban Micmacs to remain within the tribal community even as they move. The boundaries of the tribe are not geographical but personal, and therefore mobile. Urban migration has become a necessity for Micmac survival, and desirable for other reasons as well; as a result the Micmacs have incorporated it into the social and cultural fabric of their existence. Writes Guillemin:

> it takes a sociological imagination to grasp the simultaneous occurrence of mobility and cohesion which characterizes urban tribalism. To be on a constant journey and yet never really leave familiar faces behind is the essence of urban Indian culture. A tribe like the Micmac is indeed a network which has expanded its perimeters, but it has also maintained communication among its members and the sense of tribal affiliation born of a common, successful cultural strategy.[37]

The Micmacs have been successful in a particular situation, and their experience may not be generalizable. What is generalizable is the message within the Micmac case: urbanization need not always lead to detribalization; on the contrary, tribalism itself may respond creatively to the urban experience and its demands. Furthermore, it appears that for many Indians reservation and urban settings are not separate worlds, but parts of a single system within which they move, work, and interact.[38] The two parts of that system may require different responses from Indian groups and individuals, but they are intimately related. Native American communities are spatially elastic; the community grows or contracts not simply as people cross spatial boundaries, but also as they enter or leave social networks that need not be spatially defined. Tribalism is relational, not geographical. Isolation may occur in the city, but it is not a necessary aspect of urbanization. The existence of tribal and multitribal urban communities, combined with the extraordinary mobility of individual Indians, keeps many involved in relationships that in one way or another remain tribal. The move to the city is not necessarily a move away from the tribe at all, for the tribe may be a resource as mobile as the migrants themselves.

There is an irony here. Indians have long exploited the opportunities of the city on behalf of their own survival. But it is unlikely that they would have done so in such numbers as they do now without the intervention of government programs. The irony is that urbanization, originally favored in part because of its supposedly assimilative effects, has become instead part of an expanded economic and social system whose center—to a large degree—remains the reservations. Growing numbers of Indians have learned to exploit urban opportunities without losing touch with reservation homelands, thereby reducing the economic pressure on the reservations without undercutting their central social function. Assimilation certainly has occurred, but it has been by no means universal. As long as that remains the case, urbanization has improved, not diminished, the chances of tribal survival.

The strategies and outcomes suggested here are not without parallels. Research on migration has long noted the importance of kinship and other communal networks in migrant adaptations, while research on Third World urbanization in particular has paid substantial attention to the persistence in urban settings of traditional institutions and "tribal" attachments.[39] While less attention has been paid to the nature and persistence of links between migrant sending and receiving societies, the idea of migration "systems" that integrate the two and the movement between them has currency in development studies and has received more attention recently in work on migration in North America and Europe as well.[40] Tribal affiliation appears to function much like the less inclusive kinship networks that played a crucial role in other migrant adaptations in the United States and much of the Third World.

Once again, however, the diversity of the Indian experience is substantial. Some migrants do leave the tribe behind, and do so by choice, preferring a new, larger world of experience and acquaintanceship. Others do so by necessity, being too few in number to sustain tribal networks in urban places: Micmacs in Boston or Navajos in Los Angeles have possibilities other migrants may not enjoy. Still others may be profoundly ambivalent, uncertain of their allegiance to both the tribe and a more generalized Indian identity. Some simply disappear.[41] The point is that urbanism and tribalism are not antithetical. Indians do not necessarily leave their world to go to the city—only certain aspects of it. Instead, they may expand their world to make the city livable.

TRIBALISM AND SUPRATRIBALISM

What, then, of supratribalism? How is it related to the tribe? In some cases, certainly, a supratribal consciousness functions as a replacement for tribal identity and attachments. Particularly for those who lack tribal networks of support, supratribal ones can serve similar purposes. In their study of "pan-Indian" associations in the San Francisco Bay area, for example, James Hirabayashi and others suggest that Indians from nations whose social organization and culture had been substantially damaged or disorganized through subordination—Sioux, Chippewa, the Oklahoma tribes—were more likely to take part in such activities than were those from tribes whose cultures and social organizations were relatively intact—Navajos and Pueblos, for example—or those, such as some Northwest Coast Indians, for whom individual assimilation into the dominant culture was fairly well advanced. The authors speculate that those who are more acculturated or who lack supportive tribal cultures participate in "pan-Indian" activities in order to retain some measure of Indian identity, while more tribally oriented Indians take part primarily because they enjoy interacting with other Indians. One could argue with their assumptions regarding the state of certain tribal cultures and with some of their data—their view of the Sioux in San Francisco, for example, seems to contradict Krutz's observations—but for some Indians, clearly, supratribal identity and activity reflect a decline in tribal identifications, filling the space left behind.[42]

All the same, given the expansion of supratribal consciousness in recent years and the apparent lack of any correspondingly large decline in tribal attachments, it seems evident that for most Indians supratribalism represents not a replacement but an enlargement of their identity system, a circle beyond the tribe in which, also, they think, move, and act.[43] Subtribal, tribal, and supratribal identities form concentric rings around the individual, parts in a sequence of increasingly inclusive group boundaries. They emerge situationally, depending on the context and the nature of the interaction. In the city supratribal identity is most clearly an aspect of Indian-White interaction, political or social, while the tribe persists as a common basis of Indian-Indian interaction, even among those for whom supratribal identity would seem logically to be most important. A notable aspect of urban Indian bars—at least of those with multitribal clienteles—is the salience of tribal identifications in conversations, introductions, joking, and the like. It remains the most important way of knowing who you are.

On the reservation, on the other hand, while supratribal identity, thanks perhaps to non-Indian expectations, may remain a common basis of social

	City		Reservation	
	Political	Social	Political	Social
Indian-White	Supratribal	Supratribal	Usually tribal	Tribal or supratribal
Indian-Indian	Tribal	Tribal	Tribal or subtribal	Tribal or subtribal

Figure 2. Contextual Variation in Indian Identifications

interaction between Indian and White, political interaction between the two most often takes place within the framework of a specific tribal-federal relationship, giving salience to tribal as opposed to supratribal identities. At the same time, Indians interacting with each other on the reservation are more likely to act on subtribal bases, emphasizing kinship, locational, or other internal dividing lines, within the framework of a taken-for-granted tribalism (see Figure 2).

These patterns are hardly invariant, and some situations are anomalous. A number of both tribal and subtribal groups, for example, have acted on a supratribal basis even when reservation issues were at stake, in part to broaden their base of support and transform tribal issues into more general, Indian ones. What is at stake in these different interactional contexts also may vary. To assert a tribal identity in Indian-Indian social interaction in the city may have to do primarily with the categorization of persons, mentally organizing the multitribal community of which the individual is a part. To assert such an identity in Indian-White political interaction on the reservation, on the other hand, may have to do primarily with the defense of peoplehood. Not only do the identities vary, but the uses to which a single identity is put may vary as well.[44]

Nor is this situationalism unusual. As Robert Merton has pointed out, "Group boundaries are not necessarily fixed but are dynamically changing in response to specifiable situational contexts."[45] The specifics of the Indian case, like any other, have their own logic, linked to Indian circumstances.

There is another way in which tribal and Indian identities come together. It appears that the growth and politicization of a supratribal consciousness in recent years may have contributed to a resurgence of interest in tribal cultures, particularly among the young. With the growing awareness of commonalities has come a new appreciation for those distinctive qualities that make of American Indians not one but many peoples. The San Francisco Kiowas, for example, used supratribal activities to assert traditional Kiowa values and ideas, revitalizing them in the process.[46]

While they need not be contradictory, however, tribal and supratribal identities are very different. Both are in some degree products of incorporative processes. Through those processes the tribe was institutionalized as a political entity. The contemporary form is a product of external forces. But for large numbers of Indians the substance of tribalism, the conceptual content of tribal identity, is neither political nor a consequence of incorporation, but classically ethnic and cultural: real or assumed ties of blood and common provenance, shared systems of meaning, a common participation in the sacred. The tribe is its own end; the actions taken in the name of the tribe, be they political, economic, or otherwise, ideally are acts of cultural self-preservation.

Supratribalism, too, is the product of outside forces. The ways in which Indians have been incorporated into dominant economic and political systems facilitated the emergence of a supratribal consciousness; they made it possible. They also, in a very real sense, made it necessary, by placing Indians in positions—geographical and political—in which supratribalism was the only basis on which action seemed likely to be effective.

In doing so they determined much of its content. Under the rubric "pan-Indianism," supratribalism, as already noted, has been perceived variously as a kind of cultural synthesis or leveling, a blending of peoples, a search for a new identity on the part of those who have been cut off from tribal roots and traditions. In some cases, certainly, these are valid descriptions, but they scarcely apply to all. The greater part of the supratribal phenomenon is not, at root, either cultural or psychological in nature, but political. It represents not a search for an identity, but a search for a basis on which to act together in pursuit of definable political and social ends.

The result, as others have suggested, is the emergence of a new ethnic group: "American Indians" or "Native Americans."[47] But the primary political significance of supratribalism lies elsewhere, less in the making of a new group than in the making of new political possibilities. The language of dominant-group categorization and control has become the language of subordinate-group self-concept and resistance. In the construction of an "Indian" identity, Indians have enlarged their own political capacities. A supratribal consciousness represents both resource and disposition: a basis on which to mobilize diverse peoples and a tendency to view oneself and the world in particular terms, to interpret issues once viewed as local, personal, or tribal as fundamentally Indian and to act accordingly. The former enlarges the scope of political participation; the latter shapes the resultant action.

Yet both of these identities are more than the result of external circumstance alone. Group formation is a complex process, a transformation of perception and behavior that builds on the inherited ideas of the past even as it responds to present circumstances and emergent interests. Contemporary tribalism is a composite made of aboriginal conceptions, the imposed definitions and requirements of non-Indians, particularly the state, and the changing interests of particular Indian nations faced with new economic, political, and social situations. Supratribalism, too, while it lacks the aboriginal component, has come into being through an interaction of Indian and non-Indian perceptions, interests, and experience. Groups are formed in encounters between groups, in the struggle between conflicting interests and interpretations.

But some critical differences remain. It seems unlikely that supratribalism can ever be as profoundly powerful a force as the tribe. More completely the product of Indian-White interaction, it lacks the essential structures of kinship and belief—blood and the sacred—that give to many Indian tribal identities their resonant durability. In most cases it is a political, as opposed to cultural, identity that is rooted in political circumstance, not in received systems of practice and interpretation.[48] It is a product of the incorporative process; tribalism, fundamentally, is a survivor of it. And while tribalism may be an end in itself, supratribalism is an end in itself only for those who have nothing else. For the rest it is a means toward other ends, toward the survival not of "American Indians," but of Indian nations. It is an arena of identity and action within which other struggles are waged.

Certain factors mitigate the organizational and political impact of supratribalism. Intertribal enmities, many of them centuries old, yet survive. One study of Indian boarding school students in the Southwest found that "for each of the five major tribes [Apache, Hopi, Navajo, Papago, Pima] some other tribal group is regarded with greater antipathy than whites." Guillemin suggests that a dislike for other Indian groups, particularly the Iroquois, is a factor in Micmac resistance to "pan-Indianism," while Fiske argues that the Navajo tendency to refrain from participation in supratribal organizations arises in part from Navajo beliefs regarding other Indians.[49]

Newer divisions are likely to arise from conflicting sets of interests and the realities of a highly competitive political arena. An abundance of tribes and organizations compete for a scarcity of funding and other resources, and their interests are not necessarily the same. Divisions in socioeconomic status have begun to appear. Some tribes are relatively rich; others have very little. Nor are the divisions all tribally defined. A sizeable professional class has emerged in recent years among Native Americans, largely the result of improved educational opportunities, greater employment of Indians in the BIA and the Indian Health Service, and the expansion of tribal bureaucracies. One study of Indians in Phoenix comments that the distance between such professionals and the destitute "inner-city" Indian population is both economic and social; they seldom communicate and their interests are very different.[50] How widespread these cleavages are is difficult to say, but the gradual integration of Indians into the class structure of the larger society will give them increased salience, which could be crippling to Indian political action, especially in urban areas, where they are less easily overcome by the potentially unifying embrace of the tribe.

There is also a division between urban and reservation worlds. It is easy to overstate, yet despite tribal links and the systemic and bidirectional character of Indian migration, such a division is evident, historically as well as now, especially between reservation groups and more permanently settled urban Indians. Its roots lie in the struggle for control of reservation affairs and for shares in the benefits of tribal membership: land claims settlements, mineral royalties, development, and the like. As early as 1928 the Meriam Report found evidence of concern among city Indians that they might be excluded from the tribal estate. Such concerns continue. The recent rise in off-reservation populations has led some tribes to try to restrict voting and membership privileges for off-reservation members so as to keep control of the decision-making process in reservation hands.[51] Growth in urban numbers has led as well to divisions over federal services, with urban Indians demanding the same services available to reservation residents, and reservation groups fearing that such an extension will mean cutbacks in services they already receive.

Political activism has exacerbated the problem. The tactics and perceived arrogance of some urban-based Indian organizations on occasion have alienated reservation support. There is a distrust also, especially among older reservation Indians, of those who seem to have moved so far from the cultural fabric of the tribe.

At the same time, a number of urban-based organizations have actively sought reservation support. And there are convergences of interest as well. In the battle over treaty rights, for example, long the preoccupation of the reservation population, Indians from many backgrounds have found common cause.[52]

Finally, supratribal identity, like tribal identity, has many faces. For some Native Americans, to be Indian is all they have; for others, it is only one of the many things they are. Different groups have embraced Indianness in different ways and to varying degrees. Some surely are motivated by its economic advantages—on occasion there are some—while others find in it an essential basis for political action or a source of social support. The roots of an Indian identity may lie in the original misperceptions of non-Indians, but it does more than mirror the White illusion. It is today as much an Indian as a White creation and thus embraces both the unitary conception originally derived from the Europeans and the multiple realities of Indians themselves.

These divisions are obstacles not to the growth of supratribalism, but to its effectiveness as a political instrument. A supratribal consciousness provides a potent new basis for political action, and its emergence may be the most significant political development in Indian affairs in this century. Both its achievement—not yet secure—and its ongoing task lie in the balancing of the universal and the unique: the ability of many peoples to act as one. It is a delicate balance, but already it has altered the shape of Indian-White relations.

Chapter 9

Who Wants What?

A favorite—if occasionally rhetorical—question on the part of legislators and administrators dealing with Native American issues is an often plaintive "What do the Indians *want?*" The question reveals not only frustration but also the obstinate view that Indians are a largely undifferentiated population with a single set of shared interests. This view conforms to recent American political culture, which tends to assume the primacy of ethnic or racial boundaries: if you are Black, your interests must be such-and-such; if you are Jewish, they must be this or that. Yet despite the consolidational processes traced in preceding chapters, despite nearly four centuries of Indian-White interaction, the Native American population remains extraordinarily diverse. The nature of that diversity has changed, but it continues to have concrete consequences for Indian politics.

The U.S. Census counted 1.4 million American Indians, Aleuts, and Eskimos in 1980. Among them are nearly three hundred tribes, bands, pueblos, and other communities in the forty-eight contiguous states, and 200 or so more in Alaska, each with a distinctive history, and many still carriers of distinctive cultures. While Native Americans are concentrated in four states—California, Oklahoma, Arizona, New Mexico—they live throughout the country, from rural communities in Maine to the Florida Everglades, from towns in western New York to the northern plains. The Census considers more than half of them urban residents, and there are more Indians in Los Angeles County than on any reservation except the Navajo. A number of urban Indians are white-collar workers, while most reservation Indians—those with jobs—are blue collar. Some work in assembly plants in reservation industrial parks; others fish the rivers of the Pacific Northwest. Some labor on New York City or Chicago construction sites; others mine uranium in New Mexico. A huge percentage are unemployed.

The reservations themselves are diverse. They range from the vast and remote Navajo Reservation, spread across southwestern deserts, to tiny California rancherias or the Tonawanda Reservation near Buffalo, New York. Some are resource rich; others have little, if anything, to sell.

The Indian world is organizationally dense. In 1974, at the height of the activist movement, the Congressional Research Service counted more than one hundred intertribal or supratribal Indian organizations, from the American Indian Movement to the Association of American Indian Physicians, from the Native American Women's Action Council to the Small Tribes of Western Washington.[1] Add tribal organizations and the number quadruples.

Reservations, communities, locations, socioeconomic divisions, organizations, and so on—each identifies a boundary. Some are imposed from outside, fitting Indians into categories and classifications chosen and used by others to fit their own needs and logic; some are generated by Indians themselves. Each offers evidence of differentiation, or a potential basis of it, and suggests as well a potentially distinct set of interests. Their salience and significance vary, but taken together they draw a complex map of constituencies and agendas, a graphic demonstration that to speak of what "the Indians" want reflects as monocular a vision as did the early and persistent tendency to view in uniform terms the hundreds of diverse peoples who originally inhabited North America. The lesson, as Sol Tax has pointed out, "is an old one. There are no 'Indians,' but rather different communities of Indians."[2]

What has changed over time is not so much the extent as the pattern of that diversity. The European newcomers to North America encountered a vast range of peoples. As noted in preceding chapters, some of the differences among those peoples eventually disappeared; a leveling occurred, imposed by the incorporative process. An increasingly common history of Indian-White interaction, combined with transformative policies uniformly applied, produced commonalities in Indian adaptations and response. But these same processes also introduced new bases of division, leading to new constituencies and political agendas that often cut across tribal boundaries.[3] In the early years these often involved simply disagreements over how to respond to invasion: for example, between those who wished to fight and those who wished to negotiate, or between those who were willing to cooperate with early reservation agents and those who refused. As the twentieth century unfolded, quite different patterns appeared. With the development of formally constituted tribal governments, for example, a whole new constituency emerged: Indian bureaucrats, guardians not only of tribal interests, but of the fledgling governments themselves. As these governments gained in power and resources, they became objects of competition among subtribal constituencies that previously had had little to fight over. Other changes had similar results, producing Indian educators, industrial workers, city dwellers, college students, cattle ranchers, and so on, each a carrier of distinct interests in addition to those shared with their various tribespeople or with all Indians. The Indian world remained complex, but the nature of the complexity had changed.

At the same time, simply replacing the fiction of a single Indian community with the fact of multiple constituencies and groups is not enough. What is needed is a way of organizing those groups and their goals that indicates which ones are particularly significant and why. The importance of this arises from the presence of complexity itself: Indians don't always agree on what they want, and this in turn has political consequences. More generically, it is important because political action is interested action. People analyze their world and their needs and act according to their perceptions of both. For the analyst of Indian politics, then, the appropriate focus becomes Indian political agendas—who wants what?—and their implications for Indian-White relations.

CLASSIFYING INDIAN GOALS

There are a number of ways to classify Indian constituencies and their objectives, but the present concern with political implications gives particular significance to two issues. First, how and to what degree are Indian goals opposed to the prevailing structures of Indian-White relations? Second, what is the orientation of Indian goals toward the institutions and values of the larger society?

Regarding the first of these, some degree of opposition may be assumed to be inherent in those relations owing to their stratified character. Dominance and subordination tend to yield their own, fundamentally opposed interests. Dominant groups try to protect their positions; subordinate groups try to alter theirs.[4] This assumption aside, however, conflict over the structure of Indian-White relations has been chronic in those relations and remains so today. The appropriate question has to do with the nature of Indian opposition. What sort of change and how much change do Indians want in the structure of Indian-White relations, that is, in the particular set of relationships linking Indian groups to the larger society?

The second question has to do not only with Indian goals, but also with dominant-group goals for Indians. R. A. Schermerhorn has drawn attention to the importance in stratified intergroup relations of agreement and discrepancy between the goals dominant and subordinate groups each support *for subordinate groups*. The conclusion he draws is obvious but important: where there is agreement between such goals for subordinates (for example, both agree that the objective is some form of integration or some form of separation), conflict in intergroup relations will be low; where there is disagreement, conflict will be high.[5]

Dominant-group goals for Indians generally have included the assimilation of Native Americans into U.S. society-at-large. Pursuit of this goal traditionally focused on individual assimilation through the breakup of Indian group structures and communities and the eradication of indigenous

cultural practice. Since the 1930s, excepting the termination years, assimilation has been pursued more on a group, as opposed to individual, basis,
through the reproduction of dominant-group institutions and values—in particular, elected representative government, market-oriented economic organization, corporate business structures—within Indian communities. The
relevant question, then, has to do with Indian orientations toward those
institutions and the values embodied within them or, in other words, with
the degree to which Indians agree with non-Indian goals for Native American peoples.

Indian positions on these issues vary. Most Indians have some objec-
tion to the current organization of Indian-White relations. Some, for example, think tribal governments lack power; some think the Bureau of Indian Affairs controls Indian resources for its own ends; some think the
Department of the Interior pays too little attention to Indian grievances.
Nearly all, in one way or another, object to the presence of non-Indian
controls—of whatever kind—over Indian communities and decisions.

But not all those who find fault with the organization of Indian-White
relations also reject the institutions and values of the larger society. Some
see those institutions and values as appropriate for their own communities
even as they object to the way power is distributed or organized within
them. In other words, despite their objections to the distribution of
power, they accept the patterns of political and economic activity that
prevail in non-Indian society as suitable models for Indian society. Others
do not. They reject both the present organizational structure of Indian-
White relations and the ways of life of non-Indian society, believing that
its culture and institutions are inappropriate models for Indian communities. Many fall somewhere in between.

These two questions can be rephrased in terms of two dichotomous distinctions that then can be used to classify Indian goals. The first distinction is between reformative and transformative goals. Reformative goals
for the most part forgo fundamental change in the structure of Indian-
White relations in favor of a redistribution of services, resources, or rewards within that structure, as, for example, through the appointment of
Indians to positions of authority in the Indian Bureau or Interior Department, the expansion of reservation social services, or the maximization of
economic returns to Indians from natural resource development. Transformative goals, on the other hand, envision not simply a redistribution of
rewards within the prevailing structure of Indian-White relations, but also
a fundamental reordering of those relations, as, for example, through the
reopening of treaty negotiations between the United States and the Indian nations or ending the plenary power of Congress in Indian affairs.
Reformative goals seek to improve Indian welfare within the existing
structure of Indian-White relations; transformative goals seek to transform
the structure itself.

The second distinction is between integrative and segregative goals. Integrative goals, while advocating change of some sort—reformative or

transformative—in Indian-White relations, for the most part accept the appropriateness in the Indian setting of Euro-American economic and political institutions and, in general, the appropriateness of the dominant culture. In effect, they promote those institutions as means of maximizing Indian welfare. Of course the institutions themselves may be modified to account for peculiarities in the Indian case, as happened in the creation of constitutional tribal governments; likewise, the dominant culture may be neither wholly accepted nor wholly reproduced. In general, however, those institutions and, to a large extent, the culture they carry are accepted as models on which the institutional shape of Indian societies can be based. Such goals are integrative in that they endorse, in effect, the integration of Indians into the dominant institutional patterns and culture, either as individuals or as groups.

Segregative goals, on the other hand, dispute the appropriateness for Indian communities of dominant-group economic and political institutions and culture, viewing them as unresponsive to Indian needs, inimical to Indian interests, or threatening to the survival of culturally distinct Indian communities. They are segregative in that they advocate, in effect, a separation of Indian communities from the institutions of the larger society and the values they represent and the preservation or adoption of distinct institutional patterns specifically tailored to distinctive Indian needs, concerns, and historical experience. Segregative goals are fundamentally anti-assimilationist and antiacculturational.[6]

While phrased as dichotomies, these distinctions are matters of degree. Indian goals may be more or less opposed to the structure of Indian-White relations; moreover, the point at which these goals change from reformation to transformation is not always easy to find. Much the same can be said of the integrative-segregative distinction; not only do goals vary in the degree of their acceptance or rejection of dominant institutions, but the point at which modifications in those institutions become so extensive that they signify rejection instead of acceptance is likewise difficult to locate. In other words, the goals of Indian groups vary along continua defined by these two distinctions, which together offer a guide to the nature and degree of Indian opposition to the status quo. Combined in a two-by-two table, they yield four tongue-twisting categories of goals: reformative-integrative, transformative-integrative, reformative-segregative, and transformative-segregative (Figure 3).

The first of these four combinations, represented by cell A, indicates some modest opposition to the status quo and relatively little intergroup goal conflict. The last combination, represented by cell D, indicates substantial opposition to the status quo and substantial intergroup goal conflict. Cell B indicates substantial opposition to the organization of Indian-White relations but a positive orientation toward dominant-group institutions and culture, while cell C indicates considerably less opposition to the organization of Indian-White relations but a negative orientation toward dominant-group institutions and culture. This last—reformative-segre-

Orientation to organization
of Indian-White relations

		Reformative	Transformative
Orientation to institutions of larger society	Integrative	A	B
	Segregative	C	D

Figure 3. Indian Political Goals

gative goals—is probably a contradiction in terms and, therefore, a null set. To seek only moderate change in the present organization of relations is to accept, to some degree at least, the institutions of the larger society; they are manifest in that organization. One could imagine reformative-segregative goals if, for example, the structure of Indian-White relations were built solely on formal treaty relationships between substantially independent nations. In that case Indian groups could pursue segregative goals without challenging the organization itself. But those relations cannot be reduced to such terms.

Assuming that Indian groups act in support of their goals, these four cells—three if C is assumed to be irrelevant—represent both different degrees of goal conflict and different degrees of conflict in intergroup relations generally. Conflict is likely to be least between the larger society and those groups acting on goals in cell A, somewhat greater between that society and groups acting on goals in cell B, and greatest between that society and groups acting on goals in cell D.

Examples of reformative-integrative goals include those listed above under reformative goals: the appointment of Indians to the Indian Bureau or other posts in Indian affairs, expansion of reservation social services, and the maximization of economic returns from resource development. They would also include increasing jobs on or near the reservations by attracting non-Indian industry to the reservation setting, campaigns to put Indians into state or local governments, and efforts to obtain financial settlements in land claims cases. These objectives do not seriously challenge the organization of Indian-White relations, but instead seek to modify it in relatively unambitious ways or to maximize Indian welfare within it, all in the context of full participation in dominant-group economic and political institutions.[7]

Examples of transformative-integrative goals include Indian efforts to enlarge the exclusive powers of tribal governments and the tribal role in policy making, moves to place control of Indian economic resources fully in Indian hands, and efforts to extend federal Indian programs to urban Indians. Efforts to expand tribal self-government are transformative in that they seek a reorganization of Indian-White relations, replacing federal controls and influence with Indian. They are integrative in that this expansion does not reject or replace existing institutions, but expands Indian power within them. Indeed, most such efforts in effect seek the further penetration of Indian communities by those institutions. That is, they seek expanded control of tribal or reservation affairs by constitutional tribal governments modeled after the political institutions of the larger society.

The distinction between reformative and transformative goals is especially apparent in the area of economic development. Development agendas that seek simply to increase royalties or jobs are essentially reformative: rewards are increased, but the control structure and the institutional mechanisms remain largely unchanged. Ending federal veto power over Indian uses of their economic resources, on the other hand, is a transformative goal: it alters the structure itself, replacing federal control with Indian.

Urban Indians often have pursued transformative-integrative goals (change the organization; accept the institutions), in particular whenever they have sought federal services now reserved to the reservation population. The effort is transformative in that it attempts to reorganize Indian-White relations in ways that will better accommodate nonreservation and nontribal communities. It is integrative insofar as much of what they seek, as indicated by their concerns with social services, jobs, and discrimination, involves their own more complete integration as individuals into dominant economic and social arrangements.

Another example of transformative-integrative goals is Indian resistance to termination in the 1950s and early 1960s. Federal Indian policy clearly anticipated and put into motion a major change in the organization of Indian-White relations, specifically promoting the dismantling of the reservation system, the end of tribalism, and the individual assimilation of Indians into American society. In the context of policy at the time, tribal resistance to termination was transformative, even though it sought to preserve the federal-tribal relationship Congress was trying to bring to an end: it opposed the policy orientation. At the same time it was also integrative in that it favored—or at least did not oppose—dominant institutional models. The conflict, in other words, was over the organization of Indian-White relations, but the relevance of dominant-group institutions in Indian societies was not at issue.

Examples of transformative-segregative goals (change the organization and reject the institutions) include, among other things, opposition to the commercialization of reservation economies and to the tendency to model them after the economy of the larger society; efforts to replace present systems of tribal government with more traditional modes of collective decision making; to increase the autonomy of subtribal reservation communities; to expand tribal sovereignty, conceived not simply as political autonomy but also as the right and capacity of a people to maintain a distinct cultural existence; and to resurrect treaty making between Indian nations and the United States in an effort to reestablish those nations as, in effect, nation-states, dependent economically on the United States but

politically independent of it.[8] All of these envision fundamental change in
the organization of Indian-White relations and reject the political and economic institutions of the larger society, anticipating their replacement with
newly developed ones or with institutions derived more directly from the
Indian past.

All of the goals offered as examples here have appeared on the Indian
political agenda at one time or another in the last two decades; many have
been around much longer, while some are relative newcomers to the political scene. Obviously, then, the objectives of Indian political action have
been, and remain, various.

Their implications for political action vary as well. Some carry a greater
potential for conflict than others, and the nature of the conflict itself varies
according to the goals being pursued. Those who wish to transform the
entire system of Indian-White relations are not only more likely to be in
conflict with that system, but are likely to act in ways very different from
those who wish simply to modify some policy within it.

And this raises a corollary point. Goals do not exist in any meaningful
sense apart from the people who support them. A diversity of goals suggests a diversity of constituencies. It is not possible here to provide an exhaustive catalog of these Indian constituencies or communities of shared
interests, their various goals, and the changes in each over the years. What
is possible, however, is to extract from the overall pattern of change those
trends that have been most significant for Indian-White relations and
twentieth-century Indian political resurgence.

PATTERNS OF CHANGE

Two such trends have been particularly important: the accelerated entry
into politics of subtribal and supratribal constituencies and the growing
salience of transformative goals.

Three broad levels of Indian group organization might be used to classify Indian constituencies: tribal, subtribal, and supratribal. One advantage
of this set of categories is that it distinguishes among constituencies according to the degree to which they are directly represented in the institutionalized, organizational structure of Indian-White relations, a distinction that
itself has implications for political action. Those relations are organized formally on a tribal basis. That is, the formal relationship between the federal
government and Indian groups is a relationship between that government
and organized political bodies called tribes. Tribal constituencies, then, are
directly represented in that structure. Subtribal constituencies are nomi-
nally represented, but indirectly through the representational mediation of
tribal governments. Supratribal constituencies, on the other hand, have no
official representation in the formal institutional organization of Indian-
White relations.[9]

One of the striking aspects of the twentieth century is the greatly increased salience of the latter two categories of constituencies, sub- and supratribal. This is the result of major changes in Indian policy.

Since the 1930s, when the Indian New Deal recognized and encouraged constitutional tribal governments, the federal government has assumed that these governments would represent, after the fashion of the Euro-American models on which they are based, the interests of their members, superseding in this regard all other organizations. Thus tribal governments and tribal constituencies became, for practical purposes, synonymous. When the federal government asks what the Indians want, it is the goals of tribal governments they usually have in mind.

Those goals range widely, from obtaining particular services or infrastructural components for reservation populations—irrigation projects, schools, roads—to assuring high prices for mineral resources, from protecting tribal water rights to achieving major changes in federal Indian policy. In general, however, the goals of tribal constituencies, thus defined, are integrative. Their political concerns typically have more to do with the organization of Indian-White relations or with the distribution of wealth and power within those relations than with the appropriateness in Indian communities of dominant-group institutions, which, after all, they in effect represent.

Nevertheless, the formalization of these governments and the significance given them by federal policy heightened and gave shape to internal conflict. Suddenly there were centers of power on Indian reservations other than the office of the BIA's reservation superintendent. As shown in Chapter 6, the governments introduced under the IRA were controversial and tended to solidify factional conflicts. Many subtribal groups whose interests have diverged from those of the tribal government, or which have opposed the structure of tribal government itself, either have bypassed those governments or have confronted them directly, taking a larger and more visible role in politics.

More significant, what had happened through the IRA was the opening of the door to the political arena. A host of subtribal constituencies—generated by the incorporative and tribalizing processes of the preceding century—walked in.

Opening the door, however, was only half the story. With nothing at stake, with nothing to struggle for, neither tribal governments nor any other Indian actors would have taken the trouble to appear on this newly accessible political stage. In fact, the stakes were growing. The Indian New Deal not only formalized certain political structures; it also reoriented Indian policy toward the maintenance of Indian communities. Maintenance meant money. New funds for economic development and community programs were soon forthcoming. While such funds and programs remained largely under the control of the BIA, tribal governments were in position to influence to some extent at least—local policy and implementation. For the first time in a long while, *Indian* agendas began to matter.

In subsequent decades the stakes continued to grow. In 1946, attempting partly to resolve jurisdictional issues in Indian litigation, partly to compensate Indian nations for past injustices, partly to simplify the claims process, Congress passed the Indian Claims Commission Act, which established a commission to pass judgment on Indian claims against the United States. These claims were of various kinds, but in practice the commission narrowed its focus and put most of its effort into land claims. Where these claims have been settled in the Indians' favor, the commission typically has awarded Indian nations financial compensation. Between 1946 and 1977 these awards totaled more than $650 million.[10] The uses made of these funds have required congressional or Interior Department approval; nonetheless, in some cases they have added substantially to the tribal pot.

Still greater sums followed. In the 1960s, as the failures of the termination policy became apparent, the federal government began to pay greater attention to reservation economic development, and tribal income from economic activities began to increase. With the discovery of mineral and other natural resources on some reservations, natural resource development, most of it through lease arrangements with non-Indian operators, became a major source of tribal income. In the late 1940s income to all Indian tribes from mineral sources averaged about $11 million a year; from the late 1950s to the early 1970s, about $48 million; from 1978 to 1982, partly as a result of improved royalty rates and joint ventures, the yearly average rose to over $130 million.[11]

Federal funds available to Indian nations also increased, especially after passage, in 1964, of the Economic Opportunity Act, designed "to mobilize the human and financial resources of the nation to combat poverty in the United States."[12] Native Americans were included among those groups to be assisted by Office of Economic Opportunity (OEO) programs, and by 1970 more than sixty Community Action Agencies had been established on Indian reservations. These became conduits for federal monies intended to both relieve reservation poverty and improve the capacities of Indian nations to pursue their own political agendas.[13]

These programs not only brought money onto the reservations; they also opened new political channels between Indian nations and the federal government, channels not tied to the BIA. Control of funds and channels became an issue for emergent Indian constituencies and organizations. Meaningful politics was becoming possible, and the heat of intragroup competition began to rise.

These developments coincided with the rapid growth of the urban Indian population and the major expansion of a supratribal political consciousness. The former meant that there was a substantial Indian constituency that was not served effectively by tribal governments; consequently, urban Indian organizations began to move into the political arena. The latter gave an assortment of Indian constituencies, including tribal and subtribal ones, an alternative and potentially powerful basis of organization and action. Organization on an Indian, as opposed to tribal, basis potentially increased numbers, political clout, and the chances of success. Supratribal Indian organizations proliferated.

As these constituencies became more involved in politics and as it appeared that political action might get results, the ambitions of the actors
rose. Not only the constituencies but the pattern of goals—at least of those
apparent in action—began to change. Transformative goals began more
frequently to appear.

Both categories—integrative and segregative—were involved. The increase
in action oriented to transformative-integrative goals came largely in two
areas. First, urban Indian activism, emerging in the 1960s, was devoted
largely to economic and social welfare goals and to gaining federal recognition of urban problems and concerns. These efforts were transformative
in that they sought a reordering of Indian-White relations to accommodate
urban Indian communities and their interests; they were integrative in that
they sought an enlarged place for urban Indians in the institutions of the
larger society.

Second, in the last few decades tribal governments have struggled to
reduce federal controls and increase their own control over tribal and reservation affairs. These governments have a stake in the institutions of the
larger society, which provided their own formative models and in which
they are substantially embedded, but they also want to increase their
autonomy. They tend naturally, then, toward transformative-integrative goals; for the most part their political efforts have favored dominant
economic and political institutions, but have sought to place those institutions under Indian control. This has been most apparent in the 1960s and
1970s, but there were signs of it earlier, not least in tribal resistance to
the termination policy. This resistance questioned not so much the integration of Indians into the larger institutional structure as the destruction
of community that accompanied it, and advocated integration on a group,
as opposed to individual, basis.

Transformative-integrative goals are apparent also in earlier Indian actions, such as the Pueblo fight against the Bursum Bill, which asserted unrecognized Pueblo rights within the prevailing institutional structure. Even
the Society of American Indians, with its intermittent opposition to the
BIA and the reservation system, might be viewed as pursuing transformative goals, albeit emphatically integrative ones. For the most part, however, early Indian goals, particularly in the 1930s and 1940s, were
reformative. This reflects in part the influence of the IRA, which itself transformed the structure of Indian-White relations and opened up new space
for Indian political activity within that structure. The early goals of the
NCAI, for example, were largely reformative-integrative in nature: establishing Indian voting rights in some states, opposing dam construction,
certain kinds of litigation, and so on. Nor have reformative-integrative
goals become less important in recent decades. Actions in favor of increasing funding for Indian programs, expanded social services and jobs
on reservations, county redistricting, educational changes, and the like
continue to occupy a good deal of Indian political energy.

But the fact remains that since the 1950s Indians increasingly have been challenging the organization of Indian-White relations, its neglect of certain Indian concerns, and its concentration of decision-making power and administrative control in non-Indian hands. Indian goals, in other words, as represented in action, have become increasingly transformative over time.

At the same time, not all of the challenge to the organization of Indian-White relations has been so accommodating to the institutions of the larger society. Transformative-*segregative* goals—which challenge not only the organization of Indian-White relations but the institutions and values of the larger society—also have become more salient. Certain subtribal groups, particularly traditionalist ones, have pursued such goals in one way or another since before the end of military conflict, resisting through adherence to their own ways of life the encroachments of *both* the administrative apparatus of Indian affairs *and* the institutional structures and dominant cultural patterns of American society. Such goals are apparent early in Indian political resurgence in resistance to BIA stock-control programs in the 1930s, and in the early defense of peyotism. In recent years the involvement of traditionalist groups in political activity has grown as some of them have resisted the growing power of tribal governments and the increased integration of tribal communities into dominant institutional structures via expanded economic development and enlarged tribal bureaucracies.

Their concerns have been echoed by some supratribal organizations. While many early supratribal goals were largely reformative-integrative, over time they became increasingly transformative, as did those of tribal governments, especially during the termination years. In the 1960s, however, a number of supratribal groups and organizations appeared with essentially segregative goals, rejecting much of the institutions and culture of the larger society and reflecting growing Indian concern with the survival of indigenous culture and with the social impacts of development. Examples of such organizations include the American Indian Movement, the National Indian Youth Council, Survival of American Indians Association, and the American Indian Environmental Council.

The obvious question is why this growth, first in transformative goals and slightly later in more specifically segregative ones, occurs when it does. The increase seems in part to represent not so much a change in goals as the heightened political visibility of the constituencies that share them: only recently have groups with hostile agendas, such as more traditional groups, been mobilized into politics. But the goals themselves also appear to have changed over time, and certain developments in Indian policy, within Indian societies, and in the society at large all seem to have played a part.

In Indian policy the critical point may have been the sobering effects of termination, the realization that there was a fundamental opposition between federal policy and the survival of Indian nations.[14] While the conflict between the two long preceded termination, it was made explicit in the 1950s, close on the heels of the supportive policies of the Indian New Deal. It reinforced in most Indian communities a profound suspicion of federal motives and stimulated new demands for tribal control of Indian affairs and for lasting guarantees of tribal sovereignty. Only under such conditions could indigenous communities survive as geographical, political, and cultural units.

The critical development within Indian societies was the emergence, in the aftermath of World War II, of a host of new Indian political actors, in particular veterans, students, and urban Indians. All of these brought, from their own perspectives, new and highly critical viewpoints to Indian affairs. Most were a generation or more removed from those Indians who formed tribal governments under the IRA, and thus had little sense of the major change that had occurred in the 1930s. They were more likely to focus their attention on the continuing subjection of their peoples and were more likely as well to view the prevailing organization of Indian-White relations as restrictive and to attempt to move outside it. For them what was faulty in Indian-White relations included much of established Indian leadership; the National Indian Youth Council, for example, was founded in 1961 partly out of dissatisfaction with Indian leaders who were reluctant to confront major issues in Indian affairs.

Finally, events and ideas current in the larger society during the last few decades clearly had an effect on Indian thinking and political action. In the 1960s and 1970s a host of groups, from Blacks to women, from university students to gays, pursued new or unattended rights within American society, challenged the institutional structures of American life, or asserted the distinctiveness and value of identities and cultures that lay outside the perceived American mainstream. Coincidentally, these tumultuous years were the period when unprecedented numbers of Indians were coming into intimate, sustained contact with the larger society for the first time. They could hardly miss the examples of action being set by others. Urbanization also seems to have made many Indians more acutely aware of the differences between their own, tribal societies and the rest of the United States. What is taken for granted in reservation life is made conspicuous by its absence in the city, and may thereby elicit a stronger defense.[15]

CONFLICT WITHOUT, CONFLICT WITHIN

These patterns of change are indicative of growing—or at least more apparent—conflict in Indian-White relations, especially in the crucial years from the early 1960s to the late 1970s. The emergence of increasingly transformative goals, and especially of transformative-segregative ones, marks growing Indian resistance to the status quo and more apparent conflict between Indian goals and those of the larger society. They suggest that the federal Indian affairs apparatus has failed to serve important Indian needs; the segregative ones in particular suggest that those needs *cannot* be met within the institutional structures of American society. They argue that the interests of Indians and those of the dominant society are not necessarily the same and that Indians must both articulate their own interests and find new ways to serve them. Where transformative-integrative goals blame Indian problems on the political patterns of Indian-White relations, and often specifically on the federal government, segregative goals see the institutions and values of the larger society more generally at fault. One set of goals represents an agenda that is essentially political; the other, an agenda that is both political and cultural.

That this growth means that more individual Indians are taking such positions is by no means clear. It indicates simply that in the last few decades, and in particular since the early 1960s, such positions have been mobilized into politics to a greater degree than at any time since the nineteenth-century Indian wars.

The new Indian politics, however, is not simply about Indian-White relations and indigenous survivals. As this whole discussion suggests, it is also an *intra*group politics. It is made so not least by federal policy, which assumes—even insists—that there is a generalized Indian constituency with a generalized interest that can best be served by a generalized Indian policy, and thus forces Indian groups to compete for power and for the legitimacy in federal eyes that will allow them to define that constituency and articulate that interest. The stakes are high and the competition occasionally has been bitter.

But it is made so also by genuine differences among Indian groups and goals, differences that cut both within and across the boundaries of the tribe. The resultant conflicts are often prosaic enough: who gets the jobs, the money, the land, the power.[16] But at its most profound level, intragroup conflict involves the shape of Indian societies themselves, the persistent tension between those who favor integration—on whatever basis—into the institutional structures of the larger society and those who oppose it.

To propose such a simple dichotomy is seemingly to contradict the thrust of this and preceding chapters. Clearly the world of Indian politics is more complex than this. Yet it appears that in broad political terms the Native American population is increasingly divided between those with essentially integrative goals and those with essentially segregative ones. Within each category there are major differences in political agendas and styles, and the distinction itself is a simplification; but the cleavage remains.

The former group might be called "realists"; the latter, "radicals."[17] Both are engaged in the defense of peoplehood. Both are highly critical of the prevailing organization of Indian affairs. Both reject non-Indian controls over Indian lives. In other words, both have fundamentally transformative agendas in mind. But "realists" look at the larger society as the arena in which they must live and work and to the institutions of that society for political power and economic prosperity. They see no necessary conflict between being Indian or tribal and being successful within those institutions. Indeed, they see the survival of Native American communities as dependent on the skill with which Indians can exploit the opportunities offered by the larger society, through the channels that society has constructed. Their politics are in essence distributional, an Indian version of the ethnic politics of the 1960s and after, a search for ways of enhancing Indian power and welfare within a broadly pluralistic system.

"Radicals," on the other hand, to varying degrees reject that society as a meaningful context for their own lives and look to the traditions of Native American societies for models of social life and action. For some of them those traditions—transformed by time as they may be—define their daily existence; their program is one of collective cultural preservation. For others the program is one of reconstruction, an attempt to find new ways of living within indigenous practice and belief. "Radicals" tend to see an inherent and irreconcilable conflict between tribalism and Euro-American patterns of life and thought; many would insulate the one from the other in order to preserve what seems to them to be truly Indian and the fundamental strength of their communities.

It should be emphasized that these are categories, as much of goals as of actors, and not, in themselves, united constituencies or groups. They are political poles around which much of Indian politics—as intragroup politics—moves. But in this, at least, the new Indian politics is actually rather old, for the positions themselves have been around a long time, wearing other names. The "realists" of the past were those who understood the relentless character of the Euro-American advance and tried to work with it instead of against it, who took up the pen at treaty negotiations and struggled to make the best of a losing situation, who embraced the IRA governments and the new political pathways they introduced.

"Radicals" and "realists," "conservatives" and "progressives," "full-bloods" and "mixed-bloods"—the terms and historical contexts have changed, but much of the internal conflict they signify has remained stubbornly the same. What makes contemporary Indian politics new is the growing ability of Indian actors to pursue these often divergent ends within a newly opened political arena.

Chapter 10

Old Wars, New Weapons

"Indians always have been politically savvy," Vine Deloria, Jr., remarked in 1978. "What's changed is their resources."[1]

He was talking about political resources: group assets that can be invested in political action and thereby enhance the political capacity of the group.[2] At the start of the twentieth century, the Indian resource situation was grim indeed. Poor, few in number, organizationally crippled, with little in the way of bargaining chips, most Native Americans lacked the resources necessary to sustain political activity within the dominant society. Since the Indian New Deal, however, and particularly in the last few decades, there has been a marked increase in Indian political resources and, therefore, in Indian capacities for political action.

A resource is political insofar as it enhances the capacity of the group to take political action. This casts the net wide; all kinds of things have such potential one way or another, though some are more obviously political than others. Numbers, for example, have clear political potential, especially where votes or disruption are important. Education, on the other hand, is less obviously a political resource, but in certain circumstances it may enhance group political capacities.

As a general rule, the greater the extent and variety of resources, the greater the capacity of the group. But not all resources are equally valuable, and their relative value depends on a variety of factors. The nature of the political system clearly makes a difference. Numbers, for example, tend to be more useful in a democracy than in a dictatorship, although very large numbers may prevail in the latter case. Legal skills are more important in a system with an independent and powerful judiciary than in one without. In other words, the opportunity structure—the external factors which make some actions more possible or desirable—places a premium on certain kinds of resources.

Some generic qualities of resources also may be important, including

convertibility, reusability, and applicability. First, while all political resources contribute, by definition, to political capacity, some also are convertible into other resources. Numbers, for example, may have political
significance as votes or protest participants, but they cannot be easily converted into education or legal skills. Money, on the other hand, can be
converted into both. Second, some resources, such as money, are used up
in conversion to other resources or in action; others, such as leadership or
organization, can be used many times. Finally, some resources are inherently limited in application. Legal skills, for example, are useful in
litigation, but not in much else. Others, such as organization, have far
wider applicability, facilitating a broad range of actions. Other things being more or less equal, resources that are more convertible, reusable, or
broadly applicable are more valuable than those that are less so.[3] For this
reason, to pick one example, organization is a more potent political resource than money.

A more useful classification of resources can be made by function. *Direct resources* are those resources or assets that bear directly upon the
political system or on relations between actors within it. Some examples
include numbers (as mobilized in the electoral process, for example, or
a demonstration), legal skills, outside support, guns, and money. These
are group assets that can be used directly in the promotion of group interests, the enhancement of group position in the political system, or to
influence directly other actors within that system. They are in effect the
media through which action occurs: people vote, litigate, shoot each other,
disrupt the economy, and so forth.

Mobilizational resources are functionally distinct from direct resources.
Mobilization is the process of putting direct resources to work, bringing
them to bear on the political system or on other actors. Mobilizational resources, then, are those that facilitate this process. Among the important
ones are organization, social cohesion, leadership, and, again, money.

Some resources may appear in both sets. Money, for example, not only
facilitates action, but can be used directly, as in the purchase of political
concessions. Thus the distinction between the two may not be inherent
in the resources themselves, but is functional. They are what they do.

These sets of resources differ in other ways as well. Mobilizational resources, essentially by definition, tend to be higher in such things as reusability, convertibility, and applicability. They serve more ends. More
important, their value is far less affected by contextual variables than is
the value of direct resources. In other words, the kinds of direct resources
that are likely to be valuable vary among situations, depending on the
nature of the political system, the characteristics and goals of the groups
involved, and the possibilities of change. Indian efforts to increase their
control of natural resource development on reservation lands are more
likely to be advanced through legal skills or money than by numbers,
while a national struggle over treaty rights may be more favorably affected by alliance with non-Indians than by money or legal skills.

In all these cases, however, mobilizational resources remain essential. While the value of particular direct resources varies from situation to situation, the value of mobilizational resources tends to be constant. Regardless of the action to be taken, in most cases the mobilization of direct resources requires the same group assets: organization, leadership, and so on. Mobilizational resources can be translated independently, for the most part, into political capacity, while the translation of direct resources must consider the relative value of different resources in different situations and for different ends.

In the last five decades the political resource endowments of Native American groups—within both categories—have significantly changed.

DIRECT RESOURCES

Among direct resources, the major change has been in bargaining resources, outside alliance, and numbers. Unfortunately, change in the last of these has had only minor effects on Indian political capacities.

The Relative Insignificance of Numbers

As with other direct resources, the importance of numbers is contextually determined. More is certainly better than less, but how much more and how much better become apparent only in particular cases. Numbers are clearly an advantage, for example, in elections, boycotts, or marches; they are less so in litigation. Consequently, where electoral politics are a vehicle of political expression and redress, numbers are important to the enfranchised. If a group can't vote, the value of numbers declines. Likewise, where marches are possible, numbers have an impact. Where marchers typically are shot, numbers may not matter so much—at least not until, as in Iran in the last days of the shah, the numbers overwhelm the guns.

The role a group plays in the economy of the society also affects the significance of numbers, as of most political resources. Those in marginal positions wield little power; an equal number in a critical position have political clout.

Native American numbers have increased dramatically since the turn of the century, but they remain low. Indians are numerous in proportion to non-Indians only on reservations and even there they are sometimes outnumbered. Until recently they have lacked any economic or political position that would give them structural power; on or off the reservations, they are rarely concentrated in any critical sector of the nation's economy and dominate few markets other than local ones. Geographically dispersed, they virtually disappear in vast rural areas or densely populated cities. In short, numbers are not a significant political resource for most Native American groups.

This is true even in terms of the classic political weapon of the citizenry in a democracy: the vote. The franchise, like U.S. citizenship itself, came to Indians in stages. Some acquired it through allotment, some through military service or congressional dispensation, others by abandoning tribal life for individual integration into the American mainstream. It was not until 1924 that the Indian Citizenship Act made all Indians born in the United States citizens of the country, a status some Indians, then and now, have protested as imposed against their will. While some states have continued to deny Indians the franchise, by the 1960s the vote was secure for the majority of the Indian population.[4]

On the other hand, they made little use of it. The data are scanty but suggestive. The House Committee on Interior and Insular Affairs reported in 1956 that few Indians were registered to vote, and fewer voted. In Arizona's Second District only 3,200 of 24,000 voting-age Indians were registered. In Mississippi's Fifth District, only 23 out of 1,300 Choctaws were registered, while among 725 voting-age Indians on the Fort Berthold Reservation in North Dakota there were no registered voters at all. The record was better on some reservations—two-thirds of Montana's voting-age Blackfeet were registered—but overall the figures were dismal.[5]

In the 1964 presidential election, less than 30 percent of the voting-age Indian population in Arizona's Apache County turned out to vote. In the 1968 elections that county and Navajo County, each with substantial Indian populations, had registration rates well under the average for Arizona, which had the lowest rate of any state outside the South.[6]

There is some evidence that this may be changing. In one of the few systematic studies of Indian political behavior, the National Indian Youth Council found in 1982 that some 60 percent of a sample of Navajo and Pueblo adults in northwestern New Mexico were registered to vote in non-tribal elections. Political participation was positively correlated with both employment and level of education.[7] But most evidence still suggests that Indian political participation is well below the national average.

Why? Registration and voting procedures have had something to do with it. Until passage of the Voting Rights Act in 1965, literacy tests and poll taxes were common and polling places for the rural Indian population were few. In 1956 substantially fewer Navajos voted in Arizona, which had a literacy test, than in New Mexico, which didn't. Reports in the 1950s and 1960s blamed low participation on Indian indifference to what they saw as non-Indian politics and on a common Indian belief that the only governmental body that matters on the reservations is the BIA.[8] Again, these Indian perceptions may be changing as Indians become more integrated into the larger society.

On the other hand, low Indian voting figures may reflect a realistic appraisal of the vote as a resource for pursuing Indian goals. The Indian vote has limited potency. Indians make up less than 1 percent of the U.S. population. In only five states did Indians constitute 5 percent or more of the population in 1980: Alaska (16 percent), New Mexico (8.1 percent), South Dakota (6.5 percent), Arizona and Oklahoma (5.6 percent each).

In all of these the proportion had risen since 1970, but not by much. As a percentage of the voting-age population, Indians are even less significant. In only two states—Alaska (13.7 percent) and New Mexico (6.6 percent)—was this population 5 percent or more Indian, and in only six states—the five already named plus Montana—did Indians make up more than 1 percent of that population.

At the congressional district level the news is only slightly better. New Mexico's Third District leads with a voting-age population that is about 17 percent Indian; Alaska, with its single district, follows at just under 14 percent. In Arizona's Fourth District, which includes large numbers of Apaches and Navajos, 12 percent of the voting-age population is Indian, while in Oklahoma's Second District the figure is 10 percent. Only three other congressional districts have voting-age populations 5 percent Indian or more.[9] While these seven districts include a large portion of the Native American population, only in the first four are the numbers probably high enough to carry significant political weight. In other areas of Indian population concentration, such as the Pacific Northwest, California, and the Great Lakes, the proportions are lower and the clout correspondingly less.

Indian votes are occasionally decisive. The *New York Times* credited Arizona's Indians with swinging the state to Republican Howard Pyle in the 1950 gubernatorial election and considered Indians in New Mexico and Arizona important factors in the then upcoming 1952 contests. More recently, Indian votes and lobbying contributed to the 1978 defeat of Congressman Jack Cunningham of Washington, sponsor of legislation to abrogate treaty relationships between Indian nations and the United States. Claims for Indian swing votes have been made in other cases as well.[10] But swing votes are limited political instruments, dependent on close elections and a disciplined electorate. They cannot be counted on to carry the Indian political agenda.

At the local level Indian voting impact rises somewhat. In 1980 ten counties in the United States had populations at least half Indian, while twenty-eight were at least 25 percent Indian. A number of Indians have been elected to local offices around the country, and their electoral potential has been enough to inspire efforts to dilute the Indian vote. One South Dakota county was divided into separate Indian and non-Indian voting districts so as to minimize Indian influence in school board elections. In 1971 Thurston County, Nebraska, nearly 30 percent Indian, replaced its district-based system of electing county supervisors, in which Indians had dominated two of seven districts, with an at-large system that sharply reduced Indian political power. Eight years later the U.S. District Court forced Thurston to return to a district system. Non-Indian residents of Arizona's Apache County, with a population nearly three-quarters Indian, campaigned in the state legislature in 1976 to divide the single county into two, one Indian, one not, while in the mid-1980s Indians in Big Horn County, Montana, were still struggling for adequate representation in county government. "Now they want to vote," one local rancher was quoted as saying. "What next?"[11]

At all levels, however, Indians face the further problem of their own diversity. In Big Horn County, one report suggests, mutual suspicion keeps Crows and Cheyennes from supporting each other's candidates.[12] Oklahoma's Indians are numerous but divided among nearly forty tribes. Arizona's Indian population, while heavily Navajo, includes some twenty different nations. Nationally, nearly three hundred different groups have agendas of their own to pursue. Unity at the polls can be elusive.

There is another area where numbers are potentially important: protest, or unconventional action. Of course the effectiveness of protest is far more a function of structural position than of numbers. Boycotts, strikes, property takeovers, mass demonstrations, and the like gain impact primarily from their ability to disrupt the normal functioning of the society, to "rock the foundations" of some interest group or institution. The major prerequisite is positional. As Frances Piven and Richard Cloward put it, "People cannot defy institutions to which they have no access, and to which they make no contribution."[13]

Recent urban migrations have brought Indians, if not potent structural position, then at least proximity to centers of power and public opinion. Large urban concentrations, combined with often militant political tactics, have proven capable of gaining quick—if fleeting—attention from the society at large. But there simply aren't many Indians around. In recent decades and for the foreseeable future, the political capacities of Native Americans depend far more on other resources.

Bargaining Resources

Commodities possessed by one group and desired by others may be thought of as bargaining resources.[14] Examples include land, services, certain kinds of rights or exemptions, quiescence, and even approval.

The utility of bargaining resources is dependent on specific political relationships between subordinate and dominant populations. If a dominant group can simply take what it wants, then the resources in question will do poor service as bargaining chips. The owner of the resources, in other words, must have some control over their disposition.

But the resources also have to be in demand. To control what you own may be inherently good, but it gives little boost to your political capacity unless somebody else wants it.

Native Americans have almost always had commodities desired by non-Indians. Most often these have been land or its resources, although at times they included labor, military or diplomatic alliance, and even food. For a time Indians also possessed significant control over the exchange. They demanded material goods for their labor and furs and a variety of things for their lands. But as time went on, Indian power relative to White declined; as new relationships emerged, Indians lost control over the transfer process. Eventually non-Indians were dictating the terms of the exchange. Commodities that had been potent bargaining resources lost their political utility as Indian political opportunities and capacities collapsed. Expropriation followed.

By the 1920s the lands that made up the bulk of Indian bargaining resources were gone. When the opportunity structure began to change again in the 1930s as the Indian New Deal brought tribes into the political arena, it did little to improve the Indian bargaining position: not much of apparent value was left. Indeed, this very fact was one reason why the federal government opened that arena to Indian actors.

In the last thirty years, however, remaining Indian lands have turned out to be loaded with natural wealth. A series of mineral and other resource discoveries since the 1920s and especially since the 1950s, combined with the introduction of new extractive technologies, the prodigious American hunger for energy, and the emphasis since the 1970s on exploiting domestic energy supplies have brought Indian natural resources back into the calculus of American economic growth. Western Indian lands contain substantial portions of the country's strippable coal and uranium reserves, smaller but significant portions of petroleum, gas, and geothermal reserves, along with other minerals and rights to large quantities of water.[15]

The result has been a major improvement in Indian bargaining resources, the result not only of greater demand for Indian natural wealth, but also of increased Indian control over it. Since the late 1960s Native American groups, as a result of the so-called self-determination policy, various court cases, and their own political actions, have achieved substantial influence over decisions pertaining to their lands and resource endowments. As their political capacity grows, they are able to demand changes in their relationships with the larger society, essentially improving the structure of political opportunity. As that structure improves, their control over their own assets improves with it; bargaining resources become still more useful, further enhancing political capacity. This has allowed some groups to use bargaining resources on behalf of specific political goals, offering access to their economic wealth in return for jobs, royalties, and autonomy.[16]

Natural resources are not the only bargaining resources tribes possess. In recent years a small number of nations, particularly in the Northeast, have gained court support for claims to lands currently held by non-Indians. The legal right to these lands is in effect a bargaining resource, forcing the federal government to negotiate for settlement of the claims. The case of the Penobscot and Passamaquoddy claim to much of Maine is the leading example. The tribes released their claim in return for a substantial quantity of land and money. In Alaska, native claims eventually led to a massive financial and land settlement in 1971. The long-term value of these settlements remains to be seen, but they were made possible by legal claims originally held by the natives, claims that became direct resources in the political arena.

These resources have drawbacks. First, because many are tied to legal claims or nonrenewable natural resources, they don't last. Once the claims are settled and the resources sold, the chips are gone. Second, effective use generally depends on other resources: legal skills, access to information, professional expertise, money. Many Indian groups lack such resources or are inexperienced in their use. Third, they are unequally distributed. Some tribes—the Navajos, for example—are richly endowed; others have nothing. And, finally, their utility depends on forces and events outside Indian control, among them the vagaries of markets and the mood of Congress, which has the power to impose new terms of exchange on Indian peoples. Today's bargaining chip may be worthless tomorrow.

Outside Alliance

Groups that are resource poor, as some analysts have pointed out, depend on outsiders.[17] Powerless people need powerful friends.

Indians are no exception. Their political success is in part dependent on their ability to mobilize elites in their favor or, failing that, to form alliances with other groups who can force elites to respond. The task is to locate common ground on which coalitions can be built.

Over the years, Indians have found a fair number of friends. The long battle of New Mexico's Taos Pueblo Indians, for example, to gain the return of their sacred Blue Lake and surrounding lands, taken from the tribe in 1906 for inclusion in Carson National Forest, received enthusiastic early support from the local Taos community and was finally won in 1970. In the 1920s non-Indian organizations played a critical role in the defense of Pueblo lands against the proposed Bursum Bill in the U.S. Congress. In the 1940s and 1950s a number of professional anthropologists provided critical testimony before the Indian Claims Commission, most of it either directly or indirectly supporting Indian claims against the United States.[18]

Many such friends were found among organizations or groups whose primary purpose included helping Indians: Indian-assistance organizations, many still extant, with a special interest in Indian affairs. They often took the lead in defining the goals and shaping the styles of political action. In recent years, however, new kinds of alliance and support have begun to emerge. On their own initiative, Indians have been forging alliances with other groups with distinct, if related, political agendas and taking the lead in defining the issues of importance.[19]

One example is the occasional Indian alliance with the environmentalist movement. The two have often been in conflict. In the late 1960s conservationists opposed the return of Blue Lake on grounds that the Indians were incapable of managing a wilderness area and would exploit the region for economic gain. Friends of the Earth and other environmentalist organizations opposed giving the Havasupai Indians lands on the rim of the Grand Canyon for similar reasons, and wildlife conservation groups have fought treaty-guaranteed hunting, fishing, and timber rights.[20]

Despite such conflicts, Indians and environmentalists have joined forces on occasion, commonly around issues of resource extraction—especially uranium and coal mining on Indian or Indian-claimed lands—and water. The campaign to Save Black Mesa, being strip-mined for coal on Hopi land in northern Arizona, involved not only Indians but the Sierra Club, Friends of the Earth, the Environmental Defense Fund, and others. The Black Hills Alliance, formed in the late 1970s to oppose uranium mining in South Dakota's Black Hills—long claimed by the Sioux nations—brought together Indian organizations, antinuclear activists, and local ranchers. A similar coalition has protested uranium mining in northern New Mexico, while Indians, environmentalists, and non-Indian residents have opposed uranium mining in northern Wisconsin and Michigan's upper peninsula. An Indian/environmentalist coalition also fought construction of a lique-fied natural gas terminal at California's Point Conception, a Chumash Indian religious site.[21]

An important alliance has developed also between Indians, especially in urban areas, and other minorities. Signs first appeared in the civil rights campaigns of the early 1960s. In 1964 the National Indian Youth Council strongly supported the pending Civil Rights Bill, although it pointed out the unique character of the Indian situation compared to that of Blacks and other groups. A few Indians took part in the 1968 Poor People's Campaign, although Indian support generally was cool. In 1971 Indians and Chicanos joined in the founding of D-Q University, near the Davis campus of the University of California.

Such coalitions are inhibited, however, by the often distinctive character of Indian political agendas. The civil rights and antipoverty campaigns were attempts to bring minorities into the American economic and political mainstream, to secure for them opportunities and rights previously with-held. These issues are important to Indians, but, as Vine Deloria, Jr., has pointed out, the primary concern of most Indian groups has been their sur-vival as distinct and autonomous peoples. While others have fought to gain entry into the American system, Indians, even as they have struggled for jobs and services, have fought also for the right and the means to remain apart, geographically, politically, culturally.[22] Even in the cities, where Native American concerns most clearly resemble those of other poor and powerless groups, much of the Indian effort has been directed toward dis-tinguishing themselves from those groups and gaining services from the BIA and other agencies currently reserved to reservation populations.

Nevertheless, the emergence of coalition politics indicates changing Na-tive American perceptions. The growth of a supratribal consciousness and of an urban Indian population has helped Indians look beyond the tribal-federal relationship—itself unique in American society—to more pervasive social and economic relationships. In that larger context the convergence of Indian and other interests is more readily apparent.

Of course coalitions of the powerless do not necessarily produce power. Perhaps more important is another area in which Indians have seized the initiative: with the general public. At Wounded Knee and elsewhere, Indian activists showed themselves to be adept at using media to create potent political symbols and communicate broad appeals for support. While public understanding of Indian-related issues is generally slight and skewed by stereotypes, public sentiment toward Indians on the whole is generous, certainly more so that it is toward Blacks.[23] Indians play a central and heroic—if doomed—role in the popular romance of America's past. Books such as Dee Brown's *Bury My Heart at Wounded Knee* sell well to the American public. Indians took effective advantage of that receptivity in the 1960s and 1970s, forcing their concerns, in often sensational style, into the public arena.

This receptivity is itself a comment on Indian political circumstances. Indians are neither numerous nor powerful. Except in areas close to reservations, they compete for few jobs and little space; their politics challenges authorities but until recently has had little immediate or obvious impact on most Americans. A public relatively unaffected by Indian political goals can afford to give them some support. Of course this may not remain the case for long. As Indians gain even modest political muscle and apply it on behalf of land and natural resource rights, they may find themselves increasingly at odds with other interests in the political arena.

Outside alliance is important for another reason: as a constraint on authorities. In 1973, for example, the federal response to the Wounded Knee occupation was clearly moderated by the attentive gaze of a public well aware of parallels with the past.[24]

But public sentiment and support tend to be latent; they have to be aroused. The trick is to arouse such sentiment without, in the name of alliance, so diluting Indian goals that the resultant coalitions have little of importance to pursue.

MOBILIZATIONAL RESOURCES

Direct resources are useless if they can't be mobilized. However many votes, friends, guns, dollars, or bargaining chips a group has, these resources are pointless unless the group can apply them, can gather them together and focus them in goal-directed activity. The prerequisite is mobilizational resources, group assets that can organize and direct collective action.

Organizational Networks

To be more than an incidental outburst, collective action requires organization: a structure of relationships among group members that facilitates common participation in a sustained, focused political effort. Organization supports collective action in several ways. First, it forms a natural foundation for recruitment, linking potential actors with each other, providing a network of associational bonds and mutual commitments on which collective enterprise can be built.[25]

Second, it distributes ideas. Organizational networks are pathways along which ideas move, articulating the nature and source of problems, the possibilities of change, the relevant bases on which to act, the pros and cons of alternative strategies. It is a vehicle of collective consciousness and interpretation.

Finally, organization facilitates decision making and the coordination of action.

The organizational patterns of Native American groups, as already shown, have changed substantially since the beginnings of Indian-White interaction: intratribal organization has been altered and simplified, intertribal and supratribal organization has become more elaborate, organizational activity in general has proliferated. Each deserves quick review.

First, internal patterns of organization have tended to become more simple. While certain institutional structures, such as kinship and religious organization, remain vital and important among some Indian groups, they have become less complex than in the past. On the other hand, especially since the Indian Reorganization Act, tribal political organization has developed rapidly. Tribes today may not be entirely united, but they are organized in ways many never were before, often including elaborate bureaucracies and systems of representation. The political structure has replaced kinship as the most comprehensive form of group organization.

Second, intertribal and supratribal organization has proliferated. Intertribal organization has a long history; supratribal organization, on the other hand, was virtually nonexistent prior to the twentieth century. In the last four to five decades, largely as a result of changing patterns of incorporation, both the organizational links among distinct groups and the organizational structures that altogether ignore tribal distinctions have become much more numerous. Some such links have been built at the individual level, especially through intertribal marriage, but most are manifest in a variety of inter- and supratribal organizations that together constitute the organizational substructure of a single Native American population.

The picture, then, is of a collection of distinct groups whose individual organizational patterns have been simplified and which are increasingly interconnected by intertribal and supratribal networks. In a general sense there are two categories of organization: tribal or subtribal and inter- or supratribal. The two categories cut across each other. Viewed graphically, the separate tribal structures form a set of parallel networks, each fundamentally similar to the others but operating independently of them. The inter- or supratribal structures, on the other hand, which are not parallel to each other in any comparable way, cut across these tribal structures at various angles. The result is an organizational web of several dimensions.

Within these developments certain formative events stand out. The most obvious is passage, in 1934, of the IRA, which led directly to organizational frameworks within which tribes could mobilize resources, old and new, for political ends. The tribal governments that emerged in the aftermath of the IRA were a direct contribution to Indian political capacity, providing not only a means of articulating interests and a formally legitimated channel for tribal dealings with the federal government, but a way of coordinating action.[26] They in turn became bases for more comprehensive organizational development, facilitating intertribal cooperation and the identification of common goals. Organizations such as the National Congress of American Indians and the Council of Energy Resource Tribes were made possible by the existence of tribal governments, of organizations that facilitated organizational activity. The IRA initiated this process, but its ramifications far outstripped the framework it originally set up.

The second important development was the growth of a supratribal consciousness. Not only did this encourage regional and national cooperation, but it was a critical organizational element in the cities, where the tribe was politically meaningless and often insufficient as a basis of political mobilization.

These two developments have been central to the third aspect of change in Native American organizational patterns: the extraordinary growth in the last fifty years in organizational activity in general, much of it for specifically political purposes. This has occurred in stages. In the two decades following the IRA the salient development, other than the establishment of tribal governments, was the proliferation of intertribal organizations, that is, of organizations of tribes. Then, in the 1950s, there was a shift in organizational activity. The NCAI had been founded in 1944, but it was not until the following decade that nontribally defined organizations such as the Indian youth councils began to appear in large numbers. This reflected the emergence of new Indian constituencies whose thinking about Indian affairs had been shaped by supratribal as well as tribal experience. These groups and organizations, while concerned with intertribal cooperation, emphasized the mobilization of a broad Indian constituency in the service of both tribal and supratribal goals.

The organizational base expanded further in the late 1960s as organizational activity followed the Indian migration to the cities, responding to the distinctive urban Indian situation. Most of the resultant organizations have remained local, although some—the National Urban Indian Council, for example—have tried to organize urban Indians on a national basis.[27] Others, such as the American Indian Movement, founded in the cities and emerging out of urban Indian problems, eventually expanded their concerns and activity to include tribal and national Indian issues.

The 1960s and 1970s also saw increased organizational activity among issue-oriented Indian constituencies. The Coalition of Indian-Controlled School Boards, the American Indian Higher Education Consortium, and the Council of Energy Resource Tribes are three of the many examples.

These various organizations hardly constitute a united front. Some have been upstart challengers to Indian elites; others have been part of tribal and national political establishments. More than a few have started as one and become the other. While some are essentially service organizations, others are committed to a profound restructuring of the whole of Indian-White relations. At one level, however, their contributions have been the same. Together they form a dense network of organizational links and resources, both within and between Native American groups, which can facilitate and directly participate in political action.

Social Cohesion

It is not only the existence but the strength of organizational ties that determines political capacity. However organized a group may be, its capacity is reduced to the extent that group members act politically on bases other than group membership.

Because most individuals are members of many groups, not all of which share the same interests, and in addition have interests of their own, groups must compete with each other for individual allegiance and commitment. The more influential a particular group is in an individual's life, the greater is the likelihood that the group can mobilize that individual. As group membership becomes less influential, individual mobilization will be more affected by other variables, such as the particular issues involved, the costs of participation, or the mobilizational efforts of others.[28] What's missing in such circumstances is social cohesion or solidarity: literally, sticking together, the extent to which group members act on the basis of that membership.

Anthony Oberschall suggests that this is largely a function of two things: the density of ties among group members and the extent of ties between group members and other groups or the larger society. The more complex the internal organization, the easier mobilization becomes, and the more disengaged the group is from the larger society, the easier mobilization becomes. The key is integration: internal integration facilitates mobilization; external integration—that is, ties to outsiders or the larger society—retards it. Put somewhat differently, one can think of social cohesion as a function of the density and exclusivity of group ties.[29]

As already noted, the internal organization of the Indian population is dense, involving everything from elaborate kinship ties to formal tribal membership and supratribal, interest-based organizations. But this density does not lead necessarily to cohesion. While organizational links have proliferated in recent decades, so have the fault lines within the Indian population. The incorporative process has produced not only new links among groups and persons, but also new cleavages. Tribal identities are distinct and powerful; the reservation/urban divide is sometimes very real; new constituencies with new political agendas have emerged. The patterns of Indian organizational links reveal newly divergent interests.

An example: Ruffing reported that by the late 1970s, largely as a consequence of large-scale natural resource development, a "nascent labor aristocracy" had emerged on the Navajo Reservation. She saw three groups appearing there: the tribal administrators and their staffs; the new, skilled blue-collar workers; and a large residual group involved in subsistence farming, unskilled labor, petty entrepreneurship, and welfare dependency. The interests of these different groups often converge, but not always; each occupies a different position in the changing socioeconomic order of Navajo society. Robbins reported that skilled Navajo workers in the new extractive industries "exhibited few allegiances to the tribe."[30] Over time each of these groups may act less on the basis of tribal membership and more on the basis of other interests.

This pattern will surely spread as Indians become more integrated into core economic and political structures, that is, as links to the larger society proliferate. Again, the Navajo example is illustrative: the new extractive industries have given individual group members a stake in the fortunes of non-Indian organizations, in this case major corporations. Not only individual Indians are involved. In some cases corporate operations have become primary sources of tribal income. In the mid-1970s, for example, half or more of Navajo and Laguna tribal revenues came from mineral leasing and extraction, largely by non-Indian operators.[31] Joint venture arrangements, which are increasingly common, will further expand intergroup ties.

Overall, then, three concurrent developments seem to be under way. The organizational structure of the Indian population has become increasingly elaborate and dense, contributing to social cohesion. That cohesion, however, often follows new organizational lines. It may be neither tribal nor subtribal, but cross-tribal, following ties that are independent of tribal or subtribal identities. Certain of these ties may leap the Indian boundary altogether, establishing new links to non-Indian constituencies.

The diversity of the Indian population means that none of these developments is happening uniformly throughout it. Consequently, the degree of organizationally based social cohesion varies from situation to situation. In general, organizational ties tend to be most dense at the subtribal level, where kinship or other indigenous structures often serve as viable bases of interpersonal interaction and where a multiplicity of overlapping ties is likely to be found. The more isolated reservation communities often are examples. On the other hand, at the supratribal level internal organizational ties are likely to be less dense, more specific, and more fragmented and are likely to organize less of daily life.[32]

Social cohesion, however, is affected not only by the density and exclusivity of internal ties, but by their content as well. Typically such ties are ties of interest. Individuals or groups sharing a common position in the social order perceive commonalities of interest and form bonds with each other. But there are other ways to common consciousness. Propinquity and time are also the makers of groups. Collections of persons who—as a consequence of shared interests, imposed constraints, or chosen patterns of life—find themselves in extended and relatively exclusive interaction eventually become communities of culture, weaving in the course of years or generations webs of sentiment, belief, worldview, and practice that in turn help to sustain the group. Native Americans, through much of their existence, have formed just such communities and have built their identities upon them; today, many continue to do so. It is here that social cohesion is likely to be greatest, following lines of both shared interest and shared outlook, common paradigms of group identity and action and common interpretations of the larger world.

Furthermore, once established, the worldviews attached to such communities in turn reshape the perception of interests, telling group members how to interpret the situations in which they find themselves and giving to communities of culture a durability that communities of interest, in and of themselves, often lack.[33] In other words, identity itself, as a symbolic structure that defines both self and society and, therefore, relevant political interests, can serve as a basis of social cohesion in a population potentially divided by diverse circumstances.

In this, also, subtribal and tribal actors have an advantage. At the comprehensive, supratribal level, where organizational ties are most recent and least dense and identity is least embedded in a cultural community, social cohesion is more contingent, dependent upon a convergence of interests and limited opportunities for alternative courses of action. But at the tribal and, especially, subtribal levels, where organizational ties are oldest and often most elaborate and where group identity tends to be embedded in more elaborately constructed worldviews, social cohesion is likely to be more dependable and more capable of overcoming divergent interests and alternative patterns of political action.

What this suggests overall is that social cohesion will become increasingly problematic. As the new Indian politics tends to concentrate less at the subtribal level and more at the supratribal, it will have to build less on the potentially strongest ties—those embedded in self-concept, worldview, and modes of interpretation—and more on the potentially weakest—ties of readily apparent material interest attached to highly mutable circumstance.

Leadership

The mention of leadership in collective action often conjures images of charismatic or highly talented individuals who, by command, example, vision, or sheer skill, drive the movement forward, directing its energies and energizing it with their own: carriers of the fire. Such figures—the Martin Luthers, Lenins, Gandhis, or Martin Luther Kings—often have been critical to the success of collective action, but a more important resource is at issue here. Sustained political action requires a pool of persons who can interpret the problems faced by the community, are experienced and skilled at organization and at dealing with outsiders, have an impatience with the past, and have a commitment to action on behalf of collective interests. Such a pool is a resource from which leaders, in the sense of individuals who direct and coordinate action, can be drawn, but it also serves a collective and exemplary function. It provides a collective impetus toward political action and offers a core around which organizational activity and political mobilization can be built.

Two clear examples: both the Society of American Indians in the early 1900s and the voting rights campaigns and other Indian actions of the 1940s and 1950s were shaped by the emergence of just such groups. In the case of SAI it was Indians who had attended the elite boarding schools, Hampton and Carlisle, who provided the impetus and leadership for action; in the 1940s and 1950s it was veterans and students. To say that the leadership resource has expanded—which it has—is not necessarily to argue that Indian groups have more and better leaders than before, but only that there is a growing segment of the Indian population with both training and experience applicable to the political effort to find solutions to contemporary Indian problems and with an orientation toward action.

The expansion of this resource has come in waves. One of the first, as in the growth of Indian political organization, was the development of tribal governments. D'Arcy McNickle has called the new tribal governments of the 1930s "training schools."[34] Aside from teaching the practical aspects of tribal administration, the most important "training" these governments offered lay, first, in the experience of trying to establish some independence from the overbearing Indian affairs bureaucracy and, second, in the use of political tools from the dominant society in pursuit of Indian goals. Lobbying and the employment of legal counsel, for example, rapidly became part of tribal government business. In addition, tribal governments propelled many Indians into more comprehensive political activity through the regional and statewide intertribal organizations that followed in their wake.

The second wave came with World War II. As noted in Chapter 7, in the 1940s and 1950s a generation of Indian veterans moved into positions of leadership on the reservations and in Indian organizations. They brought with them not only a new sense of confidence in dealing with the non-Indian world, but also a new political awareness and an impatience with the status quo in Indian affairs. They were critical actors in the early development of the NCAI and led the battles for voting rights in the Southwest.

They were followed by yet another leadership generation, this one largely college students or of college age, who in the late 1950s and early 1960s brought a new style of action to Indian politics. Impatient with established Indian leadership, which they viewed as too timid, too wrapped up in tribal politicking, and too closely linked to the BIA, this new, younger cohort actively sought new ideas and tactics and, in general, a new assertiveness on the part of Indian people. Their politics was often confrontational and explicitly supratribal and, through organizations like the National Indian Youth Council, they began to make their way into the Indian political establishment.[35]

They, too, eventually were superseded. By the mid- to late 1960s yet another wave of Indian leadership was emerging, this time from the cities.

Urban life was a training ground of another kind. The urban experience included extensive dealings with urban bureaucracies, naturally encouraged supratribal perspectives and action, and provided close contact with the pluralist politics of the city. A leader of the American Indian Movement, itself a product of city experience, commented, "Urban Indians have seen the potential for change as exemplified by other minority groups." A member of DRUMS, the organization that eventually won restoration of the Menominees to federally protected tribal status in 1974, had this to say about the urban origins of his organization: "Menominee people outside the County were more aware of things going on with other Indians, for example, Red Power, self-determination. They were also more sophisticated or experienced with the outside world, slum lords, etc."[36] It was urban activists also who refined the confrontational style that dominated Indian politics from the mid-1960s until well into the following decade.

Another group also began to appear, if more quietly, in these decades. Part of the legacy of OEO and related federal programs was a rapidly growing group of Indian professionals: planners, program administrators, lawyers, and others. In the 1970s and 1980s their skills and experience began to be put to work in tribal government, economic development, education, and virtually every aspect of Indian affairs. Their politics, while more conventional in style than the militant activism of the 1960s and 1970s (in which some of them were involved), remained fiercely opposed to non-Indian controls over Indian communities and their futures.

Tribal governments, war experience, expanded education, urban life, the 1960s social programs, and so on—out of each came a new cohort of Indian leaders who expanded the pool of experience and ability and acted collectively as both stimulus and example of a new pattern of politics, more aggressive at almost every stage, testing new tactics in pursuit of old political ends. Each has added a new burst of energy to a political struggle already long under way.

Money

One morning in the mid-1970s a representative of Alyeska, the company building the Alaska oil pipeline, spoke to a group of newly hired workmen on the subject of relations between pipeline workers and local Indian and Eskimo communities, which recently had won a major financial and land settlement from the United States. The message to the workers: treat the natives with respect. "You may wonder," the representative said, "why they are so important. They are important because they are a people, because they were here before us and because they have a rich heritage. They are also important because they belong to regional corporations that are able to afford the finest legal counsel in the country."[37]

Money is a political resource. While it can be used directly—to buy votes, for example—its primary political function is mobilizational. It is a valuable, if not necessary, ingredient in almost every kind of political action.

Indians, however, are mostly poor. Indeed, according to Census data, rural Indians—largely the reservation population—"are in a class of poverty by themselves."[38] By most common socioeconomic indicators, including per capita income, unemployment, quality of housing, and health, reservation Indians are among the very poorest of the poor. But, as shown in Chapter 9 and as the Alaska story indicates, in recent decades some Indian groups have acquired substantial sums. Through land claims settlements, from natural resource development and other economic activity, from philanthropic sources and federal social programs, many Native American groups have seen their financial resources grow significantly in the last two decades. Some Indian political organizations have been direct beneficiaries. Tribal governments, long dependent on federal funds, received substantial new sums through the Community Action Programs of the 1960s; the National Tribal Chairmen's Association (NTCA) was founded with federal money; the Native American Rights Fund (NARF), "a national Indian interest law firm," was founded in 1970 under Ford Foundation sponsorship.[39]

Of course some of these sources are inherently unstable. Many organizations hostage to the federal funding pipeline collapsed in the Reagan years; in the mid-1980s dropping oil prices devastated the energy tribes; philanthropies moved on to other causes. But the 1960s and 1970s were boom years, and the influx of funds was an important mobilizational factor in the new Indian politics, particularly in the conventional realm—litigation, lobbying, organizational development. Indians may have been poor, but their political capacities prospered.

THE DIFFERENTIAL DISTRIBUTION OF RESOURCES

They did not prosper uniformly, however. Political resources have always been differentially distributed among Indian groups. Both history and circumstance have favored some groups over others. Bargaining resources, for example, are concentrated in the western Indian nations with accessible reserves of important natural materials. Because bargaining resources usually are also economic resources, these tribes tend to have more money. Tribes that received land claim awards and kept sizeable sums under tribal control are also better off financially than those with no claims, or whose claims were rejected, or who chose per capita distributions of awards.

Lacking not only bargaining resources and money, but size as well, smaller tribes have had to pay more attention to organizational strategies. The Inter-Tribal Council of Nevada, the Small Tribes Organization of Western Washington, and the Coalition of Eastern Native Americans, to name only a few, emerged as organizational attempts by such groups to maximize their political resources through intertribal alliance.

Differential distribution is apparent both among tribes and within them. Most political resources are concentrated in tribal governments. The capacities of subtribal, nongovernmental constituencies are typically smaller, their resources less concentrated and less completely under their control. They often compete with each other for resources that are essentially tribal in nature.

With the exception of social cohesion, this distributional problem has been most acute for so-called traditional or full-blood groups. This is in part a consequence of the nature of the resources. Their effective use depends upon active participation in the political systems of the larger society. This can be true even of organizational resources. Tribal governments, for example, which are critical organizations in the mobilization of much Indian political activity, were designed with participation in the larger political system very much in mind. But it is just such participation that many traditional tribal people—and other "radical" constituencies—reject. Their struggle is in part an attempt to purge those systems from Indian lives.

But regardless of their political agendas, traditional groups still find themselves at a disadvantage. Disproportionately concentrated among the poor, most are also isolated on reservations or in remote rural areas; ties with non-Indians are few. Opposition to tribal governments often denies them the resources those governments control. When they succeed in capturing the attention of policymakers, they may be dismissed as backward or irrelevant, enemies of progress.

The other group that lacks many of these resources is urban Indians. Their voting impact is negligible. They have few bargaining resources other than quiescence. Circumstantially outside the structure of Indian law, it is difficult for them to make the treaty-based legal claims that reservation groups can make. They typically have no income-producing land base and many are dependent on welfare. While the urban constituency is huge, half or more of the Indian population, its dispersion makes it difficult to convert size into influence. Often highly organized, urban Indians are also highly localized. Lacking other political resources, they have tended to turn both to alliance with non-Indians, especially others of the urban poor, and to unconventional forms of action.

Summed up—and oversimplified—one might say that "realists" tend to be resource rich; "radicals," to be resource poor. Of course the resource distribution has its own effect on political agendas and tactics. Those who lack conventional means of politicking may become more radical—and more highly visible—simply because their choices of action are so few.

This last point leads to another feature of political resources that has implications for Indian political action. Resources are channels. They facilitate certain kinds of action, and in so doing they tend to direct it. Direct resources represent alternative strategies: those with numbers can choose to vote; those with bargaining resources can choose to bargain; and so on. Furthermore, the availability of such resources moves groups into conventional politics. Those who reject the conventional path are usually those who lack the requisite resources. In the Indian case, unconventional action typically has been a strategy, less by choice than necessity, of certain sub-tribal constituencies and the urban poor.

Resources also shape action by placing limits upon it. An organization that is dependent on outside funding sources, for example, must begin to define the problems it proposes to confront in terms those sources can understand and with which they concur. Ultimately, the danger to Indians of federal funding lies in the tendency to replace Indian definitions of their needs with federal ones, or at least to alter those definitions in order to expedite funding. Alliance can have a similar effect; it depends on finding common ground. The increase in capacity gained from alliance is limited by its basis. As goals diverge, the utility of the resource declines, even if generalized support continues.

In other words, resources also are differentially distributed among ends. Alliance with the environmentalist movement, for example, has been possible and fruitful in opposing indiscriminate natural resource development on Indian lands; it has been much less likely when the issue has been the return of lands to Indians, which environmentalists often have opposed.

The fact that resources are also channels raises a more fundamental problem. Indian political ends are various, but they have been dominated by some salient and recurrent concerns: tribal sovereignty, treaty rights, land. For many Indians these can be subsumed under one preeminent imperative: cultural and political survival, the maintenance of peoplehood. But, as already pointed out, cultural and political survival may mean different things to different groups, and these various conceptions are served in different ways by the political resources Indians possess.

This is where the problem lies. To the extent that Indians are trying to preserve modes of action and belief very different from those of the dominant society, the resources most Indians possess can be counterproductive. Their use is a form of incorporation: they facilitate action within the systems of the dominant society. To act is to enter those systems.

This problem is most acute for traditionalists. Not only are they usually resource poor, but in terms of their own goals they have the most to lose through the integrative effects of some kinds of action. But it is a problem for other groups as well. This is illustrated by Linda Medcalf's study of lawyers representing Native Americans. Many such lawyers have consciously sought to maximize Indian political, economic, and legal power so that Native American groups can make a "meaningful choice" between assimilation into American society and the development of independent Indian reservation communities. Medcalf suggests, however, that the lawyers' activities and influence might undermine their goals. As Indians increasingly adopt the legal methods of the larger society and begin to organize, act, and think politically in ways derived from dominant-group models and traditions, those methods and modes of thought become established in Indian communities as well. Alternative conceptions of political organization, of community and social life, gradually become less imaginable and more difficult

to realize. The opportunity to make a "meaningful choice" in fact is reduced as Indian communities inadvertently come more and more to resemble non-Indian ones.[40]

Robert Nelson and Joseph Sheley see a similar danger in the bureau-
cratization of tribal governments, something encouraged by the BIA. "As
the bureaucratic 'ideology' has been increasingly legitimated," they write,
"traditional tribal approaches to problems and their solution have been
similarly delegitimated. Traditional tribal social structure has therefore suffered."[41]

Whether these developments are good or bad depends on the agendas of
the groups involved. "Radicals" are likely to see them as more of a problem than "realists" would. The point is that resources serve particular ends,
and they are not always the ends actors have most in mind.

Yet there is a bottom line. Indian political resources have changed in recent decades. While the most obvious change has been in bargaining resources, these are fairly narrowly distributed among both groups and goals.
More important has been the change in mobilizational resources and particularly in organizational facilities and networks, leadership and, for a
time at least, money. It is precisely such resources that facilitate a broad
range of actions and, therefore, have the most dramatic impact—other
things being equal—on Indian political capacities. But whatever the distribution of resources, the fundamental fact remains: in the 1960s and 1970s
those capacities had become significantly greater than they had been in a
very long time.

Part III

THE RETURN OF
THE NATIVE

Chapter 11

Lieutenant Anthony's Legacy

When the committee from Plymouth had purchased the
territory of Eastham of the Indians, "it was demanded,
who laid claim to Billingsgate?" which was understood to
be all that part of the Cape north of what they had purchased. "The answer was, there was not any who owned it.
'Then,' said the committee, 'that land is ours.' The Indians
answered, that it was." This was a remarkable assertion
and admission. The Pilgrims appear to have regarded themselves as Not Any's representatives. Perhaps this was the
first instance of that quiet way of "speaking for" a place
not yet occupied, or at least not improved as much as it
may be, which their descendants have practised, and are
still practising so extensively. Not Any seems to have been
the sole proprietor of all America before the Yankees. But
history says, that when the Pilgrims had held the lands of
Billingsgate many years, at length, "appeared an Indian,
who styled himself Lieutenant Anthony," who laid claim to
them, and of him they bought them. Who knows but a
Lieutenant Anthony may be knocking at the door of the
White House some day?

—Thoreau, *Cape Cod*[1]

Indeed. Lieutenant Anthony is back. He lay in wait, biding his time, but
now he's back, knocking at the door not only of the White House, but of
the Congress, the courts, and the American public.

You can map his progress on a chart. A chronology of Indian political
action from 1911 to 1980 effectively traces his return (Figure 4).[2] The
early signs are scattered, coming on the heels of decades of relative silence.
Scarcely more than a dozen events of significance occurred in the first
twenty of these years. The founding of the Society of American Indians

187

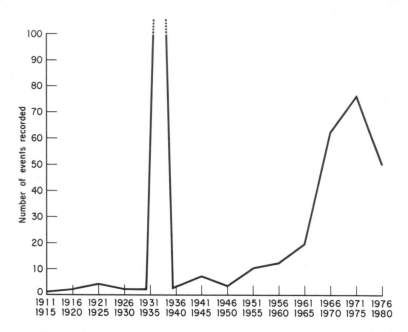

Figure 4. Indian Political Action, 1911–80. The dramatic rise in activity in the mid-1930s is almost entirely due to tribal referenda on the Indian Reorganization Act.

in 1911; the incorporation of the Native American Church in 1918; the Pueblo struggle against the Bursum Bill in the early 1920s; the founding of the Indian Defense League of America, which struggled to preserve treaty rights in western New York, in 1926: these and a few others marked the opening skirmishes in the twentieth-century Indian wars. Few and far between, they formed a beginning nonetheless.

Then the 1930s: a quantum leap upward in political activity. The key was the Indian Reorganization Act of 1934. Out of this single event came a new stage in Indian politics. Thousands of Indians went to the polls to vote on tribal adoption of the IRA. Tribe after tribe either campaigned against it or moved quickly to set up a government under its provisions or influence. Organizing a tribal government was a political act, and in the 1930s it occurred on a massive scale.

There were other events in these years. The Navajos, for example, waged a bitter campaign against livestock reductions forced on them by the BIA in an attempt to reduce overgrazing on the Navajo range; other groups went to court in defense of treaty rights. But the IRA dominates Indian-White relations in the years leading up to World War II. Through it and the battles around it, Native American political resurgence took a large step forward.

The 1940s saw a return to something slightly above the pre-IRA level of activity, but the events themselves were crucial, among them the founding of the National Congress of American Indians in 1944, the wave of litigation following the Indian Claims Commission Act of 1946, and the voting rights battles at the end of the decade.

And then the crescendo begins. More than twenty major events occurred in the 1950s. They included the youth councils in the Southwest and elsewhere, the Garrison Dam fight, continuing efforts to ensure the franchise, and the protracted battle over termination.

New tactics began to appear. In 1957 several hundred Mohawks from the St. Regis Reservation in New York traveled to the town of Massena where, claiming that the state had no sovereignty over them, they tore up summonses issued for nonpayment of state taxes. A year later the New York State Power Authority attempted to seize more than a fifth of the Tuscarora Reservation in western New York for a new reservoir. The Tuscarora chiefs ordered the surveyors and SPA officials off the reservation. When the surveyors returned the next day with a hundred riot-equipped Niagara County sheriff's deputies and state troopers, they were met by more than a hundred Indians who scuffled with police and used their bodies to block government trucks. In 1958, in Robeson County, North Carolina, angry Lumbee Indians, faced with harassment by the Ku Klux Klan, took up guns and routed a major Klan rally one night, driving the Klan from the county. In 1959 another group of Indians, several hundred strong, marched on BIA headquarters in Washington, D.C., in protest against termination, and attempted a citizen's arrest of the Indian commissioner.

What was new in the 1950s became commonplace in the 1960s. More than sixty major events occurred in the decade. The 1961 American Indian Chicago Conference kicked it off, followed shortly by the founding of the National Indian Youth Council (NIYC), first of the major militant activist organizations. By 1963 urban Indians were taking to the streets in protest against BIA policies, initiating a wave of urban Indian protest that lasted over a decade.

At about the same time Indians began organizing "fish-ins" and other demonstrations in the Pacific Northwest, part of a continuing, occasionally violent struggle to retain treaty-guaranteed fishing rights. In 1965, in northeastern Oklahoma, traditionalist Cherokee communities organized a disobedience campaign to defy state restrictions on Indian hunting. In the next few years Makahs, Lummis, and Quinaults moved to bar non-Indians from reservation lands in Washington; Indians from California's Big Ben Rancheria forcibly halted attempts to open a logging road across their reservation; Mohawks in New York boycotted local schools until the state allowed them to participate in school board elections; forty-one Mohawks were arrested for blocking a bridge between Canada and the United States in protest against violations of the 1794 Jay Treaty, which gauranteed unrestricted passage; Passamaquoddy Indians forcibly halted logging operations on disputed lands in Maine.

In 1968 the American Indian Movement (AIM) was founded in Minneapolis in an effort to halt police mistreatment of Indians in the city. By

1970 it was organizing Indians in cities across the country as well as on reservations. In November 1968 another new organization, Indians of All Tribes, seized Alcatraz Island in San Francisco Bay. They held it for nineteen months. On more than fifty occasions over the next five years Indian activists seized and occupied—for varying lengths of time—lands and buildings in nearly every part of the country, protesting government policies, land alienation, racial discrimination, uncontrolled resource development on Indian lands, and the erosion of treaty rights and tribal sovereignty. They helped make the 1970s the high-water mark of the activist movement, with well over a hundred major political events recorded for the decade. Among the more sensational: the takeover of BIA headquarters in Washington in 1972 and the violent ten-week confrontation at Wounded Knee in 1973. AIM was a major actor in both.

At least as important were less dramatic events. In the 1960s and 1970s significant numbers of Indians for the first time won elected off-reservation posts in local government. Lobbying became a common activity of tribal governments, who pursued everything from the return of tribal lands to federal funds to development programs. Indian-initiated litigation continued to increase, while regional and national organizations proliferated. A highly politicized supratribal news media appeared. Every week produced a new event, a new organization, a new issue, a new demand.

The result, by the 1970s, was a political movement of major proportions. It appeared in both urban and rural areas, among young rebels and established tribal leaders, at the polls, in the streets, in the courts, and on the dusty backroads of reservations across the country. As a political phenomenon it surpassed in scale, extent, and impact anything in Indian-White relations since the wars of the nineteenth century.

Lieutenant Anthony had returned.

PATTERNS OF POLITICAL RESURGENCE

There is ample logic in the pattern of this resurgence. The wars of the eighteenth and nineteenth centuries, followed by reservation confinement and the imposition of elaborate controls on Native American communities, left most of those communities, late in the nineteenth century, with few political opportunities and little capacity with which to pursue them. Only in the Indian Territory was there significant, sustained political activity in these years. The desperate effort of the Five Civilized Tribes to construct a political framework capable of preserving their own autonomy was unique, but it, too, failed. Thus, with the exception of some scattered claims litigation, there is essentially a hiatus in Indian political action that lasts from defeat or subjugation—different times for different nations—into the present century.

Under these conditions organized political action was perhaps possible only among those who were relatively more integrated into the American mainstream, or who could readily draw on outside resources. The major events of the early years reflected this situation. The SAI was the work of an emergent group of Indian professionals; its goals were reformative and integrative, even assimilative, in nature. On the other hand, the goals of the Indian Defense League of America were quite different. It emerged out of the effort of New York tribes to retain their treaty rights to free passage across the U.S.–Canadian border and represents direct resistance, waged largely through the courts, to dominant-group actions.[3] But again, it was the work of Indians who had lived much of their lives in interaction with Whites, in a region long dominated by Euro-Americans. Graduates of Carlisle, most famous of the elite Indian boarding schools, were heavily involved in the peyote debates and the founding of the Native American Church, which occurred in Oklahoma, home to a long history of Indian attempts to use the institutional apparatuses of the larger society for their own distinctive ends. Even the major reservation-based event of the period—the Pueblo resistance to the Bursum Bill—occurred in an unusual situation. The Pueblo systems of government had remained relatively intact and the Pueblo effort received substantial non-Indian support and assistance. In other words, Pueblo political capacities, like those of the Tuscaroras and others in western New York at the time, were atypically high.

Yet in the early decades of the twentieth century two societal developments led ultimately to new political openings. First, the demand for Indian land declined in the 1920s, and with it much of the logic of Indian subordination. Second, a non-Indian movement for reform in Indian affairs led to the Indian New Deal and the reorganization of Indian-White relations. The results were new opportunities for Indian action and new organizational resources for Indian groups.

Major constraints remained. Native Americans still lacked economic clout or any structural location that would allow them to deal with the federal government from a position of strength. Intertribal organizational links were few, while links to centers of power outside the administrative framework of Indian affairs were virtually nonexistent. The Indian nations themselves had little money that they effectively controlled and little leadership experienced both in dealings with Congress and the Indian affairs bureaucracy and in operating the institutions of Euro-American governance. On the other hand, the policy changes of the Indian New Deal dramatically expanded the political space open to Indian actors.

In the aftermath of World War II new political resources and constituencies began to emerge to take advantage of these opportunities. Returning veterans and workers brought with them new skills, a broadened experience of the non-Indian world, a growing disposition to act on a supratribal basis, an impatience with the poverty and powerlessness of the reservations, and an eagerness for action. The NCAI and other organizations not only provided additional organizational resources, but also began to bridge the gap between the tribal organizations developed in the 1930s and the nascent supratribal consciousness emerging in the 1940s and 1950s. The goals of Indian action remained, for the most part, reformative and integrative in nature—voting rights, increased levels of Indian personnel in the BIA, compensation for land claims, and so on—but the actions themselves were Indian initiated and led.

In the 1950s, presented with a major crisis—termination—this new Indian politics began to show its teeth. Facing a hostile administration and a deadly threat to the tribal estate, it became more vocal, more bold, and more supratribal in its approach and revealed a heightened sense of efficacy, a belief in the possibilities of change. This was apparent not so much in the tribal councils, which remained hobbled by BIA controls, as in the new, nontribal constituencies that began to test the political waters. The Indian students putting together youth councils in the Southwest were creating new patterns of organization and action not linked to tribal governments or the Indian establishment, moving political action out of the institutional structures of Indian affairs, a pattern soon replicated by the growing urban Indian population. And in New York, North Carolina, and elsewhere, new, more confrontational styles of action were beginning to appear.

In these decades, then, from the 1910s into the 1950s, as the opportunity structure opened, as political capacities expanded, and as new political actors emerged, a twentieth-century political resurgence gradually took shape. In the 1960s and 1970s this movement burst free of the bonds of established Indian-White relations and transformed the world of Indian affairs.

It was encouraged by broader societal developments. Critical among these was the mobilization of American Blacks. Not only did it offer tactical lessons, but the magnitude of Black mobilization and its popular support forced government authorities to respond—however inadequately—to the issues it raised. This in turn encouraged similar actions by other groups, including Native Americans. Furthermore, the social programs of the Johnson years, specifically directed to the claims of the disadvantaged, established those claims as legitimate items on the national agenda.

These developments further broadened the opportunities for Indian political action and enhanced the sense of power among Indian groups. Joined to the growing political capacities of tribes and other constituencies, to a heightened supratribalism, and to the conviction among Indians that they had to seize the initiative in Indian affairs, they produced an explosion in Indian political activity of all kinds, which continued through the 1960s and into the following decade.

And this resurgent politics had effects. It opened new channels for the expression of Indian political interests and new means of putting pressure on decision-makers. In the process it antagonized a lot of people, both Indian and non-Indian, but it brought Indian affairs out of the tribal offices, the BIA, and the Congress and placed them before a larger public. It also brought many more Indians, previously only peripherally involved in politics, into the political effort to solve their problems. And it contributed directly to a new phase of political incorporation.

THE DECLINE OF UNILATERALISM

In the early twentieth century Native Americans were almost wholly absent from the decisions that most affected their lives and their relations with non-Indian society. What had begun as bilateral relations between, in many cases, more or less equal powers, by late in the nineteenth century had become essentially unilateral relations between dominant and subordinate groups, linked in a structure designed to maintain strict controls over Indian communities. Explicit in law and ubiquitous in practice, this unilateralism became the salient feature of intergroup relations.

In the 1930s, under the influence of the IRA, a new pattern of political incorporation emerged, but the change was less profound than it appeared. In its support for indigenous political organization and action, the IRA looked very much like bilateralism, but this emergent structure of self-government was also a structure of control, strictly limiting Indian power and leaving Indians subject to the BIA and the Congress. The new bilateralism was essentially unilateralism in disguise.

What is most striking about contemporary Indian affairs is the disintegration of this unilateral relationship. Since the early 1960s there has been a breakdown in the control structure in Indian-White relations, precipitating a major crisis in Indian affairs.

Ironically, termination—an almost wholly unilateral policy—became the catalyst in the decline of unilateralism. This was partly the result of its failure to achieve what it set out to do: to reduce federal government involvement in Indian affairs and to integrate Indians into the economic mainstream of U.S. society. Its failure revealed the essential bankruptcy of the traditional federal policy approach: antitribal, patently assimilationist, unilateral. Much of the opposition to termination, both Indian and White, focused on the last of these: the lack of Indian input in its implementation. Faced with mounting criticism and accumulating evidence of failure, the federal government committed itself to a more bilateral approach. Thereafter, the theme of Indian participation in policy making and administration became common in discussions of Indian affairs, and in 1970 the government officially replaced termination with a new policy of "self-determination."

The failure of termination contributed to the breakdown of unilateralism in a second way as well: it encouraged the economic development of Indian reservations, previously of secondary importance to policymakers. Funding for reservation economic development began to climb, from less than $2 million in 1960's BIA budget to more than $10 million in 1970. The antipoverty programs of the mid-1960s reinforced the new policy emphasis and added additional funds. By the late 1960s economic develop-

ment had become the new centerpiece of Indian policy. This further promoted bilateralism as agencies other than the BIA, including the Office of
Economic Opportunity and the Economic Development Administration,
became involved in programs designed to improve reservation economies.
Political links between tribes and the federal government, previously dominated by the BIA, multiplied and became dispersed among a number of
different organizations, opening new channels for Indian input into policy
and administration.[4] Some of these new programs were specifically designed to enhance the political power of poor communities.[5]

But the single most important element in the breakdown of unilateralism
was Indian political resurgence, and in particular the activist movement of
the 1960s and 1970s. Termination again was a catalytic element, in this
case through its effect not on policymakers but on Indians. Its implementation in the face of widespread Indian opposition demonstrated the impotence of tribal governments—at least in the current situation—as vehicles for
the protection of Indian interests, the necessity of united action, and the
need to escape the politically repressive structure of Indian affairs. It was
catalytic in that it helped to focus growing Indian political capacities. Since
the 1940s those capacities had been employed largely in regional and tribal
issues. In contrast, termination presented all Native American groups with
the question of whether or not they could survive as distinct cultural or political communities. An affirmative answer required opposition not simply
to an event or program, but to the whole of Indian policy and the unilateralism at its core. The threat was comprehensive, and it drew a commensurate response.

THE INDIAN CHALLENGE

The Indian political response posed a direct challenge to the prevailing
patterns of Indian-White relations. It did so in three ways: it bypassed the
administrative structure of those relations; it attacked that structure directly; it attacked the essentially assimilationist orientation of Indian policy.

One of the notable developments of the 1960s and 1970s was the appearance of new, nontribally defined groups in the political arena: urban
Indians, subtribal constituencies, local communities, students, supratribal
organizations. Most were not formally linked to the administrative structure of Indian affairs and operated increasingly outside the system of tribal
governments and the accustomed political channels leading through those
governments to the BIA. Land seizures in the 1960s and early 1970s, protests by Iroquois activists in the late 1950s and by others in later years, the
fishing rights march on the Washington state capitol in 1964, the protest
powwows and legal battles waged by the National Indian Youth Council
and other organizations throughout the period, protests by traditional Cherokees in eastern Oklahoma in the mid-1960s—these and others are examples of sub- or supratribal groups taking politics into their own hands or

taking their concerns directly to Congress, the states, the courts, and the public.

Tribes often followed suit. Especially in intertribal organizations such as the National Tribal Chairmen's Association and the Council of Energy Resource Tribes, as well as individually, tribes formed new relationships with government agencies other than the BIA and with higher levels of the federal administration. Many set up offices in Washington, D.C., to pursue their interests directly with Congress and the executive branch, bypassing BIA lines of administrative access. Such actions moved Indian politics into new channels and engaged a wider set of decision- and policymakers.

Not only did contemporary Indian politics bypass the structure of control; through litigation and extrainstitutional action it attacked it. Tribal governments took part in this attack, challenging congressional and Interior Department prerogatives in decision making and going to court to assert claims to lands, jurisdictional rights, services, and so forth. But the attack came from elsewhere as well, and tribal governments themselves were frequent targets. In some cases—examples include the Hopis, the Navajos, and the Oglalas of Pine Ridge—Indian groups challenged the right not only of non-Indian actors but also of tribal governments to make decisions governing the affairs of subtribal communities.[6]

Others attacked the institutional structure of Indian affairs more generally, claiming that it was unresponsive to their needs and secured control of those affairs in the hands of federal bureaucrats and reservation elites. Among the proposals in the so-called Twenty Points, for example, submitted to the federal government at the end of the Trail of Broken Treaties caravan, which brought nearly one thousand Indians to Washington, D.C., in the fall of 1972, were the restoration of treaty making, the reaffirmation of treaties as the basis of Indian-federal relations, and the mandated judicial consideration of Indian interpretations of treaty rights. The proposals also included abolition of the BIA, repeal of termination legislation, and direct Indian administrative access to the White House.[7] Other Indian concerns included continuing federal control of Indian lands and resources and encroachment by the states on tribal civil and criminal jurisdictions. But whatever the specific issues, the point is the growing challenge, expressed in action, to non-Indian controls on Indian lives and resources.

In bypassing or attacking the political and administrative structures of Indian-White relations, Native Americans were attempting to overcome a position of relative powerlessness. The third aspect of their challenge has had less to do with the distribution of power or the control relationship than with the effect of that relationship on Indian communities and cultures. In recent years a number of Indian groups have attacked the assimilationist orientation of Indian policy, the effort to reproduce within Indian communities the institutions and values of the larger society. In so doing, they have confronted a central element of the control system in Indian affairs.

In all societies, albeit in widely varying degrees, social control rests to some extent on the belief among members that the existing institutions of that society are fundamentally appropriate and just and that the ideas and values they represent are essentially good and, indeed, normal.[8] The promotion of these institutions and values has long been a major component of the ongoing program of Indian assimilation, whether organized on an individual or a community basis.

This program has run into problems. Various constituencies have been involved, but most important have been the more "radical" ones, in particular traditionalist communities on some reservations and the generally younger, often urban Indians influenced both by traditional Native American cultures and worldviews and by the widespread disaffection with the dominant culture apparent among Blacks, the young, and other groups in the 1960s and 1970s.

Their targets have been diverse. Among them have been tribal political institutions introduced since the 1930s and the economic institutions and programs introduced on many reservations as economic development has moved forward. Sometimes the two have been combined. On the Navajo Reservation, for example, natural resource development programs resuscitated long-standing opposition by local communities to the loss of local autonomy and the subordination of local practices or interests to more comprehensive, tribal ones. But not only autonomy has been involved. Some Navajos have objected to the economic development process itself, seen as a long-term threat to indigenous culture and social organization, a concern shared by some Northern Cheyennes and others.[9]

More generally, a number of Indians have rejected claims by policymakers and consultants that the economic viability of Indian communities depends on the replacement of traditional tribal values with the more economistic and individualistic values of non-Indian society.[10] Many have rejected the idea that their interests and those of the larger society are necessarily the same or can best be served by the institutions of that society. Of course these are factional—often minority—viewpoints and represent only one current within diverse Indian politics. But since the 1960s they have been amply apparent among Indian groups and have been increasingly transformed into political action.[11]

To some extent this rejection of the dominant ideology or value system—in effect, of much of the dominant culture—is a recent development, especially among young Indians. But rejection of the dominant culture by portions of the Indian population is scarcely new and is rooted both in historical experience at the hands of that culture and in the often profound differences between it and various Native American worldviews and value systems. Historically much of that rejection has been expressed either in the kinds of "religious" movements described in Chapter 4 or in a sort of "lived" resistance: the tenacious adherence by some Indian communities to their own tribal values, systems of meaning, and ways of interacting with each other and the world.

These cultural patterns have significance for social control because they provide bases for resistance rooted not simply in material interests, but in received—and often radically different—conceptions of self and society. They challenge the control system at its core: in its assumptions about the primacy of economic interests and relationships and in its tendency to make policy the child of market forces. In contrast, they give primacy to the preservation of particular communities and ways of being in the world. To the extent that they survive, they offer distinctive bases for the articulation and organization of political opposition.

In the 1960s and 1970s such communities of "lived" resistance became increasingly involved in resurgent Indian activism. In some cases this was the result of particular conflicts with Whites, as over hunting rights and other issues in eastern Oklahoma and resource extraction on Navajo and Hopi lands, or with tribal governments, as at Pine Ridge in South Dakota. Also important have been termination and expanded resource development, both of which pose threats to the lands and relative isolation from non-Indian society, which in part have sustained traditional cultural practice. A third factor in the politicization of these groups is their long-standing concern with treaty rights and land preservation. Deloria argues that it was in the late 1960s and early 1970s, when Indian activists and tribal leaders began to focus on the rectification of broken treaties through land restoration, that more traditional groups began to give their support to the activist movement.[12] Whatever the cause and extent, their participation bolstered the challenge to the assimilationist program and brought to the activist movement the sanctification of cultural tradition and its living representatives.

There is another way in which Indians attacked both the structure of Indian affairs and the political institutions of the larger society, and that was in their tactics. Beginning with the Iroquois protests of the late 1950s and lasting well into the 1970s, the activist movement turned increasingly to extrainstitutional action: mass protests, civil disobedience, land seizures, building occupations, and the like, some of which became violent. Such events gained attention for Indian concerns. They also signified an important political step, "a fundamental rejection of the established institutional mechanisms for seeking redress of group grievances."[13] This rejection may have been part of an ideological stance or it may simply have reflected the unresponsiveness of those established mechanisms. In any case, it is worth asking why it occurred.

Early in this century the avenues of redress available to most Indian groups were few. Appeals to the reservation superintendent or agent just about exhausted the political inventory. Some Indians could vote, but without much effect; a few tribes mounted legal campaigns, but with only occasional success. Under the circumstances one might think the discontented would choose more dramatic modes of action. There were some isolated instances in the early decades of the century, as among full-blood draft resisters who took up arms during World War I. But everything in the Indian

situation discouraged it. Many tribespeople still had memories of the ap-
palling costs of resistance in decades past. In a world now so totally dominated by Whites, militant resistance must have seemed not only unrealistic
but suicidal.

It was probably impossible, too: the necessary organizational structures
were no longer intact and the targets were far away. Indians had only limited access to the organizations that governed them. Finally, for many Indians then and later, the only defensible course of action was to emulate
the larger society. Change would come as Indian people raised themselves
up through education, hard work, and Christianity: learning the secrets of
that society in order to achieve its power. Such reasoning frowned on defiance as a response that had failed and had no place in a changed world.
This attitude proved persistent. When some Indians in the early and mid-
1960s renounced militant protest as alien to the Indian way, they were at
odds with their own history, but they probably expressed the dominant Indian opinion of the time.

By then, however, things were changing. Defiance had become a tactic
of choice. Several factors contributed to this. Frustration certainly was part
of it, particularly among younger Indians in the 1950s and early 1960s
who were impatient with established tribal leaders and ways of doing
things. As Mel Thom, one of the founders of the National Indian Youth
Council put it, "We were concerned with direct action, Indians moving out
and doing something. The younger Indians got together in the Youth
Council because they didn't feel that the older leadership was aggressive
enough."[14] As "realists" came to dominate the new tribal governments,
some reservation groups likewise looked for new avenues of redress. This
search was especially important for more "radical" constituencies that were
at odds not only with the occupants of the new governments, but with the
governing institutions themselves.

Certainly, also, the tactics of Black protest had a powerful influence on
Indian thinking. Deloria argues that "the basic fact of American political
life—that without money or force there is no change—impressed itself upon
Indians as they watched the civil-rights movement."[15] In this connection,
and in the growth of extrainstitutional action generally, urbanization was a
critical factor. For the first time Indians were being socialized politically in
an environment in which confrontational politics was commonplace.

There was also, conscious or not, a revised calculation of costs. While
protesters in the 1960s could not expect to act with complete impunity, the
sheer magnitude of minority and student protest and the extent of public
support for it—including that of some influential groups in the society—
much reduced the range of responses available to power holders.[16]

In the last few decades, then, Native Americans challenged both the institutional structures of control and, often enough, the assimilationist orientation embedded in those structures and in Indian policy. The result was
a growing crisis in Indian affairs. As conflicts multiplied, the old system of
controls no longer could contain them. Not only could Indian compliance

with dominant-group goals no longer be assured, but Indian-White relations themselves were becoming chaotic. This development alone would have made the future of Indian-White relations uncertain, but its significance was amplified by a second one: the reemergence of intense pressures on Indian economic resources.

REEMERGENCE OF THE ECONOMIC PROBLEM

In the last few decades two convergent developments have led to a resurgent demand for Indian economic resources. First, by the 1950s and 1960s it was apparent, as a result of mineral exploration and discovery, that some of the lands remaining in Indian hands were resource rich. Second, in the late 1960s and 1970s the crisis in natural resources—and particularly energy resources—placed new and urgent demands on domestic supplies of oil, coal, gas, and minerals. With rising prices, the value of Indian resources skyrocketed; Indian lands turned out to contain riches cumulatively valued in the billions of dollars. Pressure for the accelerated development of those resources became intense.

Development activity soared. By 1980 forty-five tribes were involved in oil production in twelve states; uranium mining was under way on the Navajo, Laguna, and Spokane reservations; coal was being mined on Indian lands in Montana, Arizona, New Mexico, and Utah, with reserves elsewhere waiting to be developed; copper production had begun on the Papago reservation and molybdenum on the Colville. By 1982 fifty-two tribes had lands in mineral production.[17]

There was more at stake than minerals. Indian water resources also have felt the pressure. Long coveted by agricultural interests for irrigation and by non-Indian communities for recreational and industrial purposes, Indian water resources are now in demand as integral components of energy development, particularly in the Upper Missouri River Basin. Elsewhere the growth of western populations and intensive irrigation have strained already limited western water supplies. Growing demand has led to infringement on Indian water rights and the diversion of Indian waters to non-Indian users. In some areas falling water tables already threaten Indian economies.[18]

The fishing rights struggle in the Pacific Northwest is also driven by competition for Indian resources. Long-simmering challenges to Indian fishing rights blossomed into a major confrontation in the 1960s as growing numbers of non-Indian fishermen joined the competition for declining numbers of salmon and other fish in northwestern waters. The issue has refused to go away. In 1984 non-Indian organizations in Washington State, determined to undermine Indian fishing rights, placed Initiative 456, which sought an end to treaty rights, on the November election ballot. One organizer called it "the beginning of a national movement to repeal treaties." The initiative passed.[19]

This new scramble for Indian resources has involved a diverse collection of actors. Among the interests pushing for rapid development have been various federal agencies, including the Bureau of Indian Affairs, the Atomic Energy Commission, and the Department of Energy. A desire for energy independence combined with intermittent concerns with reservation economic development has led the government to promote quick, often cheap access to Indian lands. State governments likewise have stood to gain from development, primarily via taxes on extractive industry, while local non-Indian populations often have looked to development to stimulate local economies. Both have sought greater access to Indian resources.[20]

Pressure for development has come from Indian constituencies as well. Reservation poverty is a fact of acute concern to tribal leaders and administrators, as it is to most tribespeople. Natural resources offer some groups unprecedented economic opportunities. Resource extraction can mean jobs for unemployed reservation populations while royalties can fund tribal government and build industrial infrastructures, tribal businesses, schools, and social services. Tribal governments in particular have tended to favor rapid development as a strategy for revitalizing marginal economies. Some reservations have become heavily dependent on natural resource income. By 1970, for example, 45 percent of Navajo tribal revenues came from mineral leasing and extraction; by 1975 the figure had risen to 70 percent. Laguna Pueblo was probably equally dependent on uranium mining in the late 1970s, while Arapahoe tribal income was coming largely from oil and gas. The Colvilles, facing economic disaster in the early 1980s owing to declining timber prices, felt compelled to allow mining of molybdenum, although the decision was controversial within the tribe.[21] Such dependencies produce a vested tribal interest in development.

Another set of actors has recently taken a major role in the development drama: multinational corporations. In a discussion of development issues in southeastern Montana, James Boggs points out that while government and industry may differ on regulatory and other issues, "both share the basic goal of developing . . . energy resources with all due haste."[22] Drawn by expectations of large profits and the accessibility of Indian resources relative to those of much of the Third World, multinational corporations have begun to replace the federal government as primary development sponsors on many reservations. By the early 1980s corporations including Exxon, United Nuclear, Kerr-McGee, Amoco, Conoco, Gulf Oil, Union Carbide, International Nickel, AMAX, Arco, and others had become major actors in Indian mineral development. Native Americans were negotiating development packages directly with such corporations, within the limits of Interior Department approval. Obviously these corporations seek maximum access at minimum cost. They have been assisted by BIA leasing and development policies and by their own financial, legal, political, and informational resources, which usually exceed those of the Indian nations involved.[23]

Despite these convergences of interest, development has been a contentious business. Not all tribes have approached it with equal enthusiasm.

Some have demanded high royalties and other concessions; others have rejected certain kinds of development outright. Acoma Pueblo, for example, turned away companies eager to exploit uranium and oil deposits on the reservation, while the Northern Cheyennes placed a moratorium on coal development on their reservation and sought restrictions on development in adjacent areas. Elsewhere subtribal constituencies protested tribal development plans, often with the assistance of supratribal organizations. Hopis, for example, fought coal development at Black Mesa; Navajos tried to stop uranium mining in eastern portions of the reservation; a coalition of Native Americans and local ranchers protested uranium mining in South Dakota. Organizations such as the American Indian Environmental Council, the National Indian Youth Council, the Coalition for Navajo Liberation, and the American Indian Movement have been involved in these and other protests and have been major instigators of political and court actions to stop or alter various development plans.

The goals of these groups are diverse; few can be described as simply "antidevelopment." Concern over environmental impacts, for example, has been especially prominent in the Dakotas, Wisconsin, and New Mexico and played an important role in the Northern Cheyenne decision against coal development. The influx of non-Indian workers that often accompanies major development activity has been an issue on the Crow and Navajo reservations and elsewhere, while concern with tribal control of the development process, its timing, extent, and social effects, has been ubiquitous. Also, as noted above, resistance to certain institutions and values of the larger society and their assimilative impacts has been extended to development programs. Some Northern Cheyennes, for example, have objected to development plans that reconceptualize homeland from source of identity and spiritual power to commercial resource, while the Blackfeet have appealed a Forest Service decision to allow oil and gas development in mountains sacred to the Blackfeet nation.[24]

The effect of this diffuse but growing opposition was to move development issues to the center of both Indian-White relations and intragroup Indian politics. As a consequence access to Indian resources became more difficult, time-consuming, and costly.

What occurred in the 1960s and 1970s, then, was the reemergence of the economic problem—how to gain access to Indian resources—just when Indian political capacities were increasing and the system of controls governing Indian-White relations was in disarray. This development gave to the new Indian politics and the attendant crisis in Indian affairs their wider implications and underlined the political aspect of a resurgent "Indian problem."

Chapter 12

Indian-White Relations Revised

When subordinate groups challenge a structure of intergroup relations, authorities[1] generally have three choices. They can ignore the challenge; they can forcibly suppress it; they can undertake reform. What they do obviously will be affected by a number of factors, including the gravity of the challenge and the extent of their own political capacities. If the challenge is serious and cannot be ignored, they must find a way of containing it. If they are unable or unwilling simply to suppress it, then they must find a way to implement reforms that do not at the same time undermine their own power.

The Indian challenge was indeed serious, insofar as it both affected substantial non-Indian interests and rendered Indian-White relations chaotic. The challenge, in other words, could not be ignored. Nor could it, thanks to national political developments and the growth in Indian political capacities, simply be suppressed. And it hasn't entirely gone away.

How this problem ultimately will be solved remains to be seen, but since the early 1970s three aspects of the dominant-group response have emerged: suppression of the most radical elements in Indian resistance to the status quo; symbolic reform in response to certain Indian demands; and more substantive reform that both accommodates other Indian demands and strengthens the institutional structure of Indian-White relations.

RESPONDING TO CRISIS

In response to the militancy of the late 1960s and early 1970s the federal government launched a campaign to discredit and cripple the more radical Indian organizations, in particular the American Indian Movement, believed responsible for many of the confrontational events and much of the violence of the activist years. The BIA, FBI, and other federal agencies joined in a campaign of surveillance, organizational infiltration, and indictment directed at Indian activists and organizations. Government officials characterized activists who either chose or were forced to go outside the formal structures of Indian-White relations and political redress as renegades, urban hoodlums, criminals, youthful adventurers, and the like. As Michael Lipsky and David Olson have pointed out in another but relevant context, by denying the political character of extrainstitutional actions and suggesting that the issues raised in such actions are mere pretense, such verbal attacks undermine support for the actors and their causes.[2]

This campaign of suppression was effective. Harassment and infiltration exacerbated factional divisions within some groups and fostered crippling internal suspicions. Court cases tied up resources. As one AIM leader said in 1978, "We've been so busy in court fighting these indictments we've had neither the time nor the money to do much of anything."[3] The decline in extrainstitutional actions since the early 1970s reflects in part the success of this campaign.

The second approach has been to respond in ways that have little substantive but considerable symbolic impact. Indians have been appointed to commissions and advisory bodies that make recommendations on policy and programs but have little power. For example, responding to widespread discontent among Indian groups, in 1975 Congress established, with great fanfare, the American Indian Policy Review Commission (AIPRC). This commission, its membership and staff heavily Indian, carried out a series of studies of major issues in Indian affairs and delivered numerous recommendations for change. These were largely ignored. Such commissions or appointments give the impression that the government has responded concretely to Indian concerns at the policy level when in fact it hasn't.[4]

A similar effect is achieved by increasing Indian staffing at the BIA, especially at high levels, and by changes in Indian administration. Responding to complaints that Indian concerns carry little weight in the Interior Department, in 1977 the government established the post of assistant secretary of the interior for Indian affairs, superseding the commissioner of Indian affairs—head of the BIA—as the senior federal official concerned solely with Indian-White relations. The first appointee was an Indian. Such changes generate publicity, indicate that the government is responding to Indian grievances, and suggest that Indian influence in policy making is on the rise. This may be the case, although policy processes and administrative structures are largely unaffected, and there is no assurance that new issues or constituencies—including those among whom discontent was greatest—will receive any better hearing than before.

Importantly, there have been substantive changes as well, as authorities have responded directly to certain Indian demands. In the area of economic development, for example, dominant-group interests, confronted with newly assertive tribal governments and growing Indian concerns about development and its effects, have turned to bargaining in order to gain access to Indian resources. Among other things, higher mineral royalties, infrastructural investment, environmental protection, preferential Indian employment, and expanded Indian control over development have become common items on the bargaining table.[5]

This response is reminiscent of the eighteenth and nineteenth centuries. Then, as now, access to some Indian resources was blocked by Indian political capacities. The United States tried to solve the problem by offering Indians Euro-American civilization in return for land. The bargain has been much the same in the twentieth century. In return for access to their resources, Indians are being offered entry into the economic mainstream. The difference is that in the earlier period this bargain envisioned the breakup of the tribal community and the insertion of Indians as individuals into larger economic structures. Today the economic structures are to be reproduced in the reservation setting. The bargain, in other words, is reservation economic development in return for Indian resources.

This bargain is not solely economic. Transplanting American economic institutions and practices to the reservations is held up as the key also to Indian self-determination. The idea is that as tribes become more adept as resource developers, profit makers, and financial managers, they will gain at the same time the means of maximizing their independence.[6] It is a "realist" approach: the key to success lies in the institutions of the larger society.

Bargaining for resources, however, is only one aspect of a more general response, in particular to Indian demands for an increased measure of tribal self-government. This was made explicit in the Indian Self-Determination and Education Assistance Act of 1975 when Congress, responding to "the strong expression of the Indian people," officially committed itself to the provision of "maximum Indian participation in the Government and education of the Indian people" and to "an orderly transition from Federal domination of programs for and services to Indians to effective and meaningful participation by the Indian people in the planning, conduct, and administration of those programs and services."[7] The act encouraged tribes to take over from the BIA and other agencies programs in education, economic development, and social services or to contract for such programs with outside sources.

This legislation, presented as a major step forward, has been criticized by some as not quite living up to its promise, and at least one close reading of the act suggests that BIA and other federal controls were scarcely diminished by it and may even have been strengthened.[8] Nonetheless, there is ample evidence that in practical terms the subsequent ten years or so have been a period of genuine reform. By the mid-1970s Indian input into policy making had gained a significance it seldom had before, and tribal governments were exercising an unprecedented degree of power. Of the Lower Brule Sioux, for example, Ernest Schusky wrote, "The money now coming to the reservation is largely under the control of the tribal council rather than the BIA. For the first time the council is making numerous significant decisions. The council has determined such matters as who will be employed in housing construction, who is eligible for low rent housing, and how much rent will be paid." The tribal council, concluded Schusky, "has become a significant body of power."[9]

More generally, the financial and organizational resources of tribal governments have expanded, while their access to external decision-making structures and their influence over federal actions have increased. This has been most apparent in economic development. For the first time, tribes today wield considerable control over development decisions and have used that power to launch a variety of development strategies of their own. In other words, their effective power—on the reservations and off—has grown. While much of this is the result of court decisions in favor of tribal control, it also reflects new federal policies of self-determination: a genuine turn to bilateral relations. "In the 1960s," comments Bill Pensoneau, tribal planner for the Poncas in Oklahoma, "self-determination was a distant dream. We're a lot closer to it now."[10]

THE CONTROL FUNCTIONS OF REFORM

Reforms that increase the political power of challengers scarcely seem a promising way of restoring a control system. It is here, however, that the specific nature of those reforms becomes important. The new bilateralism is of a limited kind, built into a new political structure that, like the old, is also a structure of control, albeit a less efficient one.

The critical point is the reorganization of the political arena. While that arena has been opened to Indian actors, only certain ones have been allowed in. The increases in Indian political power and political access have been concentrated almost wholly in tribal governments. Indians have been encouraged to play an expanded role in Indian-White relations, but only through already established institutional structures. Tribal governments or those organizations that more or less officially represent them—for example, regional organizations and the National Tribal Chairmen's Association—have become the major sources of Indian input into policy making and administration, and intentionally so. In relation to the Self-Determination Act the Indian Bureau states that "the federal government is committed to accept and support tribal government judgments based on the needs and goals of their people."[11]

The logic of this is twofold. On the one hand, tribal governments are the only elected bodies exclusively representing Indian peoples and usually the only logical Indian recipients of funds and administrators of programs on the reservations. But the federally sponsored expansion of tribal government political power is also a control mechanism. As noted above, Native American political opposition is diverse. Some Indians have challenged both the organization of Indian-White relations and the appropri-

ateness for Indian communities of dominant political and economic institutions, rejecting not only non-Indian control of Indian lives and resources
but much of the dominant culture and society as well. Such groups pose
a substantial threat to the stabilization of Indian-White relations and the
smooth incorporation of Indian resources.

Others, including many tribal governments, also have challenged the
organization of Indian-White relations, but have viewed dominant economic and political institutions and values more favorably. Indeed, most
tribal governments are both creations and replicas of those institutions.
For such constituencies the institutions of the larger society are less at
issue than the ability of Indian tribes to use them to their own advantage.
What is important for them about economic development is that it take
place under Indian control; what is important about political incorporation is that it provide tribes with real power.

The reforms of the last decade have spoken to the more moderate demands of the latter constituencies and largely ignored the more radical
demands of the former. The federal government has moved toward greater
self-determination for Indian groups through a program of strengthening
tribal governments and giving them increased influence in Indian affairs.
These governments have become the dominant Indian actors in the political arena. This strategy has its risks. As the Northern Cheyenne moratorium on coal development and the 1982 Navajo tribal election[12] showed,
there is no guarantee that tribal governments, once able to choose their
own course of action, will follow the wishes of the larger society.

But the strategy also has advantages. As the powers of tribal governments have grown, so has their stake in the institutional structure of which
they are an increasingly important part. While they undoubtedly will continue to challenge the distribution of power within that structure, they are
unlikely to attack the institutions—political or economic—themselves or
to look kindly on those who do. What they will tend to become, in other
words, is protectors of the institutional status quo.[13]

Furthermore, by regarding those governments as the only legitimate
representatives of Indian interests, the federal government effectively justi-
fies ignoring political actions that bypass the tribal councils or their representatives, thereby directing action into channels that remain subject
ultimately to non-Indian controls. Thus the newly empowered tribal governments form buffers against more hostile political actors and constituencies
whose goals diverge more sharply from those of the larger society. Self-
determination in this case means tribal government determination. In 1976
Senator James Eastland, chairman of the Committee on the Judiciary,
made the federal position clear in his introduction to the invited testimony
of Doug Durham, FBI informer and one-time member of AIM: "As a
result of . . . extensive publicity . . . the public impression was that the
American Indian Movement spoke for the masses of the Indian people.
This, of course, is simply not true. The elected tribal councils speak for the
masses of the Indian people."[14]

This is not to say that tribal governments have adopted dominant-group, as opposed to Indian, interests; far from it. Most tribal councils are fiercely nationalistic defenders of the perceived interests of their peoples and remain highly suspicious and critical of the federal government. The point is that by responding to Indian demands for self-determination via an increase in the political power of tribal governments, the federal government has been able to take advantage of certain characteristics of those governments, in particular their desire to remain in power and their inherent attachment to dominant institutions. Those governments have been brought into the control system in a position of responsibility.

There are two other advantages to this response. First, it is a decentralizing strategy. One of the strengths of the activist movement has been its supratribal character. Mounted by diverse groups and often oriented to regional or local issues, it nonetheless has been a national phenomenon, challenging the whole framework of Indian-White relations and expressing not only tribal but also Indian solidarity. The response, in its emphasis on tribal government representation of Indian interests, disperses conflict and allows authorities to deal with Indian claims on a more tractable, group-by-group basis.[15]

Second, it deflects conflict from the intergroup to the intragroup arena. Disputes rooted in Indian-White relations are rechanneled into Indian-Indian relations, to be fought out among diverse Indian constituencies at the tribal or intertribal level. Thus the federal government is able to structure political activity in ways that partially protect dominant-group interests and facilitate at least some dominant-group control over hostile political actors and the pace and direction of change.

Superficially, at least, these events resemble the outcome of the IRA. Then, too, certain Indian actors—new tribal governments—were given some access to the political arena. The difference is that the arena then was more closely circumscribed and the power of those governments was small. There also were few hostile political actors of significance; the system as a whole was not under attack. Today the power given to those governments is substantial, in part because the system has been under attack and more hostile actors are both plentiful and significant.

Nonetheless, the current response may owe a lot to the IRA. Four decades of Indian experience with the governing structures set up by the IRA, along with a growing tribal council investment in those structures, have made tribal governments a better risk. As dominant institutions have become more firmly embedded in Indian communities, the federal government has been willing to give those communities a larger measure of independence.

The success of this strategy is by no means certain. The problem has been to allow greater Indian political participation without losing control of the nature and outcomes of subsequent political activity. The trouble is that the greater independence of tribal governments makes them increasingly potent political actors. Their agendas and those of the larger

society are not necessarily the same. Furthermore, outside the formal organization of Indian affairs there are still a number of Indian constituencies—urban Indians, subtribal groups, single-issue organizations—whose
distinctive political agendas, often including more hostile goals that are not
only transformative but also segregative in nature, remain largely unattended. Despite government efforts to discredit or disorganize some of
these groups and to place tribal governments between itself and them, many
retain significant political capacities of their own, particularly in the areas
of litigation and protest.

THE NEW PHASE OF INCORPORATION

What emerged in the 1970s was a new incorporative phase in Indian-White
relations. Its precise nature remains unclear—structures that are more
negotiated and less imposed may be more changeable—but the salient features are apparent. At its heart, once again, lies the incorporation of Native
American resources into the larger economy. Now, however, incorporation
is being pursued as much as possible through cooperative arrangements
instead of coercion, thanks in no small measure to the increased political
capacities of Indian groups. Furthermore, instead of excluding Indians
from that economy, incorporation in the current phase explicitly involves
their participation. This has occurred not because of the indispensability
of Indian skills, as in the fur trade, but as part of the price of access. Yet
the object remains the same: it is Indian resources, not Indians themselves,
that are fundamentally of interest to the larger society.

Certainly there is more to it than this. The policy of reservation economic development is only partly derivative of the energy crisis or the
quest for raw materials. Faced with unremitting poverty, tribal governments have demanded development, while federal concern about the dismal economic condition of the reservations has been apparent since the
Meriam Report of the late 1920s. It may be that, regardless of world
events, programs of reservation development would have had priority
in the 1970s and 1980s and might have succeeded on their own in bringing reservations and the American economy together. But world events
have given the development agenda a new urgency. Current pressure on
Native Americans to develop their resources in ways advocated by the
larger society is substantially a product of the old economic imperative,
itself a recurrent element in Indian-White relations, given new life in an
age of renewed scarcity.

Politically, the new phase of incorporation involves alterations in the
organization of Indian affairs designed to expand Indian participation and
strengthen the tribal government system, coupled with efforts to discredit
those political actors who are most hostile to the institutions and programs
of the larger society. This gives reality to the rhetoric of self-determina-

tion while maintaining some measure of external control over Indian actions. It also makes Indian tribes primary executors of policy. The pattern of incorporation is no longer forced upon Indians; in effect, it is chosen by them.

This new incorporative phase is a departure from the past. It is not so much dominant-group goals that have changed, however, nor, at its most fundamental level, is it Indian policy. What this new phase represents instead is a change of means, prompted by systemic political and economic developments and by the increased capacities of Native American groups to pursue their own ends.

LOOKING AHEAD

The 1980s have looked rather different from the two preceding decades. Certainly they have been more quiet. The militant phase of the activist movement peaked about 1973 and then began to wind down; by the end of the 1970s the more sensational events were a thing of the past. This was true of the nation as a whole; protest politics was becoming rare. But it reflected also the success of the federal strategy—both its reformist and its repressive components—and of Indian politics. The former had restored a control system of sorts; the latter had achieved a net increase in power. More radical Indian actors had been put down; more moderate ones had been supported. These latter have been by no means toothless. Backed by the federal policy of self-determination, Indian tribes have hastened to flex their new muscles, exerting influence and power on the reservations and off. The significant change has been not so much in the extent as in the tone and style of Indian politics, which have returned to more conventional and newly accessible channels.

Then, too, a good deal of Indian energy has been deflected to the tasks of survival. It has not been an easy time. The Reagan administration got high marks from many Indians when it announced its intention, early in 1983, to deal with tribes "on a government-to-government basis," promising support for tribal governments and consideration of their views. Responsibility for White House–tribal relations was moved from the Office of Public Liaison, which handles relations with interest groups, to the Office of Intergovernmental Affairs, which handles relations with state and local governments.[16] But even as the administration was committing itself to government-to-government relations, federal budget cutters were sending shock waves through Indian communities.

The Reagan administration made significant cuts in federal assistance to Native Americans. In 1983 alone aid was slashed by more than a third, from $3.5 billion to $2 billion, affecting programs on every reservation. Cancellation of the CETA program cost the Poncas two hundred jobs virtually overnight. The Intertribal Alcoholism Treatment Center in

Montana lost half its counselors and most of its beds. In 1982 the Navajo Tribe reported that yearly per capita income had declined 25 percent since 1980. The public housing and other programs had been cut.[17]

Few tribes have been able to recoup their losses. With weak economic bases, most have found themselves powerless in the face of rising unemployment, deteriorating health care, and a falling standard of living. Their options are limited. Attachments to community and homeland make many Indians unwilling simply to vote with their feet, as some administration planners would have it, and leave the reservation for greener pastures. A recent study of one reservation in Montana found many residents fearful this might be the only choice left to them by an economy in dramatic decline.[18] Nor do many Indians appear persuaded that a robust and rising national economy will solve their problems. Tribal planner Pensoneau looked at his Oklahoma reservation, where he estimated Ponca unemployment in 1984 at between 50 and 70 percent and could not find a bank willing to fund a reservation convenience store, and vented his disgust. "Trickle-down economics," he said, "feels a lot like being pissed on."[19]

On the other hand, armed with an unprecedented degree of control over the development process, in recent years Indian nations have become more intensely involved in development activity than ever before. From profit-oriented wildlife management on the White Mountain Apache Reservation in Arizona to coal mining on the Crow Reservation to a bingo parlor on Oklahoma's Tonkawa Reservation, economic enterprises are popping up all over Indian country. Some are making it, some aren't, but at least the development agenda is finally in Indian hands. At the same time, major assistance will be necessary if reservation economies are to become viable. Few reservations have the natural resources of such tribes as the Navajos, Utes, Jicarilla Apaches, and others; many are isolated from markets, transportation networks, and centers of population; skilled workers are rare. Outside investment is key, but not easy to find. In his search for funds Pensoneau encountered what he calls "a termination mentality, the idea that sometime Indians will finally disappear. They act as if we are not a part of the future."[20]

Not only are the options few, but the dangers are very real. As tribes pursue economic development, they have to negotiate some tricky problems, among them how to maximize tribal self-determination while making ever more elaborate the links between tribal communities and the surrounding society. Development can lead to its own form of dependency, and Indian nations, because of their size, are especially vulnerable. When the Anaconda Company closed its Jackpile uranium mine on the Laguna Pueblo Reservation in 1981, the tribe lost not only hundreds of jobs but one of the few sources of employment on the reservation. When the uranium and timber industries all but collapsed on Washington's Spokane Reservation in 1982, unemployment shot up to nearly 75 percent. AMAX's decision to leave the Colville molybdenum project left the tribe in desperate economic straits.[21] The trick will be to develop diversified economies that are neither corporate appendages nor hostage to the whims of a single market. The successes so far are few.[22]

A perhaps more difficult problem is how to make Indian communities economically viable without destroying either their communal character or indigenous cultural designs. Development tends not only to link Indian nations more closely to forces they cannot control, but also to produce divergent sets of interests within the tribal community and thereby to fragment it. It also tends to reorganize those communities on the basis of market needs and criteria instead of shared cultural practice or perception. "A tribe," says Gerald Wilkinson of the National Indian Youth Council, "is becoming less and less conceived of as a community held together by human relationships, either blood relations or ceremonial relations. It is being conceived of as a corporation. Corporate institutions are replacing tribal institutions such as the family, clan, ceremonial societies and so forth."[23]

The conflict is hardly new. It is the classic dilemma of Western development, making itself felt in Indian country as it has been felt around the world: the aggressive pursuit of economic efficiency and wealth is seldom kind to communal ties. Organizational structures are vehicles suited to particular ends. As Indian societies come more and more to resemble, in organizational terms and in daily practice, non-Indian ones, their choices, ironically, may be increasingly limited. Distinctive communities of culture may become more difficult to maintain.

Certainly such communities still survive on many reservations, rooted in tribal worldviews and bound together by common participation in networks of kinship and ceremonial action. For many Indians, regardless of how much has changed in the pattern of everyday life, these communities remain the *locus ultimus* of tribal identity.[24]

For these Indians and others like them, the values and activities attached to such communities are vital aspects of a received cultural practice, part of the furniture of daily life that is both commonplace and profound, resonant with the passage of generations who have continued to live in the eternally evolving way of "the people."

But this is by no means universally the case. There are many individuals whose links to such communities are distant and tenuous. A growing generation of urban Indians, for example, is being raised outside the embrace of traditional tribal culture, with few links to their own heritage except through occasional stories, the intermittent teachings of schools, and the simplifications of media presentations. Like many other migrants in American life, their cultural heritage is quickly becoming a description of a past that is no longer realized in practice.

But even in some reservation settings, it appears that the number of tribespeople participating in such communities may be in decline, with significant effects on Indian self-concepts. Cherokee anthropologist Robert Thomas argues that "few Indians under 40 see themselves as members of distinct, unique, autonomous peoples who are surrounded by a more numerous and powerful society. They see themselves simply as an American variant with a special heritage," that is, as comparable to every other American ethnic group, one more star in the pluralist heaven. Noting that many tribes no longer have native curers or medicine people, that few young Indians are learning to be ceremonial leaders, and that native language use is in dramatic decline, Thomas worries that "in some sense, Indian tribes are becoming collections of generalized tribal personalities without a truly native institutional structure nor a coherent culture, tradition, and language."[25]

Some signs point in the opposite direction. The political resurgence of the last few decades has been a cultural resurgence as well. Tribal languages are being taught in some reservation schools. Many young people are showing a new interest in their heritage. Indian writers and painters have immersed themselves in the traditions of their people, rearticulating them in new ways. The symbols of Indianness, from bumper-sticker slogans to religious fetishes, are becoming more visible, not less. Much of this trend reflects an attempt by some individuals to locate their own roots, to touch base with some identity more substantial than the dominant culture seems able to provide, an attempt to put a thicker flesh on the bones of their self-concept. The question is whether this cultural resurgence will be realized in actual patterns of life and action or will remain simply a veneer, an overlay on lives shaped to a large degree by the non-Indian world, a collection of icons that symbolize an identity and a past but organize little of contemporary life.

If there is a normative issue here—if the concern should be with cultural preservation—it is one for Indians to decide. As long as Indian communities of some sort survive, there will be Indian cultures as well, whether in new or old forms. *"We* are the Native people," wrote an Eskimo more than a decade ago. "What we do *is* the Native culture."[26] This will be as true decades from now as it was then, however that culture changes in response to new challenges. The point is that as development proceeds, as the institutions, values, and practices of the larger society become more completely reproduced and firmly implanted in Indian communities, it may become more difficult to sustain tribal identities as distinct ways of life and interpretation and not simply as political rhetorics.[27]

In such circumstances tribal communities may also become more difficult to defend politically. The protection of sovereignty and treaty rights depends to some extent on public, non-Indian support. If Indian nations come to be viewed not as carriers of distinct ways of life, involuntarily put to risk by the larger society, but simply as anachronistic legal residues of an unfortunate past, that support may disappear. In a peculiar way, distinctiveness is a form of security.[28]

Certainly there are enemies around. The "termination mentality" Pensoneau encountered is no figment of his imagination. It is apparent in comments like that of the mayor of Scottsdale, Arizona, adjacent to the

Salt River Reservation, who told the *Wall Street Journal* in 1977, "It seems to me that someday we're going to have to abandon the whole idea of Indian reservations. End them, and the Indian could be assimilated into American society."[29] This melting pot vision is an Indian nightmare.

But the termination mentality has a still more malevolent side. A movement to revoke Indian treaty rights has been under way since the late 1970s, when Congressman Jack Cunningham of Washington introduced legislation that would have abrogated treaties and ended the federal-tribal trust relationship.[30] The bill went nowhere, but the movement gradually picked up popular support, fed by growing resource-related conflicts between Indian and non-Indian interests. By 1983, responding to water issues in particular, the American Farm Bureau Federation drafted "The American Indian Property Right Act of 1983." Among its goals: "the termination of federal supervision over the trust properties of Indians, the transfer of Indian reservation lands to the several Indian tribes for disposal to members of Indian tribes, . . . termination of federal services furnished Indians because of their status as Indians."[31] While the legislation was not passed, it was indicative of what was going on, as was Initiative 456 in the state of Washington, adopted in the 1984 elections, which threatened treaty-based fishing rights.

The rhetoric of the abrogationist movement is the old rhetoric of termination: Indians should be given equal status with other Americans, set free of tribal bonds, brought into the mainstream. The leading abrogationist organization in Wisconsin in the early 1980s called itself Equal Rights for Everyone; in Montana, Montanans Opposing Discrimination.

But the issue has little to do with equality. At the heart of it is a very different and much older story: the continuing demand for Indian resources.

In the 1970s, during the seemingly endless battle over fishing rights in the Pacific Northwest, Indians in the region put out a poster that presented their own argument in compelling terms. They pointed out that in the nineteenth century, in an agreement worked out over a number of years and enshrined in treaties entered into by sovereign nations, the Indians of the Northwest gave to the United States a vast expanse of land, including much of what is now Washington and Oregon and parts of Idaho and California. In return, among other things, the United States formally recognized specific rights of those nations to fish in certain northwestern waters. It seems obvious who got the better part of this exchange, but the point is the treaties in which the exchange is enshrined and on which, to a significant degree, the survival of Native American communities depends. "We made an agreement," said the Indians' poster. "We kept our part. You keep yours."[32]

Chapter 13

"Another World is Coming"[1]

Action is a contingent process. It is derivative of circumstance, shaped by the world in which it occurs. But it also can be productive of circumstance, a shaper of worlds, refashioning its limits even as it responds to them.

This duality is amply apparent in the history of Indian-White relations. One of the striking things about that history is the rapidly declining role of Indian action. Native Americans were crucial actors in the early years; by late in the nineteenth century, however, their influence on Indian affairs was virtually nil. Their decline can be described in terms of the political opportunities they had, their capacities to exploit those opportunities, and resulting patterns of action.

In the first, or market, period, from soon after contact until the middle of the eighteenth century, there is high demand by Europeans for resources controlled by Native Americans—both economic and political—combined with relatively high Native American political capacities. The result is a substantial degree of political power in the hands of certain Indian groups. Via force, diplomacy, and trade, some of those groups are able not only to enhance their political and economic position relative to other Native Americans, but, for a time at least, also to play a central, determinative role in the development of Indian-White relations.

With the transition from the market to the conflict period, their influence begins to decline. That transition is itself largely a product of forces exogenous to the intergroup arena. It has more to do with growing colonial populations, the declining relative value of the fur trade, and altered relations among the European powers than with any particular actions by Native Americans. While they were among the architects of market structure, Indians were peripheral to its collapse.

This diminished role continues in the conflict years. By the beginning of the nineteenth century, U.S. hegemony has eliminated the intra-European competition for Indian alliance; demand for Indian economic resources remains high, but the resources at stake change. No longer furs and labor, the issue now is land. Native Americans are no longer participants in economic incorporation, but obstacles to it. At the same time Indian political capacities are in decline. The result is rapidly dwindling Native American power and diminished Indian influence on the structure of Indian-White relations. Certainly Indian military capabilities remain important in some areas until the last few decades of the century, but increasingly the relations themselves reflect other factors, in particular non-Indian economic interests and the concerns of reformers and humanitarians, all operating under the umbrella of rapidly growing U.S. military power. Indians are less and less the makers of their own world.

In the move to the reservation period this subductive process becomes extreme: both the opportunity structure—the political openings offered by the structure of relations between Indian groups and Euro-American society—and indigenous political capacities have collapsed, while Indians themselves have become objects of a repressive administrative apparatus. The result, for the most part, is political paralysis, at least in the secular realm. Forced from the political arena, most Native American groups either abandon intergroup politics altogether or turn to an assortment of cultural or religious movements in an attempt to restore some degree of order and power to their communities and lives. In this they reflect their circumstances: their alternative courses of action are few. Through such movements and in their adaptive strategies of daily living, Indians continue, in important ways, to shape their own worlds, but they play little part in the broader construction of Indian-White relations.

While the twentieth century sees a gradual reversal of the overall trend, even the more hopeful transition from the reservation period to the IRA years has little to do with Indian actions. It occurs under the influence of broader societal developments: lingering progressivism and reform sentiments, diminished demand for Indian lands, the New Deal. While the IRA opens up new opportunities for political action and initiates a major increase in Indian political capacities, Native Americans remain minor political actors. New Indian politics is clearly in the making in these years, but its influence is slight. The subsequent termination policy, itself a product of forces beyond Indian control, only serves to demonstrate the fact.

The latest transition, however, has been different, signifying a major new pattern in Indian-White relations. The move from termination to self-determination—that is, to the current stage in Indian affairs—has been in substantial measure a product of Indian actions. Those actions are themselves reflective of previous developments and events, of a half century of changes in group organization and self-concept, capacities, and opportunities. But now the circle is complete. Native Americans, who played a leading role in the early development of Indian-White relations and then were transformed by those relations and related events, since 1960 have become once again major actors in their own drama. This latest stage has

not been dictated or designed by them, but it bears the mark of their resurgent effort to claim control of their own communities and lives. It
records, in effect, the recovery of a modest degree of power: not only
the ability to act, but also a measure of leverage over the related actions
of others. The fragility of the gains—and their selective distribution—is
all too apparent, but so also is their impact: the world of Indian-White
relations is changing. More than anyone else, Native Americans made it
happen.

Yet the new Indian politics has been more than simply a broad movement for social change. It is also an arena of action, an expanding political space within which a growing number of actors and agendas is engaged. Like the arena itself, those actors and agendas are products of
a historical restructuring both of Native Americans' lives and of their
relationships with each other and with the non-Indian world. The result
is a changed but still remarkable diversity that reflects less and less the
variety of the aboriginal past and more and more the complex ways in
which Indians have been integrated into the economics and politics of
the contemporary United States. The cumulative result of this rapidly
expanding political participation has been to render an orderly set of intergroup relations disorderly, and to bring a diverse set of claims into the
political process. It is this very diversity that has at once both limited the
achievements of Indian political resurgence and made it so difficult to
contain.

Thanks in part to the resultant chaos, some of these claimants have
been more successful than others. Actors with political and economic
claims against the larger system have been accommodated so long as they
have accepted the institutional means of redress offered by that system.
Distributional politics, after all, is largely assimilated politics, however
conflictual it may be. On the other hand, actors with political and economic claims who reject those means of redress are less manageable and
generally have been suppressed. Potentially most difficult are those actors
whose claims are not primarily political or economic but cultural. They
are difficult to deal with because their claims are not negotiable; what
they are defending is their own participation in a particular cultural system that has become both method and motivation of their politics and
is fundamentally at odds with the social organization and culture of the
larger society. The most traditional groups on the reservations fit into
this category, but they have little power; except when they have joined
forces with other radical constituencies, for the most part they have been
ignored.

Looming in the background of these events and giving them their own
developmental logic has been the historical trajectory of incorporation:
the changing sets of linkages between Native Americans and larger societal structures. Certain of those linkages have been especially important:
among others, the treaty relationship, the reservation system, urbanization, the IRA. These have set the terms of action, opening up some op-

portunities and closing others, creating and distributing new resources, rearranging the actors themselves. A common thread runs through many of them: the centrality of land, the peripherality of labor. It is not the whole story, but it loosely ties together some disparate developments. It is the demand for land that leaves Native Americans on reservations and thereby contributes to their survival as nations; it is negotiation over land that leads to treaties and thereby to a distinct legal standing; it is land that ultimately gives bargaining power to late-twentieth-century tribes. Much of the pattern of incorporation, and many of its effects, can be traced to this crucial point.

That incorporative pattern in turn has been reflective of larger societal transformations: European invasion and competition, the demand for furs, U.S. agrarianism and economic development, the reform movements of the late nineteenth and early twentieth centuries, the New Deal, the cold war, the turmoil of the 1960s, the energy crisis—the list goes on. What began as a study of Indian political resurgence necessarily becomes a study of Indian-White relations and in turn a chronicle of Euro-American society. The transitions are logical and necessary: action is made comprehensible by context.

It is made comprehensible also by history, and particularly so in the Native American case. "Indians," as Sam Stanley has written,

> have a perspective toward modern life which involves their own past deeply. The treaties, which most non-Indians regard trivially, are a sacred part of their life. . . . They had their roots here thousands of years before Europeans arrived. They are acutely aware of the specific ways in which they lost possession of over 98 percent of the land to non-Indians. All of this involves history, and it is living history to Indians—handed down orally in every tribe.[2]

The historical frame of reference within which most Indians consciously act is immense. Other groups in American life—Jews, Blacks, perhaps others—may have a sense of history matching it in scope and in the immediacy with which it informs their daily lives. Uniquely for Indians, however, that sense of history is rooted here, in this land, in the geography of their present. Most forms of Indian political action are explicitly grounded in a consciousness of that history and, more often than not, are articulated in explicitly historical terms.

But there is another reason as well for the historical dimension in a study such as this. Incorporation, identity, action—such phenomena are more process than event; they cannot be accounted for in static terms. To look at only one moment, at one stage, in the unfolding of intergroup relations or collective action is to look at a single frame from a motion picture. We see a juxtaposition of elements, an alignment of actors and circumstance, but lacking knowledge of how that particular arrangement came about, we are likely to have an inadequate and perhaps erroneous idea of what is going on. We have a picture but not a story. The point is to tell the story, not simply as a narrative of events, but as an analysis of the construction and reconstruction of relationships; to produce, in other words, a historical sociology of the events themselves.

To do so is to make an inquiry into the extended and reciprocal relations between structure and action. The particular concern of historical sociology, writes Philip Abrams, is the problem of agency, "the problem of finding a way of accounting for human experience which recognises simultaneously and in equal measure that history and society are made by constant and more or less purposeful individual action *and* that individual action, however purposeful, is made by history and society."[3] The world makes us; we remake the world.

This relationship between action and structure has been the implicit theme of this study. What we have here is an intermingling of two histories, at once distinct and inseparable: the life history of a people—more precisely, of a collection of peoples—and that of an evolving and ultimately encompassing society. That intermingling has been the focal point of the analysis. It is a sociological analysis insofar as its central concern has been the ways that this encounter has shaped and been shaped by the actions of the groups involved; it is historical not only in the temporal breadth of its attention, but insofar as it has conceived the two aspects of that shaping as a single extended process, as the irregular rhythms by which a world—perhaps over very long periods of time—is continually remade.

Such, indeed, is the point of Indian political resurgence. Native Americans remake their world early and late, in the first stages of incorporation and the last. The object has been to examine the long road that leads from one time of power to the next, to show that for Native Americans, as for others, the relationship between structure and action—between incorporation and response—is a reciprocal one. People act within the limits of particular situations, but in so doing they may transform both themselves and the conditions under which they act. The next stage of Indian-White relations remains unknown, but it seems certain that, in some substantial measure, once again it will be Indian-made.

Notes

Chapter 1. The New Indian Politics

1. There are a number of useful accounts of the Wounded Knee massacre. See, for example, *Report of the Commissioner of Indian Affairs, 1890* (Washington: Department of the Interior, 1891), pp. 125–35; James Mooney, *The Ghost-Dance Religion and the Sioux Outbreak of 1890* Fourteenth Annual Report of the Bureau of Ethnology, 1892–93, Part 2 (Washington: Government Printing Office, 1896), ch. 13; Robert M. Utley, *The Last Days of the Sioux Nation* (New Haven: Yale University Press, 1963), ch. 12; U.S. Senate, *Hearings Before the Committee on the Judiciary,* "To liquidate the liability of the United States for the Massacre of Sioux Indian men, women, and children at Wounded Knee on December 29, 1890," 94th Congress, 2nd Session, 1976.

2. The most detailed account of this incident is in Akwesasne Notes, *Voices from Wounded Knee, 1973* (Mohawk Nation, Rooseveltown, N.Y.: Akwesasne Notes, 1974); see also Peter Matthiessen, *In the Spirit of Crazy Horse* (New York: Viking, 1983), ch. 3, and contemporary coverage in the *New York Times.*

3. "Black Hawk's Farewell," reprinted in Interracial Books for Children, *Chronicles of American Indian Protest* (New York: The Council on Interracial Books for Children, 1979), p. 108.

4. Clyde Warrior, "We Are Not Free," in Alvin M. Josephy, Jr., *Red Power: The American Indians' Fight for Freedom* (New York: McGraw-Hill, 1971), p. 72.

5. Quoted in Michael Paul Rogin, *Fathers and Children: Andrew Jackson and the Subjugation of the American Indian* (New York: Vintage, 1976), p. 117, and originally in James Parton, *Life of Andrew Jackson,* 3 vols. (Boston, 1966), 1:401.

6. Vine Deloria, Jr., *We Talk, You Listen* (New York: Macmillan, 1970).

7. Joseph K. Dixon, *The Vanishing Race: The Last Great Indian Council* (New York: Popular Library, 1972; orig. pub. 1913), p. 222.

8. Karl Marx, "The Eighteenth Brumaire of Louis Bonaparte," in Robert C. Tucker, ed., *The Marx-Engels Reader* (New York: W. W. Norton, 1972), p. 437.

9. Philip Abrams, *Historical Sociology* (Ithaca: Cornell University Press, 1982), p. 3.

Chapter 2. Exceptional Beginnings: The Fur Trade and Indian Labor

1. Francis Jennings, *The Invasion of America: Indians, Colonialism, and the Cant of Conquest* (New York: W. W. Norton, 1976).

2. James Lang, *Conquest and Commerce: Spain and England in the Americas* (New York: Academic Press, 1975), p. 108.

3. On Jamestown, see ibid., p. 112; on Plymouth, Francis X. Moloney, *The Fur Trade in New England 1620–1676* (Cambridge: Harvard University Press, 1931), p. 19; on New Netherlands, Francis Jennings, "Glory, Death, and Transfiguration: The Susquehannock Indians in the Seventeenth Century," *Proceedings of the American Philosophical Society* 112, no. 1 (February 1968): 23; and on the French, Robert A. Goldstein, *French-Iroquois Diplomatic and Military Relations, 1609–1701* (The Hague: Mouton, 1969), pp. 24–25, and Paul Chrisler Phillips, *The Fur Trade*, 2 vols. (Norman: University of Oklahoma Press, 1961), 1:27f. Jennings's remark on the Dutch perhaps needs qualification. While the fur trade dominated economic activity in the colony, the Dutch West India Company did experiment with other commercial ventures, in particular agriculture. But New Netherland was certainly a commercial enterprise. See Van Cleaf Bachman, *Peltries or Plantations: The Economic Policies of the Dutch West India Company in New Netherland 1623–1639* (Baltimore: The Johns Hopkins Press, 1969), pp. 54–55. The same can be said of Russian penetrations of Alaska. Writes James R. Gibson: "The maritime fur trade was the raison d'etre of Russian America. The procurement (by hunting and trading) and exportation of furs remained the principal business of the Russians until the middle of the nineteenth century." *Imperial Russia in Frontier America: The Changing Geography of Supply of Russian America, 1784–1867* (New York: Oxford University Press, 1976), p. 32.

4. Francis Jennings has pointed out that trade in furs was itself simply one case of a more general phenomenon of intersocietal exchange in which "natives worked at extractive industries to produce goods to exchange for the products of European processing industries." In the period at issue here, the primary good produced by natives for exchange with Europeans was animal hides, and the trade in hides has been referred to generally as "the fur trade." See Jennings, *The Ambiguous Iroquois Empire: The Covenant Chain Confederation of Indian Tribes with English Colonies from its Beginnings to the Lancaster Treaty of 1744* (New York: W. W. Norton, 1984), pp. 61–62.

5. Murray G. Lawson, *Fur: A Study in English Mercantilism, 1700–1775*, University of Toronto Studies, History and Economics Series, vol. 9 (Toronto: University of Toronto Press, 1943), pp. 2–8; Phillips, *Fur Trade*, 1:27, 203.

6. Harold A. Innis, *The Fur Trade in Canada: An Introduction to Canadian Economic History* (New Haven: Yale University Press, 1930), pp. 13–14; Jennings, *Invasion of America*, pp. 98–99. On consumer items sought by Indian customers, see ibid.; also Arthur J. Ray, *Indians in the Fur Trade: Their Role*

as Trappers, Hunters, and Middlemen in the Lands Southwest of Hudson Bay, 1660–1870 (Toronto: University of Toronto Press, 1974), ch. 9, and Toby Morantz, "The Fur Trade and the Cree of James Bay," in Carol M. Judd and Arthur J. Ray, eds., Old Trails and New Directions: Papers of the Third North American Fur Trade Conference (Toronto: University of Toronto Press, 1980), pp. 41–45.

7. On the Mohawk-Susquehannock conflict, see Jennings, "Glory, Death, and Transfiguration," pp. 23–25; on the English view of the Iroquois, Allen W. Trelease, Indian Affairs in Colonial New York: The Seventeenth Century (Ithaca: Cornell University Press, 1960), p. ix; on prices of English goods, ibid., pp. 217–18, and Thomas Eliot Norton, The Fur Trade in Colonial New York 1686–1776 (Madison: University of Wisconsin Press, 1974), p. 12. More generally on Iroquois-European relations in the colonial period, see Jennings, Ambiguous Iroquois Empire.

8. See, for example, Patricia Dillon Woods, French-Indian Relations on the Southern Frontier, 1699–1762 (Ann Arbor: UMI Research Press, 1980).

9. Wesley Frank Craven, The Colonies in Transition, 1660–1713 (New York: Harper and Row, 1968), p. 112; Edward Channing, A History of the United States, 6 vols. (New York: Macmillan, 1909), 1:313–14. On Pennsylvania, see Francis Jennings, "The Indian Trade of the Susquehanna Valley," Proceedings of the American Philosophical Society 110, no. 2 (December 1966): 407; on New Netherland and New York, Trelease, Indian Affairs in New York, pp. 131, 256; on Maryland, Lewis Cecil Gray, History of Agriculture in the Southern United States to 1860, 2 vols. (Gloucester: Peter Smith, 1958), 1:130.

10. Phillips, Fur Trade, 1:165–73; Lang, Conquest and Commerce, pp. 125–26; Craven, Colonies in Transition, p. 135.

11. Gray, History of Agriculture, 1:129; Philip M. Brown, "Early Indian Trade in the Development of South Carolina: Politics, Economics, and Social Mobility During the Proprietary Period, 1670–1719," The South Carolina Historical Magazine 76, no. 3 (July 1975): 118–28; Moloney, Fur Trade in New England, p. 31.

12. F. F. Rich, "Russia and the Colonial Fur Trade," The Economic History Review (Second Series) 7, no. 3 (1955): 307–8; Norton, Fur Trade in New York, p. 101; Moloney, Fur Trade in New England, p. 66.

13. Lawson, Fur, pp. 70–72; Norton, Fur Trade in New York, pp. 101–2, 120.

14. Thomas Jefferson, "Memoir of Meriwether Lewis," in Meriwether Lewis and William Clark, The History of the Lewis and Clark Expedition, ed. Elliott Coues, 3 vols. (New York: Dover, 1965; orig. 1893), 1:xxix.

15. Jennings, Invasion of America, p. 89.

16. Ibid., p. 88. On the processing of deer skins, see ibid., p. 92; and on beaver, Phillips, Fur Trade, 1:105. More generally on processing methods, see Harold E. Driver, Indians of North America, 2nd ed. (Chicago: University of Chicago Press, 1969), pp. 164–66. As Driver notes, much of the labor involved in the processing of hides, as opposed to their procurement, was done by women. Alan M. Klein has argued recently that as Indian involvement in fur production increased, women bore an ever greater share of the economic burden, and their roles in the indigenous economy became increasingly circumscribed. See Klein, "The Political Economy of Gender: A 19th Century Plains

Indian Case Study," in Patricia Albers and Beatrice Medicine, eds., *The Hidden Half: Studies of Plains Indian Women* (Washington: University Press of America, 1983), pp. 143–73.

17. Quoted in Innis, *Fur Trade in Canada,* p. 239; see also Gibson, *Imperial Russia in America.*

18. On the Huron, see Bruce Trigger, *The Children of Aataentsic: A History of the Huron People to 1660,* 2 vols. (Montreal: McGill–Queen's University Press, 1976), 1: ch. 6; on the Potawatomi, James Clifton, *The Prairie People: Continuity and Change in Potawatomi Indian Culture 1665–1965* (Lawrence: The Regents Press of Kansas, 1977), p. 52; on the Assiniboine and Cree, Ray, *Indians in Fur Trade,* ch. 3; on the Iroquois, Trelease, *Indian Affairs in New York,* pp. 118–20.

19. Clifton, *Prairie People,* p. 127. See also Arthur J. Ray, "Indians as Consumers in the Eighteenth Century," in Judd and Ray, *Old Trails and New Directions,* pp. 255–71.

20. While Indian demands for commodities played a critical role in the trade, they were by no means insatiable. In their study of Hudson's Bay Company records, Arthur Ray and Donald Freeman have shown that attempts by Bay Company traders to increase the number of furs Indians produced by offering higher prices failed to have the desired result, actually producing fewer furs as Indians found they could satisfy their needs with less. Growing Indian demands were more likely to reflect depreciation and replacement of goods and expansion of the trade itself than a propensity to maximize income. See Ray and Freeman, *'Give Us Good Measure': An Economic Analysis of Relations Between the Indians and the Hudson's Bay Company Before 1763* (Toronto: University of Toronto Press, 1978), ch. 14; also Morantz, "Fur Trade and Cree," p. 50, and E. E. Rich, "Trade Habits and Economic Motivation among the Indians of North America," *Canadian Journal of Economics and Political Science* 26 (1960): 35–53, who argues that the trade must be seen as a social as well as economic activity. Duane Champagne has attributed the lack of accumulative behavior as much to the political and economic circumstances of the trade as to Indian cultural characteristics. See his "Politics, Markets, and Social Structure: The Political and Economic Responses of Four Native American Societies to Western Impacts," Ph.D. dissertation, Harvard University, 1982.

21. James Mooney, *Historical Sketch of the Cherokee* (Chicago: Aldine, 1975; orig. 1900), p. 72; Clifton, *Prairie People,* pp. 53, 127; Charles A. Bishop, *The Northern Ojibwa and the Fur Trade: An Historical and Ecological Study* (Toronto: Holt, Rinehart and Winston, 1974), p. 12, ch. 8; John Ewers, *The Blackfeet: Raiders on the Northwestern Plains* (Norman: University of Oklahoma Press, 1958), pp. 44, 70.

22. See, for example, the discussion in William Cronon, *Changes in the Land: Indians, Colonists, and the Ecology of New England* (New York: Hill and Wang, 1983), pp. 93–97; also Sylvia Van Kirk, *"Many Tender Ties": Women in Fur-Trade Society in Western Canada, 1670–1870* (Norman: University of Oklahoma Press, 1980).

23. Norton, *Fur Trade in New York,* p. 212.

24. James Axtell, *The European and the Indian: Essays in the Ethnohistory of Colonial North America* (New York: Oxford University Press, 1981), p. 246.

25. See, for example, Ewers, *Blackfeet,* p. 66; Trigger, *Children of Aataent-*

sic, p. 208; Susan McCulloch Stevens, "Passamaquoddy Economic Development in Cultural and Historical Perspective," in Sam Stanley, ed., *American Indian Economic Development* (The Hague: Mouton, 1978), p. 340.

26. Phillips, *Fur Trade*, 1:89, 315, 496, 612, 623; see also Cronon, *Changes in the Land*, pp. 97–102.

27. Alfred Goldsworthy Bailey, *The Conflict of European and Algonkian Cultures 1504–1700: A Study in Canadian Civilization*, 2nd ed. (Toronto: University of Toronto Press, 1969), p. 56; Ray, *Indians in Fur Trade*, p. 147; Craven, *Colonies in Transition*, p. 113; Bishop, *Northern Ojibwa and Fur Trade*, ch. 8.

28. Trigger, *Children of Aataentsic*, ch. 11; Jennings, *Ambiguous Iroquois Empire*, pp. 99–100.

29. Jennings, "Glory, Death, and Transfiguration," p. 29.

30. An exception to this voluntary participation, at least for a while, was the Russian American maritime trade, where Aleuts and Konyagas, according to Gibson, were "virtually enslaved" by Russian entrepreneurs, who forced them to hunt sea otters for pelts. See *Imperial Russia in America*, pp. 8, 32.

31. Jennings, *Invasion of America*, p. 90; Richard M. Clokey, *William H. Ashley: Enterprise and Politics in the Trans-Mississippi West* (Norman: University of Oklahoma Press, 1980), p. 68; David J. Wishart, *The Fur Trade of the American West, 1807–1840: A Geographical Synthesis* (Lincoln: University of Nebraska Press, 1979), p. 125. The Blackfeet refused trappers access to their country, offering to trade but reserving the trapping role for themselves, leading eventually to violent conflict with Whites. See Ewers, *Blackfeet*, p. 57.

32. Ray and Freeman, *'Give Us Good Measure,'* pp. 262–63.

33. For a discussion of the end of competitive political conditions in North America, the emergence of British hegemony, and the significance of both for Native Americans, see Champagne, "Politics, Markets, and Social Structure."

34. Clarence L. Ver Steeg, *The Formative Years: 1607–1763* (New York: Hill and Wang, 1964), p. 183; Phillips, *Fur Trade*, 1:580–81, 612.

35. See Barbara Graymont, *The Iroquois in the American Revolution* (Syracuse: Syracuse University Press, 1972), ch. 4 and 5.

36. Reginald Horsman, *The Frontier in the Formative Years, 1783–1815* (New York: Holt, Rinehart and Winston, 1970), ch. 1 and 2.

37. Given the limited role of labor in Indian-White relations, it is understandable that little attention has been paid to it, but it remains an important part of the Indian experience in North America, both historically and, increasingly, at the present time. Some scholars recently have begun to look at it more closely. See, for example, Patricia K. Ourada, "Indians in the Work Force," *Journal of the West* 25, no. 2 (April 1986): 52–58; Cardell K. Jacobson, "Internal Colonialism and Native Americans: Indian Labor in the United States from 1871 to World War II," *Social Science Quarterly* 65, no. 1 (March 1984): 158–71; George Harwood Phillips, "Indians in Los Angeles, 1781–1875: Economic Integration, Social Disintegration," *Pacific Historical Review* 69 (August 1980): 427–51; Albert L. Hurtado, " 'Hardly a Farm House—A Kitchen Without Them': Indian and White Households on the California Borderland Frontier in 1860," *Western Historical Quarterly* 13, no. 3 (July 1982): 245–70; idem, "Controlling California's Indian Labor Force: Federal Administration of California Indian Affairs During the Mexican War," *Southern California Quarterly* 61, no. 3 (Fall 1979): 217–38; Eric Henderson, "Skilled and Un-

skilled Blue Collar Navajo Workers: Occupational Diversity in an American Indian Tribe," *Social Science Journal* 16, no. 2 (April 1979): 63–80; Rolf Knight, *Indians at Work: An Informal History of Native Indian Labour in British Columbia, 1858–1930* (Vancouver: New Star, 1978).

38. On Indian enslavement, see Almon Wheeler Lauber, *Indian Slavery in Colonial Times within the Present Limits of the United States,* Columbia University Studies in History, Economics and Public Law, vol. 54 (New York: Columbia University, 1913); Winthrop D. Jordan, *White Over Black: American Attitudes Toward the Negro, 1550–1812* (Baltimore: Penguin, 1969), pp. 69, 89–90. The South Carolina figures are from Gray, *History of Agriculture,* 1:328, 360–61. The Opechancanough invitation is recounted in J. Leitch Wright, Jr., *The Only Land They Knew: The Tragic Story of the American Indians in the Old South* (New York: The Free Press, 1981), p. 70. On slavery among Indian groups, see Driver, *Indians of North America,* ch. 19.

39. Edward H. Spicer, *Cycles of Conquest: The Impact of Spain, Mexico, and the United States on the Indians of the Southwest, 1533–1960* (Tucson: University of Arizona Press, 1962), pp. 158–59; Sherburne F. Cook, *The Conflict Between the California Indian and White Civilization* (Berkeley: University of California Press, 1976), pp. 224, 300–16.

40. Jordan, *White Over Black,* pp. 89–91; Gary B. Nash, "Red, White, and Black: The Origins of Racism in Colonial America," in Donald L. Noel, ed., *The Origins of American Slavery and Racism* (Columbus: Charles E. Merrill, 1972), pp. 146–48.

41. Jordan, *White Over Black,* p. 89; Eugene Genovese, "The Negro Laborer in Africa and the Slave South," in idem, *The Political Economy of Slavery: Studies in the Economy and Society of the Slave South* (New York: Vintage, 1967), p. 82, and pp. 72–73.

42. Marvin Harris, *Patterns of Race in the Americas* (New York: W. W. Norton, 1974), p. 12.

43. Peter H. Wood, *Black Majority: Negroes in Colonial South Carolina from 1670 through the Stono Rebellion* (New York: W. W. Norton, 1975), ch. 2.

44. Hurtado, "California's Indian Labor Force," p. 219. On the railroad, see the remarks by W. B. Dodoridge, cited in Lynne Rhodes Mayer and Kenneth E. Vose, *Makin' Tracks: The Story of the Transcontinental Railroad in the Pictures and Words of the Men Who Were There* (New York: Praeger, 1975), p. 93. On the Paiutes, see Martha C. Knack, "A Short Resource History of Pyramid Lake, Nevada," *Ethnohistory* 24, no. 1 (Winter 1977): 49–50. On the Southwest, see Spicer, *Cycles of Conquest,* p. 540.

45. Loring Benson Priest, *Uncle Sam's Stepchildren: The Reformation of United States Indian Policy, 1865–1887* (Lincoln: University of Nebraska Press, 1975), p. 115.

46. Jacobson, "Internal Colonialism and Native Americans," pp. 164–65; Donald L. Parman, "The Indian and the Civilian Conservation Corps," in Norris Hundley, ed., *The American Indian* (Santa Barbara: Clio Press, 1974), p. 143.

Chapter 3. Solving "the Indian Problem"

1. March 1, 1871, in Senate debate over an appropriation bill that would, among other things, end treaty making between the United States and the Indian nations, reported in *Congressional Globe*, 41st Congress, 3rd Session, 1871, p. 1825.

2. James Truslow Adams, *Provincial Society 1690–1763* (New York: Macmillan, 1927), p. 64.

3. Michael Paul Rogin, "Liberal Society and the Indian Question," *Politics and Society* 3 (1971): 269–312.

4. Susan Previant Lee and Peter Passell, *A New Economic View of American History* (New York: W. W. Norton, 1979), p. 21.

5. See, for example, Douglass C. North, "International Capital Flows and the Development of the American West," *Journal of Economic History* 16, no. 4 (December 1956): 493–94. The land factor also shaped technological development. "A distinctive feature of much American innovation," writes Nathan Rosenberg, "was that it was directed toward making possible the exploitation of a large quantity of such resources with relatively little labor." Rosenberg, *Technology and American Economic Growth* (New York: Harper and Row, 1972), p. 25.

6. Given the central role of land availability in agricultural expansion (to say nothing of its role in economic development generally), the lack of attention to Indian dispossession in American economic history texts is striking. Most either take the land as given or refer largely to U.S. acquisitions from European powers or Mexico, mentioning Indians only in passing or not at all. Dispossession was not merely an aspect of frontier history; it was the fundamental economic event on which much of the American future turned.

7. Mapping Indian land cessions against area-specific increases in southern cotton production during this period shows a lag time of only a few years between the two. Combining this with Douglass North's argument about the role of cotton production in early American economic growth produces a graphic demonstration of the elementary relationship between dispossession and economic development. See Stephen E. Cornell, "American Indian Political Resurgence: The Historical Sociology of Group Incorporation and Response," Ph.D. dissertation, University of Chicago, 1980, ch. 4. Indian land cessions are shown in Charles C. Royce, comp., *Indian Land Cessions in the United States,* Eighteenth Annual Report of the Bureau of American Ethnology, 1896–1897, Part II (Washington: Government Printing Office, 1899); increases in cotton production can be followed in Stuart Bruchey, comp. and ed., *Cotton and the Growth of the American Economy: 1790–1860* (New York: Harcourt, Brace and World, 1967); see also the maps in Gray, *History of Agriculture*, vol. 2. For North's argument, see Douglass C. North, *The Economic Growth of the United States, 1790–1860* (New York: W. W. Norton, 1966). Certain of his views have been challenged, although the general significance of cotton has not been seriously disputed. See the summary appraisal in Lee and Passell, *New Economic View*, pp. 146–52.

8. On Arkansas, see David L. Cohn, *The Life and Times of King Cotton* (New York: Oxford University Press, 1956), pp. 105–6; on Mississippi, Arthur H. DeRosier, Jr., *The Removal of the Choctaw Indians* (Knoxville: University

of Tennessee Press, 1970), p. 100, also p. 48. More generally, see Rogin, *Fathers and Children,* ch. 7, and pp. 174–75.

9. Weber writes: "The old economic order asked: How can I give, on this piece of land, work and sustenance to the greatest possible number of men? Capitalism asks: From this given piece of land how can I produce as many crops as possible for the market with as few men as possible?" Max Weber, "Capitalism and Rural Society in Germany," in idem, *From Max Weber: Essays in Sociology,* ed. H. H. Gerth and C. Wright Mills (New York: Oxford University Press, 1958), p. 367. Cf. Barrington Moore: "Under the pressure of circumstances, the medieval notion of judging economic actions according to their contribution to the health of the social organism began to collapse. Men ceased to see the agrarian problem as a question of finding the best method of supporting people on the land and began to perceive it as the best way of investing capital in the land." *Social Origins of Dictatorship and Democracy: Lord and Peasant in the Making of the Modern World* (Boston: Beacon Press, 1966), p. 8. This systemic conflict between capitalism and its precursors is the theme of Karl Polanyi, *The Great Transformation: The Political and Economic Origins of Our Time* (Boston: Beacon Press, 1957).

10. This point is particularly well made by Rogin, *Fathers and Children,* especially ch. 3 and 6.

11. Ibid., p. 102.

12. Robert F. Berkhofer, Jr., *The White Man's Indian: Images of the American Indian from Columbus to the Present* (New York: Knopf, 1978), p. 135; see also his subsequent discussion, pp. 135–39.

13. This brief discussion of agrarianism in America draws largely on: Drew R. McCoy, *The Elusive Republic: Political Economy in Jeffersonian America* (New York: W. W. Norton, 1980), especially ch. 1 and 2; Henry Nash Smith, *Virgin Land: The American West as Symbol and Myth* (Cambridge: Harvard University Press, 1950), ch. 11 and 12; A. Whitney Griswold, "The Agrarian Democracy of Thomas Jefferson," *American Political Science Review* 40, no. 4 (1946): 657–81; and Garry Wills, *Inventing America: Jefferson's Declaration of Independence* (New York: Doubleday, 1978).

14. Thomas Jefferson, *Notes on the State of Virginia* (New York: Harper Torchbooks, 1964), pp. 157–58.

15. Griswold, "Agrarian Democracy," p. 667; see also Wills, *Inventing America,* ch. 16.

16. John Adams, letter to James Sullivan, in *The Works of John Adams,* ed. Charles Francis Adams, 9 vols. (Boston: Little, Brown and Co., 1850–56), 9:376–77.

17. The conflict between these is beyond the scope of this discussion, but see Mary Young, "The West and American Cultural Identity: Old Themes and New Variations," *Western Historical Quarterly* 1, no. 2 (1970): esp. 156–60; also Rogin, *Fathers and Children,* pp. 101–7.

18. Quoted in Smith, *Virgin Land,* p. 37.

19. Marshall Sahlins, *Stone Age Economics* (Chicago: Aldine-Atherton, 1972), p. 76; idem, *Tribesmen* (Englewood Cliffs, N.J.: Prentice-Hall, 1968), pp. 74–75.

20. Sahlins, *Stone Age Economics,* pp. 185–86n.

21. Ibid., pp. 82–86; also Maurice Godelier, *Rationality and Irrationality in Economics* (New York: Monthly Review Press, 1972), p. 291. Of course

capitalist production shares this goal—the maintenance of a particular social structure or set of social relations, in particular the relations of production itself—but within the larger goal of the achievement of maximum exchange value and the accumulation of wealth.

22. If we take "property" to mean property in land, we can agree with Marx: "The fundamental condition of property based on tribalism . . . is to be a member of the tribe." Karl Marx, *Pre-Capitalist Economic Formations* (New York: International, 1965), p. 91. See also Sahlins, *Tribesmen*, p. 76. Actual patterns of landholding varied greatly among Native American societies. The popular view of the difference between Indian and European patterns of land-holding as that between communal and individual property is misleading as a generalization across Indian cultures, ignoring as it does both the actual range of variation among Indian groups and the important distinctions among the kinds of rights that constitute different degrees of ownership or control over land. On variation among those societies, see Driver, *Indians of North America*, ch. 16, and Ralph M. Linton, "Land Tenure in Aboriginal America," in Oliver La Farge, ed., *The Changing Indian* (Norman: University of Oklahoma Press, 1942), pp. 42–54. On the various kinds of rights in land, see in particular A. Irving Hallowell, "The Nature and Function of Property as a Social Institution," in idem, *Culture and Experience* (Philadelphia: University of Pennsylvania Press, 1955), pp. 239–41; also Imre Sutton, *Indian Land Tenure: Bibliographical Essays and a Guide to the Literature* (New York: Clearwater, 1975), p. 6.

23. For some suggestive materials, see Raymond J. DeMallie, "Touching the Pen: Plains Indian Treaty Councils in Ethnohistorical Perspective," in Frederick C. Luebke, ed., *Ethnicity on the Great Plains* (Lincoln: University of Nebraska Press, 1980), especially pp. 46–48.

24. Maurice Halbwachs, *The Collective Memory* (New York: Harper and Row, 1980; orig. pub. 1950), p. 156.

25. Joseph is quoted in Dee Brown, *Bury My Heart at Wounded Knee: An Indian History of the American West* (New York: Holt, Rinehart and Winston, 1970), p. 316; Seathl in Virginia Irving Armstrong, comp., *I Have Spoken: American History Through the Voices of the Indians* (Chicago: Sage Books, 1971), p. 79.

26. Halbwachs, *Collective Memory*, p. 130.

27. Curly is quoted in Dixon, *Vanishing Race*, p. 141. Such conceptual relationships have by no means disappeared. See, for example, N. Scott Momaday, *The Way to Rainy Mountain* (New York: Ballantine, 1969).

28. As used here, "removal" refers not only to the removal policy of the 1820s and 1830s, but also to the general relocation of Indians from their lands, which formed a prominent, if intermittent, aspect of Indian policy from the 1820s into the 1960s.

29. Berkhofer, *White Man's Indian*, p. 135.

30. See Reginald Horsman, *Expansion and American Indian Policy, 1783–1812* (Lansing: Michigan State University Press, 1967), ch. 1 and pp. 53–65.

31. Berkhofer, *White Man's Indian*, p. 145.

32. See Richard Drinnon, *Facing West: The Metaphysics of Indian-Hating and Empire-Building* (Minneapolis: University of Minnesota Press, 1980), pp. 83–84.

33. On the reservation policy, see Robert A. Trennert, *Alternative to Ex-*

tinction: Federal Indian Policy and the Beginnings of the Reservation System, 1846–51 (Philadelphia: Temple University Press, 1975); William T. Hagan, "The Reservation Policy: Too Little and Too Late," in Jane F. Smith and Robert M. Kvasnicka, eds., *Indian-White Relations: A Persistent Paradox* (Washington: Howard University Press, 1976), pp. 162–70.

34. The text of the act is given in D. S. Otis, *The Dawes Act and the Allotment of Indian Lands,* ed. Francis Paul Prucha (Norman: University of Oklahoma Press, 1973), pp. 177–84.

35. Robert Winston Mardock, *The Reformers and the American Indian* (Columbia: University of Missouri Press, 1971), p. 1.

36. Smith's statement is from Commissioner of Indian Affairs, *Annual Report, 1876* (Washington: Government Printing Office, 1876), p. ix; the remarks by Price and Gates, from "Allotment of Land in Severalty and a Permanent Land Title" and "Land and Law as Agents in Educating Indians," both in Francis Paul Prucha, ed., *Americanizing the American Indians: Writings by the "Friends of the Indian" 1880–1900* (Cambridge: Harvard University Press, 1973), pp. 89, 50–51.

37. Otis, *Dawes Act,* pp. 14, 20; Priest, *Uncle Sam's Stepchildren,* p. 217. Sectional differences were not as clear-cut as this suggests; generally, however, the reform movement drew most of its support from the East, while agitation for Indian lands came largely from the West. On sectional differences and their role in policy making in this period, see Priest, p. 86–92, 122–24; also Mardock, *Reformers and Indian,* pp. 86–100. Other considerations also figured in the Dawes legislation, including the expense of the reservation system. For comprehensive discussions of the act and its genesis and support, see Otis, *Dawes Act,* and Wilcomb E. Washburn, *The Assault on Indian Tribalism: The General Allotment Act (Dawes Act) of 1887* (Philadelphia: J. B. Lippincott, 1975).

38. William T. Hagan, *United States–Comanche Relations: The Reservation Years* (New Haven: Yale University Press, 1976), p. 233; Priest, *Uncle Sam's Stepchildren,* pp. 160–64, 239–41; Mardock, *Reformers and Indian,* pp. 214–15, 221–22.

39. Institutions of governance varied greatly in Indian societies and tended to be less formally organized than those of Europe: polity, like economy, was seldom a distinct aspect of the social order. Everywhere, however, there were organizations and structures through which group action was given shape and meaning. These presented obstacles to Euro-American designs. For a brief discussion of aboriginal political organization, see ch. 5.

40. Sovereignty is an exceedingly complex topic on which Native Americans and Euro-Americans sometimes radically differ. I use it here to refer to the powers of self-government recognized by colonial and U.S. governments. But for a substantially different conception, see James Youngblood Henderson, "Comment," in Center for the History of the American Indian, *Indian Sovereignty: Proceedings of the Second Annual Conference on Problems and Issues Concerning American Indians Today,* ed. William R. Swagerty, Occasional Papers Series, no. 2 (Chicago: The Newberry Library, 1979), pp. 56–67 and 71–84.

41. Felix S. Cohen, *Handbook of Federal Indian Law* (Washington: Government Printing Office, 1942), p. 122, citing *Worcester* v. *Georgia,* 31 U.S. (6 Pet.) 515, 599 (1832); see also Jessie D. Green and Susan Work, "Comment: Inherent Indian Sovereignty," *American Indian Law Review* 4, no. 2

(1976): 314–15; and Kirke Kickingbird, Lynn Kickingbird, Charles J. Chibitty, and Curtis Berkey, *Indian Sovereignty* (Washington: Institute for the Development of Indian Law, 1977).

42. Charles J. Kappler, comp., *Indian Affairs: Laws and Treaties,* 5 vols. (Washington: Government Printing Office, 1904–41), vol. 2: Treaties (pub. 1904), "Treaty with the Wyandot, etc., 1785," Art. 2, p. 7, and Art. 9, p. 8; "Treaty with the Wyandot, etc., 1789," Art. 3, p. 19; "Treaty with the Cherokee, 1785," Art. 9, p. 10; "Treaty with the Kaskaskia, 1803," Art. 2, p. 67.

43. See the account in Grant Foreman, *Indian Removal: The Emigration of the Five Civilized Tribes of Indians* (Norman: University of Oklahoma Press, 1953). For a summary of treaty making in these years, see Cohen, *Handbook,* pp. 53–62.

44. Kappler, *Treaties,* "Treaty with the Cherokee, 1835," Art. 5, p. 442.

45. 5 Stat. 135 (1837); Green and Work, "Inherent Indian Sovereignty," p. 322.

46. Cohen, *Handbook,* p. 76.

47. Kappler, *Treaties,* "Treaty with the Navaho, 1849," Art. 9, p. 584. The wording is slightly different in the Ute treaty. See ibid., "Treaty with the Utah, 1849," Art. 7, p. 586; also, for example, "Treaty with the Apache, 1852," Art. 9, p. 599.

48. 11 Stat. 329 (1858), Sec. 2. Emphasis added.

49. Kappler, *Treaties,* "Treaty with the Seneca, Tonawanda Band, 1857," Art. 5, p. 769.

50. See the treaties with the Oto and Missouri Indians, Omahas, Shawnees, Iowas, Sauk and Fox, Kickapoos, Kaskaskias, and Peorias, etc., in 1854, and others then and thereafter, all in ibid. The 1862 legislation is 12 Stat. 427 (1862), Secs. 2 and 3.

51. Kappler, *Treaties,* "Treaty with the Cherokee, 1866," Arts. 6 and 12, pp. 944–46.

52. On the end of treaty making, see Laurence F. Schmeckebier, *The Office of Indian Affairs: Its History, Activities, and Organization* (Baltimore: The Johns Hopkins Press, 1927), pp. 55–59, 64–65; also the debate itself, *Congressional Globe,* 41st Congress, 3rd Session, 1871. The law is 16 Stat. 544 (1871), Sec. 1.

53. Quoted in Clark Wissler, *Indians of the United States* (New York: Doubleday, Doran & Co., 1940), p. 227.

Chapter 4. "They Carry Their Lives on Their Finger Nails"

1. "The Apaches were once a great nation; they are now but few, and because of this they want to die and so carry their lives on their finger nails." Cochise, Chiricahua Apache, 1871. From A. N. Ellis, "Recollections of an Interview with Cochise," *Kansas State Historical Society Collections* 13, (1913–14): 391–92, quoted in Armstrong, *I Have Spoken,* p. 96.

2. Quoted in Mooney, *Ghost-Dance Religion,* p. 861.

3. William M. Denevan, "Introduction," in Idem, ed., *The Native Population of the Americas in 1492* (Madison: University of Wisconsin Press, 1976), p. 7.

4. Chiparopai, a Yuma woman, quoted in T. C. McLuhan, *Touch the Earth:*

A Self-Portrait of Indian Existence (New York: Promontory, 1971); orig. in Natalie Curtis, *The Indian's Book: Songs and Legends of the American Indians* (New York: Dover, 1969; orig. pub. 1907), p. 569.

5. See Henry F. Dobyns, "Native American Population Collapse and Recovery," in W. R. Swagerty, ed., *Scholars and the Indian Experience: Critical Reviews of Recent Writing in the Social Sciences* (Bloomington: Indiana University Press, 1984), pp. 28–29.

6. J. M. Mooney, *The Aboriginal Population of America North of Mexico,* ed. John R. Swanton, Smithsonian Miscellaneous Collections 80, no. 7 (Washington: Smithsonian Institution, 1928); Alfred L. Kroeber, "Native American Population," *American Anthropologist* 36 (1934): 1–25. For more recent estimates, see Henry F. Dobyns, "Estimating Aboriginal American Population," *Current Anthropology* 7, no. 4 (1966): 395–416; idem, "Brief Perspective on a Scholarly Transformation: Widowing the 'Virgin' Land," *Ethnohistory* 23, no. 2 (1976): 95–104; idem, "Native American Population Collapse," pp. 20–22; Russell Thornton and Joan Marsh-Thornton, "Estimating Prehistoric American Indian Population Size for United States Area: Implications of the Nineteenth Century Population Decline and Nadir," *American Journal of Physical Anthropology* 55 (1981): 51; and the essays in Denevan, *Native Population of Americas.*

7. Sherburne F. Cook, "The Significance of Disease in the Extinction of the New England Indians," *Human Biology* 45, no. 3 (1973): 504–5; on the Massachusetts, idem, *The Indian Population of New England in the Seventeenth Century* (Berkeley: University of California Press, 1976), pp. 31–32; on the Western Abenaki, Dean R. Snow, *The Archeology of New England* (New York: Academic Press, 1980), p. 34; on the Huron, Jennings, *Invasion of America,* p. 25.

8. E. Wagner Stearn and Allen E. Stearn, *The Effect of Smallpox on the Destiny of the Amerindian* (Boston: Bruce Humphries, 1945), pp. 15, 93, 94; Edward M. Bruner, "Mandan," in Edward H. Spicer, ed., *Perspectives in American Indian Culture Change* (Chicago: University of Chicago Press, 1961), p. 187.

9. Jennings, *Invasion of America,* p. 30. A detailed discussion of the effects of European diseases, especially smallpox, on New World populations is given in Alfred W. Crosby, Jr., *The Columbian Exchange: Biological and Cultural Consequences of 1492* (Westport, Conn: Greenwood Press, 1972).

10. Virginia P. Miller, "Aboriginal Micmac Population: A Review of the Evidence," *Ethnohistory* 23, no. 2 (Spring 1976): 117–26; Richard W. Stoffle and Michael J. Evans, "Resource Competition and Population Change: A Kaibab Paiute Ethnohistorical Case," *Ethnohistory* 23, no. 2 (Spring 1976): 173–97; Sherburne F. Cook, *The Population of the California Indians, 1769–1970* (Berkeley: University of California Press, 1976), p. 199.

11. Henry F. Dobyns, "The Decline of Mescalero Apache Indian Population from 1873 to 1913," *Papers in Anthropology* 18, no. 2 (Fall 1977): 61–69.

12. Cook confronts the issue directly in the California case, estimating the effect of disease at five times that of physical assault and warfare, in terms of numbers lost, and argues that the part played there by disease was significantly less than in other parts of the continent. Cook, *Conflict Between California Indian and White Civilization,* pp. 18, 216.

13. Decline was not necessarily continuous. Jeanne Kay argues, for exam-

ple, that the fur trade actually led to population increases among the Menominee, Winnebago, and Sauk and Fox, all midwestern nations. Kay, "The Fur Trade and Native American Population Growth," *Ethnohistory* 31, no. 4 (1984): 265–87.

14. This is Driver's conclusion, based on the Annual Reports of the Indian Commissioner; see Harold E. Driver, "On the Population Nadir of Indians in the United States," *Current Anthropology* 9, no. 4 (1968): 330; also Henry F. Dobyns, *Native American Historical Demography: A Critical Bibliography* (Bloomington: Indiana University Press, for the Newberry Library, 1976), pp. 56–57. Thornton and Marsh-Thornton argue for a nadir population of only two hundred twenty-eight thousand. See their "Estimating Prehistoric Population Size," p. 48.

15. H. Craig Miner, *The Corporation and the Indian: Tribal Sovereignty and Industrial Civilization in Indian Territory, 1865–1907* (Columbia: University of Missouri Press, 1976), pp. 24–28, 40, and ch. 5.

16. See Hagan, "Reservation Policy," p. 190.

17. Spicer, *Cycles of Conquest*, pp. 543–49.

18. Ernest L. Schusky, *The Forgotten Sioux: An Ethnohistory of the Lower Brule Reservation* (Chicago: Nelson-Hall, 1975), pp. 73–74; Hagan, *United States–Comanche Relations*, 127–28; Donald J. Berthrong, *The Cheyenne and Arapaho Ordeal: Reservation and Agency Life in the Indian Territory, 1875–1907* (Norman: University of Oklahoma Press, 1976), p. 327; Loretta Fowler, *Arapahoe Politics, 1851–1978: Symbols in Crises of Authority* (Lincoln: University of Nebraska Press, 1982), pp. 87–96.

19. See the analysis in Leonard Albert Carlson, "The Dawes Act and the Decline of Indian Farming," Ph.D. dissertation, Stanford University, 1977.

20. Cf. Mina Davis Caulfield: "Following Marx, when I use the term 'exploitation of land and natural resources,' I intend the meaning that the original users of these resources have been deprived of their right to make their own cultural uses of them, rather than the economist's meaning that the resources simply have been utilized." "Culture and Imperialism: Proposing a New Dialectic," in Dell Hymes, ed., *Reinventing Anthropology* (New York: Vintage, 1974), p. 191.

21. Both quotes from Thomas J. Morgan, "Statement on Indian Policy," in Prucha, *Americanizing the American Indian*, p. 75.

22. William T. Hagan, *Indian Police and Judges: Experiments in Acculturation and Control* (New Haven: Yale University Press, 1966), pp. 137–38. Robert Utley remarks of the Oglalas of the Pine Ridge Reservation: "The chiefs rightly viewed the Indian police force as a menace to their supremacy" and tried to prevent its organization. Utley, *Last Days of the Sioux*, p. 28.

23. Hagan, *Indian Police*, ch. 6 and p. 120.

24. Roy W. Meyer, *History of the Santee Sioux: United States Indian Policy on Trial* (Lincoln: University of Nebraska Press, 1967), p. 230. For other examples of the use and abuse of agents' powers, see Fowler, *Arapahoe Politics*, pp. 96–98; Hagan, *United States–Comanche Relations*, pp. 153–54; and Schusky, *Forgotten Sioux*, p. 156. For an account that reveals the difficult situation many agents faced, trying to please both the BIA and, in some cases, their Indian wards, see Robert L. Bee, *Crosscurrents along the Colorado: The Impact of Government Policy on the Quechan Indians* (Tucson: University of Arizona Press, 1981), ch. 3.

25. Commissioner of Indian Affairs, *Annual Report, 1901* (Washington: Government Printing Office, 1901), pp. 5–6.

26. See, for example, Utley, *Last Days of the Sioux,* pp. 28–29.

27. Spicer, *Cycles of Conquest,* pp. 408–9.

28. Raymond J. DeMallie, "Pine Ridge Economy: Cultural and Historical Perspectives," in Stanley, *American Indian Economic Development,* p. 257. On the same problem in an earlier period, see Utley, *Last Days of the Sioux,* p. 29.

29. Discussing the agents' efforts to shape chief selection on the Cheyenne-Arapaho Reservation, Donald J. Berthrong writes, "In the eyes of an Indian agent a chief was particularly valuable if he was a member of a Christian church and if he sent his children to school, lived with only one woman, cut his hair, wore white man's clothing, labored on his allotment, did not visit for weeks with his friends and relatives, did not drink liquor, did not attend the Sun Dance, and did not spend 'frivolously' his lease and interest money on feasts and presents." *Cheyenne and Arapaho Ordeal,* pp. 338–39.

30. Robert W. Young, "The Rise of the Navajo Tribe," in Edward H. Spicer and Raymond H. Thompson, eds., *Plural Society in the Southwest* (New York: Interbook, 1972), pp. 185–86. For other examples of similar processes, see Spicer, *Cycles of Conquest,* pp. 409–10; Schusky, *Forgotten Sioux,* p. 184; Fowler, *Arapahoe Politics,* p. 98.

31. Not all Native American groups experienced the same degree of political interference. Particularly in the Southwest, as among the Pueblos, much of the native structure of self-government survived.

32. Such efforts were ubiquitous, if intermittent, during the reservation years. Among the studies that devote attention to them are Fowler, *Arapahoe Politics,* and Bee, *Crosscurrents along the Colorado.*

33. These efforts are discussed in Allen G. Applen, "An Attempted Indian State Government: The Okmulgee Constitution in Indian Territory, 1870–1876," *Kansas Quarterly* 3, no. 4 (Fall 1971): 89–99; Amos Maxwell, "The Sequoyah Convention," *Chronicles of Oklahoma* 28, no. 2 (Summer 1950): 161–92, and idem, "The Sequoyah Convention (Part II)," *Chronicles of Oklahoma* 28, no. 3 (Autumn 1950): 299–340; and Angie Debo, *And Still the Waters Run: The Betrayal of the Five Civilized Tribes* (Princeton: Princeton University Press, 1940). Contemporary journalistic reports include "Red Men in Council," *New York Times,* June 20, 1888, p. 5, and "A Federation of Indians," *New York Times,* June 27, 1888, p. 1. White efforts to establish an Indian state, and Indian responses to these efforts, are chronicled in Annie H. Abel, "Proposals for an Indian State, 1778–1878," *Annual Report of the American Historical Association,* 1907, 1:87–104. Somewhat removed from these efforts, but notable in their own right, were the attempts of "full-blood" members of the Five Civilized Tribes in the early 1900s to form national governments separate from the established tribal ones, to resist federal government controls and the breakup of their lands, and to resuscitate traditional social organization and culture. See John Bartlett Meserve, "The Plea of Crazy Snake (Chitto Harjo)," *Chronicles of Oklahoma* 11 (September 1933): 899–911; Daniel F. Littlefield, Jr., "Utopian Dreams of the Cherokee Fullbloods: 1890–1934," *Journal of the West* 10, no. 3 (July 1971): 404–27; and Robert K. Thomas, "The Redbird Smith Movement," in William N. Fenton and John Gulick, eds., *Symposium on Cherokee and Iroquois Culture,* Bureau of Ameri-

can Ethnology, Bulletin 180 (Washington: Smithsonian Institution, 1961), pp. 159–66.

34. See Duane Champagne, "Social Structure, Revitalization Movements and State-Building: Social Change in Four Native American Societies," *American Sociological Review* 48, no. 6 (December 1983): 754–63.

35. Mooney, *Ghost-Dance*, pp. 771–72. In his prophecy and teachings Wovoka seems to have drawn not only on indigenous Paiute culture, in particular shamanistic traditions, but also on certain Christian ideas with which he was familiar and on the legacy of earlier religious movements in the region, including a similarly prophetic movement, also known as the Ghost Dance, that occurred in the same area in 1870. See the discussion in Bryan Wilson, *Magic and the Millennium* (London: Heinemann, 1973), pp. 283–94.

36. Mooney, *Ghost-Dance*, ch. 10; Alexander Lesser, *The Pawnee Ghost Dance Hand Game: Ghost Dance Revival and Ethnic Identity* (Madison: University of Wisconsin Press, 1978; orig. pub. 1933), p. 62.

37. Dan L. Thrapp, *General Crook and the Sierra Madre Adventure* (Norman: University of Oklahoma Press, 1972), ch. 1 and 2. I have followed Mooney, *Ghost-Dance*, p. 704, on the spelling of the prophet's name.

38. Hagan, *United States–Comanche Relations*, pp. 105–8; James L. Haley, *The Buffalo War: The History of the Red River Indian Uprising of 1874* (Norman: University of Oklahoma Press, 1976), ch. 5.

39. Alvin M. Josephy, Jr., *The Nez Perce Indians and the Opening of the Northwest*, abr. ed. (New Haven: Yale University Press, 1971), pp. 424–26; Wilson, *Magic and Millennium*, pp. 278–83.

40. Mooney, *Ghost-Dance*, ch. 2 and 3; Wilson, *Magic and Millennium*, p. 279.

41. See, for example, Raymond J. DeMallie, "The Lakota Ghost Dance: An Ethnohistorical Account," *Pacific Historical Review* 51, no. 4 (November 1982): 391, 397–98.

42. Lesser, *Pawnee Ghost Dance Hand Game*; James A. Clifton, "Sociocultural Dynamics of the Prairie Potawatomi Drum Cult," *Plains Anthropologist* 14, no. 44 (May 1969): 92–93. For a relevant typology of social movements sensitive to the transformative/accommodationist distinction, see David F. Aberle, *The Peyote Religion among the Navaho* (Chicago: Aldine, 1966), ch. 19.

43. Anthony F. C. Wallace, *The Death and Rebirth of the Seneca* (New York: Knopf, 1970), ch. 8 and 9.

44. See, for example, Edgar E. Siskin, *Washo Shamans and Peyotists: Religious Conflict in an American Indian Tribe* (Salt Lake City: University of Utah Press, 1983); George Spindler and Louise Spindler, *Dreamers Without Power: The Menomini Indians* (New York: Holt, Rinehart and Winston, 1971); Aberle, *Peyote Religion*. On the phenomenon as a whole, the central resource is Weston La Barre, *The Peyote Cult*, 4th ed. (New York: Shocken, 1975).

45. Eugene D. Genovese, *From Rebellion to Revolution: Afro-American Slave Revolts in the Making of the Modern World* (Baton Rouge: Louisiana State University Press, 1979), p. 7.

46. See Eugene D. Genovese, *Roll, Jordan, Roll: The World the Slaves Made* (New York: Pantheon, 1974), pp. 161–284.

47. Accounting for the pattern of participation in such movements remains a tricky business. A number of variables may be involved, including at least:

societal stress, the range of alternative courses of action, and cultural com-
patibility. The Sioux, for example, showed no interest in the 1870 Ghost Dance,
when their own societies remained largely intact and their capacities for negotiation, war, and other adjustments remained substantial. The 1890 prophecies,
on the other hand, fell on fertile ground and were taken up by nations that had
run out of choices. The Navajos, however, may have rejected the Ghost Dance
for quite different reasons. In Navajo cosmology the dead were to be feared;
no one wanted their return. In contrast, the resurrection of the dead was an idea
long embedded in the belief systems of the Paiutes and their northern neigh-
bors, who had quickly taken up Wovoka's teachings. See Anthony F. C. Wallace, "James Mooney and the Study of the Ghost-Dance Religion," in Mooney,
Ghost-Dance, abr. ed. (Chicago: University of Chicago Press, 1965), p. viii.
A number of authors have argued similarly that the pattern of diffusion of
peyotism was affected in part by the varying importance of visions in aboriginal
cultures. See La Barre, *Peyote Cult,* p. 201. Some additional factors are exam-
ined by Michael P. Carroll, "Revitalization Movements and Social Structure:
Some Quantitative Tests," *American Sociological Review* 40, no. 3 (June
1975): 389–401; and Russell Thornton, "Demographic Antecedents of a Revitalization Movement: Population Change, Population Size, and the 1890
Ghost Dance," *American Sociological Review* 46, no. 1 (February 1981):
88–96. The most interesting recent attempt to deal with the issue is by Duane
Champagne, who systematically considers both contextual and internal variables, in particular the nature and extent of structural differentiation within
various Native American societies. See his "Social Structure, Revitalization
Movements and State-Building"; also his *Strategies and Conditions of Political
and Cultural Survival in American Indian Societies,* Occasional Paper No. 21
(Cambridge: Cultural Survival, 1985).

48. Indian concepts of power are complex. For some useful discussions, see
Raymond J. DeMallie and Robert H. Lavenda, "Wakan: Plains Siouan Concepts of Power," and Albert L. Wahrhaftig and Jane Lukens-Wahrhaftig, "The
Thrice Powerless: Cherokee Indians in Oklahoma," both in Raymond D. Fogelson and Richard N. Adams, eds., *The Anthropology of Power* (New York:
Academic Press, 1977), pp. 153–65 and 225–36; Rosalie Wax and Murray
Wax, "The Magical World View," *Journal for the Scientific Study of Religion*
1 (1962): 179–88; and Walter B. Miller, "Two Concepts of Authority," *American Anthropologist* 57, no. 2 (1955): 271–89.

49. Anthony F. C. Wallace, "Revitalization Movements: Some Theoretical
Considerations for their Comparative Study," *American Anthropologist* 58
(1956): 264–81.

50. Morgan, "Statement," p. 75.

51. Roberta Ash, *Social Movements in America* (Chicago: Markham, 1972),
p. 143.

Chapter 5. The Transformations of the Tribe

1. John G. Neihardt, *Black Elk Speaks: Being the Life Story of a Holy Man
of the Oglala Sioux* (Lincoln: University of Nebraska Press, 1961), p. 200.

2. "Tribe" is a problematic term. Its complexities have troubled anthropologists and students of political development for years and there is little consensus

on its meaning. Some eschew its usage altogether; others have tried in various ways to specify it; still others see it as politically pregnant but technically useless. In much of the Third World it is pejorative; among most Native Americans it is not only in everyday use but often carries substantial emotional or spiritual significance. On the latter point, see the remarks in Russel Lawrence Barsh and James Youngblood Henderson, *The Road: Indian Tribes and Political Liberty* (Berkeley: University of California Press, 1980), pp. vii–viii. On the term in general, see Morton H. Fried, *The Notion of Tribe* (Menlo Park: Cummings Publishing, 1975); and June Helm, ed., *Essays on the Problem of Tribe* (Seattle: University of Washington Press, 1968).

Definitional and usage issues, however, are peripheral to the current enterprise. Indians traditionally have been divided, through either aboriginal history or contact and conflict with non-Indians, into groups referred to by non-Indians and, eventually, by Indians as "tribes." Whether or not these groups fit techical definitions of "tribe," and whether or not the term is analytically advantageous, are not at issue here. What is of interest is the collectivities to which "tribe" has come to refer and the ways they have changed in the historical course of Indian-White interaction.

3. Clyde Kluckhohn and Dorothea Leighton, *The Navaho,* rev. ed. (Cambridge: Harvard University Press, 1974), p. 121.

4. Clifton, *Prairie People,* p. 59.

5. Confederation and alliance, in some cases more formal and enduring than in others, apparently were relatively common in some parts of the continent both before and after contact. Yet these organizations generally had only limited authority over constituent groups. Even in the Iroquois case, perhaps the most elaborate and durable of all, the bulk of political power in daily affairs remained at the village level. See, for example, Lowell John Bean, "Social Organization in Native California," in Lowell John Bean and Thomas C. Blackburn, eds., *Native Californians: A Theoretical Retrospective* (Socorro: Ballena Press, 1976), pp. 103–4; and Anthony F. C. Wallace, "Political Organization and Land Tenure among the Northeastern Indians, 1600–1830," *Southwestern Journal of Anthropology* 13, no. 4 (1957): 301–21. On the distribution of authority within the League of the Iroquois, see Wallace, *Death and Rebirth,* p. 40.

6. E. Adamson Hoebel, *The Cheyennes: Indians of the Great Plains* (New York: Holt, Rinehart and Winston, 1960), pp. 49–50.

7. Summary treatments of aboriginal political organization include Driver, *Indians,* ch. 17; and Robert H. Lowie, "Some Aspects of Political Organization among the American Aborigines," *Journal of the Royal Anthropological Institute of Great Britain and Ireland* 78 (1948, pub. 1951), pp. 11–24. See also Elizabeth Colson, "Political Organizations in Tribal Societies: A Cross-Cultural Comparison," *The American Indian Quarterly* 10, no. 1 (Winter 1986): 5–19. For some more detailed regional surveys, see Charles Callender, "Great Lakes-Riverine Sociopolitical Organization," in William C. Sturtevant, ed., *Handbook of North American Indians* Vol. 15: Northeast (Washington: Smithsonian Institution, 1978), pp. 610–21; Charles Hudson, *The Southeastern Indians* (Knoxville: University of Tennessee Press, 1976), ch. 4; and Spicer, *Cycles of Conquest,* ch. 14.

8. Edward H. Spicer, "Persistent Cultural Systems," *Science,* 174 (November 19, 1971): 796.

9. A. L. Kroeber, "Nature of the Land-Holding Group," *Ethnohistory* 2, no. 4 (1955): 303–5. Relevant here is Walker Connor's effort to extricate the nation from the tendency to confuse it with the state: "Defining and conceptualizing the nation is much more difficult because the essence of a nation is intangible. This essence is a psychological bond that joins a people and differentiates it, in the subconscious conviction of its members, from all other people in a most vital way. The nature of that bond and its well-spring remain shadowy and elusive . . . the nation is a self-defined rather than an other-defined grouping." Walker Connor, "A Nation is a Nation, is a State, is an Ethnic Group, is a . . . ," *Racial and Ethnic Studies* 1, no. 4 (1978): 379–80.

10. Ernest Wallace and E. Adamson Hoebel, *The Comanches: Lords of the South Plains* (Norman: University of Oklahoma Press, 1952), p. 22.

11. Robert H. Lowie, *Indians of the Plains* (Garden City: Natural History Press, 1963), p. 94; Morris E. Opler, "An Outline of Chiricahua Apache Social Organization," in Fred Eggan, ed., *Social Anthropology of North American Tribes*, enlarged ed. (Chicago: University of Chicago Press), p. 176: idem, "Jicarilla Apache Territory, Economy, and Society in 1850," *Southwestern Journal of Anthropology* 27, no. 4 (1971): 309; Harry W. Basehart, "Mescalero Apache Band Organization and Leadership," in Keith H. Basso and Morris E. Opler, eds., *Apachean Culture History and Ethnology* (Tucson: University of Arizona Press, 1971), pp. 37, 42. On the Hopi, see Fred Eggan, *Social Organization of the Western Pueblos* (Chicago: University of Chicago Press, 1950), ch. 2; on the Colorado River groups, Spicer, *Cycles of Conquest*, p. 377.

12. Lowell John Bean, *Mukat's People: The Cahuilla Indians of Southern California* (Berkeley: University of California Press, 1975), p. 85; Clifton, *Prairie People*, pp. 20–24; Callender, "Great Lakes-Riverine," p. 617; David H. Corkran, "Cherokee Pre-History," *North Carolina Historical Review* 34, no. 4 (1957): 455–66.

13. Spicer, *Cycles of Conquest*, p. 384.

14. Verne F. Ray, *Cultural Relations in the Plateau of Northwestern America* (Los Angeles: The Southwest Museum, 1939), p. 14.

15. Harold Hickerson, "The Chippewa of the Upper Great Lakes: A Study in Sociopolitical Change," in Eleanor Burke Leacock and Nancy Oestreich Lurie, eds., *North American Indians in Historical Perspective* (New York: Random House, 1971), pp. 169–99; Champagne, "Politics, Markets, and Social Structure," ch. 3.

16. Robert F. Berkhofer, Jr., *Salvation and the Savage: An Analysis of Protestant Missions and American Indian Response, 1787–1862* (New York: Atheneum, 1976), pp. 63–64, 82–87.

17. For examples of occasional consolidation for defense, see Spicer, *Cycles of Conquest*, pp. 377–78, on rancheria peoples of the Southwest, and p. 408, on the Pimas. On the Mandan and Hidatsa, see Alfred W. Bowers, *Hidatsa Social and Ceremonial Organization*, Bureau of American Ethnology, Bulletin 194 (Washington: Smithsonian Institution, 1965), pp. 23–25.

18. Sutton, *Indian Land Tenure*, pp. 192–93. See also DeMallie, "Touching the Pen," pp. 38–53.

19. Sutton, *Indian Land Tenure*, p. 186.

20. The situation was complicated further by mutual incomprehension. White misperceptions of Indian societies had pervasive effects on Indian policy,

which usually was formulated and implemented in profound ignorance. In particular, Whites often failed to understand the complexities of Indian group structures and the nature of authority in Native American societies. Indians, on the other hand, were usually little more enlightened about Europeans, and in particular about European concepts of property, sale, and law. Moreover, as DeMallie has shown, the process of negotiation itself took place at the bottom of a cultural chasm: lengthy treaty councils that appeared to have produced agreement often meant one thing to the Indians, quite another to the Whites. Frequently neither side fully understood what the other wanted or was thinking. See DeMallie, "Touching the Pen."

21. Berkhofer, *Salvation and Savage*, p. 133.

22. Clifton, *Prairie People*, p. 119.

23. Fowler, *Arapahoe Politics*, pp. 32–34; Basehart, "Mescalero Band Organization," p. 36; Stoffle and Evans, "Resource Competition and Population Change," p. 190; Young, "Rise of the Navajo Tribe," p. 184.

24. Michael D. Green, "'We Dance in Opposite Directions': Mesquakie (Fox) Separatism from the Sac and Fox Tribe," *Ethnohistory* 30, no. 3 (1983): 129–140.

25. See, for example, Clifton, *Prairie People*, p. 169.

26. Spicer, *Cycles of Conquest*, pp. 408–12.

27. This theme emerges from a number of recent works on Native Americans, among them Karen I. Blu, *The Lumbee Problem: The Making of an American Indian People* (Cambridge, U.K.: Cambridge University Press, 1980); Thomas Buckley, "Yurok Realities in the Nineteenth and Twentieth Centuries," Ph.D. dissertation, University of Chicago, 1982; Clifton, *Prairie People;* Fowler, *Arapahoe Politics;* Fred W. Voget, *The Shoshoni-Crow Sun Dance* (Norman: University of Oklahoma Press, 1984); Albert L. Wahrhaftig, "In the Aftermath of Civilization: The Persistence of the Cherokee Indians in Oklahoma," Ph.D. dissertation, University of Chicago, 1975; Willard Walker, "Cherokee Curing and Conjuring, Identity, and the Southeastern Co-Tradition," in George Pierre Castile and Gilbert Kushner, eds., *Persistent Peoples: Cultural Enclaves in Perspective* (Tucson: University of Arizona Press, 1981). See also Sol Tax, "Acculturation," in Anthony F. C. Wallace, ed., *Men and Cultures* (Philadelphia: University of Pennsylvania Press, 1960).

28. On San Carlos, see Spicer, *Cycles of Conquest*, p. 409; on the Santees, Meyer, *History of the Santee Sioux*, pp. 153–54.

29. On the Comanches, see Hagan, *United States–Comanche Relations*, pp. 133, 154–55; on the Nez Perce, Deward E. Walker, Jr., *Conflict and Schism in Nez Perce Acculturation: A Study of Religion and Politics* (Pullman: Washington State University Press, 1968), pp. 15, 45–54.

30. Henry F. Dobyns, "The Indian Reorganization Act and Federal Withdrawal," *Applied Anthropology* 7, no. 2 (Spring 1948): 37.

31. On occasion those subtribal identities themselves received support from government practice. Kluckhohn and Leighton argue that a Navajo tribal consciousness has been substantially the result of being dealt with by the United States as a single unit; at the same time, they say, the administrative structure of the reservation has helped to sustain regional and other subtribal identities. *Navaho*, pp. 122–23.

32. Nancy Oestreich Lurie, "The Indian Claims Commission Act," *Annals of the American Academy of Political and Social Science* 311 (May 1957); 62.

For an example, see Elizabeth Colson, *The Makah Indians: A Study of an Indian Tribe in Modern America* (Minneapolis: University of Minnesota Press, 1953), pp. 61–82. Such efforts did not always succeed. One federal commission urged that the Arapahoe and the Sioux be settled together in hopes that the Arapahoe would be "lost as a tribe." The Arapahoe successfully resisted, but eventually were settled with the Shoshones on the Wind River Reservation in Wyoming. Fowler, *Arapahoe Politics*, p. 56.

33. On the Yakimas, see "Treaty of 1855," in Robert E. Pace, comp., *The Land of the Yakimas* (Toppenish, Wash.: Yakima Indian Nation, 1977), p. 9; also "Treaty Summer Changed Yakimas," *Yakima Nation Review* (Toppenish, Washington) 9, no. 3 (June 23, 1978): 1. On Warm Springs, see Jack Hunt, "Land Tenure and Economic Development on the Warm Springs Indian Reservation," *Journal of the West* 9, no. 1 (1970): 93–109. It should be noted that in both these cases the present tribal governments are structured in ways that recognize the original constituent peoples. Thus the Yakima Tribal Council has fourteen members, although among the people themselves the tribal and band distinctions have largely disappeared, while the council of the Confederated Tribes of Warm Springs originally included, among others, a representative from each of the three original groups on the reservation.

34. Ronald L. Trosper, "Native American Boundary Maintenance: The Flathead Indian Reservation, Montana, 1860–1970," *Ethnicity* 3, no. 3 (September 1976): 267. While in these cases political consolidation was accompanied over time by the growth of new, inclusive tribal identities, this has not always been so. The Shoshone and Arapahoe, for example, were forced in 1878 to share the originally Shoshone Wind River Reservation in Wyoming. The social distance between the two groups, who were traditional enemies and shared neither language nor culture, has remained large, although for administrative purposes they have been treated as one tribe. See Fowler, *Arapahoe Politics*.

35. For some summary discussions of Indian factionalism, see P. Richard Metcalf, "Who Should Rule at Home? Native American Politics and Indian-White Relations," *Journal of American History* 61, no. 3 (December 1974): 651–65, and Robert F. Berkhofer, Jr., "Native Americans," in John Higham, ed., *Ethnic Leadership in America* (Baltimore: The Johns Hopkins University Press, 1978), especially pp. 123–28.

36. The full-blood/mixed-blood terminology, while common among both Indians and non-Indians, implies a biological distinction and is therefore misleading. The difference has far more to do with culture than biology, referring generally to the perceived extent to which an individual's life is organized and lived in Indian versus non-Indian ways, much the more salient concern among Native Americans. While the terminology's original meaning doubtless was biological, referring to the mixing of Indian and White, few Indian nations ever paid much attention to biological "purity"; on the contrary, most were eager to adopt outsiders as means of sustaining group numbers, with culture, not genealogy, as the subsequent measure of membership. In the conflict and reservation years, of course, there may well have been a substantial correlation between cultural practice and blood quantum, but that was less and less the case as time went on. For a useful discussion, see Robert E. Daniels, "Cultural Identities among the Oglala Sioux," in Ethel Nurge, ed., *The Modern Sioux: Social Systems and Reservation Culture* (Lincoln: University of Nebraska Press, 1970), pp. 198–245.

37. On conflict for influence with reservation agents, see, for example, Schusky, *Forgotten Sioux*, pp. 71–72. On the role of missionaries and religious factionalism, see Berkhofer, *Salvation and Savage*, ch. 7; Daniel K. Richter, "Iroquois versus Iroquois: Jesuit Missions and Christianity in Village Politics, 1642–1686," *Ethnohistory* 32, no. 1 (1985): 1–16; and Walker, *Conflict and Schism*, pp. 54–73. For one of many examples of exploitation of factionalism in negotiations with Indians, see Josephy, *Nez Perce*, ch. 8. Of course Indians could be equally opportunistic. See, for example, Miner, *Corporation and Indian*, pp. 44–47.

38. Fragmentation was not everywhere the case. The Arapahoe, for example, managed to sustain a flexible, adaptive approach to crisis which, over an extended period, largely avoided the crippling factionalism that many nations experienced. See Fowler, *Arapahoe Politics*.

Chapter 6. New Music, New Partners, A New Dance

1. Ira Katznelson, *Black Men, White Cities: Race, Politics, and Migration in the United States, 1900–30, and Britain, 1948–68* (Chicago: University of Chicago Press, 1976), p. 24.

2. Arthur L. Stinchcombe, *Constructing Social Theories* (New York: Harcourt, Brace, and World, 1968), p. 173. Cf. Samuel P. Huntington, *Political Order in Changing Societies* (New Haven: Yale University Press, 1968), ch. 1.

3. See the discussion in M. G. Smith, "Pluralism in Precolonial African Societies," in Leo Kuper and M. G. Smith, eds., *Pluralism in Africa* (Berkeley: University of California Press, 1971), pp. 96–97.

4. Carlson, "Dawes Act and Indian Farming," pp. 51–52; J. P. Kinney, *A Continent Lost—A Civilization Won: Indian Land Tenure in America* (Baltimore: Johns Hopkins Press, 1937), pp. 294–96; United States Census, *Statistical History of the United States* (Washington: U.S. Department of Commerce, 1960), pp. 236–37, 278.

5. An excellent account of these events is in Kenneth R. Philp, *John Collier's Crusade for Indian Reform, 1920–1954* (Tucson: University of Arizona Press, 1977), ch. 2. Lawrence is quoted by Philp, p. 34. The Pueblo statement is given in Joe S. Sando, *The Pueblo Indians* (San Francisco: The Indian Historian Press, 1976), p. 96.

6. Randolph C. Downes, "A Crusade for Indian Reform, 1922–1934," *Mississippi Valley Historical Review* 32, no. 3 (December 1945): 342.

7. Lewis Meriam and Associates, *The Problem of Indian Administration* (Baltimore: Johns Hopkins Press, 1928), pp. 3–5.

8. Ibid., p. 86. Emphasis added.

9. John Collier, *Indians of the Americas* (New York: New American Library, 1948), pp. 154–55; Lawrence Kelly, *The Assault on Assimilation: John Collier and the Origins of Indian Policy Reform* (Albuquerque: University of New Mexico Press, 1983); Stephen J. Kunitz, "The Social Philosophy of John Collier," *Ethnohistory* 18, no. 3 (Summer 1971): 213–29.

10. On the evolution of the IRA from original proposal to final version, see Lawrence C. Kelly, "The Indian Reorganization Act: the Dream and the Reality," *Pacific Historical Review* 44, no. 3 (August 1975): 293–99. As for tribal approval: Collier himself, following a series of conferences with Indians,

added an amendment to the proposed bill allowing any tribe to exclude itself via a referendum. See Philp, *Collier's Crusade,* p. 156.

11. U.S. Statutes at Large, 48 Stat. 984 (1934). The quote is from Section 16. Oklahoma Indians and Alaska natives originally were excluded from the IRA. The Oklahoma Indian Welfare Act and the Alaska Reorganization Act, both passed in 1936, extended its provisions to them.

12. Graham D. Taylor, *The New Deal and American Indian Tribalism: The Administration of the Indian Reorganization Act, 1934–45* (Lincoln: University of Nebraska Press, 1980); Kenneth R. Philp, "Termination: A Legacy of the Indian New Deal," *Western Historical Quarterly* 14, no. 2 (1983): 170–71.

13. The exact number of tribes approving and rejecting the IRA is difficult to pin down. See Kelly's comparison of the standard sources, "Dream and Reality," pp. 301–2. Also see his discussion, ibid., 303–5, of the numbers of Indians voting and the subsequent adoption of constitutions and corporate charters. The number of tribes organizing under the IRA has increased over the years. By 1980, of the approximately 280 Indian entities in the lower forty-eight states recognized as eligible for federal services, slightly more than half were organized under the IRA and the Oklahoma Indian Welfare Act. However, a substantial number of those not so organized were very small California groups; the proportion of Indians, as opposed to groups, so organized was much higher. See U.S. Department of the Interior, Bureau of Indian Affairs, Tribal Government Services, "Memorandum: Organizational Status of Federally Recognized Indian Entities," May 1, 1979. The IRA is no less controversial among Indians today. For some representative views, see Kenneth R. Philp, ed., *Indian Self-Rule: First-Hand Accounts of Indian-White Relations from Roosevelt to Reagan* (Salt Like City: Howe Brothers, 1986), Part 1.

14. Along with the IRA, the Alaska Reorganization Act, and the Oklahoma Indian Welfare Act, the legislative components of the Indian New Deal also included the Johnson-O'Malley Act, passed in 1934, which authorized the secretary of the interior to provide financial assistance to Indians in the area of social welfare, health education, and agriculture, and the Arts and Crafts Board Act, passed in 1935, which authorized the establishment of an Indian Arts and Crafts Board to promote the marketing of Indian art and craft work and to encourage the preservation of the crafts themselves.

15. Spicer, *Cycles of Conquest,* p. 352.

16. Ibid., 412–13. On the role of American models in the drafting of tribal constitutions, see Frank Ducheneaux, "The Indian Reorganization Act and the Cheyenne River Sioux," *American Indian Journal* 2, no. 8 (August 1976): 9–10.

17. The first quote is given by Henry F. Dobyns, "Therapeutic Experience of Responsible Democracy," in Stuart Levine and Nancy O. Lurie, eds., *The American Indian Today* (Baltimore: Penguin, 1968), p. 269. The second is from John Collier, "The Genesis and Philosophy of the Indian Reorganization Act," in William F. Kelly, ed., *Indian Affairs and the Indian Reorganization Act: The Twenty Year Record* (Tucson: University of Arizona, 1954), p. 2.

18. Henry F. Dobyns made the point years ago: "The IRA provides an irreducible minimum of segregation in setting up a tribal entity. This hard core is what will remain if all other Indian characteristics are lost. Yet the other feature of the IRA is that in fitting this tribal entity into the larger American

framework, the Indians will be assimilating themselves." Dobyns, "Indian Reorganization Act and Federal Withdrawal," p. 37.

19. Collier, "Genesis and Philosophy," p. 3.

20. See, for example, Fowler, *Arapahoe Politics,* ch. 4.

21. In its provisions for tribal government the IRA at least partially resembles what Katznelson has called repressive reforms (although, given the genuine increase in Indian political capacity, the word "repressive" overstates the present case), that is: "reforms that appear to restructure relationships to widen choice but are actually extensions of and/or the creations of new mechanisms of social control." Katznelson, *Black Men, White Cities,* p. 198.

22. Indian Reorganization Act, 48 Stat. 984 (1934), Section 19.

23. Graham D. Taylor, "The Tribal Alternative to Bureaucracy: The Indian's New Deal, 1933–1945," *Journal of the West* 13, no. 1 (January 1974): 135.

24. The Indian Bureau was aware of this problem and attempted in various ways to come to grips with it, but without much success. See Taylor, *New Deal and Tribalism,* ch. 5.

25. See, for example, Philp's description of the attempt to help the Hopis design a tribal government suited to their particular social organization and culture, *Collier's Crusade,* pp. 166–67.

26. Robert A. White, "Value Themes of the Native American Tribalistic Movement among the South Dakota Sioux," *Current Anthropology* 15, no. 3 (September 1974): 284.

27. See Spicer, *Cycles of Conquest,* p. 419.

28. Taylor, *New Deal and Tribalism,* p. 76.

29. See, for example, Triloki Nath Pandey's discussion of political conflict on the Zuni Reservation, "Images of Power in a Southwestern Pueblo," in Fogelson and Adams, *Anthropology of Power,* pp. 195–215.

30. Taylor discusses factionalism and the IRA at length in *New Deal and Tribalism,* ch. 4. For other examples of these problems, see Clifton, *Prairie People,* pp. 408–10, 432–33; Spicer, *Cycles of Conquest,* pp. 412–15. A former tribal chairman of the San Carlos Apaches remarks that even after the adoption of a tribal constitution at San Carlos, "Superintendent Kitch was still the boss." See Clarence Wesley, "Tribal Government under the IRA," in Kelly, *Indian Affairs and Reorganization Act,* p. 26. William Y. Adams discusses the perception of tribal government as serving non-Indian interests among Shonto Navajos in the 1950s in *Shonto: A Study of the Role of the Trader in a Modern Navajo Community,* Bureau of American Ethnology, Bulletin 188 (Washington: Smithsonian Institution, 1963), pp. 65–68. A variation on this situation, in which tribal government is perceived as representing a particular community more than the tribe as a whole, is discussed in Bobby Thompson and John H. Peterson, Jr., "Mississippi Choctaw Identity: Genesis and Change," in John W. Bennett, ed., *The New Ethnicity: Perspectives from Ethnology,* Proceedings of the American Ethnological Society, 1973 (St. Paul: West Publishing, 1975), pp. 191–92. On the Hopi, see Emory Sekaquaptewa, "Preserving the Good Things in Hopi Life," in Spicer and Thompson, *Plural Society in Southwest,* pp. 239–60.

31. Edward P. Dozier, "Factionalism at Santa Clara Pueblo," *Ethnology* 5, no. 2 (April 1966): 182–83.

32. The reference to the Sac and Fox is from a letter to Indian Commissioner John Collier, 1938; to the Blackfeet, from Charles Heacock, "Report on

Proposed Amendment for Representation on the Blackfeet Tribal Council,"
1945, both cited in Taylor, "Tribal Alternative," p. 136. On Pine Ridge, see
DeMallie, "Pine Ridge Economy," p. 261, and Ira H. Grinnell, *The Tribal
Government of the Oglala Sioux of Pine Ridge, South Dakota* (Vermillion:
Government Research Bureau, University of South Dakota, 1967), p. 44. There
were exceptions to this pattern. On the Northern Cheyenne Reservation, for
example, it was the full-bloods who eventually took control of the council. See
Taylor, *New Deal and Tribalism,* p. 60. Not all factional conflict over government revolves around the mixed-blood/full-blood axis, which is often a simplification of much more complex political divisions. For an example of other kinds
of conflict and of change in the factional axis over time, see Walker, *Conflict
and Schism,* ch. 6.

33. DeMallie, "Pine Ridge Economy," p. 274. See also Robert K. Thomas,
"Powerless Politics," *New University Thought* 4, no. 4 (Winter 1966/67): 48,
and cf. Gary Witherspoon on the Navajo: "In intra-group relations no individual, regardless of position or status, has the right to impose his will on the
group. Likewise, the group does not have the right to impose its will on the
individual. Unanimity is the only acceptable basis of collective action. Although a system of majority rule has been imposed on the Navajos for half a
century, the extent to which the principle of unanimity continues to pervade
almost all social and political deliberations is amazing." *Language and Art in
the Navajo Universe* (Ann Arbor: University of Michigan Press, 1977), p. 83.

34. Duane Champagne, "Bureaucratic Domination, Political Differentiation
and the Stability of American Indian Tribal Governments," unpublished manuscript, 1987.

35. Henry F. Manuel, Juliann Ramon, and Bernard L. Fontana, "Dressing
for the Window: Papago Indians and Economic Development," in Stanley,
American Indian Economic Development, p. 542; Wahrhaftig and Lukens-
Wahrhaftig, "Thrice Powerless," p. 230; Gail Landsman, "Ganienkeh: Symbol
and Politics in an Indian/White Conflict," *American Anthropologist* 87 (December 1985): 832 (on Mohawks). The Pine Ridge figure is cited in DeMallie,
"Pine Ridge Economy," p. 276.

36. On the Navajo, see Adams, *Shonto,* and Mary Shepardson, "Navajo
Ways in Government: A Study in Political Process," *American Anthropological
Association Memoir,* No. 96 (June 1963). On the Hopi, see Richard O. Clem-
mer, "Truth, Duty, and the Revitalization of Anthropologists: A New Perspec-
tive on Cultural Change and Persistence," in Dell Hymes, ed., *Reinventing
Anthropology* (New York: Vintage, 1974), pp. 213–47; and Shuichi Nagata,
"Opposition and Freedom in Moenkopi Factionalism," in M. Silverman and
R. F. Salisbury, eds., *A House Divided? Anthropological Studies of Factional-
ism* (Newfoundland: Institute of Social and Economic Research, Memorial
University of Newfoundland, 1977), pp. 146–70. On the Shoshone-Goshute,
see Richard O. Clemmer, "Channels of Political Expression among the Western
Shoshone-Goshute of Nevada," in Ruth M. Houghton, ed., *Native American
Politics: Power Relationships in the Western Great Basin Today* (Reno: Bureau
of Governmental Research, University of Nevada, 1973), pp. 7–16. It is interesting that the Arapahoes, who have escaped much of the crippling factionalism
other tribes have experienced, rejected the IRA and struggled instead to adopt
new political practices without losing their own, consensus-based governing tradition. See Fowler, *Arapahoe Politics.* A number of other groups also have

managed to combine traditional and Euro-American forms of government, even within the structures set up by the IRA. See, for example, Nancy Owens and Ken Peres, "Overcoming Institutional Barriers to Economic Development on the Northern Cheyenne Reservation," Northern Cheyenne Research Project, Lame Deer, Montana, 1980.

37. See, for example, the later chapters in Clifton, *Prairie People.*

38. Warren L. d'Azevedo, "Some Recent Studies of Native American Political Relations in the Western Great Basin: A Commentary," in Houghton, *Native American Politics,* pp. 107–8.

39. Vine Deloria, Jr., *God is Red* (New York: Dell, 1973), p. 255.

40. For an example of how such rewards may motivate tribal identification, see Patricia C. Albers and William R. James, "On the Dialectics of Ethnicity: To Be or Not to Be Santee (Sioux)," *Journal of Ethnic Studies* 14, no. 1 (Spring 1986): 14–15.

Chapter 7. Toward a Supratribal Consciousness

1. Hazel W. Hertzberg, *The Search for an American Indian Identity* (Syracuse: Syracuse University Press, 1971), p. 1.

2. See Berkhofer, *White Man's Indian,* pp. 23–25.

3. See Robert K. Thomas, "Pan-Indianism," in Levine and Lurie, *American Indian Today,* pp. 129–30; also Deloria, *God is Red,* pp. 217 and 365–66.

4. By "supratribalism" I refer to a generalized Indian identity and to the tendency on the part of Indians in certain situations to organize or act on the basis of that identity as opposed to particular tribal identities. The investigation of this and similar tendencies is hardly new. With a few exceptions, however, it has been the cultural and religious manifestations of the phenomenon, grouped in academic circles under the rubric "pan-Indianism," that have aroused interest. Only recently has political "pan-Indianism" received much attention. Because "pan-Indian" tends to conflate cultural and political phenomena, and because the reference here is to aspects of collective identity and action, I believe "supratribal" is the more appropriate term. Furthermore, "pan-Indian" has drawn objections from Indians, who seldom use the term and, according to Deloria, "abhor it." See Vine Deloria, Jr., "The Rise and Fall of the First Indian Movement: A Review Article," *Historian* 33, no. 4 (August 1971): 661. To my knowledge, as a description of Indian political objectives, "supratribal" was first used by Lurie and, as a description of Indian organizations, by Spicer. See Nancy O. Lurie, "An American Indian Renaissance?" in Levine and Lurie, *American Indian Today,* pp. 309, 315–16; and Edward H. Spicer, *A Short History of the Indians of the United States* (New York: D. Van Nostrand, 1969), p. 144. I have taken the liberty of adding an "ism" and enlarging the scope of the term.

For early discussions of "pan-Indianism" as a cultural phenomenon, see James H. Howard, "Pan-Indian Culture of Oklahoma," *The Scientific Monthly* 81, no. 5 (1955): 215–20; Evon Z. Vogt, "The Acculturation of American Indians," *Annals of the American Academy of Political and Social Science* 311 (May 1957): 145–46; Ernest Schusky, "Pan-Indianism in the Eastern United States," *Anthropology Tomorrow* 6 (December 1957): 116–23; James Hirabayashi, William Willard, and Luis Kemnitzer, "Pan-Indianism in the Urban Setting," in Thomas Weaver and Douglas White, eds., *The Anthropology of Urban Environments* (Washington: Society for Applied Anthropology, 1967), pp. 77–87. Interestingly, one of the first discussions of a comprehensive Indian identity approached it as a specifically political phenomenon: Margaret Mead, *The Changing Culture of an Indian Tribe* (New York: Capricorn Books, 1966; orig. pub. 1932), pp. 66–69. Among more recent treatments of "pan-Indianism" that pay some attention to its political aspects, the important ones include Hertzberg, *Search for Identity*, Part I; Thomas, "Pan-Indianism," primarily pp. 135–40; and Nancy Oestreich Lurie, "The Contemporary American Indian Scene," in Leacock and Lurie, *North American Indians*, pp. 418–80. Of these, only Thomas traces its historical emergence.

5. "To the Cherokee," says Robert Thomas, "Englishmen and Creeks were . . . simply different kinds of outsiders." "Pan-Indianism," p. 130.

6. Brief summaries of these alliances can be found in Shirley Hill Witt, "Nationalistic Trends Among American Indians," in Levine and Lurie, *American Indian Today*, pp. 94–98; and in Spicer, *Short History*, ch. 1 and 2. There are substantial literatures on all of them. The Narragansett, Miantunnomoh, is quoted in Armstrong, *I Have Spoken*, p. 3. For an example of colonial attempts to inhibit intertribal alliance, see Wright, *Only Land They Knew*, p. 125.

7. See Reginald Horsman, *Race and Manifest Destiny: The Origins of American Racial Anglo-Saxonism* (Cambridge: Harvard University Press, 1981), especially ch. 6 and 10.

8. Hertzberg, *Search for Identity*, p. 2.

9. Charlot and Daykauray are quoted in Armstrong, *I Have Spoken*, pp. 56, 99.

10. Mooney, *Ghost-Dance Religion*, p. 777.

11. James F. Downs, *The Two Worlds of the Washo* (New York: Holt, Rinehart and Winston, 1966), p. 103.

12. Aberle, *Peyote Religion*, ch. 19.

13. Mooney commented in 1918: "The Indian, under the influence of this peyote religion, has given up the idea that he and his tribe are for themselves alone, and is recognizing the fact of the brotherhood of the Indian race particularly, and beyond that the brotherhood of mankind." Quoted in Hertzberg, *Search for Identity*, p. 252. On the emergence of the Native American Church, see ibid., ch. 10 and 11. While certainly the most significant, the 1918 incorporation was not the first formal organization of peyotism in the United States. On earlier incorporations, see La Barre, *Peyote Cult*, pp. 167–74. The Indian Shaker Church also incorporated some years earlier, but with somewhat less Indian input and a good deal less external impact; see H. G. Barnett, *Indian Shakers: A Messianic Cult of the Pacific Northwest* (Carbondale: Southern Illinois University Press, 1957), p. 113.

14. Lurie, "Contemporary American Indian Scene," pp. 449–51; Gertrude Prokosch Kurath, "Pan-Indianism in Great Lakes Tribal Festivals," *Journal of American Folklore* 70 (April–June 1957): 181. Paredes, however, felt the Chippewa participants he studied more or less ignored the Pan-Indian aspects of the powwow. See J. Anthony Paredes, "Chippewa Townspeople," in J. A. Paredes, ed., *Anishinabe: 6 Studies of Modern Chippewa* (Tallahassee: University Presses of Florida, 1980), p. 389. My own observations on the Bad River Ojibwa Reservation in Wisconsin suggest that both circles of identity

receive reinforcement: Bad River Ojibwas viewed their powwow as an opportunity both to renew ties with Indians from other nations, celebrating a common identity, and to display the distinctive qualities of their own community and its traditions. Field notes, Bad River Ojibwa Reservation, 1981.

15. Berkhofer, *White Man's Indian*, p. 26.

16. See Berkhofer's discussion in ibid., esp. pp. 49–55 and 62–69; also J. W. Burrow, *Evolution and Society: A Study in Victorian Social Thought* (Cambridge, U.K.: Cambridge University Press, 1966), ch. 5–7.

17. A representative selection of such writing is available in Prucha, *Americanizing the American Indians*.

18. Theodore Fischbacher, *A Study of the Role of the Federal Government in the Education of the American Indian* (San Francisco: R & E Research Associates, 1974), p. 99.

19. "Report of the Indian School Superintendent," in Commissioner of Indian Affairs, *Annual Report, 1886* (Washington: Government Printing Office, 1886), p. 89, Table A. After 1890 the emphasis shifted back to day schools. By 1901 the number of government day schools exceeded boarding schools, 138 to 113, although 47 mission boarding schools also remained in operation. See Estelle Fuchs and Robert J. Havighurst, *To Live on This Earth: American Indian Education* (New York: Anchor, 1973), p. 225; also Fischbacher, *Government in Education*, pp. 146–47.

20. Thomas Morgan, *Indian Education*, U.S. Bureau of Education, Bulletin No. 1, 1889 (Washington: Government Printing Office, 1890), p. 12. Morgan hoped Indian students would be "weaned from the reservation"; however, many graduates returned to their communities and at least one school, Hampton, encouraged them to do so. See Wilbert H. Ahern, " 'The Returned Indians': Hampton Institute and its Indian Alumni, 1879–1893," *Journal of Ethnic Studies* 10, no. 4 (Winter 1983): 101–24.

21. Fischbacher, *Government in Education*, pp. 105, 147; Margaret Connell Szasz, *Education and the American Indian: The Road to Self-Determination Since 1928*, 2nd ed. (Albuquerque: University of New Mexico Press, 1977), p. 10.

22. Hertzberg states flatly, "Pan-Indianism would have been impossible without English as a lingua franca." *Search for Identity*, p. 303; see also pp. 15–20, where she discusses the impact of Indian education on early supra-tribal developments. Weston La Barre argues that schoolboy friendships and the spread of English greatly facilitated the diffusion of peyotism. La Barre, *Peyote Cult*, p. 113.

23. Richard La Course, personal communications. La Course has found urban Indian publications from as early as the mid-nineteenth century, and of course tribal journalism goes back further still, but these school publications seem to have been the first to deal self-consciously with the Indian population as a whole.

24. See especially Morgan, *Indian Education*.

25. Hertzberg, *Search for Identity*, p. 20. See also Sally J. McBeth, *Ethnic Identity and the Boarding School Experience of West-Central Oklahoma American Indians* (Washington: University Press of America, 1983), pp. 125–26. Day schools were less effective in producing these results, hindered in their efforts by the daily return to kin, custom, and native tongue. Then, too, their students usually came from a single tribe.

26. Given in Hertzberg, *Search for Identity*, p. 80. Part I of Hertzberg's book is a detailed history of the SAI and is the basis of its treatment here.

27. Ibid., pp. 81–82.

28. Ibid., p. 109

29. Both statements are quoted in ibid., pp. 63–64 and 139–40. There were other Indian organizations of the period that shared this general outlook. See, for example, Philip Drucker, *The Native Brotherhoods: Modern Intertribal Organizations on the Northwest Coast*, Bureau of American Ethnology, Bulletin 168 (Washington: Smithsonian Institution, 1958).

30. Deloria, "First Indian Movement," p. 661.

31. Hertzberg, *Search for Identity*, p. 96.

32. Compiled from Meriam, *Problem of Indian Administration*, pp. 355–56, 402–3.

33. On this point, see Hertzberg, *Search for Identity*, pp. 299–300.

34. On the AIF, see Laurence M. Hauptman, "The American Indian Federation and the Indian New Deal: A Reinterpretation," *Pacific Historical Review* 52, no. 4 (1983): 378–402.

35. "Register of Delegates at the National Convention of American Indians held in Denver, Colorado, November 15–18, 1944"; Article II, NCAI Constitution, as printed in "Proceedings of the First Convention of the National Congress of American Indians," p. 54; "Preamble" in ibid. All in Records of the National Congress of American Indians, National Anthropological Archives, Smithsonian Institution, Washington, D.C. (hereafter NCAI Records).

36. The quote is from Department of the Interior, *Annual Report of the Secretary of the Interior, 1944* (Washington: Government Printing Office, 1944), p. 237; the figures are from idem, *Annual Report of the Secretary of the Interior, 1945* (Washington: Government Printing Office, 1945), pp. 249–50.

37. Alden Stevens, "Voice of the Native: Arizona's and New Mexico's redskins could swing the election in those two states," *New York Times*, November 2, 1952. The NCAI was founded with an explicit awareness of the political resource returning veterans represented and a desire to make use of it. See letter from Mark L. Burns, President, National Council of American Indians, to "Tribal Councils and Indian Leaders," October 16, 1944, regarding the upcoming first convention of NCAI, NCAI Records.

38. Quoted in Clayton R. Koppes, "From New Deal to Termination: Liberalism and Indian Policy, 1933–53," *Pacific Historical Review* 46, no. 4 (November 1977): 556.

39. On these various constituencies and their views, see Koppes, "New Deal to Termination"; Lurie, "Contemporary Indian Scene," pp. 456–57, 461; Philp, "Termination," pp. 170–71.

40. Commission on Organization of the Executive Branch of the Government, *Social Security and Education; Indian Affairs: A Report to the Congress* (Washington: U.S. Government Printing Office, 1949), pp. 63–67; idem, "Report of the Committee on Indian Affairs to the Commission on Organization of the Executive Branch of the Government," n.p., October 1948, p. 54.

41. Arthur V. Watkins, "Termination of Federal Supervision: The Removal of Restrictions over Indian Property and Person," *Annals of the American Academy of Political and Social Science* 311 (May 1957): 48–49.

42. Details of termination legislation are given in Charles F. Wilkinson and

Eric R. Biggs, "The Evolution of the Termination Policy," *American Indian Law Review* 5, no. 1 (1977): 139–84.

43. See, especially on this last point, ibid., pp. 153–54.

44. Quoted in Harold E. Fey and D'Arcy McNickle, *Indians and Other Americans: Two Ways of Life Meet*, rev. ed. (New York: Perennial Library, 1970), p. 145, from an August 2, 1952, memorandum directed to "All Bureau Officials."

45. Deborah Shames, coord. ed., *Freedom with Reservation: The Menominee Struggle to Save Their Land and People* (Madison: National Committee to Save the Menominee People and Forests, 1972); Nancy Oestreich Lurie, "Menominee Termination: From Reservation to Colony," *Human Organization* 31, no. 3 (Fall 1972): 257–70. The quote is from Spindler and Spindler, *Dreamers Without Power*, p. 202.

46. Lurie, "Contemporary Indian Scene," p. 456. See also Larry W. Burt, *Tribalism in Crisis: Federal Indian Policy, 1953–1961* (Albuquerque: University of New Mexico Press, 1982), ch. 9. NCAI opposition to termination can be followed in issues of its Washington Bulletin in the late 1940s and 1950s (NCAI Records). Not all Indians opposed the termination policy. Those living off the reservations in particular saw advantages in the dissolution and distribution of the tribal estate. See, for example, the discussion and table in Jean A. Maxwell, "Colvilles on the Verge of Development," in Joseph G. Jorgensen, ed., *Native Americans and Energy Development II* (Boston: Anthropology Resource Center and Seventh Generation Fund, 1984), pp. 158–60.

47. D'Arcy McNickle, *Native American Tribalism: Indian Survivals and Renewals* (New York: Oxford University Press, 1973), p. 117. For a detailed report and history of the conference itself, see Nancy Oestreich Lurie, "The Voice of the American Indian: Report on the American Indian Chicago Conference," *Current Anthropology* 2, no. 5 (1961): 478–500.

48. Secretary of the Interior Fred E. Seaton in a radio address, September 18, 1958, quoted in S. Lyman Tyler, *A History of Indian Policy* (Washington: Department of the Interior, 1973), p. 180; Richard M. Nixon, "Message to Congress on Indian Affairs," in Josephy, *Red Power*, pp. 213–30. On the restoration of the Menominee, see Nicholas C. Peroff, *Menominee Drums: Tribal Termination and Restoration, 1954–1974* (Norman: University of Oklahoma Press, 1982).

49. Szasz, *Education and American Indian*, pp. 114, 135; "More U.S. Indians Going to College," *New York Times*, September 7, 1958.

50. My brief account of these developments is based on Stan Steiner, *The New Indians* (New York: Dell, 1968), ch. 3 and 4, and on conversations with Herbert Blatchford in Albuquerque, March 1979, and Robert Thomas in Detroit, June 1979. The figures on the 1960 youth conference are from Steiner, p. 35.

51. In conversation, Detroit, June 1979. In a 1974 policy statement, NIYC confirmed its long-standing position combining tribal and supratribal concerns: "We believe that one's basic identity should be with his tribe . . . we believe that tribalism is what has caused us to endure. Our purpose is not to create one kind of Indian but to make young Indian people more effective members of their tribal communities. NIYC will make itself into an effective institution

that will foster brotherhood among tribes." Quoted in *Wassaja*, February 1974, p. 4.

52. See especially Howard, "Pan-Indian Culture of Oklahoma."

Chapter 8. The Politics of Indianness

1. Robert E. Park, "The City: Suggestions for the Investigation of Human Behavior in the Urban Environment," in Robert E. Park and Ernest W. Burgess, *The City* (Chicago: University of Chicago Press, 1925), p. 40.

2. On Indian labor in Tucson in the 1850s, see the statement by a U.S. Survey Service officer stationed in the city at the time, cited in W. Miller Barbour, "Tucson: A Study of Race Relations," mimeo, Tucson Urban League Service Council, 1954, p. 35. On Barrio Libre, see Bernice Cosulich, *Tucson* (Tucson: Arizona Silhouettes, 1953), p. 267.

3. Richard La Course, personal communication; Bureau of the Census, *U.S. Census of the Population, 1900;* Meriam, *Problem of Indian Administration,* ch. 12.

4. Joseph G. Jorgensen, *The Sun Dance Religion: Power for the Powerless* (Chicago: University of Chicago Press, 1972), pp. 113–14, 121–23.

5. For example, National Resources Board, "Indian Land Tenure, Economic Status, and Population Trends," Supplementary Report of the Land Planning Committee (Washington: Government Printing Office, 1935).

6. Tyler, *History of Indian Policy*, p. 159.

7. Commissioner of Indian Affairs, *Annual Report, 1906* (Washington: Government Printing Office, 1906), pp. 6–16.

8. See the Annual Report of the Commissioner of Indian Affairs for the years 1931–1938; also Cardell K. Jacobson, "Internal Colonialism and Native Americans: Indian Labor in the United States from 1871 to World War II," *Social Science Quarterly* 65, no. 1 (1984): 164–65.

9. The early development of the relocation program is described in Elaine M. Neils, *Reservation to City: Indian Migration and Federal Relocation*, Research Paper No. 131 (Chicago: University of Chicago Department of Geography, 1971), ch. 2. On the vocational training program, see Alan L. Sorkin, "Some Aspects of American Indian Migration," in Howard M. Bahr, Bruce A. Chadwick, and Robert C. Day, eds., *Native Americans Today: Sociological Perspectives* (New York: Harper and Row, 1972), p. 468.

10. American Indian Policy Review Commission (hereafter AIPRC), *Report on Urban and Rural Non-Reservation Indians* (Washington: Government Printing Office, 1976), p. 23.

11. Neils, *Reservation to City*, p. 55, Table 8. Her source is U.S. Bureau of the Budget, *The Budget of the United States for the Fiscal Year Ending June 30*, 1953–1966.

12. Commission on Organization of the Executive Branch of the Government, "Report of Committee on Indian Affairs," p. 100; Watkins is quoted in Hilda Bryant, "Loneliness is the White Man's City," *Seattle Post-Intelligencer,* December 14, 1969, cited in Howard M. Bahr, "An End to Invisibility," in Bahr et al., *Native Americans Today*, p. 409. James E. Officer argues that pressures for termination and for relocation came from different sources and sentiments; see his "The American Indian and Federal Policy," in Jack O. Waddell

and O. Michael Watson, eds., *The American Indian in Urban Society* (Boston: Little, Brown and Co., 1971), pp. 46–47. On the other hand, Philleo Nash, a member of President Truman's White House staff and later Commissioner of Indian Affairs under President Kennedy, claims that "relocation was part of the termination policy followed by the Truman administration." See his comments in Philp, *Indian Self-Rule*, p. 164.

13. "Is Relocation Running Away with the Bureau?" National Congress of American Indians, *Bulletin*, June 1955, p. 4. NCAI Records. There were many Indians, however, who saw relocation as a viable solution. See Kenneth R. Philp, "Stride Toward Freedom: The Relocation of Indians to Cities, 1952–1960," *Western Historical Quarterly* 16, no. 2 (1985): 176–77.

14. Peter Z. Snyder, "The Social Environment of the Urban Indian," in Waddell and Watson, *Indian in Urban Society*, p. 220; see also the interview with Alfred Dubray, Brule Sioux, in Joseph T. Cash and Herbert T. Hoover, "The Indian New Deal and the Years that Followed: Three Interviews," in Peter Iverson, ed., *The Plains Indians of the Twentieth Century* (Norman: University of Oklahoma Press, 1985), pp. 130–31.

15. Bureau of the Census, *Census of the Population, 1980,* United States Summary, General Social and Economic Characteristics (Washington: Government Printing Office, 1980), Tables 128, 124.

16. Earlier examples include Vogt, "Acculturation of American Indians," p. 146; and Howard, "Pan-Indian Culture of Oklahoma," pp. 215–20. The quote is from Hirabayashi et al., "Pan-Indianism in Urban Setting," p. 86.

17. Meriam, *Problem of Indian Administration*, pp. 720–23; Hertzberg, *Search for Identity*, ch. 9; Phillips, "Indians in Los Angeles," pp. 427–51; comments by Herbert Blatchford in *Indian Voices: The First Convocation of American Indian Scholars* (San Francisco: Indian Historian Press, 1970), p. 340.

18. John A. Price, "The Migration and Adaptation of American Indians to Los Angeles," *Human Organization* 27, no. 2 (1968): 168–75.

19. See the discussion of urban Indian institutions in John A. Price, "The Development of Urban Ethnic Institutions by U.S. and Canadian Indians," *Ethnic Groups* 1, no. 2 (1976): 107–31; and Shirley J. Fiske, "Urban Indian Institutions: A Reappraisal from Los Angeles," *Urban Anthropology* 8, no. 2 (1979): 149–71.

20. AIPRC, *Report on Urban Indians*, pp. 19, 97–105; on the data in the report, see Joseph H. Stauss, "A Critique of the Task Force Eight Final Report to the American Indian Policy Review Commission: Urban and Rural Non-Reservation Indians," in *New Directions in Federal Indian Policy: A Review of the American Indian Policy Review Commission* (Los Angeles: American Indian Studies Center, University of California, Los Angeles, 1979), pp. 88–98.

21. AIPRC, *Report on Urban Indians*, pp. 41, 76–78. See also Herbert Blatchford's discussion of Indian centers in *Indian Voices: First Convocation*, pp. 336–39.

22. On the functions of urban Indian enclaves, cf. Snyder, "Social Environment of Urban Indian," p. 219; also Bruce A. Chadwick and Joseph H. Stauss, "The Assimilation of American Indians into Urban Society: The Seattle Case," *Human Organization* 34, no. 4 (1975): 359–69. Sam Stanley and Robert K. Thomas have written that new immigrants to American cities "must find interstices in the existing institutional structure in which to build formal or informal

organizations of their own. American Indians in cities are trying very hard to build together some kind of community life, or ethnic group perhaps, but against tremendous odds. They are a small minority, scattered throughout the metropolitan area, and struggling desperately to avoid becoming a part of the anonymous mass." Sam Stanley and Robert K. Thomas, "Current Demographic and Social Trends Among North American Indians," *Annals of the American Academy of Political and Social Science* 436 (March 1978): 116.

23. Joann Westermann, "The Urban Indian," *Current History* 67 (December 1974): 262; Joan Ablon, "Relocated American Indians in the San Francisco Bay Area: Social Interaction and Indian Identity," *Human Organization* 23, no. 4 (1964): 300; Price, "Migration and Adaptation," pp. 174–75.

24. The general argument about organizational dynamics is made by Michael T. Hannan, "The Dynamics of Ethnic Boundaries in Modern States," in John W. Meyer and Michael T. Hannan, eds., *National Development and the World System: Educational, Economic, and Political Change, 1950–1970* (Chicago: University of Chicago Press, 1979), pp. 253–75. It has been applied to the Indian case, though not specifically to Indian urbanization, by Joane Nagel, "The Political Mobilization of Native Americans," *Social Science Quarterly* 19, no. 3 (July 1982): 37–45.

25. Much the same point is suggested by Bahr: "the migration of Indian people to cities, rather than 'submerging' them in the mainstream, has created conditions which have enhanced Indian identity and have led to the establishment of a Pan-Indian power base." Bahr, "End to Invisibility," p. 410.

26. Joan Ablon, "American Indian Relocation: Problems of Dependency and Management in the City," *Phylon* 26 (Winter 1965): 362–71. The BIA figures are from Sorkin, "Aspects of Indian Migration," p. 246; Navajo figures are given in Price, "Migration and Adaptation," p. 171.

27. Blatchford in *Indian Voices: First Convocation,* p. 336; William H. Hodge, "Ethnicity as a Factor in Modern American Indian Migration: A Winnebago Case Study with Reference to Other Indian Situations," in Helen I. Safa and Brian M. du Toit, eds., *Migration and Development* (The Hague: Mouton, 1975), p. 33. For examples, see Jeanne Guillemin, *Urban Renegades: The Cultural Strategy of American Indians* (New York: Columbia University Press, 1975); William H. Hodge, *The Albuquerque Navajos* (Tucson: University of Arizona Press, 1969); Joseph Mitchell, "The Mohawks in High Steel," in Edmund Wilson, *Apologies to the Iroquois* (New York: Vintage, 1960), pp. 1–36. On urban–reservation commuting generally, see Lurie, "Contemporary Indian Scene," in Leacock and Lurie, *North American Indians,* p. 440; Blatchford in *Indian Voices: First Convocation,* pp. 335–36; Sol Tax, "The Impact of Urbanization on American Indians," *Annals of the American Academy of Political and Social Science* 436 (March 1978): 128. Data in these sources are supported by my observations and conversations with Indians in Tucson and Minneapolis, which indicated substantial numbers of part-time, highly mobile urban residents.

28. Blatchford, *Indian Voices: First Convocation,* p. 336.

29. These remarks draw largely on my own observations and conversations with Indians and others in Minneapolis, Seattle, Tucson, Albuquerque, and northern Wisconsin. As far as I know, there have been no studies of the effects of urban returnees on reservation population self-concepts. According to Constance Sutton and Susan Makiesky, this lacuna has been apparent in migration

studies generally, which have paid little attention to the effects on sending societies of changing migrant self-concepts or ideology. These authors' work is exceptional in this regard and suggestive of what I believe to be the case among American Indians. For the more general point about migration studies, see Sutton and Makiesky, "Migration and West Indian Racial and Ethnic Consciousness," in Safa and du Toit, *Migration and Development*, pp. 114–15. Their discussion of the "feedback effects" of West Indian migration to Britain and the United States is on pp. 132–39. For similarly suggestive material from Africa, see John Middleton, "Political Incorporation among the Lugbara of Uganda," in Ronald Cohen and John Middleton, eds., *From Tribe to Nation in Africa: Studies in Incorporation Processes* (Scranton: Chandler, 1970), pp. 65–67, suggesting that returning migrants contributed to the growth of a generalized ethnic awareness among rural Lugbara groups.

30. American Indian Press Association, *American Indian Media Directory*, 1974 ed. (Washington: American Indian Press Association, 1973). The history of Indian media is given in James E. Murphy and Sharon M. Murphy, *Let My People Know: American Indian Journalism* (Norman: University of Oklahoma Press, 1981). The quote is from "Media Milestone: Indian Journalists Mark 150th Year of Publishing," *Red Current* 1, no. 1 (Spring 1978): 1.

31. American Indian Press Association, *Media Directory*, p. 2.

32. Interview with Richard La Course, November 1978; "Those AIPA Days," *Red Current* 1, no. 1 (Spring 1978): 12.

33. This is clear from conversations with Richard La Course, then editor of the *Yakima Nation Review* and former news director of AIPA, in September 1978, and from interviews with Rupert Costo, editor of *Wassaja*, and Andy de los Angeles of *Northwest Indian News*, both in November 1978, and Charles Trimble, organizer of AIPA, in April 1979.

34. James E. Officer, "Federal Policy and the Urban Indian," in Jack O. Waddell and O. Michael Watson, eds., *American Indian Urbanization* (Lafayette: Institute for the Study of Social Change, Purdue University, 1973), p. 9; J. Milton Yinger and George Eaton Simpson, "The Integration of Americans of Indian Descent," *Annals of the American Academy of Political and Social Science* 436 (March 1978): 137, 148–49; Lynn C. White and Bruce A. Chadwick, "Urban Residence, Assimilation and Identity of the Spokane Indian," in Bahr et al., *Native Americans Today*, pp. 239–49.

35. Ablon, "Relocated American Indians," pp. 296–304; Chadwick and Stauss, "Assimilation of American Indians," pp. 359–69. The quote is from the abstract, p. 359. See also Joseph H. Stauss and Bruce A. Chadwick, "Urban Indian Adjustment," *American Indian Culture and Research Journal* 3, no. 2 (1979): 23–38. Bernard E. Anderson and Donald F. Harvey, "American Indian Labor Mobility: A Problem of Cross Cultural Adjustment," mimeo (Flagstaff, 1970), cited in White and Chadwick, "Urban Residence," pp. 241–42. Gordon V. Krutz, "Compartmentalization as a Factor in Urban Adjustment: The Kiowa Case" and "Transplanting and Revitalizing of Indian Cultures in the City," pp. 101–16 and 130–39, both in Waddell and Watson, *American Indian Urbanization*. The quotes are from, respectively, pp. 133, 103, and 138. Mary Patrick, "Indian Urbanization in Dallas: A Second Trail of Tears?" *The Oral History Review* (1973), pp. 50, 56; Abraham Makofsky, "Tradition and Change in the Lumbee Indian Community of Baltimore," *Maryland Historical Magazine* 75, no. 1 (March 1980): 55–71; W. T. Stanbury, *Success and Failure: Indians in*

Urban Society (n.p.: University of British Columbia Press, 1975), ch. 10. For a more general critique of the assimilationist argument, see C. Hoy Steele, "The Acculturation/Assimilation Model in Urban Indian Studies: A Critique," in Norman R. Yetman with C. Hoy Steele, eds., *Majority and Minority: The Dynamics of Race and Ethnicity in American Life,* 3rd ed. (Boston: Allyn and Bacon, 1982), pp. 282–89. The conclusions cited above are supported by my own field data from Minneapolis, Seattle, and Tucson.

36. Stanley and Thomas, "Demographic and Social Trends," pp. 116, 117. On socialization and generational change in the city, see also L. S. Kemnitzer, "Familial and Extra-Familial Socialization in Urban Dakota Adolescents," in Nurge, *Modern Sioux,* pp. 246–67.

37. Guillemin, *Urban Renegades,* p. 293.

38. Cf. Lurie: "Unlike the usual migrants, Indian people do not seem to perceive urban work as a break with the rural past, but merely as an extension of the peripheries of the territory which can be exploited economically." Nancy O. Lurie, "Historical Background," in Levine and Lurie, *American Indian Today,* p. 73. Kemnitzer argued that Dakota migrants in San Francisco participate in just such a system. See his "Urban Dakota Adolescents," p. 251. While both these authors' remarks are based on 1960s data, there is little to suggest that the phenomenon has disappeared. See also Hodge, "Ethnicity as a Factor," pp. 33–34.

39. See, for example, Tamara K. Hareven, *Family Time and Industrial Time* (Cambridge, U.K.: Cambridge University Press, 1982), ch. 5; Joan M. Nelson, *Access to Power: Politics and the Urban Poor in Developing Nations* (Princeton: Princeton University Press, 1979), pp. 215–18; Charles Tilly and C. Harold Brown, "On Uprooting, Kinship, and the Auspices of Migration," *International Journal of Comparative Sociology* 8, no. 2 (September 1967): 139–64.

40. See, for example, J. Van Velsen, "Labor Migration as a Positive Factor in the Continuity of Tonga Society," *Economic Development and Cultural Change* 8, no. 3 (1960): 265–78; Phillip Mayer, *Townsmen or Tribesmen: Conservatism and the Process of Urbanization in a South African City* (Cape Town: Oxford University Press, 1961), ch. 18; Tamara K. Hareven, "The Invisible Bridge: Immigrants and Their Communities of Origin," paper presented at the Harvard-Draeger Conference on Population Interactions between Poor and Rich Countries, Cambridge, Massachusetts, October 1983. The appropriate comparative referents for an understanding of certain aspects of Indian urbanization—and Indian identity as well—often are less the experiences of other American migrants than Third World examples.

41. See, for example, J. Anthony Paredes, "Chippewa Townspeople," pp. 324–96.

42. Hirabayashi et al., "Pan-Indianism," pp. 84–85; Patricia Locke, "Indian Urban Communities," unpublished manuscript; Price, "Migration and Adaptation," pp. 174–75.

43. A study of Mississippi Choctaws notes that "contact with members of other tribes and with the mass media image of Indians has resulted in younger Choctaws beginning to see their identity as Indian, rather than exclusively Chata [the Choctaw term for themselves]. It is important to note that identity as Indian is not replacing identity as Chata, but rather is in addition to Chata identity." Thompson and Peterson, "Mississippi Choctaw Identity," p. 190.

44. For a similar point regarding urbanization and African "tribalism," see

Max Gluckman, "Anthropological Problems Arising from the African Industrial Revolution," in Aidan Southall, ed., *Social Change in Modern Africa* (London: Oxford University Press, 1961). The situational character of Indian identities is noted by James H. Stewart, "Urbanization, Peoplehood and Modes of Identity: Native Americans in Cities," in George E. Carter and James R. Parker, eds., *Identity and Awareness in the Minority Experience*, Selected Proceedings of the 1st and 2nd Annual Conferences on Minority Studies (La Crosse: Institute for Minority Studies, University of Wisconsin, 1975), pp. 108–36.

45. Robert K. Merton, *Social Theory and Social Structure*, enlarged ed. (New York: The Free Press, 1968), p. 340.

46. Krutz, "Transplanting Indian Cultures," p. 137. This resurgence of interest in tribal cultures was foreseen early on by Schusky, "Pan-Indianism in Eastern U.S.," p. 123. It was amply apparent among Indian adolescents with whom I worked at the Southwest Indian Youth Center in Tucson, Arizona, in 1973.

47. Thomas, "Pan-Indianism," pp. 128–29, 139; Stanley and Thomas, "Demographic and Social Trends," pp. 119–20.

48. Cf. Frances Svensson, "Ethnicity versus Communalism: The American Indian Movement and the Politics of Survival," in Jeffrey A. Ross and Ann Baker Cottrell, eds., *The Mobilization of Collective Identity: Comparative Perspectives* (Lanham: University Press of America, 1980), pp. 65–88.

49. Joe R. Feagin and Randall Anderson, "Intertribal Attitudes Among Native American Youth," *Social Science Quarterly* 54, no. 1 (1973): 129; Guillemin, *Urban Renegades*, p. 157; Shirley Fiske, "Intertribal Perceptions: Navajo and Pan-Indianism," *Ethos* 5, no. 3 (Fall 1977): 358–75.

50. Joyotpaul Chaudhuri, *Urban Indians of Arizona*, Arizona Government Studies, No. 11, Institute of Government Research, University of Arizona (Tucson: University of Arizona Press, 1974), pp. 25–28.

51. Meriam, *Problem of Indian Administration*, p. 739; Officer, "Federal Policy and Urban Indian," p. 9; Neils, *Reservation to City*, pp. 127–28. Jean A. Maxwell reports that several tribal council members on the Colville Reservation owe their positions to off-reservation constituents, who both outnumber reservation voters, and tend more to vote as a block. See Maxwell, "Colvilles on Verge of Development," p. 166.

52. Both the urban/reservation tension and the felt need to overcome it are apparent in an interview with Greg Frazier, head of the National Urban Indian Council, in "Urban Indians Enter the Political Arena," *American Indian Journal* 6, no. 8 (August 1980): 15–18. For an interesting account of reservation/nonreservation factional conflict, see Clifton, *Prairie People*, ch. 12 and 13.

Chapter 9. Who Wants What?

1. Congressional Research Service, *Indian and Indian-Interest Organizations* (Washington: Congressional Research Service, 1974).

2. Tax, "Impact of Urbanization," p. 134.

3. For a case study of just this process, see Miner, *Corporation and Indian*.

4. Cf. Frank Parkin, *Marxism and Class Theory: A Bourgeois Critique* (New

York: Columbia University Press, 1979); also Ralf Dahrendorf, *Class and Class Conflict in Industrial Society* (Stanford: Stanford University Press, 1959), pp. 174–76.

5. R. A. Schermerhorn, *Comparative Ethnic Relations: A Framework for Theory and Research* (New York: Random House, 1970), pp. 77–78, 82–83.

6. Segregative constituencies are more distinctive for their cultural than their political agendas: it is not so much political separation as cultural that they seek, although they typically advocate a high degree of tribal autonomy. This is not meant to suggest that integrative Native American goals are pro-assimilation; few of them are. What they envision is more substantial participation in the larger system without loss of Indian or tribal identities. They do not really deal with questions of assimilation, turning their attention more to questions of access and distribution. Segregative goals, in contrast, explicitly confront the assimilationist tendency.

7. Of course ends may also be means. Reformative-integrative goals, such as electing an Indian to Congress, may be means to transformative-integrative ones, such as passing legislation that would revise the formal structure of Indian-White relations. As Steven Lukes points out, "What counts as an end is always relative to a particular way of drawing conceptual boundaries." Lukes, "Power and Structure," in idem, *Essays in Social Theory* (New York: Columbia University Press, 1977), p. 12.

8. On this last point, see Vine Deloria, Jr., *Behind the Trail of Broken Treaties: An Indian Declaration of Independence* (New York: Dell, 1974), especially ch. 6–9.

9. Neither these various constituencies nor their goals are mutually exclusive. Individuals and groups typically are part of more than one constituency at a time. Likewise, the goals of one may be shared on occasion by others. It should be noted also that there is a fourth type of constituency that does not appear in previous chapters: what might be called "unrecognized tribal" constituencies. These are groups that claim tribal status but are not recognized by the federal government as tribes with whom that government has formal relations and who are entitled, therefore, to federal services. Like supratribal constituencies, they lack official representation in the formal structure of Indian-White relations. Insofar as their political agendas are focused on issues of recognition and representation, they resemble some urban Indian actors.

10. Nancy O. Lurie, "The Indian Claims Commission," *Annals of the American Academy of Political and Social Science* 436 (March 1978), p. 101. This is a good deal of money but, as the Interior Department at one point noted, it is only a tiny fraction of the total value claimed and less than the annual budget of the BIA in most years. See Barsh and Henderson, *The Road*, p. 94n.

11. See U.S. Department of the Interior, *Mineral Revenues: The 1982 Report on Receipts from Federal and Indian Leases* (Washington: Minerals Management Service, Department of the Interior, 1983), pp. 38, 45; Henry W. Hough, *Development of Indian Resources* (n.p.: Indian Community Action Program, Arizona State University, University of South Dakota, University of Utah, 1967), p. 118, Figure III-B; Sar A. Levitan and William B. Johnston, *Indian Giving: Federal Programs for Native Americans* (Baltimore: Johns Hopkins University Press, 1975), p. 20.

12. Pub. Law 88–452, 88th Congress, Second Session, 1964.

13. See Monroe E. Price, "Lawyers on the Reservation: Some Implications

for the Legal Profession," *Law and the Social Order* 1969, no. 2 (1969): 177–78; and the discussion of Community Action Programs in J. David Greenstone and Paul E. Peterson, *Race and Authority in Urban Politics: Community Participation and the War on Poverty* (Chicago: University of Chicago Press, 1976), pp. 2–6.

14. Lurie, "Contemporary Indian Scene," p. 455.

15. This point has been made to me by Indians on a number of occasions and was evident among adolescents I worked with at the Southwest Indian Youth Center in Tucson, Arizona, in 1973.

16. Conflict over these issues involves not only distribution itself, but also questions of entitlement. The mixed-blood/full-blood distinction, for example, which for many Indians indicates primarily a cultural divide, has been used also by both Indians and Whites as a biological means of determining rights to economic and political resources and rewards. For certain purposes the federal government determines who is and is not an Indian—and the consequent distribution of certain resources—through blood quanta.

17. These terms are mine. I have surrounded them with quotation marks in order to emphasize that fact and because the terms themselves are fraught with meaning. My own usage refers to the degree of change sought by each set of constituencies. I have used "realists" not because I think such constituencies are more in touch with reality than others, but because their agendas generally accept the dramatic changes that already have occurred in Native American societies and seek ways of working with non-Indian society and not against it. Most emphatically reject assimilation in the sense of disappearance into an American melting pot, but promote cooperation with the larger society as it presently exists. I use "radicals" likewise to refer to the greater degree of change sought or opposition expressed by these other constituencies, whose agendas and ideas are more substantially at odds with those of the prevailing social order. Gail M. Gerhart uses "realists" and "rebels" in similar ways in her discussion of the internal politics of Black resistance in South Africa. See her *Black Power in South Africa: The Evolution of an Ideology* (Berkeley: University of California Press, 1978), pp. 39–44.

Chapter 10. Old Wars, New Weapons

1. In conversation, Tucson, Arizona, 1978 (author's field notes).

2. Resources have long been central considerations in the sociology of power. See, in particular, Robert Bierstedt, "An Analysis of Social Power," *American Sociological Review* 15 (December 1950): 730–38; and Hubert M. Blalock, Jr., *Toward a Theory of Minority-Group Relations* (New York: Capricorn, 1970), ch. 4. They have received increased attention recently from the "resource mobilization" approach to collective action, which emphasizes the distribution of resources among collective actors and the ways those actors gather and invest those resources in action. Despite the centrality of the concept in this work, however, resources themselves often have been left loosely defined or not at all; consequently the approach sometimes has suffered from a conflation of group position (political opportunity) and group assets (political capacity). See, for example, the list of resources in Jo Freeman, "Resource Mobilization and Strategy: A Model for Analyzing Social Movement Organization Ac-

tions," in Mayer N. Zald and John D. McCarthy, eds., *The Dynamics of Social Movements* (Cambridge: Winthrop Publishers, 1979), p. 174. For a general discussion and critique of the resource mobilization perspective, see Doug Mc-Adam, *Political Process and the Development of Black Insurgency, 1930–1970* (Chicago: University of Chicago Press, 1982), ch. 2; and J. Craig Jenkins, "Resource Mobilization and the Study of Social Movements," *Annual Review of Sociology* 9 (1983): 527–53.

3. These properties and other aspects of resource utility are discussed at some length in James S. Coleman, *Resources for Social Change: Race in the United States* (New York: Wiley-Interscience, 1971), pp. 2–5 and Part III, and in Terry N. Clark, "The Concept of Power," in Terry N. Clark, ed., *Community Structure and Decision-Making: Comparative Analyses* (San Francisco: Chandler, 1968), pp. 58–67.

4. See Helen Peterson, "American Indian Political Participation," *The Annals of the American Academy of Political and Social Science* 311 (May 1957): 121.

5. U.S. Congress, House Committee on Interior Insular Affairs, *Present Relations of the Federal Government to the American Indian* (Washington: Government Printing Office, 1959), pp. 157, 175–79.

6. Penn Kimball, *The Disconnected* (New York: Columbia University Press, 1972), p. 191. Participation in tribal elections often has been low as well. Less than 30 percent of eligible voters took part in tribal elections on the Pine Ridge Sioux Reservation in South Dakota in 1969. See DeMallie, "Pine Ridge Economy," p. 276; also, on the Papagos, Manuel et al., "Dressing for the Window," p. 542.

7. National Indian Youth Council, "American Indian Political Attitudes and Behavior Survey: Data Report," National Indian Youth Council, Albuquerque, New Mexico, January 1983, p. x. How many actually did vote is not reported. The survey also found higher voter participation in tribal elections; see p. xi.

8. Peterson, "Political Participation," p. 124; U.S. Congress, *Present Relations*, pp. 157–74; U.S. Commission on Civil Rights, *1961 Commission on Civil Rights Report*, Book 5: Justice (Washington: Government Printing Office, 1961), p. 138; Steiner, *New Indians*, pp. 240–41.

9. Population figures are from U.S. Bureau of the Census, *Census of the Population: 1980*, vol. 1, *Characteristics of the Population*. The voting-age population figures are based on 1980 Census data, reported in Michael Barone and Grant Ujifusa, *The Almanac of American Politics 1984* (Washington: National Journal, 1983), p. 1316. In both cases the Alaska figures include Eskimos and Aleuts.

10. Stevens, "Voice of the Native"; author's field notes, Yakima Reservation, Washington, November 1978; Peterson, "Political Participation," p. 124; Steiner, *New Indians*, pp. 235–36.

11. Steiner, *New Indians*, pp. 238–39; "Tribes Win Ruling in District Voting," *Wassaja*, September 1979, p. 24; Steve Auslander, "Apache County: When the Indians Take Over . . . ," *Arizona Daily Star*, October 31, 1976; Lorna Thackeray, "Indians fight for voter districts," *Billings Gazette*, November 19, 1985, p. 5-A; the rancher is quoted in "Whites vs. Indians in Montana, where racism still reigns," *San Francisco Examiner*, October 5, 1986, p. A-4.

12. Wilbur Wood, "Second Battle of Big Horn: Indian Voting Rights Suit," *The Nation*, October 25, 1986, p. 406.

13. Frances Fox Piven and Richard A. Cloward, *Poor People's Movements: Why They Succeed, How They Fail* (New York: Vintage, 1979), p. 23.

14. Obviously votes could be considered a bargaining resource. I have treated them separately here for two reasons: first, the topic requires fairly lengthy treatment; second, votes are individually held while my concern here is with resources generally controlled by the group. Blalock calls these resources "competitive": those "that attach to minority individuals by virtue of their possessing something that dominant-group members positively want." The usage is similar here, except that the resources at issue are possessed by groups. See Blalock, *Theory of Minority-Group Relations*, pp. 118–19.

15. Estimates of the extent of Indian natural resources vary, but see, for example, Lorraine Turner Ruffing, "The Role of Policy in American Indian Mineral Development," in Roxanne Dunbar Ortiz, *American Indian Energy Resources and Development*, Development Series No. 2 (Albuquerque: Native American Studies, University of New Mexico, 1980), p. 51, where she estimates that Indian lands include about a quarter of U.S. reserves of strippable coal, 11 percent of uranium, and 3 percent of oil. Recent estimates from the Council of Energy Resource Tribes have been somewhat higher: as much as a third of strippable coal, 40 percent of privately held uranium, and 4 percent of oil and natural gas. See David R. Bomberry, "Foreword," in Jorgensen, *Native Americans and Energy Development II*, p. 7.

16. See the discussion in Stephen Cornell, "Crisis and Response in Indian-White Relations, 1960–1984," *Social Problems* 32, no. 1 (October 1984): 44–59; also James P. Boggs, "Adversarial Politics and Indian Tribal Involvement in NEPA: A Case Study," in Charles C. Geisler et al., eds., *Indian SIA: The Social Impact Assessment of Rapid Resource Development on Native Peoples*, Monograph #3 (Ann Arbor: Natural Resources Sociology Research Lab, University of Michigan, 1982), pp. 57–79; and "The Indians, The Royalties, and the BIA," *Civil Rights Digest* 10, no. 2 (Winter 1978): 26–31. This development is discussed more fully in Chapter 12.

17. See, for example, J. Craig Jenkins and Charles Perrow, "Insurgency of the Powerless: Farm Worker Movements (1946–1972)," *American Sociological Review* 42 (April 1977): 249–68; and Michael Lipsky, *Protest in City Politics: Rent Strikes, Housing and the Power of the Poor* (Chicago: Rand McNally, 1970).

18. John J. Bodine, "Blue Lake: A Struggle for Indian Rights," *American Indian Law Review* 1, no. 1 (Winter 1973): 25–26; on the fight against the Bursum Bill, see Philp, *Collier's Crusade*, ch. 2; on anthropologists and the Claims Commission, see Lurie, "Indian Claims Commission" (1957), pp. 60–62.

19. Cf. Gerlach and Hine's discussion of the change in "influence flow" from White dominance to Black in the evolution of the Black Power movement. Luther P. Gerlach and Virginia H. Hine, "The Social Organization of a Movement of Revolutionary Change: Case Study, Black Power," in Norman E. Whitten, Jr. and John F. Szwed, eds., *Afro-American Anthropology: Contemporary Perspectives* (New York: The Free Press, 1970), pp. 395–96.

20. Bodine, "Blue Lake," p. 29; advertisement by Friends of the Earth opposing Havasupai land grant, *New York Times*, July 8, 1974; "U.S. Urged to Strip Indians of Special Sporting Rights," account of National Wildlife Federation convention, *New York Times*, March 17, 1975.

21. See Suzanne Gordon, *Black Mesa: The Angel of Death* (New York: John Day Company, 1973); Richard O. Clemmer, "Black Mesa and the Hopi," in Joseph G. Jorgensen et al., eds., *Native Americans and Energy Development* (Cambridge, Mass.: Anthropology Resource Center, 1978), pp. 17–34; "The Black Hills Alliance," *Akwesasne Notes* 11, no. 2 (Spring 1979), p. 28; Committee on Native American Struggles, "Union Carbide Leaves the Black Hills," *CONAS Newsletter* 6, no. 1 (Winter 1982): 3–4; Tom Barry, "New Mexico Pueblos Confront the Atomic Age," *American Indian Journal* 5, no. 12 (December 1979): 11–17; Al Gedicks, "Resource Wars in Chippewa Country," in Jorgensen, *Native Americans and Energy Development II*, pp. 184–86.

22. See *Indian Voices* (Chicago), April 1964, p. 10; Vine Deloria, Jr., *Custer Died for Your Sins: An Indian Manifesto* (New York: Avon, 1970), pp. 180–83.

23. Max Weber was an early observer of this fact. See his "Ethnic Groups," in Max Weber, *Economy and Society: An Outline of Interpretive Sociology,* ed. Guenther Roth and Claus Wittich, 2 vols. (New York: Bedminister Press, 1968), 1:386.

24. The historical symbolism of Wounded Knee was undoubtedly a factor in the decision by Indian activists to precipitate a confrontation there, not only as a result of the famous massacre of 1890 but also because of the recent popular success of Dee Brown's book. See DeMallie, "Pine Ridge Economy," p. 305. See also Terri Schultz, "Bamboozle Me Not at Wounded Knee," *Harper's,* June 1973, pp. 46–48, 53–56, for an interesting, though biased, view of the occupation as an exercise in media manipulation.

25. Social movement participants, says McAdam, "are recruited along established lines of interaction." *Political Process and Black Insurgency,* p. 44. See also Anthony Oberschall, *Social Conflict and Social Movements* (Englewood Cliffs, N.J.: Prentice-Hall, 1973), ch. 4; and Donald Von Eschen, Jerome Kirk, and Maurice Pinard, "The Organizational Substructure of Disorderly Politics," *Social Forces* 49 (June 1971): 529–44.

26. See, for example, Faun Mortara's discussion of the IRA's effect on the ability of the Pyramid Lake Paiutes to fight proposed congressional legislation that would have reduced Paiute lands. "Political Resources Available through the Wheeler-Howard Act: A Case Study," in Houghton, *Native American Politics,* pp. 52–58.

27. See, for example, "National Urban Indian Council" (pamphlet) and "What, Why, When Who and How of N.U.I.C." (press release), both from National Urban Indian Council, Denver, no date, in possession of author, and the interview with Greg Frazier of the National Urban Indian Council, "Urban Indians Enter the Political Arena," *American Indian Journal* 6, no. 8 (August 1980): 15–18.

28. See Bruce Fireman and William A. Gamson, "Utilitarian Logic in the Resource Mobilization Perspective," in Zald and McCarthy, *Dynamics of Social Movements,* pp. 8–44.

29. See Oberschall, *Social Conflict,* pp. 119–21; also Craig Calhoun, "The Radicalism of Tradition," *American Journal of Sociology* 88, no. 5 (March 1983): 886–914.

30. Lorraine Turner Ruffing, "The Navajo Nation: A History of Dependence and Underdevelopment," *Review of Radical Political Economics* 11, no. 2 (Summer 1979): 36; Lynn A. Robbins, "Energy Developments and the Navajo

Nation," in Jorgensen, *Native Americans and Energy Development,* p. 42. See also Henderson, "Blue Collar Navajo Workers," pp. 63–80.

31. Lorraine Turner Ruffing, "Navajo Economic Development: A Dual Perspective," in Stanley, *American Indian Economic Development,* p. 34; Lisa Young, "What Price Progress? Uranium Production on Indian Lands in the San Juan Basin," *American Indian Law Review* 9 (1981): 1–50.

32. Arthur Stinchcombe, building on some ideas from Raymond Breton, argues that the extent of the individual's identification with or loyalty to the group depends in part on the degree of institutional completeness of the group, that is, on the ability of the group to provide an effective and complete design for living. See Arthur L. Stinchcombe, "Social Structure and Politics," in Fred I. Greenstein and Nelson W. Polsby, eds., *Handbook of Political Science,* vol. 3 (Reading, Mass.: Addison-Wesley, 1975), pp. 601–5; and Raymond Breton, "Institutional Completeness of Ethnic Communities and the Personal Relations of Immigrants," *American Journal of Sociology* 60 (1964): 193–205.

33. These issues are discussed in detail in Stephen Cornell, "Communities of Culture, Communities of Interest: On the Variable Nature of Ethnic Ties," paper presented at the annual meetings of the American Sociological Association, New York City, August, 1986; also see Calhoun, "The Radicalism of Tradition." On paradigms of action, or "root paradigms," see Victor Turner, "Religious Paradigms and Political Action: Thomas Becket at the Council of Northampton," in idem, *Dramas, Fields, and Metaphors: Symbolic Action in Human Society* (Ithaca: Cornell University Press, 1974), pp. 63–64; and, for an illustrative case, Blu, *Lumbee Problem.*

34. McNickle, *Native American Tribalism,* p. 95.

35. See the discussion in Chapter 7.

36. The first quote is from an interview conducted by Richard La Course (author's field notes, 1978); the second is given in Peroff, *Menominee Drums,* p. 176.

37. Reported in Michael Rogers, "The Dark Side of the Earth," *Rolling Stone,* May 22, 1975, p. 54.

38. Department of Health, Education and Welfare, *A Study of Selected Socio-Economic Characteristics of Ethnic Minorities Based on the 1970 Census. Volume III: American Indians* (Washington: Department of Health, Education and Welfare, 1974), p. v. While there has been some positive change in subsequent years, in the mid-1980s the statement remained essentially valid.

39. Native American Rights Fund, *Annual Report, 1977* (Boulder: Native American Rights Fund, 1977), pp. 3, 18.

40. Linda Medcalf, *Law and Identity: Lawyers, Native Americans, and Legal Practice* (Beverly Hills: Sage Publications, 1978), ch. 6, but see also the comments on culture and Indian lawyers in Philip S. Deloria, "The Era of Indian Self-Determination: An Overview," in Philp, *Indian Self-Rule,* p. 206.

41. Robert A. Nelson and Joseph F. Sheley, "Current BIA Influence on Indian Self-Determination: A Criminal Justice Planning Illustration," *The Social Science Journal* 19, no. 3 (July 1982): 77. For an example of a similar process, in which the demands of supportive lawyers for a more structured organization with which to work eventually undermined the effectiveness of a traditionalist social movement, see Albert L. Wahrhaftig and Jane Lukens-Wahrhaftig, "New Militants or Resurrected State? The Five County Northeastern Oklahoma Cherokee Organization," in Duane H. King, ed., *The Chero-*

kee Indian Nation: A Troubled History (Knoxville: University of Tennessee Press, 1979), pp. 239–40.

Chapter 11. Lieutenant Anthony's Legacy

1. Henry David Thoreau, *Cape Cod* (New York: The Library of America, 1984; orig. pub. 1865), p. 878. The internal quotations are from a historical pamphlet, published by the town of Eastham, which Thoreau read on his journey through the area.

2. See Cornell, "American Indian Political Resurgence," Appendix; updated, Harvard University, 1988. This chronology has some significant shortcomings. The history of Native American political activity is poorly documented, particularly in the early years of this century. Much of what Indians have done has gone either unrecorded or noted only in obscure journalistic and official sources and has been missed by this survey. Additionally, the chronology largely excludes litigation, a major form of Indian political activity, but one difficult to chronicle precisely. Consequently, Figure 4 should be viewed as a representation of the overall shape of Indian political resurgence and not as a precise record of events. The major sources of the chronology include: *New York Times,* 1886–1978, surveyed through *The New York Times Index; Facts on File,* 1941–1978; Commissioner of Indian Affairs, *Annual Reports, 1900–1940;* Barbara A. Leitch, ed., *Chronology of the American Indian* (St. Clair Shores: Scholarly Press, 1975); Indians of All Tribes, *Alcatraz Is Not an Island* (Berkeley: Wingbow Press, 1972); Vine Deloria, Jr., "The Rise of Indian Activism," in Jennings C. Wise, *The Red Man in the New World Drama,* ed. Vine Deloria, Jr. (New York: Macmillan, 1971), ch. xxvi; Steiner, *New Indians;* Jack Forbes, "The New Indian Resistance?" *Akwesasne Notes* 4, no. 3 (1972): 20–22; issues of the Washington *Bulletin,* published by the National Congress of American Indians; issues of *Indian Voices,* a newsletter published at the University of Chicago from 1962 to 1968; issues of *Akwesasne Notes,* published at the Mohawk Nation in New York; issues of *Americans Before Columbus,* newspaper of the National Indian Youth Council, published in Albuquerque; issues of *Yakima Nation Review,* published at Toppenish, Washington. These and other sources were used to revise the chronology and bring it up to date through 1980. Of course the events included vary in significance. This is more a record of volume than of impact.

3. See Barbara Graymont, ed., *Fighting Tuscarora: The Autobiography of Chief Clinton Rickard* (Syracuse: Syracuse University Press, 1973), ch. 5.

4. This point was first made to me by Herb Blatchford. It is amply apparent in Bee, *Crosscurrents Along Colorado,* ch. 5; see also George P. Castile, "Federal Indian Policy and the Sustained Enclave: An Anthropological Perspective," *Human Organization* 33 (Fall 1974): 219–28. On changes in federal funding, see Neils, *Reservation to City,* p. 55, Table 8.

5. Greenstone and Peterson, *Race and Authority,* pp. 2–6. Some of the antipoverty programs implemented on Indian reservations are discussed in Sar A. Levitan and Barbara Hetrick, *Big Brother's Indian Programs—With Reservations* (New York: McGraw-Hill, 1971), ch. 6.

6. Clemmer, "Truth, Duty, and Revitalization," pp. 213–47; Joseph G. Jorgensen and Richard O. Clemmer, "On Washburn's 'On the Trail of the

Activist Anthropologist': A Rejoinder to a Reply," *Journal of Ethnic Studies* 8, no. 2 (Summer 1980): 85–94; Robbins, "Energy Developments and the Navajo Nation," pp. 35–48; DeMallie, "Pine Ridge Economy," pp. 237–312.

7. Akwesasne Notes, *Trail of Broken Treaties: "B.I.A., I'm Not Your Indian Anymore,"* 2nd ed. (Rooseveltown: Akwesasne Notes, 1974), pp. 63–88.

8. See Max Weber, *The Theory of Social and Economic Organization* (New York: The Free Press, 1947), p. 325; also Frank Parkin, *Class Inequality and Political Order* (New York: Holt, Rinehart and Winston, 1971), p. 83. I use the term "social control" in the sense used by Ira Katznelson, who quotes Joseph Roucek: "Social control takes place when a person is induced or forced to act according to the wishes of others, whether or not in accordance with his own individual interests." Katznelson, *Black Men, White Cities,* p. 105. I am reading "person" as "group."

9. Robbins, "Energy Developments and Navajo Nation," pp. 45–47; Allen V. Kneese and F. Lee Brown, *The Southwest Under Stress: National Resource Development in a Regional Setting* (Baltimore: Johns Hopkins University Press, 1981), pp. 214–15; Shiprock Research Center, *Annual Report* (Shiprock: Shiprock Research Center, 1977); Bruce Johansen and Roberto Maestas, *Wasi'chu: The Continuing Indian Wars* (New York: Monthly Review Press, 1979); Northern Cheyenne Tribe, *The Northern Cheyenne Air Quality Redesignation Report and Request* (Lame Deer: Northern Cheyenne Tribe, 1977); Patrick C. West, "Tribal Control and the Identity-Poverty Dilemma," in Geisler, *Indian SIA,* pp. 80–92.

10. A BIA statement to Congress in the late 1960s captures the general spirit of this viewpoint. "Indian economic development," stated the BIA, "can proceed only as the process of acculturation allows." You are poor, in other words, because you are Indian. Bureau of Indian Affairs, "Economic Development of Indian Communities," in Joint Economic Committee, U.S. Congress, *Toward Economic Development for Native American Communities* (Washington: Government Printing Office, 1969), p. 333. See also Robert L. Bennett, "Economic Development as a Means of Overcoming Indian Poverty," in ibid., pp. 102–18; Kent Gilbreath, *Red Capitalism: An Analysis of the Navajo Economy* (Norman: University of Oklahoma Press, 1973), ch. 5; and Boise Cascade Center for Community Development, *Indian Economic Development: An Evaluation of EDA's Selected Indian Reservation Program,* vol. 1 (Boise: Boise Cascade Center for Community Development, 1973). More recently, the Presidential Commission on Indian Reservation Economies (PCIRE) flagged, among other things, consensus-based decision making and cultural prohibitions against individual accumulation of wealth as obstacles to development. PCIRE, *Report and Recommendations to the President of the United States* (Washington: Government Printing Office, 1984), Part 1, p. 41; Part 2, pp. 33, 36–37, 117.

11. I know of no systematic data summarizing Indian viewpoints on these issues. The views outlined here are implicit in much Indian political activity of the 1960s and 1970s and have been expressed by a number of Indian organizations and individuals. My impressions of these views have been shaped by tribal and supratribal newspapers and other sources and by conversations with a number of Indian participants in and observers of political activity during this period, among them Pat Ballanger, Herb Blatchford, Duane Champagne, Richard La Course, Bill Pensoneau, and Gerald Wilkinson. But see also, for example, Clemmer, "Black Mesa and Hopi," pp. 17–34; Johansen and Maestas,

Wasi'chu; and Russell Means, "Marxism is a European Tradition," *Akwesasne Notes* 12, no. 3 (1980): 17–19.

12. Deloria, *Trail of Broken Treaties,* p. 40.

13. McAdam, *Political Process and Black Insurgency,* p. 57.

14. Quoted in Steiner, *New Indians,* p. 40.

15. Deloria, *Trail of Broken Treaties,* p. 23.

16. Ultimately Indian use of extrainstitutional action as a political strategy comes up against a difficult problem: the lack of structural power. It is scarcely coincidental that much of the disruptive political activity by Indians in the late 1960s and early 1970s was directed at the BIA. It was a target principally, of course, because of its history as a kind of Indian colonial office. But it is also one of the few bureaucratic structures where Indian action has impact. It is vulnerable to them, and not much of the political structure is.

17. John Butler and Richard La Course, "45 Indian Tribes in a Dozen States Form Heartland of Indian Oil Production," *The CERT Report* 4, no. 11 (Sept. 13, 1982): 1–7; Daniel H. Israel, "New Opportunities for Energy Development on Indian Reservations," *Mining Engineering* (June 1980): 651–57; U.S. Department of Interior, *Mineral Revenues,* p. 39.

18. For some discussions, see Norris Hundley, Jr., "The Dark and Bloody Ground of Indian Water Rights: Confusion Elevated to Principles," *Western Historical Quarterly* 9 (1978): 455–82; Kneese and Brown, *Southwest Under Stress,* ch. 3 and 4; "The Acceptable Cost," *Akwesasne Notes* 9, no. 3 (Summer 1977): 18–20; Robert D. Dellwo, "Recent Developments in the Northwest Regarding Indian Water Rights," *National Resources Journal* 20, no. 1 (January 1980): 101–20; Charles Bowden, *Killing the Hidden Waters* (Austin: University of Texas Press, 1977).

19. The quote is from an interview with Jim French of KIRO Radio, Seattle, March 1984. A chronology of the fishing rights conflict is given in *Northwest Indian News* (Seattle) 10, no. 1 (August 1979), p. 4. For a detailed and more up-to-date analysis, see Fay G. Cohen, *Treaties on Trial: The Continuing Controversy over Northwest Indian Fishing Rights* (Seattle: University of Washington Press, 1986); she discusses Initiative 456, pp. 185–86.

20. On the federal position, see Winifred T. Gross, "Tribal Resources, Federal Trust Responsibility: United States Energy Development Versus Trust Responsibilities to Indian Tribes," *American Indian Law Review* 9 (1981): 309–43; also Ronald L. Trosper, "American Indian Mineral Agreements: Literture Search and Reform Proposals," in American Indian Policy Review Commission, *Report on Reservation and Resource Development and Protection* (Washington: Government Printing Office, 1976), pp. 137–47. On the state level, see Kneese and Brown, *Southwest Under Stress;* Young, "What Price Progress?" pp. 1–50.

21. Ruffing, "Navajo Economic Development," p. 34; Young, "What Price Progress?" pp. 44–45; Barry, "Pueblos Confront Atomic Age," pp. 11–17; Fowler, *Arapahoe Politics,* p. 232; Maxwell, "Colvilles on Verge of Development," pp. 162–65. AMAX, the molybdenum developer in the Colville case, eventually pulled out of the deal.

22. Boggs, "Adversarial Politics," p. 72.

23. See, for example, "Energy Agreements Affected by Joint Venture Bill," *The CERT Report* 4, no. 11 (Sept. 13, 1982): 19–20; Israel, "Opportunities for Energy Development"; Lorraine Turner Ruffing, "Navajo Mineral Develop-

ment," *American Indian Journal* 4, no. 9 (September 1978): 2–16; Richard Nafziger, "Transnational Energy Corporations and American Indian Development," in Roxanne Dunbar Ortiz, ed., *American Indian Energy Resources and Development*, Development Series No. 2 (Albuquerque: Native American Studies, University of New Mexico, 1980), pp. 9–38; Boggs, "Adversarial Politics."

24. On Indian opposition in these cases and others, see Tom Barry and Beth Wood, "Uranium on the Checkerboard: Crisis at Crown Point," *American Indian Journal* 4, no. 6 (1978): 10–13; Barry, "Pueblos Confront Atomic Age"; Duane Champagne, "Socio-cultural Reponses to Coal Development: A Comparison of the Crow and Northern Cheyenne," unpublished manuscript, 1983; Clemmer, "Black Mesa and Hopi"; Charles C. Geisler, "Land Ownership, Control and Use as Sources of Social Impacts: The Sokaogon Chippewa Case," in Geisler, *Indian SIA*, pp. 200–35; Johansen and Maestas, *Wasi'chu;* Kneese and Brown, *Southwest Under Stress*, ch. 10; Northern Cheyenne Tribe, *Air Quality Report;* Robbins, "Energy Developments and Navajo Nation"; Nancy J. Owens, "Can Tribes Control Energy Development?" in Jorgensen, *Native Americans and Energy Development*, pp. 49–62; Ruffing, "Role of Policy in Mineral Development"; Chandler C. Smith, "Optimizing Development Impacts on Indian Reservations," in Geisler, *Indian SIA*, pp. 41–56; Civil Rights Digest, "Indians, Royalties, and BIA,"; CONAS Newsletter, "Union Carbide Leaves Black Hills"; Rubie Sootkis and Anne Terry Straus, "A Rock and a Hard Place: Mineral Resources on the Northern Cheyenne Reservation," *Chicago Anthropology Exchange* 14, no. 1 and 2 (1981): 27–35; Jim Robbins, "Fighting Over the Oil in Hallowed Ground: Montana Blackfeet Appeal a Ruling," *New York Times*, December 28, 1986, p. E-12. More generally, see the discussion in Donald L. Fixico, "Tribal Leaders and the Demand for Natural Energy Resources on Tribal Lands," in Iverson, *Plains Indians of Twentieth Century*, pp. 221–23.

Chapter 12. Indian-White Relations Revised

1. Authorities are defined here in Gamson's terms as "those who, for any given social system, make binding decisions in that system." William A. Gamson, *Power and Discontent* (Homewood: Dorsey Press, 1968), p. 21. In the case of Indians in the United States, this means the Bureau of Indian Affairs, the Department of the Interior, Congress, and the federal courts.

2. Michael Lipsky and David J. Olson, "The Processing of Racial Crisis in America," *Politics and Society* 6, no. 1 (1976): 88, 91. On the federal campaign against Indian organizations, see Richard La Course, "FBI, BIA Probing Indian Movement," *Race Relations Reporter* 5 (September 1974): 1–4; U.S. Senate, Committee on the Judiciary, *Revolutionary Activities Within the United States: The American Indian Movement* (Washington: Government Printing Office, 1976); Johansen and Maestas, *Wasi'chu;* Rex Weyler, *Blood of the Land: The Government and Corporate War Against the American Indian Movement* (New York: Everest House, 1982); Peter Matthiessen, *In the Spirit of Crazy Horse* (New York: Viking, 1983).

3. In conversation, Minneapolis, 1978 (author's field notes).

4. Cf. Lipsky and Olson, "Processing of Racial Crisis," pp. 79–103.

5. See Ruffing, "Role of Policy in Mineral Development."

6. This point on occasion has been explicit. One report prepared for the BIA in the early 1970s was titled *Finance and Management: The Key to Indian Self-Determination* (by William J. Ewasiuk et al., prepared by the Department of Agricultural Economics and Economics, Montana State University, Bozeman, Montana, 1973). See also Bureau of Indian Affairs, "Economic Development of Indian Communities," in U.S. Congress, *Toward Economic Development, p. 333;* and PCIRE, *Report and Recommendations.*

7. U.S. Congress, "Public Law 93–638: The Indian Self-Determination and Education Assistance Act," *United States Statutes at Large,* Vol. 88, Part 2, 1976: 2203, 2204.

8. Russel Lawrence Barsh and Ronald L. Trosper, "Title I of the Indian Self-Determination and Education Assistance Act of 1975," *American Indian Law Review* 3 (1975): 361–95; see also Nelson and Sheley, "Current BIA Influence," pp. 76–77. On Indian reactions to the act, see Edmund J. Danziger, Jr., "A New Beginning or the Last Hurrah: American Indian Response to Reform Legislation of the 1970s," *American Indian Culture and Research Journal* 7, no. 4 (1984): 69–84. A detailed overview of the act and its consequences is in Michael P. Gross, "Indian Self-Determination and Tribal Sovereignty: An Analysis of Recent Federal Indian Policy," *Texas Law Review* 56 (1978): 1195–1244.

9. Ernest L Schusky, "Development by Grantsmanship: Economic Planning on the Lower Brule Sioux Reservation," *Human Organization* 34 (Fall 1975): 235; see also Bee, *Crosscurrents Along Colorado,* ch. 5.

10. In conversation, January 1985. On the increase in Indian control of reservation economic development, see Joseph P. Kalt, "The Redefinition of Property Rights in American Indian Reservations: A Comparative Analysis of Native American Economic Development," Energy and Environmental Policy Center, John F. Kennedy School of Government, Harvard University, Discussion Paper Series (May 1987).

11. Bureau of Indian Affairs, *Handbook for Decision-Makers on Title I of the Indian Self-Determination and Education Assistance Act* (Washington: Bureau of Indian Affairs, 1975), p. 3.

12. In 1982 Navajos elected a new tribal chairman, Peterson Zah, evidently less committed than his predecessor, Peter MacDonald, to a rapid development strategy. In 1986, in a close election, MacDonald won the chairmanship back from Zah.

13. Viewed in these terms, tribal governments bear at least some resemblance to urban political machines, which, as Katznelson observes, controlled "both the input and output sides of politics; they provided an organized, coherent access link to government, and acted as the key distributor of political rewards." The rewards controlled by tribal governments, however, as Schusky's remarks, quoted earlier, suggest, are often both political and economic. See Ira Katznelson, "The Crisis of the Capitalist City: Urban Politics and Social Control," in Willis D. Hawley and Michael Lipsky, eds., *Theoretical Perspectives in Urban Politics* (Englewood Cliffs, NJ.: Prentice-Hall, 1976), p. 224.

14. U.S. Senate, *Revolutionary Activities Within United States, p. 2.*

15. Ira Katznelson makes a similar point about responses to urban Black challenges in much the same period. See Katznelson, *City Trenches: Urban Politics and the Patterning of Class in the United States* (New York: Pantheon, 1981), ch. 7.

16. Office of the Press Secretary, The White House, "Fact Sheet: Indian Policy Statement," Washington, D.C., January 14, 1983.

17. The overall spending drop was reported in *New York Times,* October 30, 1983, Section IV, p. 5. The figure on Ponca job loss is from Bill Pensoneau, tribal economic planner, telephone conversation, October 1984. Cutbacks in Montana are reported in Majel R. Bird, "The Effects of 'Reaganomics' on the Northern Cheyenne Reservation," unpublished, no date, p. 14. The Navajo cutbacks and income figures were reported in Hazel W. Hertzberg, "Reaganomics on the Reservation," *The New Republic,* November 22, 1982, p. 17.

18. Bird, " 'Reaganomics' on Northern Cheyenne Reservation," pp. 7, 9.

19. In conversation, Ponca Reservation, Oklahoma, August 1984.

20. In telephone conversation, January 1985.

21. See "Hard Times Mount for Spokane Tribe," *New York Times,* January 6, 1983; Chris N. Gjording, S.J., "Update, February 1983," in Jorgensen, *Native Americans and Energy Development II,* pp. 170–74.

22. One example is a "mini-conglomerate" run by the Eastern Band of Cherokees in North Carolina. The Cherokee Boy's Club—it began as a youth organization—today runs a charter bus service, makes school lunches, collects garbage on and off Cherokee lands, has a construction company, and operates a laundry service for both Indian and non-Indian customers. See the script of Odyssey Productions' television program, "The New Capitalists: Economics in Indian Country," Odyssey Productions, Portland, Oregon, 1984.

23. Gerald Wilkinson, "The Native American Family," unpublished manuscript.

24. Writing about traditional Oglalas today, William K. Powers argues that "the boundary which delineates Oglala society from non-Indians, or even non-Oglalas, is ideational." Powers, *Oglala Religion* (Lincoln: University of Nebraska Press, 1977), p. 204.

25. Robert K. Thomas, "The Vanishing Indian," *Americans Before Columbus* (Albuquerque: newspaper of the National Indian Youth Council) 14, no. 2 (1986): 7–8.

26. Frederick Seagayuk Bigjim and James Ito-Adler, *Letters to Howard: An Interpretation of the Alaska Native Land Claims* (Anchorage: Alaska Methodist University Press, 1974), p. 85. Emphasis added.

27. Cf. Svensson, "Ethnicity Versus Communalism."

28. Sam Deloria makes a similar point in his "Era of Self-Determination," pp. 192–93.

29. Quoted in Arlen J. Large, "Tribes in Transition," *Wall Street Journal,* August 23, 1977, p. 1.

30. HR 13329 (1978), Native American Equal Opportunity Act. See also "Cunningham Rewrites Abrogation Bill," *Yakima Nation Review* (Toppenish, Washington), Autumn National Edition, 1978, p. 12.

31. Richard La Course, "Farm Bureau Revives 'Termination,' " *The CERT Report,* Prototype Edition, early 1983, p. 16. The text of the bill is given in ibid., p. 17.

32. Several versions of this poster have appeared in the Northwest. The quote is from one issued by the Quinault Education Project, Quinault Indian Nation, Tahola, Washington, no date.

Chapter 13. "Another World is Coming"

1. Gerald Wilkinson, Executive Director of the National Indian Youth Council, quoted in Stan Steiner, *The Vanishing White Man* (New York: Harper and Row, 1976), p. 297.

2. Sam Stanley, "Introduction," in Stanley, *American Indian Economic Development,* p. 6.

3. Abrams, *Historical Sociology,* p. xiii.

Selected Bibliography

All works referred to in the text are included in the notes. Because a complete, separate bibliography would be prohibitively long, what follows is a highly selective list of those works of particular importance in the conception and evolution of this book.

Philip Abrams, *Historical Sociology* (Ithaca: Cornell University Press, 1982).

Akwesasne Notes, *Trail of Broken Treaties: "B.I.A., I'm Not Your Indian Anymore,"* 2nd ed. (Mohawk Nation, Rooseveltown, N.Y.: Akwesasne Notes, 1974).

Russel Lawrence Barsh and James Youngblood Henderson, *The Road: Indian Tribes and Political Liberty* (Berkeley: University of California Press, 1980).

Robert L. Bee, *Crosscurrents along the Colorado: The Impact of Government Policy on the Quechan Indians* (Tucson: University of Arizona Press, 1981).

Robert F. Berkhofer, Jr., *The White Man's Indian: Images of the American Indian from Columbus to the Present* (New York: Knopf, 1978).

Leonard Albert Carlson, "The Dawes Act and the Decline of Indian Farming," Ph.D. dissertation, Stanford University, 1977.

Center for the History of the American Indian, *Indian Sovereignty: Proceedings of the Second Annual Conference on Problems and Issues Concerning American Indians Today,* ed. William R. Swagerty, Occasional Papers Series, No. 2 (Chicago: The Newberry Library, 1979).

Duane Champagne, "Politics, Markets, and Social Structure: The Political and Economic Responses of Four Native American Societies to Western Impacts," Ph.D. dissertation, Harvard University, 1982.

James Clifton, *The Prairie People: Continuity and Change in Potawatomi Indian Culture 1665–1965* (Lawrence: The Regents Press of Kansas, 1977).

Sherburne F. Cook, *The Conflict Between the California Indian and White Civilization* (Berkeley: University of California Press, 1976).

William Cronon, *Changes in the Land: Indians, Colonists, and the Ecology of New England* (New York: Hill and Wang, 1983).

Vine Deloria, Jr., *Behind the Trail of Broken Treaties: An Indian Declaration of Independence* (New York: Dell, 1974).

————, "The Rise of Indian Activism," in Jennings C. Wise, *The Red Man in the New World Drama*, ed. Vine Deloria, Jr. (New York: Macmillan, 1971).

Raymond J. DeMallie, "The Lakota Ghost Dance: An Ethnohistorical Account," *Pacific Historical Review* 51, no. 4 (November 1982).

————, "Touching the Pen: Plains Indian Treaty Councils in Ethnohistorical Perspective," in Frederick C. Luebke, ed., *Ethnicity on the Great Plains* (Lincoln: University of Nebraska Press, 1980).

Henry F. Dobyns, "The Indian Reorganization Act and Federal Withdrawal," *Applied Anthropology* 7, no. 2 (Spring 1948).

Donald L. Fixico, "Tribal Leaders and the Demand for Natural Energy Resources on Tribal Lands," in Peter Iverson, ed., *The Plains Indians of the Twentieth Century* (Norman: University of Oklahoma Press, 1985).

Loretta Fowler, *Arapahoe Politics, 1851–1978: Symbols in Crises of Authority* (Lincoln: University of Nebraska Press, 1982).

Charles C. Geisler et al., *Indian SIA: The Social Impact Assessment of Rapid Resource Development on Native Peoples*, Monograph No. 3 (Ann Arbor: Natural Resources Sociology Research Lab, University of Michigan, 1982).

Jeanne Guillemin, *Urban Renegades: The Cultural Strategy of American Indians* (New York: Columbia University Press, 1975).

William T. Hagan, *United States–Comanche Relations: The Reservation Years* (New Haven: Yale University Press, 1976).

A. Irving Hallowell, "The Nature and Function of Property as a Social Institution," in idem, *Culture and Experience* (Philadelphia: University of Pennsylvania Press, 1955).

Hazel W. Hertzberg, *The Search for an American Indian Identity* (Syracuse: Syracuse University Press, 1971).

Francis Jennings, *The Invasion of America: Indians, Colonialism, and the Cant of Conquest* (New York: W. W. Norton, 1976).

Joseph G. Jorgensen, ed., *Native Americans and Energy Development II* (Boston: Anthropology Resource Center and Seventh Generation Fund, 1984).

————, *The Sun Dance Religion: Power for the Powerless* (Chicago: University of Chicago Press, 1972).

Charles J. Kappler, comp., *Indian Affairs: Laws and Treaties*, 5 vols. (Washington: Government Printing Office, 1904–41).

Ira Katznelson, *City Trenches: Urban Politics and the Patterning of Class in the United States* (New York: Pantheon, 1981).

Weston La Barre, *The Peyote Cult*, 4th ed. (New York: Schocken, 1975).

Michael Lipsky and David J. Olson, "The Processing of Racial Crisis in America," *Politics and Society* 6, no. 1 (1976).

Steven Lukes, "Power and Structure," in idem, *Essays in Social Theory* (New York: Columbia University Press, 1977).

Nancy O. Lurie, "The Contemporary American Indian Scene," in Stuart Levine and Nancy O. Lurie, eds., *The American Indian Today* (Baltimore: Penguin, 1968).

Drew R. McCoy, *The Elusive Republic: Political Economy in Jeffersonian America* (New York: W. W. Norton, 1980).

H. Craig Miner, *The Corporation and the Indian: Tribal Sovereignty and In-*

dustrial Civilization in Indian Territory, 1865–1907 (Columbia: University of Missouri Press, 1976).

James Mooney, *The Ghost-Dance Religion and the Sioux Outbreak of 1890*, Fourteenth Annual Report of the Bureau of Ethnology, 1892–93, Part 2 (Washington: Government Printing Office, 1896).

Elaine M. Neils, *Reservation to City: Indian Migration and Federal Relocation*, Research Paper No. 131 (Chicago: University of Chicago Department of Geography, 1971).

Douglass C. North, *The Economic Growth of the United States, 1790–1860* (New York: W. W. Norton, 1966).

Paul Chrisler Phillips, *The Fur Trade*, 2 vols. (Norman: University of Oklahoma Press, 1961).

Kenneth R. Philp, *John Collier's Crusade for Indian Reform, 1920–1954* (Tucson: University of Arizona Press, 1977).

————, ed., *Indian Self-Rule: First-Hand Accounts of Indian-White Relations from Roosevelt to Reagan* (Salt Lake City: Howe Brothers, 1986).

Frances Fox Piven and Richard A. Cloward, *Poor People's Movements: Why They Succeed, How They Fail* (New York: Vintage, 1979).

Karl Polanyi, *The Great Transformation: The Political and Economic Origins of Our Time* (Boston: Beacon Press, 1957).

William K. Powers, *Oglala Religion* (Lincoln: University of Nebraska Press, 1977).

Michael Paul Rogin, *Fathers and Children: Andrew Jackson and the Subjugation of the American Indian* (New York: Vintage, 1976).

Charles C. Royce, comp., *Indian Land Cessions in the United States*, Eighteenth Annual Report of the Bureau of American Ethnology, 1896–1897, Part II (Washington: Government Printing Office, 1899).

Marshall Sahlins, *Stone Age Economics* (Chicago: Aldine-Atherton, 1972).

R. A. Schermerhorn, *Comparative Ethnic Relations: A Framework for Theory and Research* (New York: Random House, 1970).

Ernest L. Schusky, *The Forgotten Sioux: An Ethnohistory of the Lower Brule Reservation* (Chicago: Nelson-Hall, 1975).

Rubie Sootkis and Anne Terry Straus, "A Rock and a Hard Place: Mineral Resources on the Northern Cheyenne Reservation," *Chicago Anthropology Exchange* 14, no. 1 and 2 (1981): 27–35.

Edward H. Spicer, *Cycles of Conquest: The Impact of Spain, Mexico, and the United States on the Indians of the Southwest, 1533–1960* (Tucson: University of Arizona Press, 1962).

Sam Stanley, ed., *American Indian Economic Development* (The Hague: Mouton, 1978).

Sam Stanley and Robert K. Thomas, "Current Demographic and Social Trends among North American Indians," *Annals of the American Academy of Political and Social Science* 436 (March 1978): 111–20.

Stan Steiner, *The New Indians* (New York: Dell, 1968).

Imre Sutton, *Indian Land Tenure: Bibliographical Essays and a Guide to the Literature* (New York: Clearwater, 1975).

W. R. Swagerty, ed., *Scholars and the Indian Experience: Critical Reviews of Recent Writing in the Social Sciences* (Bloomington: Indiana University Press, 1984).

Sol Tax, "Acculturation," in Anthony F. C. Wallace, ed., *Men and Cultures* (Philadelphia: University of Pennsylvania Press, 1960).

Graham D. Taylor, *The New Deal and American Indian Tribalism: The Administration of the Indian Reorganization Act, 1934–45* (Lincoln: University of Nebraska Press, 1980).

Robert K. Thomas, "Pan-Indianism," in Stuart Levine and Nancy O. Lurie, eds., *The American Indian Today* (Baltimore: Penguin, 1968).

Albert L. Wahrhaftig and Jane Lukens-Wahrhaftig, "The Thrice Powerless: Cherokee Indians in Oklahoma," in Raymond D. Fogelson and Richard N. Adams, eds., *The Anthropology of Power* (New York: Academic Press, 1977).

Deward E. Walker, Jr., *Conflict and Schism in Nez Perce Acculturation: A Study of Religion and Politics* (Pullman: Washington State University Press, 1968).

Anthony F. C. Wallace, *The Death and Rebirth of the Seneca* (New York: Knopf, 1970).

Index

271